Original French edition:
"Ton corps dit: "Aime-toi!""
First printing: 1997
CAN ISBN 2-920932-15-2

Copyright © 2001 by Lise Bourbeau
First edition/Second Printing
National library of Canada
National library of Quebec
ISBN 2-920932-17-9

Worldwide distributor
Lotus Brands Inc.
P.O. Box 325
Twin Lakes, WI
53181 USA
Tel: 262-889-8501 or 1-800-824-6396
Fax: 262-889-2461
email: lotuspress@lotuspress.com
www.lotuspress.com

Publisher
Les Editions E.T.C. Inc.
1102 Boul. La Salette
Saint-Jerome (Quebec)
J5L 2J7   Canada
Tel: 450-431-5336; Fax: 450-431-0991
Email: info@leseditionsetc.com
www.leseditionsetc.com

LISE BOURBEAU

AUTHOR OF THE BEST-SELLER

LISTEN TO YOUR BODY, your best friend on Earth

Your body's telling you:

Love yourself!

The most complete book on metaphysical causes of illnesses & diseases

ÉDITIONS E.T.C. INC

Acknowledgments

A special thanks to those who taught me about metaphysics, especially Louise Hay of California who was the first female metaphysician to introduce me to this marvelous philosophy.

Thanks to the *Listen To Your Body* team that has worked in tandem with me for several years and is always there to support and advise me in my endeavor to perfect my technique of decoding illnesses and diseases.

Thanks to Monica Shields, Odette Pelletier, Bette Davies, Alan Shields, Nathalie Raymond, Susan Proulx and Sue Tinkle who contributed to the editing and typesetting of this book.

Finally, I would like to express my utmost gratitude to those who shared with me sincere and candid testimonials to their own healing. Because of their generosity of spirit, I have gained the understanding and the insight that I now share with you.

LISE BOURBEAU

Table of contents

"A wise man should consider that health is the greatest of human blessings and learn how, by his own thought, to derive benefit from his illnesses."

"Natural forces within us are the true healers of disease."

"Each person is unique and it is the person, not the disease, that has to be taken care of."

"It is more important to know what kind of person has a disease than to know what kind of disease a person has."

"If someone wishes for good health, one must first ask oneself if he is ready to do away with the reasons for his illness. Only then is it possible to help him."

Hippocrates (father of medicine)

Introduction

After many years of research and development in the field of metaphysics, specifically the correlation between the physical and the metaphysical, I have decided to share my insights with you in this easily accessible reference guide. Its purpose is to help you understand more fully the causes of illnesses and disease. I will speak directly to you, person to person, throughout the book so that you will identify more easily with the information on a personal level.

I have chosen to use the word *metaphysical* rather than *psychosomatic* because of the implications of the definitions. *Psychosomatic* is defined as "pertaining to, or caused by phenomena that are both physiological and psychological." The term psychosomatic carries with it a common misconception that it relates to disease that is "all in one's head" or "in the imagination." Thus, I prefer to look at illness and disease from a balanced, metaphysical perspective.

Over the years, I've learned a great deal through my teachings. The more I teach, the more I learn. In sharing this knowledge throughout the years, the light spreads farther, making everything clearer inwardly and outwardly.

When illness or **dis-ease** is indicated, the body is communicating to us that our way of thinking (although

11

unconscious) is out of harmony with what is beneficial to our being. Illness indicates the need for change in our belief system and tells us that we have reached our physical and psychological limits.

The science of metaphysics has resurfaced since the advent of psychoanalysis. Sigmund Freud discovered that the body and the psyche are irrevocably linked. One of his most famous students, Carl Jung, said, *"In the same way that the conscious and unconscious are in constant interaction, the body and the mind are in constant interaction."* This statement, more than 50 years old, is affirmed by some of the world's greatest minds. Researchers in the field such as Wilhelm Reich, John Pierrakos, Fritz Pearls, Louise Hay and many others have contributed greatly to the resurgence of the body of information that constitutes metaphysical science.

Unfortunately, traditional modern medical practices (and some alternative therapies) take the position that illness is an obstacle to happiness and should be fought as an enemy attacking the body. The focus is on ridding the body of symptoms, which is like removing the little red light on the dashboard of a car that indicates a problem. Without signals, much more serious problems can develop. Symptoms are signals from the body that a specific area needs attention!

I have discovered, instead, (to my good fortune) that illness is a gift whose purpose is to bring back the equilibrium in our being. The physical body does not create illness because the physical body can do nothing by itself. What maintains its life is our soul, our inner self. Illness is a direct result of the imbalance of the inner realm that is manifested in the physical body. Therefore, a sick body seeks only to find its way back to the natural state of vibrant health. It is so for the mental and emotional levels also.

"What on earth is she talking about?! How am I supposed to believe this? Where does she get this?" As an intelligent, objective human being, I'm sure you are asking yourself these questions. As an intelligent objective human being, you will read on with an open mind, an open heart, and discover your own truth. By opening this book, you indicate that you are already motivated to walk the path to vibrant health. I will, in good conscience and with all sincerity, present you with well-documented and researched information from which you may assimilate what is comfortable and useful to you. You have nothing to lose in considering this approach, but be forewarned that you may resist strongly, as your ego is not going to like this information. This approach will require you to surrender to your intuition, to listen to the voice of your soul as it speaks to you through your body. Your core belief system may be challenged and your ego will have to move over so that your whole being can find its rightful place in fullness and in vitality. That is why I decided to add the following section on the EGO so that you understand, every time I mention it, what it really means.

Section 1

The ego

The EGO is the culmination of your interpretation of events in your life that have taken too much space over the years, so much so that the ego overpowers you and smothers your essence. Most people actually believe that the ego is who they are. Believing that your ego is the *real* you will undermine any attempt you will make at achieving balance. You must understand that the ego is the false self - the one that is made up as you go along.

Your perceptions build your ego, brick by brick, over your lifetime. Each event, pleasant or unpleasant, is filed in your memory database, and from each event you will draw a conclusion that is then filed in your belief system file. Before entering into a similar event, you refer to your database and determine whether the event will be positive or negative, thereby determining whether it is to be enjoyed or avoided.

Many of the experiences you've accumulated throughout lifetimes, and subsequently filed in your databases, are no longer relevant. They are, nonetheless, continually referred to. They all have a different voice and talk to you continuously. Each time you refer to them, believe them, and let them rule your life, you nourish them - they become bigger and bigger. Most beliefs accumulated since childhood are no longer helpful, though they might have been at one time. But it is important to realize that when you first *believed* your ego, you did so because you thought that belief would help you to be happier.

A good example would be a child who experienced difficulty learning to read. His teacher or parents may have said, *"You're not good at anything; you're too ab-sent-minded; you'll never amount to much..."* The child not only suffers from such comments, but he believes them, so there will always be a small voice inside him - and inside the man this child will become - that says: *"You're not good at anything..."* Every time he wants to learn or take on something new, this part of him (the be-lief), convinced that it's helping him avoid suffering, will prevent him from taking on this new experience. Deep in the subconscious, this thought has become part of the be-lief system this man will refer to all of his life. The same thought thereby becomes part of his ego self. He will make excuses like *"I'm not interested"* or *"I've changed my mind"* or *"It's not the right time yet"* when taking on anything new. Excuses will shield him from being told that he's not good at anything.

The ego is made up of hundreds of these beliefs. If you are not aware of their irrelevance, they will over-whelm you and prevent you from ever achieving the needs essential to expressing your "I AM."

The ego is also the greatest obstacle to your health! Once the ego is allowed to run your life, it will prevent you from being what you need to be and doing what you want to do, consequently blocking various parts of the physical body that could have helped you achieve those desires.

I recall a particular case in which a young woman came to see me with a bad case of tendonitis of the right arm. When I asked her what, specifically, the tendonitis was preventing her from doing, she replied that she could not play tennis. She could have told me that it was keeping her from holding her child or from housework or many other things, but in this case, I knew that she had an underlying belief that was preventing her from playing tennis. (Discovering what the illness is preventing us from doing is a big help in determining the cause or the belief behind that illness.) I asked her what her intentions were when she began to play tennis. *"I began to play for fun,"* she replied *"I was taking life too seriously. I've got business obligations and two children at home and needed to play a little."*

She then told me that she allowed herself to be talked into joining three other women who had decided to form two teams to play weekly. The game, which had started out as fun, became a serious competition. Whenever she missed a ball or made an error in the game, her tennis partner criticized her and commented on the quality of her game. It wasn't fun anymore. For fear of offending her teammate, she did not stick up for herself. Rather than tell the woman directly that she didn't want to play tennis competitively, she developed tendonitis to prevent playing at all.

Deep down, she knew she needed more play in her life, but because she *believed* that life was serious business, her ego had to find a way to make that true. It was her ego that attracted her to these competitive partners and eventually caused the tendonitis. The belief (ego) won. It made sure that she would be unable to play and could get down to serious business. She then realized that her mother had the same belief: *Life is serious and there is never time to play.*

Had she known how to listen more clearly to her body, the tendonitis would not have been a signal to stop playing tennis, but a signal that it was time to change her attitude about the game. It is common to believe that pain is a signal to stop doing something. Beware! That reaction is the ego's trick so that you will not discover the belief. Why? Because the ego is convinced it knows best and is helping you prevent suffering!

Be particularly alert when your discomfort seems only physical. Here are a few examples of situations that seem to stem from simple, physical causes:

- An illness caused by a vitamin deficiency that vanishes when the vitamins are ingested;

- You fall and break an arm;

- You overeat and get indigestion;

- Overexertion from any particular activity that is still felt as muscle pain several days later.

It is very tempting to believe that these events have purely physical causes. Since it's impossible to separate the physical body from the emotional and mental, I suggest you not be influenced by your ego, as it always wants to find an exterior cause for anything that is wrong. There are underlying reasons for all of the above situations that the ego doesn't want you to discover. For you to understand those reasons, you will have to take personal responsibility for them, and the ego will have none of that! How will the ego maintain control if you refuse to lay blame on external factors or influences?

Remember that the ego is not real - you have created it yourself with your mental energy. It is incapable of knowing the needs of your true self!

All people from all walks of life, in all cultures, have belief systems that are influenced by their families, friends, communities, societies and their own individual interpretation of events that have formed their lives. No human being is immune to the influence of the ego.

As all living things, the ego has a primal instinct for self-preservation; however, it can only exist and maintain control when you allow your beliefs to determine your life. This concept is discussed in greater detail in my other books.

If you believe that illnesses, accidents and disorders are relevant only to the physical self, you are disassociating yourself from your mental, emotional and spiritual aspects, thereby refusing to acknowledge the majority of what makes you who you really are! You have only to recall a situation where you've experienced instinctive reactions (such as your heart racing when you are afraid or that feeling in the pit of your stomach when you anticipate something you may be dreading); these automatic reactions are not coming from the physical body, but are transferred to the physical body through thoughts or emotions. The physical body cannot possibly be separated from the mental and emotional bodies. These three make up the material envelope of our spiritual self.

The most frequent causes of illness are negative attitudes and emotions, guilt, the need for attention, or the need to escape an unpleasant situation. Those who are vulnerable to the suggestion that illness is "contagious" will attract illness because they expect to be sick as a result of circumstances. If they believe, for example, that a draft will result in a cold, they will "get" a cold when exposed to a draft.

With each illness or disorder, your body is reminding you to love yourself (thus the title of this book). Through genuine self-love, you allow your heart to guide you to wellness and wholeness. The ego does not know how to lead you there because it is made of mental energy. The mental body contains and uses only memory.

To love yourself is to give yourself permission to live as you choose - to love others is to give them permission to live as *they* choose and to let them carry out their own experiments.

When you love yourself, you accept yourself as you are at any moment - in all your humanity - with fears,

20

weaknesses, desires, beliefs and aspirations that are all facets of who you are. You do not judge yourself or your actions as right or wrong, correct or incorrect, but accept every moment as an experience from which you will learn, thereby facing the consequences of your actions and decisions (whether pleasant or unpleasant). In this way, you will achieve and maintain the balance necessary for optimal health because you do not let your ego decide what is right or wrong.

Before any mental transformation can arise, you must unconditionally accept who you *are*, and determine the mental attitude that blocks you to the point of creating a physical problem. For this reason, I have included a list of questions to ask yourself that pertains to each particular disease or disorder listed herein. They will help you explore the reasons behind any physical problem.

Your physical body will be happy to adjust to the inner transformation. Remember that your physical body is a direct reflection of the state of your inner self. I often hear my clients tell me that they don't understand why a particular illness or disorder doesn't improve or disappear, even after they understand the reason behind it. It is not enough to merely understand and accept the reason: the most important step is to accept and forgive *yourself*. (Simple steps for forgiveness are given at the end of this book.)

PLEASE NOTE: I do not advocate avoidance of medical intervention! Discovering and addressing the metaphysical cause of your illness does not mean that you are not to consult a physician. It is much easier to

21

explore the inner realms when you are not distracted by physical pain, so, by all means, get the help you need to ease the situation so that you can explore in comfort.

Thankfully, the medical profession is slowly recognizing that we are not only physical beings, but also complex and multi-dimensional beings comprised of subtle bodies connected to a physical body. Medical practitioners in our western culture are finally acknowledging this connection - knowledge that has always been accepted by eastern cultures. You may be pleasantly surprised to find a doctor who is prepared to listen and treat you as a whole person. You may also benefit from a number of alternative methods of treatment. Take responsibility for the cause of your illness and find out as much as you can about traditional and alternative therapies so you can make an informed decision about treatment. You can custom-design the most effective and proactive treatment for your own health and well being. It is liberating to realize that you are responsible for your own health - you do have choices.

There has been a global shift in energy brought on by the year 2000. The "Age of Aquarius" is upon us and, whether or not you acknowledge it, this new era is the opening to a new world. Humanity is shedding the old skin of a world dominated by the mind, or the collective ego. We will go forward into the New Millennium with a new understanding and a new mindset - the shift to a more spiritual existence for all Humans Being. Embracing this transformation will bring an ease and balance to your life on all levels. Ignoring this shift will result in difficulty and stagnation in your physical, mental, emotional and spiritual bodies. Open your mind, open your heart and allow yourself to receive the flow of loving, healing Universal energy that is rightfully yours.

Section 2

Overview

Here are the answers to many questions that people frequently ask me and ask themselves.

How is a congenital disease explained metaphysically?

Remember that we are all souls who have chosen to incarnate on this earth for many lifetimes. Just as we may awaken one morning to find an illness still present that had not healed the previous day, so we may carry an illness with us from one lifetime to the next.

The soul may choose to experience congenital disease as a life lesson that has been carried over from unresolved inner conflict or imbalance in another life. Or the soul may choose to experience a particular illness in order to learn the necessary lessons it requires for its own growth in this particular lifetime. Usually, the person suffering from a congenital disease is more accepting of his condition than are his family and friends. It is important that the parents of a child with a congenital illness not blame themselves for the illness. On a soul level, the child has chosen and taken personal responsibility for the illness, knowing full well the purpose and the lesson to be learned.

This person must discover what this disease prevents him from being and doing; this will help him understand its message. I highly recommend that he ask himself the questions at the end of this book.

How is hereditary or genetic disease explained metaphysically?

What is inherited is not the disease, but the way of thinking. From a metaphysical perspective, a person with a hereditary disease has actually chosen the parent with whom he has a shared lesson to learn in this lifetime. Generally, a parent's refusal to accept circumstances manifests itself through the guilt carried by that parent and the consequent grievance the child carries toward the parent. Aside from blaming the parent, it is common for a child in this situation to do everything possible to avoid becoming anything like the parent. This conscious and/or subconscious animosity creates an ongoing discomfort and emotional problems for both the parent and the child.

The person suffering from a hereditary disease is receiving the following message: Accept your choice of parents because this is a great opportunity for you to progress in your spiritual awareness. Until this acceptance is achieved, the hereditary or genetic disease usually continues to be passed on from generation to generation.

How is an epidemic explained metaphysically?
When the same thing affects thousands of peo-
ple, do they all have the same lesson to learn?

Throughout time, epidemics have had a way of sweeping through populations like a sickle through a field of grain, quickly and effectively felling large numbers of people. The duration and extent of the epidemic are directly proportional to the particular belief system that maintains it. Metaphysically, those who are affected by such widespread disease are allowing themselves to be overrun by the way of thinking prevalent at the time. This is true especially in times of plague that takes many lives in a very short period of time - sometimes within weeks or months.

Illnesses currently occurring in epidemic proportions are cancer, AIDS, diabetes, muscular dystrophy, heart disease, and asthma, among others. These conditions are flourishing despite the tremendous discoveries made through the research of pharmaceutical companies and the scientific community. We can see many similar beliefs among those who have the same disease. We can only conclude that there must be another way to deal with this. This other way is none other than self-love and true forgiveness. The steps of forgiveness are well defined at the end of this book.

Why is it that the onset of most disease is at mid-
dle age, even though we have carried a particular
belief system throughout our lives?

27

Illness occurs when we reach our physical limitations. That point varies from person to person and is determined by the level of energy reserves. The physical body is affected once the emotional and mental limits have been reached.

Our energy reserves, and the number of times we accumulate negative emotional experiences, determine when we will reach our limits. Let's take, for example, a child who experiences an unjust act. Each unjust experience will awaken and add to the child's inner wound. One day, when he has reached his limit of injustice, the illness will appear.

Is it possible to get better without understanding the underlying metaphysical cause of one's physical problem?

Of course! This happens all the time. It is possible to do the work of acceptance or forgiveness internally without even being aware of it. According to research, human beings are fully conscious no more than 10% of the time; that means our awareness of our own mental and emotional state lies dormant at least 90% of the time. However, if we do not acknowledge and release the old inner wound, and we get better *only* because we believe in the medical treatment or keep a positive 'mental' attitude, the cure will be temporary. The next event that triggers and reawakens the old inner wound will reawaken the dis-ease or disorder.

What are the factors that determine whether a disease will manifest as a simple illness or something more serious - even fatal?

The primary determining factor is our interpretation of events during childhood. If the inner pain was mild, disease will not be as serious. If the inner pain was perceived as devastating or endured in isolation (in situations where we had no one to turn to), the resulting illness will be much more severe. The degree of seriousness of the disease is directly proportional to the depth of emotional pain. Primal emotional injuries such as rejection, abandonment, humiliation, betrayal and injustice are often buried deep within the subconscious and left to fester into adulthood.

What is the nature of inflammatory disease in relation to the metaphysical?

After having heard about and reading the works of Dr. Geerd Hamer, a German doctor, I found the results of his research in what he calls NEW MEDICINE to be very interesting. According to Dr. Hamer, inflammation or infection (any illness ending with the suffix "itis") is the result of the body's resolution of an inner conflict. As soon as the conflict is gone or resolved, the body (with help from the brain) puts itself on the road to recovery and it's at that moment that the infectious or inflammatory disease appears. Example: an employee who can't stand his boss and decides to go on vacation just to get away. As soon as he gets there and starts to feel good, he develops sinusitis for no apparent reason.

29

(A biological conflict is a violent shock that makes us feel powerless, and is endured in isolation. It's a difficult conflict that catches us off guard. Everyday conflicts are easier deal with because we often see them coming and can prepare ourselves psychologically.)

Fundamentally, human pain has its biological meaning: to immobilize the organism and the affected organ for optimal healing.

Once the body has begun the healing process and developed inflammation, it is not inappropriate to seek medical attention. Be sure, however, to resolve any underlying conflict with love and forgiveness or any medical solution will be purely superficial and temporary.

According to Dr. Hamer, of the 1,000 and some documented diseases, half are *warm* diseases and the other half *cold* diseases. Warm diseases, such as inflammation, indicate that the conflict is resolved and the body is in the process of healing. Cold diseases are those in the first phase that occur when conflict is yet unresolved. With resolution come warmth and the beginning of the healing process.

Pain exists as much in the cold phase as in the warm phase. Stomach ulcers or sore legs would be the kind of pain in a cold illness and inflammation; infection and edema would belong to a warm illness.

The theories of New Medicine are very interesting. The works of Dr. Hamer, Dr. Siegel, Dr. Simonton and others expand new horizons for all of us. Results of their research have been extraordinary, meshing the traditional with resourceful, innovative and holistic thinking. How do you know who beholds the truth? Listen carefully to your intuition and you will find the balance of traditional and New Medicine that will be appropriate and most effective for you.

To the works of Dr. Hamer I want to add that we must not only distance ourselves from the conflict, but also resolve it so that it will not return. In the example in which the employee developed sinusitis on his vacation: in order for him to achieve *permanent* healing from the sinusitis, he must become aware of its cause. Without acknowledging the source and forgiving both himself and his boss, he will likely develop chronic sinusitis. Distancing will provide only temporary relief. Resolution, on the other hand, will result in permanent healing.

Suggestions for using alphabetical guide

Note that illnesses and diseases are listed in alphabetical order. Once you have found the name of an illness, take the following steps:

1. When you find the particular illness or disease (listed alphabetically) you are suffering from, read the metaphysical description.

2. Write down or mentally note what affects or concerns you the most about what you have read.

3. Read the key questions at the back of the book in order to accurately pinpoint the causes of the disease.

4. Take the necessary time to read carefully and digest the conclusion of this book, which is the most important part. Only when you truly understand the cause will you be able to set into motion the internal and external forces that will transform your health.

5. I strongly suggest you read the two preceding sections frequently, as they pertain to all of the individual diseases listed.

Alphabetical reference guide to the metaphysical significance of illnesses and diseases

ABORTION

PHYSICAL BLOCK

Abortion is the induced termination of pregnancy before the fetus can survive outside the womb, which is usually not performed after the fourth month. A *spontaneous abortion* is another word for *miscarriage*, in which the fetus is rejected and expelled by the body, usually lifeless and with the placenta. A *therapeutic abortion*, on the other hand, is a voluntary termination of the pregnancy that is performed on a live fetus by a physician after careful deliberation regarding the impact of a full-term pregnancy on the physical and psychological health of the mother.

EMOTIONAL BLOCK

A spontaneous abortion (or miscarriage) is the result of an unconscious choice made between the mother and the soul of the baby she is carrying. There is a soul-level communication between mother and child in which either or both parties have decided to end the incarnation at this particular time. The soul of the child may have decided to choose another incarnation or to come to this same mother at a different point in time. The mother may have decided that she is not ready for the pregnancy at this time and communicated this to the child who, in turn, withdraws its life force from the fetus to return, quite possibly, to the same mother at a more appropriate time in another pregnancy.

37

If the mother has chosen to terminate the pregnancy through abortion, it is usually out of fear. If complications arise as a result of the abortion, guilt often is the cause. It is important that the mother explain her feelings clearly to the soul of this fetus. She must express her fear in an open and heartfelt manner; love and accept herself and her limitations. Otherwise the guilt she may carry for refusing to bring her child into the world will spawn a number of long-term physical and psychological complications.

In choosing a *therapeutic abortion* rather than a spontaneous one, the mother has transferred her decision to terminate the pregnancy to the medical professional, rather than taking full responsibility herself. In this way, she may feel less guilty, as she has validated her need to end the pregnancy by getting a "professional opinion."

An *abortion* or *miscarriage* often coincides with a project that *aborted*, or did not succeed. This woman cannot or will not bring her creation to term.

MENTAL BLOCK

I have had the opportunity to observe many young women at various stages in this process who ended up with long-term problems in the genital area after having an abortion. They feel guilt over ending the life of the child and punish themselves (unconsciously). Some of these women retain a distended abdomen indefinitely, indicating the carrying of a "psychological baby." If you have had an abortion, it is very important that you come to terms with your reasons for doing so. Understand that tak-

A

ing the pregnancy to full term was beyond your limits and accept your decision and yourself.

I believe that when a woman becomes pregnant, powerful life lessons are presented to her. If you are currently considering an abortion, I highly recommend that you get in touch with your reasons for terminating the pregnancy and realize that they may be based in fear. Try to get past the fear and put yourself in the hands of the Divine. Realize that fear creates limitation and without it, you will make your decision with clarity. Too often we believe we have reached our limits, but in reality we are much stronger than we think.

It is imperative that you take some time to yourself before making this decision. Do not listen to the rationale that others will give you. Listen to your heart. Speak to the tiny soul inside you; only the two of you together can make the right decision. If delaying the incarnation of this small being is the right decision, you will feel a peace come over you in doing so. If you abort based on your own fear, the rejection of the child will come back as karma that you will have to deal with as a consequence. Clear and open communication with the child will bring about the right decision.

Do not judge yourself harshly in terms of making a right or wrong decision. There is no right or wrong, rather there are consequences regardless of the choice you make. Give yourself the right to not always finish what you've started. Recognize and accept your true limitations and be gentle with yourself.

SPIRITUAL BLOCK AND CONCLUSION

To uncover the spiritual block that keeps you from responding to the needs of your BEING, refer to the "KEY QUESTIONS" at the back of this book. In answering these questions, you will come in touch more easily and accurately with the true cause of your physical problem.

ABSCESS

PHYSICAL BLOCK

An *abscess* is a localized mass of pus that can erupt anywhere on the surface of the body. In the case of a warm abscess (by far the most common), the purulent gathering develops quickly and is accompanied by the four signs of inflammation: cyst, redness, warmth and pain. The slow formation of liquid and no apparent sign of inflammation, on the other hand, characterize a *cold abscess*.

EMOTIONAL BLOCK

Presence of an abscess indicates repressed anger that is brought to the surface during moments of despair, feelings of powerlessness and lack of success. The pleasure of living is being drowned in sadness and anger. Abscesses are also painful, indicating that guilt is felt in the face of the anger. To determine the root of the anger, note the location of the abscess. If it's on a leg, the anger can be interpreted as frustration about the direction your life is taking, anxiety about the future or about going forward. Read the following and also refer to the relevant location.

MENTAL BLOCK

Just as the physical body must be kept clean to avoid infection, so must your thoughts be cleansed. Is it possible that you have unhealthy thoughts about yourself or about someone else? Are you angry with someone about something that happened in the past and have wanted to express this anger, but suppressed it instead to the point where you can no longer control yourself? There is probably some shame related to a fear that's festering inside you. See SECTION 2.

SPIRITUAL BLOCK AND CONCLUSION

To uncover the spiritual block that keeps you from responding to the needs of your BEING, refer to the "KEY QUESTIONS" at the back of this book. In answering these questions, you will come in touch more easily and accurately with the true cause of your physical problem.

ACCIDENT

PHYSICAL BLOCK

Because an *accident* is an unpredictable event, we often believe it happens by pure chance. Increasingly, we are being told, "there are no accidents." Nothing happens by coincidence. I believe that chance and accidents are tools the Universe (GOD) uses to get our attention. Just make note of what part of the body has been injured and how seriously. These are important considerations when trying to understand the metaphysical cause of the accident. Read the following and also refer to the relevant location.

EMOTIONAL BLOCK

Accidents are interpreted unconsciously as punishment, as on a deeper level we blame ourselves and accuse our inner-self. We feel responsible for what goes on around us. For example: a mother, tending to her chores, hears her child calling from the next room. She feels the child can wait and, continuing with her chores trips and hurts her leg. If she asks herself *"What was I thinking just now?"* she realizes that she was accusing herself of being a neglectful mother. Hurting her leg was punishment for being such a mother, one that did not want to *go* to her child. Accidents are a way to neutralize our guilt, to punish ourselves. Unfortunately, all of this goes on unconsciously.

MENTAL BLOCK

Your definition of guilt needs to be revised. According to our legal system, a person is declared guilty when it has been proven, beyond a shadow of a doubt, that harm was intended. Each time you blame yourself or feel guilty about something, ask yourself if you intended to do harm. If not, stop accusing yourself in your mind. This will help you to stop punishing yourself with "accidents."

In the example above, do you think the mother intended to harm her child? Nothing happened that she needs to punish herself for. When someone is actually guilty, the law of cause and effect will prevail and will exhibit itself in his character. A wise and responsible person is one who rec-

42

ognizes when he is at fault, and asks forgiveness of the person he has wronged or hurt. In doing so, he creates harmony that will come back to him as harmony and acceptance. This is Divine Justice.

If your accident was an unconscious way of giving yourself a "break," it is important to remember that you could have accomplished the same thing without injuring yourself physically. It would be much less painful to simply make your request known.

If your injury is significant and painful, such as a FRACTURE, it is an indication that you are consciously or unconsciously suppressing violent thoughts directed at someone else. By nature, violent thoughts cannot be contained and may instead turn inward against yourself. Liberate yourself by communicating your feelings to the other person, forgiving yourself for having the thoughts in the meantime.

See also FRACTURE, BURN or SPRAIN as it applies to your situation.

SPIRITUAL BLOCK AND CONCLUSION

To uncover the spiritual block that keeps you from responding to the needs of your BEING, refer to the "KEY QUESTIONS" at the back of this book. In answering these questions, you will come in touch more easily and accurately with the true cause of your physical problem.

ACHILLES' TENDON

See HEEL PAIN or HEEL SPUR and add to the definition that you want to show your power.

ACNE

PHYSICAL BLOCK

Acne eruptions are generally limited to the fatty tissue on the skin of the face, shoulders and upper back. Usually beginning around puberty and limited to adolescence, acne problems may also carry into adulthood as far as the thirties and forties, when the skin begins to dry. Common acne heals without scarring, but nodular acne, which occurs deep in the epidermis, may last many years and leave deep, permanent scarring.

EMOTIONAL BLOCK

Acne is a way to distance ourselves from others so we won't be looked at too closely. This skin problem affects those with low self-esteem. They do not like themselves, don't know how to love themselves, and are generally very sensitive, withdrawn souls. This is why acne so often affects teenagers, because they ask too much of themselves and are easily ashamed. Instead of having to hide from others, they repel others with their skin problem.

Acne can also be a problem among teenagers who are struggling to please one or both parents. It is difficult for

44

A

them to accept themselves, because they are in the process of defining who they are.

MENTAL BLOCK

If you are an adolescent struggling with acne, take some time to examine the way you perceive yourself. Determine what attitude is keeping you from being your true self, from expressing your individuality. Perhaps you believe you should be just like your same-sex parent, or you are so opposed to his/her way of thinking that you are doing everything in your power to be the opposite. Meanwhile, you are not being yourself. How do others see you? Do they see you the same way you see yourself?

If you are struggling with acne as an adult, look back at your adolescence and determine what happened at that time that had a lasting emotional effect on you. Acne that persists into adulthood indicates a need to change your self-perception.

If your acne erupted in adulthood, it may be that you have successfully (until now) repressed old hurts received in adolescence in order to avoid suffering from them. This would be especially true of psychological injuries that affected your individuality. Determine what happened just before the onset of the acne that triggered the adolescent memories. Remember that your body is using the acne to help free you from the hurts that have festered inside you all these years. You can no longer suppress them and it takes a lot of energy to keep the pain of an emotional wound buried. Your body is telling you to love and accept yourself - to see your inner beauty. It is releasing the toxic thoughts that you have buried all these years.

See also FACIAL and SKIN DISORDERS.

SPIRITUAL BLOCK AND CONCLUSION

To uncover the spiritual block that keeps you from responding to the needs of your BEING, refer to the "KEY QUESTIONS" at the back of this book. In answering these questions, you will come in touch more easily and accurately with the true cause of your physical problem.

ADDISON'S DISEASE

Addison's disease is caused by depletion in adrenal hormones, which can result in problems with skin pigmentation. Refer to ADRENAL GLAND and SKIN DISORDERS. People affected by this disease often suffer from HYPOGLYCEMIA, so please refer to it as well.

ADENITIS

Adenitis is an inflammation of the lymph glands. Refer to swollen GLANDS and add suppressed anger to its description.

ADENOIDS

PHYSICAL BLOCK

The *adenoids* are lymphoid tissue growths in the upper part of the throat, behind the nose. In childhood, the adenoids may become overdeveloped (hypertrophy) and cause nasal obstruction, causing the child to breathe through the mouth.

EMOTIONAL BLOCK

A child suffering from swollen adenoids is characteristically ultra-sensitive with a strong sense of premonition. This child can sense disharmony between parents long before the parents realize there is any problem. The child's reaction is to block his own feelings so that he is not hurt. He refrains from discussing his fears with anyone and becomes isolated. A nasal obstruction represents thoughts or emotions the child is holding onto for fear of being misunderstood.

MENTAL BLOCK

This child believes that he is in the way or unwelcome. He may believe he is the cause of the problems he feels around him. It is important that he validates and absolves himself of blame by discussing this with someone he can trust, so that he can begin to realize that others can love him whether or not others understand him.

SPIRITUAL BLOCK AND CONCLUSION

To uncover the spiritual block that keeps you from responding to the needs of your BEING, refer to the "KEY QUESTIONS" at the back of this book. In answering these questions, you will come in touch more easily and accurately with the true cause of your physical problem.

ADENOMA

An *adenoma* is a benign tumor. See TUMOR.

ADHESIONS

PHYSICAL BLOCK

Adhesions are the result of inflammation that the body has developed in order to resist an assault. Growths of fibrous tissue accumulate and harden, joining organs that are normally separate. These adhesions can establish themselves on or between any number of organs and their location is an indication as to the reason for the disease.

EMOTIONAL BLOCK

Adhesions develop in individuals who have become "hardened" or "tough" - those who hold strongly to ideas to fend off attack. These immovable ideas take up too much room and prevent you from feeling.

MENTAL BLOCK

In order to be able to create these unnecessary tissues in your body, the belief system you've created has to have been in place for a number of years. You can let go of those beliefs that are hurting you. Understand that you do not need to harden in order to be loved and accepted.

SPIRITUAL BLOCK AND CONCLUSION

To uncover the spiritual block that keeps you from responding to the needs of your BEING, refer to the "KEY QUESTIONS" at the back of this book. In answering these questions, you will come in touch more easily and accurately with the true cause of your physical problem.

ADRENAL GLAND PROBLEMS

PHYSICAL BLOCK

The two *adrenal glands* (also called *suprarenal glands*) are situated one above each kidney and serve a number of functions. In a state of emergency, they secrete adrenaline, a hormone necessary to alert the brain, accelerate the heartbeat, and mobilize the reserve sugars to provide energy sufficient for fight or flight. They also secrete cortisone, which plays an important role in the metabolism of sugars and as an anti-inflammatory. They are also instrumental in maintaining electrolyte balance in the body. Problems with the adrenal glands can have profound ramifications on the entire human organism.

EMOTIONAL BLOCK

The adrenals link the physical body to the *root chakra* (energy center). They furnish you, as an individual, with the energy necessary to maintain faith in Mother Earth and in her capacity to provide you with fundamental needs. This refers to anything that regards *having*.

Adrenal problems indicate that you are burdened with unrealistic and unfounded fears surrounding your material life. You are afraid of making the wrong move and lack confidence in your own ability to meet your material needs. You probably exhibit a fertile imagination, doubt your self-worth and become annoyed at yourself for not being more vital and dynamic.

Hypofunction, or underproduction of adrenaline, occurs when you've failed to respect your personal limitations and have exhausted your adrenals. You want nothing more than to simply rest. This is the body's way of telling you that you need to rest your mind, to let go and to trust the Universe's ability to take care of you. Know that it has always taken care of every living thing that allows it to do so.

Adrenal *hyperfunction*, or overproduction of adrenaline, is a sign that you are keeping your adrenal glands in a state of alert as if you had to face an emergency when, in reality, this is happening in your imagination. There is a loss of grounding and a lack of coherence.

MENTAL BLOCK

A

Your body is trying to get the message across to you that you're not alone to provide for yourself; what you have learned so far is not the only means to survival. It is your inner self (and not your mind) that knows and remains in touch with your innermost needs. Learn to trust this intelligence and understand that it will provide for you. Your most fundamental needs will be fulfilled. Rather than expending all of your energy worrying, learn to simply be grateful for all that you now have. Develop reverence and gratitude; these will become your links to your inner power. Once you've tapped into this resource, your energy will be renewed and you will go forward with an unshakable and renewed strength and vitality.

SPIRITUAL BLOCK AND CONCLUSION

To uncover the spiritual block that keeps you from responding to the needs of your BEING, refer to the "KEY QUESTIONS" at the back of this book. In answering these questions, you will come in touch more easily and accurately with the true cause of your physical problem

---

AEROPHAGIA

PHYSICAL BLOCK

Aerophagia is a condition that has been brought on by excessive inhalation of air either voluntarily or involuntarily. Repeated belching occurs as the body tries to rid itself of the accumulation of air, often resulting in the dilation of the esophagus and stomach as well as vomiting.

EMOTIONAL BLOCK

If you are suffering from aerophagia, you probably often feel anguished. You try desperately to breathe in life all at once and overextend yourself, thereby not living according to your true nature and limits.

MENTAL BLOCK

Since air is symbolic of life, it is probable that you believe you must breathe life into everyone around you and consequently take in enough air for everyone! A physical imbalance is bound to occur, as the body cannot possibly process this amount of air. What do you do to breathe life into everyone?

If you suffer from this condition, you need to realize that, in order to maintain health, you need to take in only what is required for your own being. You will find yourself enjoying life from a much more balanced perspective.

SPIRITUAL BLOCK AND CONCLUSION

To uncover the spiritual block that keeps you from responding to the needs of your BEING, refer to the "KEY QUESTIONS" at the back of this book. In answering these questions, you will come in touch more easily and accurately with the true cause of your physical problem.

AGORAPHOBIA

PHYSICAL BLOCK

Agoraphobia provokes a feeling of anguish as soon as you leave a protective area or person to find yourself in an open space or public place. It's the most prevalent of all phobias. Women are twice as likely to have it as men, although many men who have it hide their agoraphobia with alcohol. They would rather become alcoholics than admit that they have an uncontrollable fear. The agoraphobic complains often of anxiety and especially anguish to the point of panic.

Such an agonizing situation brings on physiological reactions such as heart palpitations, dizziness, tense or weak muscles, sweating, respiratory difficulty, nausea, incontinence, etc. that can lead to panic. Agoraphobia can also produce cognitive reactions (feelings of oddness, fear of losing control, going crazy, being publicly humiliated, dying, etc.) and behavioral reactions such as fleeing anxiety-ridden situations and any place that seems to be too far from the person or place which is seen as "safe."

EMOTIONAL BLOCK

Agoraphobics experience such overpowering fear that they avoid situations where they feel they cannot readily escape. For this reason, the agoraphobic must venture out with someone they can trust - a "safe" person - or know that there is a "safe" place nearby they can run to. There are those who will justify never going outside at all. In reality, the anticipated disasters rarely happen.

The majority of agoraphobics were very dependent on their mothers when they were young and felt responsible for her happiness or for helping her in her role as a mother. Agoraphobics can help themselves emotionally by dealing with the skewed relationship they have developed with their mothers.

MENTAL BLOCK

Agoraphobics ultimately fear death and madness. After having counseled them for many years in my workshops, I have developed a theory that has helped several hundred of them. Most agoraphobics' fears come from their childhood years and have been experienced in isolation. Death or madness of someone close to them affected them enormously. They may have had a brush with death themselves or an unnerving sense of emotional instability was pervasive in the home where fear of death or insanity was ever present.

Most agoraphobics and those who treat them fail to realize that this fear of death is not only the fear of physical death, but of *change*. Change is symbolic of the death of what exists, and all forms of change can cause tremendous anguish for the agoraphobic. The passage from childhood to adolescence, from adolescence to adulthood, from single to married, the death or birth of someone close to them - even a move to a new location, a pregnancy, accident, or separation, can be catastrophic. This fear can be con-

A

trolled for many years, until the moment they reach their limit and it then becomes conscious.

Most agoraphobics possess a lively and vivid imagination. They imagine situations well beyond the scope of reality, and then believe themselves incapable of facing these situations. It is this enormous excess of mental activity that makes them fear madness/insanity. They dare not speak of it to others, for fear of seeming crazy. It is imperative to understand that it is not madness but badly managed over-sensitivity.

If you are agoraphobic, understand that you are not mad and that you are not going to die from this. You were simply extremely sensitive as a child and so susceptible to other peoples' emotions that you felt responsible for their happiness or misfortune. Subsequently, you became finely tuned psychically in order to watch out for them in their presence. Even now when you are in a public place you tend to collect all the emotions of others and become overwhelmed. These emotions do not belong to you! You are not responsible for them; let them go! You must learn as soon as possible what a responsible person is. This theory is fundamental in all my teachings.

Refer also to HYPOGLYCEMIA, very common in agoraphobics.

SPIRITUAL BLOCK AND CONCLUSION

To uncover the spiritual block that keeps you from responding to the needs of your BEING, refer to the "KEY QUESTIONS" at the back of this book. In answering

55

these questions, you will come in touch more easily and accurately with the true cause of your physical problem.

AIDS

PHYSICAL BLOCK

AIDS, or *acquired immune deficiency syndrome*, is defined primarily by what appears to be severe immune deficiency, and is distinguished from virtually every other disease by the fact that it has no constant, specific symptoms. AIDS is an umbrella term for any or all of some twenty-five previously known diseases and symptoms. These include cancer, rheumatism, sarcoma, pneumonia, diarrhea, dementia, mycosis, tuberculosis, fever, herpes, neurological malfunction or deficiency, candidiasis, toxoplasmosis, weight loss, night sweats, rashes and swollen lymph glands. If HIV antibodies are detected, or the patient is seropositive, these diseases converge as AIDS; if not, they are diagnosed simply for what they are. There have been a number of books written by scientists about this disease and it is the subject of much controversy. It is most important, however, to understand that being HIV positive does not necessarily lead to an AIDS diagnosis.

EMOTIONAL BLOCK

AIDS is linked directly with self-love. It occurs when we are unable to love ourselves, and especially when we are unable to accept our own gender, preferring to be born the opposite sex. AIDS, however, is not partial to either gen-

A

der and ravages both heterosexual and homosexual populations. In Africa, Asia and the Indies, for example, the heterosexual population is most affected because of rampant prostitution and unprotected sexual behavior. Unfortunately, more and more children are being born with AIDS.

Although many people still view AIDS as a sexually transmitted disease, in reality it is a disease contracted by those who, because they cannot love themselves, compensate by embracing the illusion of love and acceptance on a sexual level. They live with a deep-seated low self-worth and perpetual sense of guilt and disappointment that causes them to become dependent on others for self-validation. This, of course, always leads to disappointment. Thus, a cycle is created of guilt and disappointment that leads to self-punishment. They feel that an illness will neutralize the guilt. As they use sex to feel loved when they believe they are unlovable, to punish themselves, they undermine their own sexuality.

MENTAL BLOCK

If you will only begin to believe that you deserve to live, AIDS need not be fatal. Understand that every disappointment you've experienced is due simply to your own unmet expectations about love. You've been looking for love in all the wrong places! Being loved is not the answer; you need to love, especially yourself. Believe enough in your own self worth, in the extraordinary being that YOU ARE.

Your body is telling you that it's urgent that you learn to love and accept yourself *as you are,* with a full and open heart. It's interesting to note that AIDS patients are generally extremely sensitive and compassionate people with enough love inside them to fill the planet. Tap some of that wellspring of love for yourself! It's critical that you accept yourself and your sex. On the most profound soul level, you chose your gender in order to experience and learn powerful life lessons, whether or not they pleased those around you, including your parents. They have lessons to learn from you, too, including those surrounding your sexuality. You are meant to approach these lessons with love and acceptance, as you honor the choices your soul has made. The most important lesson is to see to your own evolution and to grow in a soil of unconditional love. This is the only reason for being, for all human beings.

SPIRITUAL BLOCK AND CONCLUSION

To uncover the spiritual block that keeps you from responding to the needs of your BEING, refer to the "KEY QUESTIONS" at the back of this book. In answering these questions, you will come in touch more easily and accurately with the true cause of your physical problem.

AIRSICKNESS

See MOTION SICKNESS.

ALIENATION

See INSANITY

ALLERGIES

PHYSICAL BLOCK

An *allergy* is defined as the body's overreaction to a foreign substance, usually after previous contact with this substance. The reaction can be acute and dissimilar to the reaction that was observed on first contact. The body has developed an immunological hypersensitivity that can be either localized to a specific area of the body or systemic, affecting the entire body.

EMOTIONAL BLOCK

If you are allergic, you may have a strong dislike for someone else and can no longer tolerate that person. You have difficulty adapting to a person or situation and are far too easily influenced by others, especially by those you want to impress. You are frequently over-sensitive, defensive and easily intimidated.

Know that you are dealing with internal conflict. Part of you loves something or someone while another part of you forbids it. You may feel love for someone but are uncomfortable that you've become emotionally dependent on him or her. One part of you wants to be in their presence and another part of you says you should do without.

You find yourself finding fault with them. Often, those with allergies had two parents that held opposing views in a number of areas, which caused conflict in the child. Allergies can easily become an attention-getting device, especially if the allergy is severe or life threatening and requires a great deal of attention to keep it in check.

MENTAL BLOCK

If you suffer from allergies, figure out what the situation is or for whom you feel enmity and yet seek his or her approval. Generally, this is a person to whom you feel very close. You think if you behave according to their expectations you will be truly loved. Realize that you have allowed yourself to become dependent upon the approval or acknowledgment of this person. It is important to remember that being submissive will not bring you love.

It is interesting to note that we often become allergic to foods we enjoy, for example, dairy products. We love ice cream but can't eat it because we are allergic to dairy. If you are allergic to a certain food, is it possible that you have difficulty allowing yourself to savor the pleasure that comes from the good things in life?

If you are allergic to dust or to an animal, is it possible that you feel easily attacked by others? Why do you think people want to attack you? I suggest you examine your own thoughts about aggression. In general, the fears we have regarding others are a reflection of what's going on inside of us.

A

Wouldn't your life be simpler and much more pleasurable if you could get the attention of those you love without making yourself sick? It is your belief system that is locking you into this pattern. Instead of believing your allergy is triggered by outside influences, I suggest you think about what happened in the 24 hours prior to the allergic reaction. It's in your best interest to find out which person you are finding intolerable. Since you can't change others, your only option is to see them through the eyes of love and accept them as they are. You will find they will accept you as you are in return and you will receive the attention you seek in a healthy manner.

SPIRITUAL BLOCK AND CONCLUSION

To uncover the spiritual block that keeps you from responding to the needs of your BEING, refer to the "KEY QUESTIONS" at the back of this book. In answering these questions, you will come in touch more easily and accurately with the true cause of your physical problem.

ALOPECIA

PHYSICAL BLOCK

Alopecia is the partial or complete loss of hair that usually occurs on the scalp, but can occur anywhere on the body, including the eyebrows and extremities. Hair can fall out in various patterns, the most common of which is called *male pattern baldness*, or *hereditary alopecia*. See BALDNESS.

Alopecia areata is a sudden loss of various circumscribed areas of hair for no apparent reason or secondary to systemic disease. *Alopecia universallis* is loss of hair over the entire body. See HAIR LOSS.

Scarring alopecia ultimately leaves the affected skin surface smooth and usually unable to regenerate hair.

EMOTIONAL BLOCK

Hair on the head and body provide a layer of protection to the skin. Loss of all or even a portion of hair indicates a cutting-off of psychological protection. Whether the result of accident or intent, hair loss indicates that you no longer feel protected and are experiencing fear from which you cannot escape on your own. You have difficulty asking for help from others and may be overly protective of others to hide your own sense of vulnerability.

MENTAL BLOCK

Alopecia is a message from your body to get back in touch with your true nature, or your I AM. You have lost your sense of your own divinity. Realize that your inner God constantly protects you. Determine whether or not those around you are really in need of your protection, and realize that you no longer need to feel you are within a hair's breadth of danger yourself. Learn to ask for help when in need. Allow yourself to be fearful and admit it openly.

See HAIR PROBLEMS.

SPIRITUAL BLOCK AND CONCLUSION

A

To uncover the spiritual block that keeps you from responding to the needs of your BEING, refer to the "KEY QUESTIONS" at the back of this book. In answering these questions, you will come in touch more easily and accurately with the true cause of your physical problem.

ALZHEIMER'S DISEASE

PHYSICAL BLOCK

This disease generally appears in older people and is characterized by a gradual loss of memory. Those affected by this disease can easily remember events of the distant past but have great difficulty remembering more recent events. It is what is called fixed amnesia, in which the affected person forgets events as they happen because they are incapable of retaining them in their memory banks.

EMOTIONAL BLOCK

Alzheimer's disease is used to escape the reality of the present. Those afflicted with this disease are often the type to have taken care of everything. They had a wonderful memory that they were very proud of and even liked to show off. It was often misused, however, by storing trivial details that others thought unimportant. These people often felt bound to others and felt that others weren't taking care of them as they would have liked. Today, this disease relieves them of responsibilities and helps them control others, especially those that care for them.

MENTAL BLOCK

Usually, it is not the person afflicted with Alzheimer's that wants to be cured; it's those around them. The person being cared for believes it is their only method of revenge. They have suffered some situation in silence for many years and now have a good excuse for doing as they please.

If you are suffering from Alzheimer's, it is important to know that you can get the attention you need from others without going about it this way. Understand that you can be accepted and loved even if you do not want to take care of everything and remember every detail. It's okay to simplify your life. Talk to someone you can confide in about your experiences, present and past. If you decide to live life at its fullest, think of the good years ahead.

If you are reading this description as it pertains to someone else, I suggest you have him or her read it over for themselves.

SPIRITUAL BLOCK AND CONCLUSION

To uncover the spiritual block that keeps you from responding to the needs of your BEING, refer to the "KEY QUESTIONS" at the back of this book. In answering these questions, you will come in touch more easily and accurately with the true cause of your physical problem.

A

AMEBIOSIS

Amebiosis is an infection of the large intestine with inter-mittent diarrhea. See INTESTINAL DISORDERS and DIARRHEA.

AMNESIA

PHYSICAL BLOCK

Amnesia is a complete or partial loss of memory. As op-posed to Alzheimer's disease, the person who suffers from amnesia is incapable of remembering the facts that their memory had previously stored.

EMOTIONAL BLOCK

Amnesia is an alibi of sorts, allowing the rejection of one or more memories that are too painful to deal with.

MENTAL BLOCK

If you find yourself in this state, know that regaining con-tact with your spiritual self will give you the strength to overcome your past limitations. It is your mental self that has been unable to deal with the memories and has led you to choose this alternative. You may not have been able to face your memories in the past, but it is quite possible that you may be able to do so now. Begin by taking the time to reprogram your mental self and believe that you can over-come anything, and then find a way by asking for help.

SPIRITUAL BLOCK AND CONCLUSION

To uncover the spiritual block that keeps you from responding to the needs of your BEING, refer to the "KEY QUESTIONS" at the back of this book. In answering these questions, you will come in touch more easily and accurately with the true cause of your physical

ANDROPAUSE

This is a natural phenomenon characterized by a decrease in sexual function that can happen to men (usually over the age of 60) and is considered an element of *"Male Menopause."* See MENOPAUSE.

ANEMIA

PHYSICAL BLOCK

Anemia is marked by a low number of red blood cells. Red blood cells are necessary for the distribution of oxygen (O_2) to the cells throughout the body and, in part, for removing carbon dioxide (CO_2). The signs of anemia are: pale skin and mucous membranes, accelerated respiration and heartbeat, and marked fatigue. There can also be headaches, vertigo, and buzzing in the ears (signs of lack of oxygen to the brain).

EMOTIONAL BLOCK

A

In metaphysics, blood represents the love of life. The anemic person has lost this love of life. He also has difficulty accepting his incarnation, possibly to the point of losing his will to live. He becomes discouraged and feels hopeless, losing touch with his needs and desires. Eventually, an anemic person feels that he is just withering away.

MENTAL BLOCK

If you currently suffer from anemia, you need to reestablish contact with your ability to shape your life, without depending on others. Become conscious of the negative thoughts that are pushing joy away from you. Let the child in you come out - the one who wants to play and take life less seriously.

SPIRITUAL BLOCK AND CONCLUSION

To uncover the spiritual block that keeps you from responding to the needs of your BEING, refer to the "KEY QUESTIONS" at the back of this book. In answering these questions, you will come in touch more easily and accurately with the true cause of your physical problem.

ANEURYSM

PHYSICAL BLOCK

An *aneurysm* occurs when a weakened area in the wall of a blood vessel dilates to the point of ballooning. Blood rushing through this area of the vein or artery puts pressure on the aneurysm, at the risk of rupturing it. If the aneurysm is in the throat, symptoms include cough or difficulty in swallowing. If it is abdominal, it may be accompanied by pain and digestive complaints. The area itself is generally palpable. A *cerebral aneurysm* is generally considered to be a consequence of late-revealing congenital malformations. If so see SECTION 2.

EMOTIONAL BLOCK

An aneurysm may occur after we have experienced great emotional trauma, generally concerning family. This prevents us from pursuing relationships as before. Those suffering from an aneurysm experience or want to experience a breaking apart of some form of relationship, even if it will break their heart. They may feel guilt about that decision, often unconsciously. They have let their feelings fester too long, and when they have reached their limit, they decide to break the relationship.

MENTAL BLOCK

An aneurysm is an urgent message from your body to stop piling up internal pain. Make a decision NOW to talk about what you're going through with the people involved, rather than keeping it all bottled up inside of you. You may not want to expose your sensitivity, but you don't have much choice; either you talk or you let it kill you. Let go of your stubbornness; it is driving you to make radical decisions that are not good for you. Your heart wants the opposite. Realize the emotional pain that over-

A

whelms you is built of negative thoughts. Open up, express your pain and regain the closeness and the love that you once enjoyed. Know in your heart that you deserve this.

SPIRITUAL BLOCK AND CONCLUSION

To uncover the spiritual block that keeps you from responding to the needs of your BEING, refer to the "KEY QUESTIONS" at the back of this book. In answering these questions, you will come in touch more easily and accurately with the true cause of your physical problem.

ANGINA

Angina is a disease marked by acute inflammation of the throat or tonsils. See TONSILLITIS.

ANGINA PECTORIS

Angina pectoris is characterized by severe paroxysmal chest pain associated with an insufficient supply of oxygen to the heart. This lack of oxygen damages the myocardium, the major muscle of the heart, triggering the pain. The angina is experienced as heaviness, squeezing or suffocating. If the pain is intense, it can radiate to the shoulder, left arm, jaw, neck and even the wrists.

See HEART DISORDERS and add that Angina Pectoris is an indication that you are afraid of going through more grief or disheartening experiences in life so withdraw from living life to the fullest. You have been over-whelmed by life's concerns and feel suffocated and trapped.

ANGUISH

Anguish is defined as unfounded fear or, when a trigger actually does exist, the anguish is stimulated by some-thing that would bring little or no reaction in a normal per-son. It causes you to shrink from perceived obstacles in your life. You no longer want to deal with everyday strug-gles as they overwhelm you and you lack the confidence in your ability to deal with them.

I have been able to establish over many years that the vast majority of patients complaining of anguish actually are suffering, to varying degrees, with agoraphobia. See AG-ORAPHOBIA.

ANKLE PROBLEMS

Lack of flexibility, *swelling* or *pain* in the ankle area are all symbolic of a fear of going forward or of making a move in a different direction. See FOOT PROBLEMS. If you have *broken* or *sprained* an ankle, see ACCIDENT, SPRAIN and FRACTURE.

ANOREXIA

A

PHYSICAL BLOCK

Anorexia occurs mainly in young women (and is becoming more prevalent among young boys), marked by an aversion to food that has long-term repercussions in terms of general health. Early indications are skin pallor and weight loss. Often an anorexic also suffers from *Bulimia*, which occurs when he or she can no longer continue the self-deprivation that characterizes anorexia, so they begin a pattern of bingeing on food and forcing themselves to vomit. This disorder most frequently affects late adolescent and young adult women. Purging can have very serious health consequences. It depletes the body of water and potassium and can even result in death.

EMOTIONAL BLOCK

The anorexic, in rejecting food (the symbol of our nurturing Mother Earth), is rejecting his or her own mother. In rejecting the mother, the principle female role model, they are also rejecting their own feminine aspect. It is essential that the anorexic woman re-examine her life and embrace her femaleness, rather than try to escape it. Basically, the anorexic is not very grounded and easily drifts off into the surreal existence beyond the physical instead of accomplishing what they were sent to do on this planet. They no longer have a taste for food because they have closed the door to their desire to live on this earth.

71

MENTAL BLOCK

If you suffer from anorexia, you must first of all examine your perception of your mother. Know, deep in your heart, that she did her best in raising and nurturing you to the best of her ability and according to her knowledge at the time. Respect her and accept her as another human being, with the fears and limitations we all have. Your mother may have failed you in any number of areas, but your perception of these events, not the events themselves, is causing your pain. You alone have the power to change this perception. Accept your mother and the way she nurtured you and in doing so, you will welcome the woman in you and become whole again. Your appetite for food and for life will be renewed.

If needed, see BULIMIA.

SPIRITUAL BLOCK AND CONCLUSION

To uncover the spiritual block that keeps you from responding to the needs of your BEING, refer to the "KEY QUESTIONS" at the back of this book. In answering these questions, you will come in touch more easily and accurately with the true cause of your physical problem.

ANORGASMIA

Anorgasmia is characterized by the ongoing absence of orgasm in sexual relations. See ORGASM.

ANUS PROBLEMS

A

PHYSICAL BLOCK

The *anus* is the terminating orifice of the digestive tract and can be the site of benign or malignant *lesions,* BLEEDING, ABSCESS, PAIN, ITCHING.

EMOTIONAL BLOCK

Since the anus is the "end" of, in the metaphysical sense, it represents the end of an idea, a relationship or some process. If you experience *pain in the anal area*, you may be feeling guilty about wanting to end something or wanting to do nothing more about it. Indeed, if the pain prevents you from sitting comfortably, your body is letting you know that you want to *just sit down and do nothing*. However, *anal itching* represents unfulfilled desires to bring something to an end.

If you have an abscess in this area, see ABSCESS and take into consideration that there is a problem with ending something.

Anal bleeding is similar to the metaphysical significance of an abscess but also indicates a loss of *joie de vivre*. It is usually related to repressed anger and frustration.

MENTAL BLOCK

It is crucial to let go of the past. Allow yourself to put an end to whatever you are carrying around with you. Put

73

down the baggage and go forward without the burden of the past so you can go on to something new with joy, love and harmony. Understand that you are capable of making your own decisions without the need for others to make them for you. Take the time to talk to that inner voice that's making you doubt yourself. Tell it that you can take care of yourself and make your own decisions because you're ready to face the consequences.

See also HEMORRHOIDS.

SPIRITUAL BLOCK AND CONCLUSION

To uncover the spiritual block that keeps you from responding to the needs of your BEING, refer to the "KEY QUESTIONS" at the back of this book. In answering these questions, you will come in touch more easily and accurately with the true cause of your physical problem.

ANXIETY

PHYSICAL BLOCK

Anxiety is a groundless fear. The person who suffers from it lives in a painful state of waiting for some unknown and unseen danger.

EMOTIONAL BLOCK

Anxiety prevents us from effectively living in the present. We base our concerns on events and experiences that happened in the past - either to us or to others - and use this ac-

A

cumulated knowledge to worry about the future. Our fertile imaginations are our constant companions. They make us imagine improbable events as we keep tireless watch for signs that would prove we have every right to worry.

MENTAL BLOCK

As soon as you feel anxiety building up inside of you, become conscious that your imagination (which is getting the upper hand) is preventing you from enjoying the present moment. Decide that you have nothing to prove. You are what you are with all of your faults and your strengths, just like everyone else. Learn to trust your intuition and know that it will guide you faithfully if you will let it lead you into unknown territory. Begin to have more faith in those around you. Let others help you in their own way. *Anxiety attacks* can also be provoked by AGORAPHOBIA, I suggest you refer to its description.

SPIRITUAL BLOCK AND CONCLUSION

To uncover the spiritual block that keeps you from responding to the needs of your BEING, refer to the "KEY QUESTIONS" at the back of this book. In answering these questions, you will come in touch more easily and accurately with the true cause of your physical problem.

APHASIA

PHYSICAL BLOCK

Aphasia is the loss of the ability to speak or understand speech and is usually the result of a cerebral lesion. It may be accompanied by *partial paralysis*.

EMOTIONAL BLOCK

A person suffering with aphasia is someone who, in the past, expressed readily what they thought, but not what they felt. They tend to be controlling with those around them and busy themselves with the affairs of others. They have difficulty showing gratitude or even anger. They are angry with themselves because they know if they could express their feelings they would be more approachable and, ultimately, more lovable.

Because they are unable to manage their own feelings or the feelings of others, those suffering from aphasia tend to shut themselves off and may develop an accompanying deafness.

MENTAL BLOCK

This condition arises because you can no longer continue with the same attitude. Stop thinking that you have to share your innermost thoughts and feelings in order for others to know what you feel towards them. There are other ways they can find out.

A

Learn to be comfortable enough to give yourself permission to express your TRUE SELF and not just what has been collected from your belief system or what others expect from you.

See also BRAIN DISORDERS and PARALYSIS.

SPIRITUAL BLOCK AND CONCLUSION

To uncover the spiritual block that keeps you from responding to the needs of your BEING, refer to the "KEY QUESTIONS" at the back of this book. In answering these questions, you will come in touch more easily and accurately with the true cause of your physical problem.

APHONIA

PHYSICAL BLOCK

Aphonia is a condition characterized by faintness of the voice or loss of the voice. If pain or inflammation is present, LARYNGITIS is more likely the cause.

EMOTIONAL BLOCK

Aphonia can occur following an emotional shock that batters your sensitivity to the point that you force yourself to talk even though you are unable to express what your heart wants to say. The extra effort required to communicate your feelings creates distress that leaves a void, blocking any sound from escaping the throat.

77

MENTAL BLOCK

Don't feel you need to speak to make your presence felt or to be acknowledged; rather get in touch with your feelings, listen to your heart and allow only truthful and loving words to come out. Once you're in tune with your heart, you will find it easier to express yourself. Putting pressure on yourself to talk is not necessary to feel accepted and loved.

SPIRITUAL BLOCK AND CONCLUSION

To uncover the spiritual block that keeps you from responding to the needs of your BEING, refer to the "KEY QUESTIONS" at the back of this book. In answering these questions, you will come in touch more easily and accurately with the true cause of your physical problem.

APNEA

PHYSICAL BLOCK

Apnea is an involuntary cessation of breathing. The person suffering from apnea resumes breathing momentarily as the body's need for oxygen becomes immediate. Without the intake of oxygen, a build-up of carbon dioxide would ultimately result in asphyxiation and death.

EMOTIONAL BLOCK

Frequent apnea will create a feeling of anguish about whether the next episode will be your last. It is important

A

to determine when the interrupted breathing took place. Since it usually happens while at rest, this indicates that life has been cut off (oxygen) and rest is being held back (carbon dioxide).

MENTAL BLOCK

If you suffer from apnea while you're resting, you need to undergo an attitude adjustment and learn to relax. Do you feel that you are no longer alive when you're resting or inactive? If apnea occurs while you are at work, you may want to ask yourself the same question relating to your job.

SPIRITUAL BLOCK AND CONCLUSION

To uncover the spiritual block that keeps you from responding to the needs of your BEING, refer to the "KEY QUESTIONS" at the back of this book. In answering these questions, you will come in touch more easily and accurately with the true cause of your physical problem.

APPENDICITIS

PHYSICAL BLOCK

Appendicitis is an inflammation of the appendix. It can begin as a nagging in the lower abdomen and escalate to pain that radiates throughout the abdomen, accompanied by digestive problems such as intestinal seizure, absence of stools, an inability to tolerate food, nausea and vomiting. A *ruptured appendix* can result in PERITONITIS.

EMOTIONAL BLOCK

Inflammation is always a condition of repressed anger due to insecurity and dependence on others. If you are suffering from appendicitis, ask yourself if there is an authority figure in your life that unnerves you or causes you to become emotionally inflamed but you don't dare to let it out. You feel trapped. You will find that this emotional inflammation will occur just prior to the physical inflammation you are experiencing.

MENTAL BLOCK

As appendicitis can accelerate to fatality, it is critical to deal with the cause as soon as possible, before you burst. Identify the emotions you are repressing and allow yourself to diffuse them with love and acceptance. Don't wait any longer to express how you really feel. Your body is not telling you to run away from the situation that angers you and from the fear it awakens but to put love into this situation while considering your limits and those of others. Also see SECTION 2.

SPIRITUAL BLOCK AND CONCLUSION

To uncover the spiritual block that keeps you from responding to the needs of your BEING, refer to the "KEY QUESTIONS" at the back of this book. In answering these questions, you will come in touch more easily and accurately with the true cause of your physical problem.

ARM PROBLEMS

PHYSICAL BLOCK

The *arms* are constantly in use - to help us get around, to reach out and touch, pick up and hold onto anything and anyone. They are used in work and play, in taking care of others and ourselves and, generally, as an extension of ourselves. Therefore, a problem occurring in the arm can affect one or many of these functions.

EMOTIONAL BLOCK

Pain in the arms signals that you feel you are no longer useful and you doubt your capacities. Or it could be that you have difficulty holding someone close to you. You may be feeling some guilt surrounding this issue. You should take a close look at why you can't take a loved one in your arms. What could happen?

Which arm is causing you pain? Be aware that the *right arm* signifies giving and the *left*, receiving or acquiring. Perhaps you don't feel worthy of being someone's right arm?

It may be that you feel you have all that you need to embrace a new situation but you've been influenced by others or by your thoughts and you're preventing yourself from grasping the situation fully.

Since the arms are an extension of the heart region, they are used to express love. Rather than feeling the weight of

81

obligation, embrace the person or opportunity with open arms, as this is the natural reaction of the heart. It is not by chance that the arms were placed at this precise spot on the body.

MENTAL BLOCK

If you doubt your ability or your usefulness, realize that this mindset is the result of listening to a little voice in your head that is bred by the ego. Trust that the Universe only gives you what you can handle and that you will reach your goals with a quiet confidence and capability. Discard painful ways of thinking and energize yourself by embracing your life fully.

If, for example, you are afraid of being someone's "right arm," examine your fears and determine if they are really justified. Doubt and fear are your only obstacles to reaching out and touching your goals. If you would observe someone like you, what are the traits you would admire? Admire them in yourself and you will discover you are energized far more than when you are filled with self-doubt.

If you find it difficult to show affection and there is a resulting ache or pain in your arms, your body is giving you a signal to reach out and demonstrate how you really feel. This doesn't mean you always have to but give yourself the right to change your way of expressing love to others. It is not your nature to be a cold, unfeeling person.

If your pain is in the ELBOW, refer to that section.

SPIRITUAL BLOCK AND CONCLUSION

To uncover the spiritual block that keeps you from responding to the needs of your BEING, refer to the "KEY QUESTIONS" at the back of this book. In answering these questions, you will come in touch more easily and accurately with the true cause of your physical problem.

ARTERIAL THROMBOSIS

See THROMBOSIS.

ARTERIES

PHYSICAL BLOCK

Arteries are the main blood vessels that carry the blood ejected from the heart toward the various tissues of the body (veins are the vessels that return blood from all parts of the body to the heart). They may become obstructed or constricted, blocking blood flow.

EMOTIONAL BLOCK

Because the arteries carry fresh, oxygenated blood directly from the heart, they both physically and symbolically embody the life force. If you are experiencing obstruction or constriction of these vessels, you are subconsciously blocking the joy in your life. There is an inefficient flow of communication and/or movement in one or several areas of your life. Are you having problems interacting socially? Are your thoughts generally positive and enriching? Is it difficult for you to express what is in your heart? Are you afraid to involve yourself in situations that would bring you joy and happiness?

MENTAL BLOCK

It's time to look inside your heart and discover what would truly make you happy. Take small steps toward your own happiness by allowing yourself simple pleasures regularly. Life need not be complicated. Let life flow in and around you freely - it's far too important to be taken so seriously!

SPIRITUAL BLOCK AND CONCLUSION

To uncover the spiritual block that keeps you from responding to the needs of your BEING, refer to the "KEY QUESTIONS" at the back of this book. In answering these questions, you will come in touch more easily and accurately with the true cause of your physical problem.

ARTERIOSCLEROSIS

Arteriosclerosis is a chronic circulatory disease in which the walls of the arteries thicken and harden. See ARTERIES and HEART DISORDERS and add that an accumulation of sadness and criticism provokes the inner hardening that causes this illness.

A

ARRHYTHMIA

If you suffer from *arrhythmia*, or irregular heartbeat, see HEART DISORDERS but with this nuance: it is likely that you are irregular in your attitude. Enjoyment is at a high then it's low. Why can't it always be at a high? What would happen? Don't forget, you must first accept what you are before transformation can take place.

ARTHRITIS

See RHEUMATOID ARTHRITIS or OSTEOARTHRITIS.

ASPHYXIA

PHYSICAL BLOCK

Asphyxia is the rapid onset of a state of unconsciousness or ultimate death caused by a lack of oxygen or an increase of carbon dioxide in the blood.

EMOTIONAL BLOCK

Asphyxia is the result of the chronic suppression of paralyzing fear. You may have succeeded in controlling this fear up until now but your fear has been awakened suddenly by a traumatic event and you can no longer control it.

MENTAL BLOCK

It is imperative that you re-establish contact with your powerful internal strength, knowing that you are the sole architect of your own life. Become the master of your thoughts and realize that you have magnified this fear in your own mind. You have handed your power over and led yourself to believe that this demon you have created from your own subconscious is actually capable of snuffing out your life. Take a deep breath and become your own self. Since this affects the lungs, see LUNG DISORDERS

SPIRITUAL BLOCK AND CONCLUSION

To uncover the spiritual block that keeps you from responding to the needs of your BEING, refer to the "KEY QUESTIONS" at the back of this book. In answering these questions, you will come in touch more easily and accurately with the true cause of your physical problem.

ASTHMA

PHYSICAL BLOCK

Asthma is an intermittent illness characterized by episodes of narrowing of the bronchial tubes of the lungs, resulting in a form of suffocation. Symptoms include pressure in the chest, wheezing, shortness of breath and often a feeling of panic. Between attacks, breathing is normal and the thorax is quiet.

EMOTIONAL BLOCK

A

If you are asthmatic, you will find you usually have no problem inhaling but have difficulty exhaling. Your body is signaling that you want to take on too much. You take on more than you can do and have great difficulty giving some back. You will not admit any limitation, even to yourself. You want to seem stronger than you are just to be loved by others. You also want things to be done your way, and when that doesn't happen, an asthma attack is just the excuse you need to not be as strong as you seem.

MENTAL BLOCK

Your asthma attacks are sending you an urgent message. The internal approach of "taking on too much" is poisoning and suffocating you. Liberate yourself. Love and accept yourself with all your weaknesses and limitations. You are human; simply take your place in the human family. There is no need to overwhelm others with your feats *or* your illness. See ALLERGIES and LUNG DISORDERS.

SPIRITUAL BLOCK AND CONCLUSION

To uncover the spiritual block that keeps you from responding to the needs of your BEING, refer to the "KEY QUESTIONS" at the back of this book. In answering these questions, you will come in touch more easily and accurately with the true cause of your physical problem.

ASTIGMATISM

PHYSICAL BLOCK

Astigmatism is a refraction error due to an uneven curvature of the cornea, blurring portions of your visual field and distorting what you see.

EMOTIONAL BLOCK

Astigmatism reveals conflict between your internal and external or social life. You are unable to see things objectively or the way others see them, which causes inner conflict. You have greater difficulty accepting change when others suggest it than when you suggest it, and dislike being imposed upon by others, especially when it affects your routine. You are also emotionally sensitive and easily hurt by others.

MENTAL BLOCK

Why are you afraid to see things from another point of view? Perhaps you decided at an early age to see things your own way and not be influenced by the views of others. This approach may have been useful in a particular situation but can be quite blinding in the larger picture! Realize it is possible to disagree with others without diminishing your own self-worth and you will resolve any inner conflict you may have along with any conflict you may have with others. In this way, you will see your way clear to a place of inner peace.

See also EYE DISORDERS.

A

SPIRITUAL BLOCK AND CONCLUSION

To uncover the spiritual block that keeps you from responding to the needs of your BEING, refer to the "KEY QUESTIONS" at the back of this book. In answering these questions, you will come in touch more easily and accurately with the true cause of your physical problem.

AUTISM

PHYSICAL BLOCK

Autistic children appear to live in their own world. They have poor communication skills, exhibit bizarre reactions to people and objects in their environment, and show an aversion to cuddling, even an abhorrence of physical contact. They retreat emotionally, often becoming mute and refusing food. There is sometimes an absence of the use of "I" in sentences and difficulty making eye contact.

EMOTIONAL BLOCK

Research shows that the cause of autism begins before the age of 8 months. I feel the autistic child has a very strong karmic connection, mostly with their mother. On a soul level, these children have chosen autism to escape their reality. It is probable that their relationship with their mother in a past life was painful and difficult and they are reacting in this lifetime with a vengeful attitude, refusing food and affection from the mother and also refusing this incarnation.

If you are the mother of an autistic child, read them this passage and be aware that the child can absorb a great deal. They are fully present on a soul level and will understand.

MENTAL BLOCK

The autistic child must be helped to accept his or her incarnation. They possess all the skills to succeed and grow in this lifetime or would not have chosen to be here. Many autistic children display profound gifts and extraordinary talent. They are deeply sensitive souls that need extra nurturing to convince them they are equipped to embrace their lives. It is important that the parents of an autistic child not blame themselves, but accept that the child has chosen autism as a life experience. Only he can decide to pull through. Does he want to continue running away from life or does he want to take advantage of the life he has.

Parents of autistic children have been blessed with an experience through which they can learn their own valuable life lessons. They can benefit enormously by discovering something about themselves - observing what is difficult and building on that.

If you have an autistic child, let him choose what he wants to do with his life (pull through or not), and provide the child a safe, loving and nurturing environment that will allow him to evolve. This is loving unconditionally. Share

A

this passage with him while including him in the reading of the text. Be aware that the child can absorb a great deal.

SPIRITUAL BLOCK AND CONCLUSION

To uncover the spiritual block that keeps you from responding to the needs of your BEING, refer to the "KEY QUESTIONS" at the back of this book. In answering these questions, you will come in touch more easily and accurately with the true cause of your physical problem.

BABY MEASLES

See ROSEOLA.

BACK (HOLLOW)

See LORDOSIS.

BACK PAIN

PHYSICAL BLOCK

The back is made up of many muscles, but when we speak of back pain, we usually speak about the spine. The spinal column is a stacking of 33 vertebrae, distributed as follows: cervical, dorsal, lumbar and sacral. The following description of back pain covers the areas dorsal, lumbar and sacral. Refer to COCCYX and NECK problems elsewhere in this book.

EMOTIONAL BLOCK

Pain or disability in the lower back (sacral region) at the base of the spine indicates fear of losing your freedom when others need your help. Your freedom is "sacred." Often enough, you fear for your own survival.

Pain and discomfort from the fifth lumbar vertebra (the lower back) to the eleventh DORSAL vertebra (waist) denotes fear of material loss. The back provides the greatest support for the physical body; therefore, any back prob-

93

lem indicates that you don't feel enough support. The lower back is connected to the *having* in your life (having a home, money, a spouse, children, a good job, a diploma, etc.). You believe you must have it all in order to feel supported, but you don't want to admit this to yourself or others. You want to do everything by yourself. You also tend to be very active because you think that it is the best way to *have* things.

Upper back pain (from the tenth dorsal vertebra (the waist) to the cervical, or neck area) represents emotional insecurity. *Doing* is very important to you. It's your way of showing and giving love to others. If someone *does* something for you, you feel loved and secure. However, your back pain might provide you the perfect excuse not to do *everything* for others, as you may fear that by doing too much, others won't help you anymore.

You expect a lot from others and when your expectations are not met you may feel you have a lot on your back. You have difficulty asking for help or support from others. When you do finally decide to do so and don't receive the help, you feel 'stuck' and your back worsens.

Upper back pain could also mean that you feel somebody is watching you, that they're on your back all the time.

MENTAL BLOCK

Pain in the lower back: stop believing that by helping others you will lose your freedom. Acknowledge your limitations and express them to others. Remember, you reap what you sow; if you want to reap help, you have to have sown it in the past. You may begin to realize that you are afraid that others will not be there for you or that they might take advantage of you as before. These fears keep you from giving, which consequently prevent you from receiving. If you feel your survival is at stake, realize that it is simply your emotional dependence that generates this fear and keeps you from believing that you can't survive alone. You have all the tools to take care of yourself.

Pain in the lumbar region indicates a need to accept that it is all right to need and love material things or whatever it takes to feel secure and supported. You have to allow yourself these things if you one day want to feel secure without them.

Instead of feeling that no one cares about what you want, I suggest you start voicing your requests - knowing, however, that others are under no obligation to acquiesce. They might not understand your needs the way you do. What is important to you may be of no importance to them. If you give yourself the right to need certain things, it will be easier for you to explain these needs to others.

To relieve pain in your upper back and neck, stop believing that you need to expend your energies to ensure others' happiness. When you want to give to others, give purely for the pleasure of giving. You don't need to be the emotional support for anyone.

Realize, also, that others don't have to do everything in order for you to be happy. It's not that they don't care about you they are merely focusing on what is important to them. Voice your needs by telling them that you realize you still need them to do things for you in order for you to feel their love but that one day you won't need that kind of love anymore because you will love yourself enough.

SPIRITUAL BLOCK AND CONCLUSION

To uncover the spiritual block that keeps you from responding to the needs of your BEING, refer to the "KEY QUESTIONS" at the back of this book. In answering these questions, you will come in touch more easily and accurately with the true cause of your physical problem.

BAD BREATH

PHYSICAL BLOCK

BAD BREATH, or *halitosis*, is an unpleasant odor emanating from the mouth. Normally our breath is odorless. If INDIGESTION or GUM PROBLEMS causes bad breath, refer to the pertinent listing. The following definition is for bad breath that is not caused by a pathological disorder.

EMOTIONAL BLOCK

When bad breath seems to float from the depths of the body, it indicates the presence of tremendous internal pain, thoughts of hatred, vengeance or extreme anger that seethe below the surface and are directed toward those who have hurt you. You find such toxic thoughts to be shameful and prefer to stay unaware, but you must realize that you are killing yourself slowly in the process. The re-

B

ality of the situation is this: your bad breath is pushing away the people you want most to be close to.

MENTAL BLOCK

If you wonder whether you have bad breath, ask those you trust for their honesty. If they confirm your suspicions, it's important that you determine whether it has a pathological cause. If your halitosis proves to have no physical cause, your body is sending you a dire message that you must adjust a very unhealthy attitude. There is no wound so deep it cannot be healed by true forgiveness. Let go of the brooding shame and sense of powerlessness fermenting inside you and accept that you are worthy of love. Rediscover your capacity for giving and receiving love. See the steps to forgiveness explained at the end of this book.

SPIRITUAL BLOCK AND CONCLUSION

To uncover the spiritual block that keeps you from responding to the needs of your BEING, refer to the "KEY QUESTIONS" at the back of this book. In answering these questions, you will come in touch more easily and accurately with the true cause of your physical problem.

BALDNESS

PHYSICAL BLOCK

Baldness is hair loss that may result in total or partial absence of hair.

EMOTIONAL BLOCK

Baldness is the result of an abuse of power or trying to control others. The balding person often has little respect for others' opinions and feels their own belief system is the right one. This person wants and loves to be obeyed. This kind of personality belongs to someone who is out of touch with their own I AM, which diminishes the quality of their relationships and builds up negative inner feelings.

MENTAL BLOCK

Your body is sending you a message that you need to recognize and accept yourself for who you are. There is no need to impose your point of view on others. If you have an authoritarian personality, accept that and live in harmony with it instead of denying it. A person in a position of authority has no need to flaunt their power. Simply acknowledging your personality traits will empower you and you will become more like your true self rather than the person others think you should be or who *you* think you should be. See also HAIR PROBLEMS.

SPIRITUAL BLOCK AND CONCLUSION

To uncover the spiritual block that keeps you from responding to the needs of your BEING, refer to the "KEY QUESTIONS" at the back of this book. In answering these questions, you will come in touch more easily and accurately with the true cause of your physical problem.

BASEDOW'S DISEASE

See GRAVE'S DISEASE.

BEDWETTING

PHYSICAL BLOCK

Occasional *bedwetting* may occur in children following a nightmare, emotional trauma or during very sound sleep. This is normal. *Persistent bedwetting*, on the other hand, is often a sign of underlying emotional stress. Bedwetting is considered persistent after the age of three when the muscles controlling the bladder functions should be developed enough to handle the task.

EMOTIONAL BLOCK

Persistent bedwetting may be symptomatic of repressed fear of one's father (the authority figure) or by the person who plays the paternal role in the child's life. The child does not fear his father physically but lives in fear of displeasing him and not living up to his expectations. During sleep, the child's subconscious releases these emotions and the body, in turn, may release the urine. To this child, the shame of displeasing his father is reflected in the shame of wetting his bed.

MENTAL BLOCK

These children need nurturing and encouragement - not coddling, but simple, positive reinforcement. They are already very hard on themselves and need to be assured that they are loved regardless of academic performance, "mistakes" in behavior (including the bedwetting itself) or whatever the particular issues are that surround them. Focus on their strengths, their talents and abilities and their unique personality, so that they will begin to relax and accept themselves. They need to be told that what they believe to be the expectations of their parents' (mostly the fathers) are ill founded.

SPIRITUAL BLOCK AND CONCLUSION

To uncover the spiritual block that keeps you from responding to the needs of your BEING, refer to the "KEY QUESTIONS" at the back of this book. In answering these questions, you will come in touch more easily and accurately with the true cause of your physical problem.

BELCHING

PHYSICAL BLOCK

Belching, or burping excessively or chronically, may be a symptom of air being gulped in with food and becoming trapped in the esophagus to escape, audibly, while you are still eating or shortly afterward.

If the stomach produces gases that escape after a meal because the food is being poorly digested or if there has been excessive intake of food, see AEROPHAGIA

EMOTIONAL BLOCK

Swallowing air instead of taking it in through the respiratory tract indicates a sudden fear. This fear might have been awakened by a thought or by a certain situation that came up and is probably linked to the intake of food or drink.

It also indicates a refusal to accept nourishing thoughts, thoughtful gestures and compliments that could build your self-esteem. You reject them because you believe there is something to fear behind these compliments.

MENTAL BLOCK

Excessive or chronic belching is a signal from the body that you need to feel more at ease and to accept yourself, regardless of the expectations of others. You will begin to appreciate what others see in you and finally begin to accept what they offer you, as well as what you have to offer.

SPIRITUAL BLOCK AND CONCLUSION

To uncover the spiritual block that keeps you from responding to the needs of your BEING, refer to the "KEY QUESTIONS" at the back of this book. In answering these questions, you will come in touch more easily and accurately with the true cause of your physical problem.

BELL'S PALSY

Bell's palsy, also known as facial palsy, is a paralysis of the muscles that control expression on one side of the face resulting from damage to the facial nerve. Full paralysis on one side will leave you looking expressionless, as you will have virtually no movement of the muscles on the paralyzed side from the forehead to the mouth. The corner of your mouth may droop and you may have difficulty retaining saliva on that side of your mouth. The eye on your affected side may close only partially.

Note that this disorder tends to occur when you refuse to face something that you feel is "in your face," metaphorically speaking. See FACIAL DISORDERS and PARALYSIS.

BLACKHEAD

See PIMPLES.

BLADDER DISORDERS

The *bladder* serves as a reservoir into which urine flows after it is discharged through the two ureters. Urine is contained in the bladder between each urination. Disorders of the bladder include INFECTION, CYSTITIS, TUMOR, INCONTINENCE and CANCER. Refer to the particular disorder and read the following:

As all bodily fluids are linked to the emotional body, or the body of desires, bladder disorders are linked with the capacity to delay gratification. If the disorder prevents or impedes urination, it indicates that you rigidly control your desires and are afraid to let them out. If the disorder results in incontinence, or an inability to retain urine, your body is telling you that you can't control your desires; that you lack judgment and want your expectations to be met immediately. Refer also to KIDNEY DISORDERS.

B

BLEEDING

See HEMORRHAGE. The urgency of the message from your body diminishes when bleeding is less severe.

BLOOD CELL DISORDERS

PHYSICAL BLOCK

White blood cells circulate, not only in the bloodstream, but also in body tissue. They are designed to defend the body aggressively against disease. *Red blood cells* maintain proper levels of hemoglobin, the protein that contains iron and carries oxygen to body tissues.

EMOTIONAL BLOCK

On an emotional level, a white blood cell problem signifies difficulty in fending for yourself and fear of asserting yourself. A white blood cell count that is too high indicates an aggressive personality. You are quick to take of-

103

fense. A low white cell count indicates the opposite - you tend to give up easily.

A low red cell count results in anemia. See ANEMIA.

MENTAL BLOCK

If your white blood cell count is low, it's high time you regained confidence in your own talent and abilities. You are the only one who can change your life. Your perception of yourself may not be realistic. If you have no inherent faith in yourself, ask those close to you how they perceive you. If you are unable to step outside of your own perception, you are at risk of seeing life as a tiresome burden and becoming increasingly depressed. Your heart is crying out: *"I want some joy in my life!"* Your inner strength is lying dormant until you have enough faith to simply reach in and tap it.

If your white blood cell count is high, realize that you don't have to fight tooth and nail for others to know and love you for who you really are. Fighting is exhausting! Your body is sending you an important message to get in touch with your true self-worth before your aggressive alter ego takes over completely.

SPIRITUAL BLOCK AND CONCLUSION

To uncover the spiritual block that keeps you from responding to the needs of your BEING, refer to the "KEY QUESTIONS" at the back of this book. In answering these questions, you will come in touch more easily and accurately with the true cause of your physical problem.

BLOOD DISORDERS

PHYSICAL BLOCK

Blood is the fluid that is circulated by the heart through the vascular system carrying oxygen and nutrients throughout the body and wastes to excretory channels. Once all nutrients and waste materials are delivered, the blood is cleansed through the filtering process carried out by the lymph fluid. Blood is formed from cells suspended in liquid, or plasma. The quality of the blood reflects the overall health of the body and its integrity is vital to homeostasis, as it serves to administer to and manage the entire physical body. It also serves as *informant*, transporting and distributing hormones. The following definition applies to all problems affecting the quality of blood and its different functions.

EMOTIONAL BLOCK

On a physical level, blood serves to manage and oversee the body's processes. Blood disorders, therefore, indicate difficulty in administering and managing your life according to your true needs. Living true to yourself means experiencing life with acceptance and joy. Over-dramatizing situations and a tendency to be myopic or unable to see a larger picture can make your life unmanageable. It may be that you have lost your *joie de vivre* because of a profound sense of something lacking.

You worry too much and have a tendency to let your blood boil over situations that involve other people. Your

105

overemotional and over-reactive tendencies actually block your sensitivity.

Blood represents the life force and, as such, must be continually free flowing and vital. Having too much composure can also block your sensitivity. Keeping your cool may be interpreted as insensitivity or cold-bloodedness, because your feelings are hidden from others.

MENTAL BLOCK

The vitally important role of blood on a physical level reflects the level of importance of joy and self-acceptance in the management of your life. Blood disorders are an urgent message from your body that you need a profound shift in your self-image. You are worth much more than you think. The quality of your life depends on your realization of your own worth and of your true needs.

You are in need of a good transfusion of unconditional love, which is the main element to improve the quality of your blood. Accept and love yourself unconditionally, as if you were someone you really cared about. In nurturing yourself in this way, the quality of your life will improve.

As blood feeds your body, so must you feed your own soul. It is up to you to manage your life; no one can do it for you. Instead of waiting for help because you think you can't do it alone, make a list! Make a list of your talents and abilities and what you've accomplished in your life up to now. Communicate with that inner voice that knows your needs and little by little you will realize that you are the most important person in your life. You are on Earth for the purpose of your own evolution, no one else's. Only **you** can see to this.

B

SPIRITUAL BLOCK AND CONCLUSION

To uncover the spiritual block that keeps you from responding to the needs of your BEING, refer to the "KEY QUESTIONS" at the back of this book. In answering these questions, you will come in touch more easily and accurately with the true cause of your physical problem.

BODY HAIR

See ALOPECIA.

BOIL

A *boil,* otherwise known as a *furuncle*, is a sub-cutaneous, infectious and painful inflammation that forms a pus-filled abscess, usually centered on a hair follicle. See the metaphysical definition of ABSCESS and add to it that boils are indicative of repressed fury, anguish, frustration and apprehension in the face of a "poisonous" situation.

BONE DISORDERS

PHYSICAL BLOCK

Bones are the dense, semi-rigid, porous, calcified connective tissue of the skeleton that serve to support, protect and participate in the movement of the body. Bone disorders include all disorders with the prefix OSTEO (as in *osteoporosis*). For broken bones, refer to FRACTURE.

EMOTIONAL BLOCK

On both a physical and metaphysical level, bones represent support. Bone disorders are invariably linked with a fear of not being sufficiently supported or fear of not sufficiently supporting others. Bone disorders indicate that we don't feel "solid" enough to take car of our own lives.

Do you often feel obliged to support others? Do you feel you need to have others dependent on you to prove to yourself and others that you are worthy or useful? If so, you may deem yourself valueless when not helping someone. This explains why osteoporosis occurs in our later years, after a lifetime of supporting others.

Bone disorders can also result if you fear authority, due to an underlying lack of faith in your own self-worth. It may be that you have become authoritative yourself in reaction to your fear of being controlled by others.

MENTAL BLOCK

B

Bone disorders are a message from your body to acknowledge your own inner strength. Your body is telling you to stabilize yourself, to regain your balance by allowing yourself to experience simple pleasures without guilt. You have everything you need to create a stable life, without having to depend on others for support.

When we study to learn something, we say we need to *bone up* on the subject. It's time for you to *bone up* on who you are and not identify yourself through others. True self-validation comes from within, so get to know yourself and discover your strengths. Stop believing that you are not enough of this or too much of that. Those in positions of authority are not better or worthier than you. Unearth your own wealth of talents and abilities. If you're not sure what they are, ask those who know you well.

Bone disorders that finish with *"itis"* (inflammatory disease) indicate repressed anger. See SECTION 2.

SPIRITUAL BLOCK AND CONCLUSION

To uncover the spiritual block that keeps you from responding to the needs of your BEING, refer to the "KEY QUESTIONS" at the back of this book. In answering these questions, you will come in touch more easily and accurately with the true cause of your physical problem.

BRAIN DISORDERS

PHYSICAL BLOCK

Refer also to HEADACHE and MIGRAINE headache, the most common brain disorders.

Among the most serious brain problems are *cerebral trauma,* resulting from a blow to the head or other trauma; *cerebral thrombosis* brought on by the obstruction or the rupture of an artery; and finally, *brain tumor*, whether benign or malign, which develops at the expense of other brain tissues.

EMOTIONAL BLOCK

All problems relating to the brain are a manifestation of misalignment with the I AM (the essence of the individual). The mind and spirit are closely interwoven, so trauma experienced by the brain indicates a traumatized spirit. As the brain is the most important organ of the body and is therefore well protected by the armor of the skull, so must the spirit, or I AM, be protected from injury or trauma. Evaluate your frame of mind and pay close attention to the events and issues that surrounded it prior to the onset of the head trauma. A strong identity and a conscious reverence for your true self (rather than the self others expect you to be) will protect your brain and your mind from any physical or emotional injury.

B

MENTAL BLOCK

As the brain controls the physical body, so the mind pilots the psychological body. A brain trauma, regardless of its cause, is an urgent message to become more in tune with your true self. You may be out of alignment with your individual identity and must take charge of your life. It is imperative that you maintain a balanced frame of mind and, in turn, a framework for the nurturing of your own soul. You may believe that you have not suffered by ignoring your true self, but your body is telling you in no uncertain terms that this is not the case.

SPIRITUAL BLOCK AND CONCLUSION

To uncover the spiritual block that keeps you from responding to the needs of your BEING, refer to the "KEY QUESTIONS" at the back of this book. In answering these questions, you will come in touch more easily and accurately with the true cause of your physical problem.

BREAST PROBLEMS

PHYSICAL BLOCK

Breasts are milk secreting glandular organs on the chest of a woman. The most common breast problems are PAIN, *hardening,* MASTITIS, CYSTS, TUMORS and CANCER.

EMOTIONAL BLOCK

The breasts are directly linked to mothering, whether of our children, our family, our spouse or the world in general. Breast disorders, whether experienced by a man or a woman, indicate insecurity about our ability to provide for others or protect them. You may treat others as if they still need their mother, pushing yourself to seem maternal so that you can be a good parent. Perhaps you do too much for others to the detriment of your own needs, leaving no time to feed your own soul and causing subconscious resentment because you are always at their beck and call. You have also become controlling and manipulative in your mothering.

Breast disorders can also occur when you tend to ask too much of yourself, or if you've become overly cautious. If you are right-handed, the right breast is linked to your partner, your family, or those close to you. Your left breast is linked more closely with your child, or your inner child. If your left hand is dominant, the opposite is true.

If your breast problems are strictly esthetic, your body is telling you that you are overly concerned with the image you project in reference to your motherhood. Acknowledge, honor and accept the type of mother you are and accept your limitations.

MENTAL BLOCK

In order to achieve a balanced perspective regarding your mothering, you must embark on a journey of forgiveness with your own mother. If your mothering methods are

B

proving unsatisfactory, there is a direct correlation with the way you were mothered. Rather than pushing yourself or whining about what you are going through, begin to realize that you weren't put on this earth to protect and feed everyone you love.

If others ask you for help and it is within your power to help, don't hesitate. But do it with love, joy and pleasure, not out of a sense of obligation or with resentment. If helping at a given time is beyond your limitations in any way, or you just don't want to do it, admit it both to yourself and to them and allow yourself to step back. As your life changes, so will the borders of your limitations. If you understand this, you can diffuse that oppressive sense of obligation and learn to be a little gentler with yourself. Let go of those you love and allow them the independence they need to be self-sufficient. Your maternal love will always be there to sustain them, without your feeling obliged to actively mother them.

SPIRITUAL BLOCK AND CONCLUSION

To uncover the spiritual block that keeps you from responding to the needs of your BEING, refer to the "KEY QUESTIONS" at the back of this book. In answering these questions, you will come in touch more easily and accurately with the true cause of your physical problem.

BRIGHT'S DISEASE

This disease is a progressive lack of kidney function, accompanied by *hypertension* and then an increased level of

113

urea in the blood. It is also called *Chronic Nephritis*. See KIDNEY DISORDERS, HYPERTENSION and NE-PHRITIS.

BRONCHITIS

PHYSICAL BLOCK

Characterized by soreness and constriction in the chest, *bronchitis* is a common viral infection of the bronchi and the trachea, the principal air passages in the chest. The greater bronchia moves air toward the lungs, while the lesser bronchia (bronchioles) contract and relax more subtly in specific areas of the breathing passage. With bronchitis, mucous membranes of the bronchia become inflamed and the management of air becomes impaired.

EMOTIONAL BLOCK

Metaphysically, the bronchia are representative of family. Bronchitis often occurs when you are going through family crisis or experiencing the disruptive chaos of quarreling. You begin to feel a sense of violation of your space. As you become irritated with the situation around you, you want to cut off contact with others who are irritating you, but guilt sets in and you dare not branch out on your own. Your life is not what you want it to be but you don't share this with anyone. The situation may feel helpless and discouraging, but it is important that you take your rightful place in the family instead of waiting for someone to give it to you.

MENTAL BLOCK

If you are suffering from bronchitis, it is imperative that you live your life with more joy. Realize that no family lives in complete harmony all the time. You don't have to share your family's opinions. Go ahead and branch out, be true to yourself and allow yourself to react to others honestly and without guilt. Reaffirm your birthright by defining yourself and your space and allow others to live their lives in their own way. See SECTION 2.

SPIRITUAL BLOCK AND CONCLUSION

To uncover the spiritual block that keeps you from responding to the needs of your BEING, refer to the "KEY QUESTIONS" at the back of this book. In answering these questions, you will come in touch more easily and accurately with the true cause of your physical problem.

BRONCHIAL PNEUMONIA

See BRONCHITIS and PNEUMONIA.

BRUISE

A *bruise* is a visible bluish or purplish mark or patch occurring beneath the surface of unbroken skin resulting from the rupture of blood vessels in the deeper layers of subcutaneous tissues, usually caused by a blow or pressure. In healing, the color of the bruise gradually fades away into a yellowish hue, as a result of the formation of bile pigments and the disintegration and gradual absorption of blood.

Refer to ACCIDENT and add to it that the bruised person feels guilty about being weak or fragile in certain situations. Bruising shows a lack of tenderness (or fluidity) in one's movements due to impulsiveness.

BRUXISM

Bruxism is the grinding of teeth. See DENTAL DISORDERS.

BULIMIA

PHYSICAL BLOCK

Symptoms of *bulimia* are recurrent episodes of binge eating. Paired with *anorexia*, it is often called the binge and purge disorder and involves the consumption of excessive amounts of food (usually high-calorie sweets) in a short time. The gorging may continue until a feeling of fullness or a stomachache develops. When the individual fears gaining weight, self-induced vomiting is common.

EMOTIONAL BLOCK

Bulimia is an eating disorder at the opposite end of the spectrum from Anorexia. Bulimics, metaphorically speaking, want to devour their mothers, as they fear being abandoned (whereas anorexics fear rejection). Although

116

B

they need to free themselves from their mother emotionally, their fear of abandonment overrules and they become obsessively needy. Ironically, at the same time they may feel that their mother runs their lives and denies them the right to love their father, which makes them very angry.

Since bulimia is a lack of self-control, it is logical to presume that the bulimic prevented themselves from loving and accepting their mother for who she is. This disorder is indicative of a great deal of confusion regarding their female aspect. Whether the bulimic is a man or a woman, they have difficulty coming to terms with their femaleness (which is represented, ultimately, in their mother). This often happens to people who do not feel their own needs and who prevent themselves from getting what they want.

MENTAL BLOCK

As a child, the bond with your mother was very strong and you were an important part of each other's lives. Adults who have undergone healthy psychological development have put their relationship with their mother in perspective and are able to carry on and nurture themselves. A bulimic is afraid to carry on "alone" and is caught in the trap of needing but not wanting the "mothering" that they no longer really require. They have not learned to nurture themselves. It may be that you were ashamed of your mother in some way when you were younger. Examine your feelings and your thoughts surrounding this issue with your mother. On close examination, you may discover that your mother had a similar problem with the parent of your sex and that she loved you more than you think. Your mother is not the problem, your perception of her is.

SPIRITUAL BLOCK AND CONCLUSION

To uncover the spiritual block that keeps you from responding to the needs of your BEING, refer to the "KEY QUESTIONS" at the back of this book. In answering these questions, you will come in touch more easily and accurately with the true cause of your physical problem.

BURN

PHYSICAL BLOCK

Burn is the destruction of body tissue by fire, the sun, chemicals, heated objects or fluids, electricity or radiation. It can range in severity from minor to life threatening.

EMOTIONAL BLOCK

From a metaphysical perspective, burns are aggressive and violent events in the face of guilt and punishment. The degree of the burn (first, second or third) has a direct correlation to the degree of guilt, and the location of the burned tissue reveals the burning issues surrounding it.

MENTAL BLOCK

A burning sensation indicates a burning attitude. Who or what is making you flaming mad? As you would prevent a forest fire by snuffing out the flames, so you must snuff out anger in your own life with a gentle tolerance toward yourself and others. Guilt and punishment have no place in your life and offer nothing positive to contribute to your wholeness.

Since a burn usually happens by accident, I refer you to ACCIDENT.

SPIRITUAL BLOCK AND CONCLUSION

To uncover the spiritual block that keeps you from responding to the needs of your BEING, refer to the "KEY QUESTIONS" at the back of this book. In answering these questions, you will come in touch more easily and accurately with the true cause of your physical problem.

BURNOUT

PHYSICAL BLOCK

Burnout is defined as exhaustion due to long-term stress. It is a trendy expression used by doctors and therapists who often confuse it with depression. Symptoms mimic those of depression and include extreme tiredness, loss of vitality and desire. Anxiety may set in due to a feeling of being overwhelmed by the demands of everyday life. Often described as *job burnout*, it indicates inhibition about your work.

If you suffer from burnout, you feel as if you just don't have the fuel or the energy to go on. You may feel you are fighting something too big for you. This problem is especially common among workers in large corporations as well as in teaching, nursing, and any profession in which the worker is seen as a small cog in a big wheel.

See the description of DEPRESSION to make sure you know the difference.

EMOTIONAL BLOCK

By my observation, burnout occurs in those who place greater importance on *doing*, rather than *being*. They feel they have something to prove to their same-sex parent. Many of them spend their entire lives, even into later adulthood, seeking the recognition they feel will validate them. This behavior only leaves them feeling controlled and powerless and they become human *doings* rather than human *beings*. How exhausting!

These people are thought of as hard workers, but they often feel taken for granted. They have a lot of expectations and feel very lonely when no one acknowledges everything they are doing. They become discouraged and say to themselves: *"What's the use? Nobody notices anyway."* Having no sense of self-worth and needing the unattainable validation of others to fuel them, they simply lose their power and burn out.

MENTAL BLOCK

If you recognize the symptoms of burnout in your own life, free yourself immediately by simply accepting yourself as you **are**. You alone made the decision early in your life that you needed to "do more" in order to be loved. Only you can change this. Realize that you don't have anything to prove to anyone! Not even to yourself.

If you think your parent asked too much of you, you're wrong. Your parent was only showing you what you expected from yourself. Later in life, you transferred this way of thinking to your job and believed that the more you would do, the more you'd be appreciated and loved.

From this moment on, do your best on the job and talk openly with your superiors about their expectations. You may have been operating under incorrect assumptions. At work and in your personal life, you have the right to say no when you are being given more than you can handle. Don't let a poor self-concept undermine your productivity or the quality of your work, but know your limitations and be true to yourself. By doing so, you will be far less critical of yourself and of others. You will radiate confidence and peace of mind that will, surprisingly, increase your competence and overall performance (to say nothing of the quality and enjoyment of your life). Remember also that a happy person can endlessly renew his energy. You are not suffering from burnout because you are exhausted from lack of energy; on the contrary, you lack energy because you lack the capacity for loving yourself.

SPIRITUAL BLOCK AND CONCLUSION

To uncover the spiritual block that keeps you from responding to the needs of your BEING, refer to the "KEY QUESTIONS" at the back of this book. In answering

these questions, you will come in touch more easily and accurately with the true cause of your physical problem.

BURSITIS

PHYSICAL BLOCK

The bursa is a sac-like membrane found in many joints that acts as a cushion between the bone and the fibrous tissues of the muscles and tendons, facilitating movement by limiting friction. When a bursa becomes inflamed, the resultant disorder is termed *bursitis*. Symptoms include swelling and pain in the elbow, knee, shoulder or other joint. The area may also feel quite warm to the touch.

EMOTIONAL BLOCK

Bursitis results from holding back anger, specifically the stifled urge to hit someone. The perfectionist who feels anger is inappropriate and instead internalizes the inflammation often endures Bursitis. You may also feel angry with and have a hard time accepting yourself. Bursitis located in the shoulder is interpreted as an unexpressed need to strike someone we feel responsible for. Located in the knee, it indicates an unexpressed desire to kick someone. If bursitis has developed as the direct result of a specific activity, such as a sport, you will find an underlying attitude is visible in the way you hit the golf ball, tennis ball, or whatever is being hit. Whether you are observing your own behavior or someone else's, you will notice bitterness and frustration underlying the game.

MENTAL BLOCK

B

I you're suffering from bursitis, it's very important that you realize that you don't have to put up with a situation to the point of physical suffering. Hitting someone will not solve the problem but expressing your feelings will do you a lot of good. Don't feel sorry for yourself, it won't help.

Remember the example I mentioned in the introduction? The woman realized that she didn't want to play tennis competitively but for her own enjoyment. When she found herself in a competitive situation anyway, she berated herself for not being true to her own needs. Her joint inflammation appeared after she quit playing because she had internalized her frustration. Had she thought the situation through and become clear about her own needs, discussing them with the friends she was playing with, they may all have realized that they needed to relax and just enjoy themselves. See SECTION 2.

See also SHOULDER, ELBOW, KNEE and JOINT DISORDERS.

SPIRITUAL BLOCK AND CONCLUSION

To uncover the spiritual block that keeps you from responding to the needs of your BEING, refer to the "KEY QUESTIONS" at the back of this book. In answering these questions, you will come in touch more easily and accurately with the true cause of your physical problem.

BUTTOCK PROBLEMS

PHYSICAL BLOCK

The buttocks, or *gluteus maximus*, are the major muscles that form the rounded, fleshy part of the rump. They play a primary role in the mobility of the legs. Pain in the buttocks is generally muscular, but specific and acute pain, especially when sitting, may be referred to the coccyx. See COCCYX.

EMOTIONAL BLOCK

Pain in the buttocks indicates a desire to control a person or a situation in which you feel you may get your "butt kicked." This may be in relation to some material aspect, such as your work, finances, or future plans. You find it difficult to play the secondary role in this situation.

MENTAL BLOCK

Pain in the buttocks indicates a need to get off it - let go and realize that you do not have control of what others choose to do, even though your ideas may be valid. Allow others to make decisions for themselves without having to consult you. Also realize that there is no need to feel you must protect yourself from others.

SPIRITUAL BLOCK AND CONCLUSION

To uncover the spiritual block that keeps you from responding to the needs of your BEING, refer to the "KEY

124

QUESTIONS" at the back of this book. In answering these questions, you will come in touch more easily and accurately with the true cause of your physical problem.

B

CALCULUS

Refer to STONES.

CALF PROBLEMS

The *calf* is the back part of the leg between the knee and the ankle. The fleshy calf muscle powers the lower leg and provides strength and mobility. See LEG problems but add the following: pain in the calf is an indication that, although you want to move forward *quickly and vigorously*, your fear is stopping you from doing so.

CANCER

PHYSICAL BLOCK

This is now a general term for more than 100 diseases that are characterized by abnormal and uncontrolled cell division. It may spread to other parts of the body through the lymphatic system or the blood stream. Read the following and realize that the part of the body affected by the *cancer* will give you a clue as to the psychological implications.

EMOTIONAL BLOCK

Cancer is the result of significant emotional wounding that was experienced in isolation during childhood. The most common emotional wounds that can manifest as serious physical disease are rejection, abandonment, humil-

127

iation, betrayal and injustice. Some people have endured a number or combination of these wounds.

If you suffer from cancer, you're probably a very loving person that wants to live in a loving world, so much that you completely repressed your feelings of bitterness, resentment and even hatred towards one of your parents. You may even have blamed God for what you went through and still blame Him for the state of your life. These suppressed feelings are not even acknowledged, let alone dealt with and released, so they are left to accumulate and gather in the body, to grow every time something awakens the emotional wound. Once emotional critical mass has been reached, the cancer will surface.

MENTAL BLOCK

Forgive yourself for having angry and vengeful thoughts towards one or both of your parents. You are human; you're allowed to suffer. Forgive and love the child in you who has suffered silently and who had no one in whom to confide.

Forgiveness is the great healer. The only thing your soul needs is love and forgiveness. Visualize if you will, all of your emotional baggage in one bag that you have carried with you all your life. It's time to simply **put down the bag.** There is no need to punish yourself any longer or to feel guilty for having these thoughts. You must stop thinking that you're unkind if you hate someone. You're not unkind - you're human. Self-forgiveness is the greatest challenge for the cancer patient. Refer to the end of this book and follow the steps to true forgiveness.

SPIRITUAL BLOCK AND CONCLUSION

To uncover the spiritual block that keeps you from responding to the needs of your BEING, refer to the "KEY QUESTIONS" at the back of this book. In answering these questions, you will come in touch more easily and accurately with the true cause of your physical problem.

CANDIDIASIS

Candidiasis is a fungous infection usually caused by *Candida albicans*. It most commonly involves the oral mucous membranes (*oral candidiasis* or THRUSH) and the vagina (*vaginal candidiasis*).

Oral Candidiasis (or thrush) occurs most often in infants and children, characterized by small whitish eruptions on the mouth, throat, and tongue, and usually accompanied by fever, colic, and diarrhea. See MOUTH PROBLEMS.

Vaginal candidiasis is often associated with common yeast infections. See VAGINAL DISORDERS. The presence of a vaginal infection indicates regret (regarding past sexual behavior) and a desire to express innocence and purity. Note that infection always represents repressed anger.

CANKER SORE

A *canker sore* is a small ulceration either in the mouth or in the genital mucous membrane. Refer to MOUTH

129

PROBLEMS and keep in mind that canker sores result from an overreaction to those around you, causing you to block communication of your feelings.

CARPAL TUNNEL SYNDROME

Carpal tunnel syndrome is a disorder caused by compression of a nerve in the carpal tunnel (where the nerve passes through the wrist). It is characterized by discomfort and weakness in the hand. See WRIST PROBLEMS.

CARSICKNESS

See MOTION SICKNESS.

CATATONIC STATE

A *catatonic state* is a phase of schizophrenia where the person is unresponsive. The tendency to assume a fixed posture and inability to move or talk are characteristic of this phase. See PSYCHOSIS and SCHIZOPHRENIA.

CATARACTS

PHYSICAL BLOCK

Cataracts are defined as clouding of the clear lens of the eye and are the leading cause of blindness. We can develop cataracts at any age, but they are most common among the elderly. Early symptoms include blurred or double vision and the appearance of spots in the visual field.

EMOTIONAL BLOCK

Cataracts indicate an emotional and psychological cloud-ing of perception of what's going on in and around you. Clarity is slowly diminished as you retreat into a morose obscurity that covers up your view of your own failure. You prefer not to see a failure or an end to something.

MENTAL BLOCK

The private, veiled retreat of the cataract reflects a deeply personal decision to withdraw in fear of a particular situa-tion, for example a personal downfall or breakdown, fail-ure or bankruptcy that obscures the good in your life. It is easier to find refuge behind a veil of denial. Realize that your perception is what is clouded and trust that the situa-tion you are trying to hide from is not as bad as you think.

SPIRITUAL BLOCK AND CONCLUSION

To uncover the spiritual block that keeps you from re-sponding to the needs of your BEING, refer to the "KEY QUESTIONS" at the back of this book. In answering these questions, you will come in touch more easily and accurately with the true cause of your physical problem.

CAVITIES

See DENTAL DECAY.

CELLULITE

PHYSICAL BLOCK

Cellulite is a fatty deposit causing a dimpled or uneven appearance, as around the thighs and buttocks. It occurs more frequently in women than men.

EMOTIONAL BLOCK

Cellulite indicates an accumulation of stored ideas, a blocking of creativity. It occurs in women who have a poor self-image and lack the confidence to express their creativity. To find the part of your life lacking in creativity, read the description of the body part affected by cellulite.

You are easily influenced by others and will not expose yourself emotionally, as what others think of you is too important. This creates a "Catch-22" wherein you become self-conscious and further suppress your creativity. The appearance of cellulite also indicates a subconscious need to control those close to you, but without wanting them to know it. You withhold this need to control and convince yourself that this is healthy.

MENTAL BLOCK

If you are burdened by cellulite ask yourself why you're afraid to acknowledge your full worth as a vibrant, creative human being. If you are prepared to be honest with yourself, you'll begin to realize that you're afraid to attract the positive attention that comes from being a talented, creative and productive person. Fear of success underlies this condition - a fear of taking control of your life and making the most of your abilities. Instead, you take on a soft, flabby persona that undermines success and ultimately, your own happiness and fulfillment. If you prevent yourself from creating, you're probably preventing others from doing the same.

Let go of the past, *be here now* and live fully as you are meant to. You are unique and very special - and deserving of all you desire. Take your place in the spotlight and allow yourself to reach your full potential. See SECTION 2.

SPIRITUAL BLOCK AND CONCLUSION

To uncover the spiritual block that keeps you from responding to the needs of your BEING, refer to the "KEY QUESTIONS" at the back of this book. In answering these questions, you will come in touch more easily and accurately with the true cause of your physical problem.

CHEEK PAIN

See FACIAL DISORDERS. It should also be stated that you prefer a slap in the face rather than risk losing the love of someone close to you.

CHEST PAIN

PHYSICAL BLOCK

The *chest* is the upper part of the torso that houses the heart and lungs. The following text is related only to chest pain.

EMOTIONAL BLOCK

Metaphysically, the chest represents family. Chest pain denotes pain experienced following an unrealized need to cuddle against the chest of a parent. It may also indicate that you are holding back from being cuddled by someone else. All pain is caused by a sense of guilt following either self-accusation or a belief that someone else is not taking adequate care of another family member.

MENTAL BLOCK

Your body is telling you to love and accept yourself for who you are, with all your faults, your weaknesses and limitations. You need not depend on others for your own happiness, as you are able to love yourself wholly and without reservation.

SPIRITUAL BLOCK AND CONCLUSION

To uncover the spiritual block that keeps you from re-sponding to the needs of your BEING, refer to the "KEY QUESTIONS" at the back of this book. In answering

these questions, you will come in touch more easily and accurately with the true cause of your physical problem.

CHICKEN POX

Chicken pox, or *varicella*, is one of the most common childhood diseases and probably one of the least serious. It is marked by fever and skin eruptions that may appear all over the body, especially the trunk and extremities. See CHILDHOOD DISEASES.

CHILDHOOD DISEASES

PHYSICAL BLOCK

Common *childhood diseases* include CHICKEN POX, WHOOPING COUGH, MUMPS, ROSEOLA, RUBELLA (or GERMAN MEASLES) and MEASLES (or RUBEOLA). Refer also to the pertinent listing.

EMOTIONAL BLOCK

It's interesting to note that the majority of childhood diseases tend to affect the eyes, nose, ears, throat and skin. Childhood diseases are physical manifestations of psychological distress. The child is experiencing inner turmoil about what is going on around him and is repressing his anger. He finds it difficult to openly express his feelings - either he doesn't know how or the adults around him may not allow him to do so. Such diseases will often occur when the child feels he isn't getting enough attention (or isn't being admired enough). If the disease exhibits REDNESS OF THE SKIN, refer to it also.

MENTAL BLOCK

If you are caring for a sick child, even a young baby, explain to them that this disease is an expression of how they are feeling about the world around them and that it's perfectly normal to have difficulty adjusting to a new world. Regardless of the age of the child, talking to them in this way will soothe their soul and the information will be assimilated on a soul level.

Nevertheless, it's important that the child realize that *all of us* arrive on the planet with belief systems from past lives and the baggage that goes with them, including limitations, fears and desires. Help the child understand that those around them also have their own worries and preoccupations and are not always able to pay as much attention to them as the child would like. The child has every right to express his anger, fear, and sadness, even though the adults may not appreciate it. The child is not responsible for the reactions and behaviors of adults. All of us are a work in progress and perpetually trying to adjust.

Refer to the specific disease in question.

SPIRITUAL BLOCK AND CONCLUSION

To uncover the spiritual block that keeps you from responding to the needs of your BEING, refer to the "KEY QUESTIONS" at the back of this book. In answering

these questions, you will come in touch more easily and accurately with the true cause of your physical problem.

CHILLS

PHYSICAL BLOCK

Chills are defined as an attack of feeling very cold even if not exposed to cold temperatures.

EMOTIONAL BLOCK

Chills are symptomatic of feeling psychologically over-extended. You find it difficult to relax and have an underlying fear of warming up to others, even though it may not appear to be so. The fear of being too engaging and of being taken advantage of is chilling you.

MENTAL BLOCK

If you are feeling chilled, become aware of which part of your body is cold. This will give you insight into which area of your life holds the fear. You will then be able to more clearly define why you are unable to let go and warm up to a particular situation. Your body is telling you to trust more, to obsess less about others, and to minimize the dramatic behavior that you tend to exhibit. Stop worrying about what "might happen." Live in the moment and give yourself permission to be the warm person you really are.

SPIRITUAL BLOCK AND CONCLUSION

To uncover the spiritual block that keeps you from responding to the needs of your BEING, refer to the "KEY QUESTIONS" at the back of this book. In answering these questions, you will come in touch more easily and accurately with the true cause of your physical problem.

CHOKING FIT

See LUNG DISORDERS.

CHOLERA

Cholera is an acute and epidemic disease in which bacteria invades the small intestine. Severe diarrhea results in dehydration and loss of critical enzymes and potassium. See INTESTINAL DISORDERS. If you are suffering from cholera, it is important to stop considering yourself as a nuisance or a bad person. You are not a "plague" to others.

CHOLESTEROL

Cholesterol is a necessary lipid, or fat, that acts as a lubricant for the body just as oil lubricates the engine of a car. Its primary function is to provide a protective barrier along the walls of the blood vessels to protect them from the continual flow of the blood. The liver synthesizes the amount of cholesterol the body requires. *A high level of cholesterol* in the blood is called *hypercholesterolemia.* Excess cholesterol coming from the food you eat is absorbed into the bile and into the small intestine for elimination. When this natural process is blocked, the surplus cholesterol remains trapped in the circulatory system, ultimately forming deposits under the skin, on the tendons, in the curve of the cornea and the eyelids and, most dangerously, on the arterial walls. This buildup in the arteries is called ARTERIOSCLEROSIS. See ARTERIES.

CIRCULATORY PROBLEMS

See ARTERIES.

CIRRHOSIS

PHYSICAL BLOCK

Cirrhosis is a disease resulting in complete impairment of the physiological functions of the liver. Alcoholism is cited as the principle cause (90% of all cases for men and 75% for women). Symptoms of cirrhosis include extreme fatigue, loss of appetite, slow digestion, heartburn, itching, rashes, constipation or diarrhea, alternating color of the stools, fever and indigestion. Suddenly there is abdominal swelling, pain, vomiting of blood, swelling of the body in general and jaundice. Advanced stages lead to very severe symptoms.

Since cirrhosis is the most significant liver disease, it is urgent that you make a major change in your life. Your body is telling you that you have reached your physical, emotional and mental limits and only you can do something about it. Your way of living is killing you. You must stop rebelling and believing life is unfair. See LIVER DISORDERS.

CLAUSTROPHOBIA

PHYSICAL BLOCK

Claustrophobia is the neurotic fear of enclosed spaces (a feeling of anguish as soon as one find himself in an enclosed space). It seems to be the opposite of agoraphobia (a feeling of anguish as soon as one leaves a protective area or person to find himself in an open space or public place), but the same person often experiences both phobias. See AGORAPHOBIA if necessary.

EMOTIONAL BLOCK

People who feel imprisoned and worry too much about the work that must be done often exhibit claustrophobia. They suppress their own desires and feelings of anger.

MENTAL BLOCK

In feeling claustrophobic, your body is showing you your inner obsession with wanting to do everything perfectly. It's time you open the prison door, you alone will hold the key once you let go of your obsessions and realize you are human and have fears, limits and weaknesses like everyone else.

SPIRITUAL BLOCK AND CONCLUSION

To uncover the spiritual block that keeps you from responding to the needs of your BEING, refer to the "KEY QUESTIONS" at the back of this book. In answering these questions, you will come in touch more easily and accurately with the true cause of your physical problem.

CLAVICLE PROBLEMS

See COLLARBONE.

CLEFT LIP / HARELIP / CLEFT PALATE

Failure of the lip to fuse together during fetal development results in a condition called *cleft lip* (or *harelip*). When the roof of the mouth also has failed to close, this is termed a *cleft palate*. See MALFORMATIONS.

COCCYX PROBLEMS

PHYSICAL BLOCK

The *coccyx*, or *tailbone*, is actually the "tail end" of the spinal column. It is comprised of five primary coccycal vertebrae fused into one. If the coccyx has been traumatized due to bruising or fracture, it can be very sensitive - especially in a seated position.

EMOTIONAL BLOCK

The coccyx represents fundamental needs. If you suffer from pain in this region, you lack confidence in the Universal Intelligence and its ability to help you with your fundamental needs. You want to be taken care of but don't want to admit that to others or to yourself. If you feel pain in the tailbone while in a sitting position, it is likely you feel guilty about sitting around, waiting for someone else to take charge of your life. You feign independence by appearing active.

It may be that you feel guilty for parking yourself near others who are busy, or for sitting idly as you have fun (at the movies, taking a class, etc.). Because you have a dependent mindset, you assume others are depending on you as well.

MENTAL BLOCK

First, get in touch with your thoughts and acknowledge the fact that you want someone else to take care of you because you have no confidence in your own abilities or in the guidance of the Universe. Is there something wrong in admitting it? It's OK to need someone's support. Don't judge yourself so harshly. This does not mean that you will be dependent forever. Perhaps the Universe has given you this person to lean on for a while until you regain your strength and confidence. Denial of your dependence will only increase it. Allow yourself to be dependent in the moment, for it's only temporary. Such self-love will help you develop more autonomy.

142

Secondly, check with your loved ones before deciding that others depend on you and that you can't have fun without their consent. See if that's true. In the process, you will allow everyone involved to express their own needs and desires.

SPIRITUAL BLOCK AND CONCLUSION

To uncover the spiritual block that keeps you from responding to the needs of your BEING, refer to the "KEY QUESTIONS" at the back of this book. In answering these questions, you will come in touch more easily and accurately with the true cause of your physical problem.

COLD (COMMON)

See COMMON COLD.

COLD SORE

PHYSICAL BLOCK

Cold sores, also known as *herpes simplex*, are the result of a viral infection affecting the skin, producing painful blisters, usually around the mouth.

EMOTIONAL BLOCK

Cold sores signify harsh judgment of someone of the opposite sex, with a tendency toward a generally harsh judgment of the opposite sex as a whole and thinking of someone or something specific as repulsive. Cold sores provide an excuse to avoid intimate physical contact with a certain someone with whom you are angry, perhaps because he/she humiliated you. You have come close to expressing this anger, but recoiled at the last minute and left it unexpressed.

MENTAL BLOCK

A cold sore is a message from your body that you need to discard a critical and unhealthy attitude toward the opposite sex. Recurring cold sores are an urgent message that you are subconsciously distancing yourself from the opposite sex when you actually desire the opposite - to be close to them with a healthy, mutual acceptance. Although you may think you are punishing them by developing cold sores, you are, in truth, only harming yourself.

SPIRITUAL BLOCK AND CONCLUSION

To uncover the spiritual block that keeps you from responding to the needs of your BEING, refer to the "KEY QUESTIONS" at the back of this book. In answering these questions, you will come in touch more easily and accurately with the true cause of your physical problem.

COLIC

The disease is so named from its being seated in or near the colon. It is a severe paroxysmal pain in the abdomen, due to spasm, obstruction, or distention of some one of the hollow viscera. The pain can be diffuse or localized.

When *colic* is intense, it can cause diarrhea. See DIAR-RHEA and INTESTINAL DISORDERS.

COLITIS

Colitis is a disorder that involves inflammation of the colon. Symptoms include acute abdominal pain, diarrhea alternating with constipation, general fatigue and irregular fever. See DIARRHEA, CONSTIPATION and INTESTINAL DISORDERS. Remember that wherever inflammation occurs, anger is indicated. See SECTION 2.

COLLARBONE PROBLEMS

PHYSICAL BLOCK

The *collarbone*, or *clavicle*, is the long bone that extends diagonally, connecting the sternum to the scapula, or shoulder. Fractures and sprains of the collarbone are common, although pain in this area is often experienced for no apparent reason.

EMOTIONAL BLOCK

All problems relating to bone tissue are manifestations of frustration about issues relating to structure, or authority. When pain or injury occurs in the collarbone, it is an indication that you are having difficulty asserting yourself and have an unexpressed need to toss out ideas that are being imposed upon you. You feel obligated to do what you are told to do, rather than what you want to do.

145

MENTAL BLOCK

It's important for you to grasp that you have the right to your own opinion and are justified in expressing it. If you continue to let your fears get in the way, you will remain intimidated by others, especially those in positions of authority. Since pain is associated with guilt, you probably feel guilty about wanting to express yourself but not having the courage to do it.

Even if you allowed one or both of your parents to dictate to you when you were a child, you need not carry the same mindset with you into adulthood. By expressing yourself and making your requests, you will realize that your fears were unfounded. Find strength in courage and you will quickly come to realize that it's a lot easier than you thought to express yourself.

See BONE DISORDERS and if necessary, see also ACCIDENT, FRACTURE or SPRAIN.

SPIRITUAL BLOCK AND CONCLUSION

To uncover the spiritual block that keeps you from responding to the needs of your BEING, refer to the "KEY QUESTIONS" at the back of this book. In answering these questions, you will come in touch more easily and accurately with the true cause of your physical problem.

COLON DISORDERS

The *colon* is part of the digestive system located between the small intestine and the rectum. It extracts moisture from food residues before they are excreted. See INTESTINAL DISORDERS.

COLOSTOMY

A *colostomy* is a surgical operation that creates an opening from the colon to the surface of the body to function as an anus. This is a surgical procedure that is usually performed following cancer of the colon. See ANUS, INTESTINAL DISORDERS and CANCER.

COMA

PHYSICAL BLOCK

Coma is a state of prolonged unconsciousness and resulting loss of related functions such as motility and physical sensitivity, including a variety of metabolic disturbances. The person appears to be asleep but unresponsive to internal or external stimuli. On a kinetic level, it is believed that the silver thread linking the physical to the metaphysical body has been partially severed.

EMOTIONAL BLOCK

The comatose person has chosen to remain in the twilight zone between life and death in order to delay making a de-

147

cision between the two. They fear the unknown realm of death and letting go of their loved ones and of the life they have built.

MENTAL BLOCK

If someone close to you is in a coma, it is important for you to understand that you are able to communicate with that person and be there to help them make their decision. Read them this passage and help them understand that their fear of the unknown is normal and that they are free to make whatever choice is most beneficial to their own soul. They can decide to stay or go, knowing that any unfinished business will be dealt with in their next incarnation.

SPIRITUAL BLOCK AND CONCLUSION

To uncover the spiritual block that keeps you from responding to the needs of your BEING, refer to the "KEY QUESTIONS" at the back of this book. In answering these questions, you will come in touch more easily and accurately with the true cause of your physical problem.

COMMON COLD

PHYSICAL BLOCK

A *common cold* is a viral infection characterized by inflammation of the mucous membranes lining the upper respiratory passages and usually accompanied by malaise, fever, chills, coughing, and sneezing. It is also called *coryza*.

EMOTIONAL BLOCK

A cold will often manifest as a result of congestion on a mental level, especially when there's so much going on in your head that you don't know which way to turn. You have the feeling that someone or some situation is either walking all over you or is being thrust upon you. You also tend to get so caught up in unimportant details that you don't know where to begin. This is frustrating for you because you want to see everything completed, even before you've begun. You've gotten *a-head* of yourself. The mental confusion that results blocks your view of your needs and you are unable to live in the moment. It may be that there is someone that you just can't stand; the cold is your body reacting to your wish to keep this person away from you.

MENTAL BLOCK

The most common misconception regarding a cold is that catching a chill will result in a cold. The more popular a belief system, the more influence it will have over a society. Even if you are unaware that you have accepted a belief system, your body is in touch with your subconscious and reacts to the belief you have internalized. It's interesting to note that, although popular belief deems that a cold can be caught, only those who believe it seem to catch one! It's important, therefore, to stop letting yourself be influenced by the mainstream mindset. The more we stop following popular belief systems, the less influence they will have on a global level.

As every illness has a purpose, however, a cold serves to tell you that external forces too easily influence you. The onset of a cold is a message from the body that it's time for you to let go; stop worrying needlessly about every little thing. You don't have to become insensitive in order to accomplish what you need to do. Blaming someone else or some situation for your discomfort is not the answer either; desensitizing yourself in order to distance yourself from them will not help you sort out your priorities. See NOSE PROBLEMS.

SPIRITUAL BLOCK AND CONCLUSION

To uncover the spiritual block that keeps you from responding to the needs of your BEING, refer to the "KEY QUESTIONS" at the back of this book. In answering these questions, you will come in touch more easily and accurately with the true cause of your physical problem.

CONCUSSION

Concussion is defined as an injury to any soft body structure, but usually pertains to the brain. A concussion is generally the result of a blow to the head. It should be noted that head trauma is a manifestation of emotional shock or trauma or feelings of being overwhelmed. See ACCIDENT and BRAIN DISORDERS.

CONGENITAL DISEASE

Congenital disease is defined as existing from the time of birth, or being present as if by nature, but not hereditary. It establishes itself in the body during the physical formation of the body in the womb and is present at birth. See SECTION 2.

CONJUNCTIVITIS

Conjunctivitis, more commonly known as *pink eye*, is an irritating inflammation of the conjunctive, the mucous membrane that lines the eye and eyelid. Symptoms include discharge from the eye that hampers opening the eyelids in the morning, swelling of the eyelid, and redness of the eye. It is a superficial problem and vision usually remains relatively normal.

See EYE DISORDERS and note that the presence of conjunctivitis indicates a discomfort in seeing something that arouses anger and a desire to close your eyes to prevent seeing it. If you are experiencing this condition, learn to see the situation with your heart, rather than your eyes. Inflammation in the eyes is your body's way of telling you to rediscover your natural enthusiasm for life, to see things from a position of clarity. See SECTION 2.

CONN'S SYNDROME

This condition is characterized by disturbances in salt-water balance and symptoms of weakness, muscular cramps, twitching, convulsions and sometimes paralysis; usually caused by a benign tumor of the cortex of the adrenal gland that leads to excess secretion of aldosterone (a steroid hormone secreted by the adrenal cortex). See ADRENAL GLAND PROBLEMS.

CONSTIPATION

PHYSICAL BLOCK

Constipation refers to the difficulty or infrequency in the passage of stools due to sluggish action of the bowels. Although "normal" bowel rhythm may vary from person to person, one thing is agreed: the condition is present when the passage of stools is difficult and the stools are dry and hard.

EMOTIONAL BLOCK

The primary function of the bowel is to evacuate what is no longer useful to the body. In metaphysical terms, optimal health hinges on the release of old ideas that are being carried around. Constipation also indicates lack of expression of one's ideas or feelings for fear of displeasing others, being "wrong," or risking the loss of something or someone.

If you are stingy or attached to material things, you probably have difficulty letting go physically as well. Constipation can occur when you feel you are being forced to part with your coveted time or money. When you do give of these things (out of guilt), it is not willingly and you would have preferred to hold on to them.

Constipation can result from the stress brought on by an inability to let go of a past incident, which importance has since been exaggerated by dark thoughts or feelings of anger, frustration, suspicion, humiliation or jealousy.

MENTAL BLOCK

If you suffer from constipation, your body is giving you a powerful message that it's time to let go! Stale ideas and old belief systems will accumulate and eventually poison you, so "out with the old and in with the new!" Feed your mind with fresh thoughts and ideas. Don't restrain yourself any longer with fear of losing someone or something. It would be worth it to find out if you would truly be a loser if you expressed yourself or did what you want. Now, isn't that a better attitude to have?

SPIRITUAL BLOCK AND CONCLUSION

To uncover the spiritual block that keeps you from responding to the needs of your BEING, refer to the "KEY QUESTIONS" at the back of this book. In answering these questions, you will come in touch more easily and accurately with the true cause of your physical problem.

CONTUSIONS

Contusions are darkish black and blue marks on the skin, formed usually without a cut, due to blood that leaks out of capillaries and into surrounding tissues after an injury. The blood collects under the skin, causing the discoloration. See ACCIDENT. Bruising occurs more easily when you are run down physically and emotionally or feeling injured and worn out by life. It is a physical manifestation of a bruised and traumatized spirit.

CONVULSIONS

PHYSICAL BLOCK

The term *convulsion* encompasses a variety of violent and involuntary contractions of the voluntary muscles, from mild to severe, sometimes associated with loss of consciousness.

EMOTIONAL BLOCK

Convulsions cause physical harm to the body. Subconsciously allowing this to happen to your body indicates that you are also harming yourself on an emotional and mental level. There is tremendous internal upheaval. Generally, you are mostly passive around others and turn any violent thoughts inward toward yourself. Even if you were a young child when you began to experience convulsions, they were an expression of suppressed and internalized violence. Note that these feelings may be carried over from the imprinted memories of past lives. The soul will carry unresolved conflict with it until it is addressed and diffused.

MENTAL BLOCK

If you suffer from convulsions, your body is telling you that you can no longer contain this internal violence. Understand that it is perfectly normal for a human being to carry repressed violence and that the goal for all of us is to learn to channel as well as offset it. Psychological research concludes that violent tendencies are relics of our most primal survival instincts. There is no need to remain completely passive and compliant simply in order to meet the expectations of others. You owe it to yourself to recognize your limits and not keep all your anger inside, as you will be the one to suffer. Love yourself and others will love you as well.

If you care for a baby or child who suffers from convulsions, I suggest you read them the above paragraph along with the explanation that all illness begins from inside them. As they are yet unable to rationalize, they will *feel* what you are telling them. Babies and young children are much more in tune with the vibrations of those around them and assimilate information very quickly on an energy level. Generally speaking, inner processing of wisdom occurs more easily in young children than in adults.

SPIRITUAL BLOCK AND CONCLUSION

To uncover the spiritual block that keeps you from responding to the needs of your BEING, refer to the "KEY QUESTIONS" at the back of this book. In answering these questions, you will come in touch more easily and accurately with the true cause of your physical problem.

CORN

PHYSICAL BLOCK

A *corn* is a thickening of the epidermis at some point, especially on the toes, by friction or pressure. It is usually painful and troublesome. The substance of a corn usually resembles horn, but where moisture is present, as between the toes, it is white and sodden.

EMOTIONAL BLOCK

Metaphysically speaking, corns represent apprehension about the future and restraint of natural enthusiasm, resulting in the impediment of any effort to go forward. If a callus appears on the hand, there is some resistance being expressed about a situation in the present.

MENTAL BLOCK

The appearance of corns is a message from the body that you are resisting something. You may lack the confidence to continue on a certain path. Determine the basis for your apprehension. Are you afraid of displeasing someone you care about? Are you afraid of failing to meet your own expectations? Stop trying to keep your desires and capabilities in tow and take the necessary steps toward what you want.

SPIRITUAL BLOCK AND CONCLUSION

To uncover the spiritual block that keeps you from responding to the needs of your BEING, refer to the "KEY QUESTIONS" at the back of this book. In answering these questions, you will come in touch more easily and accurately with the true cause of your physical problem.

CORNEA (ULCERATED)

See EYE DISORDERS, noting that an *ulcerated cornea* is an indication that reality has become very painful to look at. The person sees life too somberly.

CORONARY THROMBOSIS

See THROMBOSIS.

CORYZA

See COMMON COLD.

COUGH

PHYSICAL BLOCK

A *cough* is a reflex action brought on by an irritation of the respiratory tract. Its purpose is to expel mucus or foreign bodies that threaten to obstruct the passageways. I refer here to coughs that occur without apparent physical cause

157

and not those brought on by asthma, flu, cold, laryngitis, etc.

EMOTIONAL BLOCK

If you have a more or less frequent cough without apparent physical cause, you likely tend to be easily irritated. You are your own worst critic. Your body is telling you that your heart would like to see you more tolerant, especially toward yourself.

Even if you are irritated by someone else or by some external situation, it is triggering your self-criticism. Sneezing is linked to external irritation, but coughing is linked with something irritating inside you.

MENTAL BLOCK

Each time you cough without apparent reason, take a moment to evaluate what you are thinking. Everything happens so quickly and automatically within you that you are not conscious of the number of times you criticize yourself and fail to accept yourself as you are. This impedes your deep inhalation of life and the sense of fulfillment and satisfaction that comes with it. **You are much more than you think you are.** The moment you become aware of an inner irritation, be gentle with yourself. Treat yourself as you would like to be treated by others. You'll find it's a breath of fresh air!

SPIRITUAL BLOCK AND CONCLUSION

To uncover the spiritual block that keeps you from responding to the needs of your BEING, refer to the "KEY QUESTIONS" at the back of this book. In answering these questions, you will come in touch more easily and accurately with the true cause of your physical problem

CRAMPS (MENSTRUAL)

See MENSTRUAL CRAMPS or DISORDERS

CRAMPS

PHYSICAL BLOCK

Cramps are involuntary and sudden contractions of the muscles, causing tightness and varying degrees of pain and discomfort. Under normal conditions, muscles are bundles of specialized cells that are able to contract and relax, creating movement. Muscle groups that most commonly experience cramping are those of the legs, feet, stomach and intestines.

EMOTIONAL BLOCK

Cramping of any part of the body indicates a fear and a desire to grab hold of someone or something.

MENTAL BLOCK

Be aware of which part of the body is actually experiencing the painful muscle contraction and what that part is used for. If the cramp is in your leg, you are probably afraid to go ahead with a project or to go to work. What or whom do you want to cling to so tightly? The fear and tension you feel are causing you to feel contracted instead of experiencing a relaxed state of mind. For further information and clarity, look up the affected body part.

SPIRITUAL BLOCK AND CONCLUSION

To uncover the spiritual block that keeps you from responding to the needs of your BEING, refer to the "KEY QUESTIONS" at the back of this book. In answering these questions, you will come in touch more easily and accurately with the true cause of your physical problem.

CROHN'S DISEASE

Crohn's disease (or *Ileocolitis*) is a chronic inflammation of the colon or final segment of small intestine, producing diarrhea, nausea, fever, pain and weight loss. If the distal ileum becomes inflamed, the condition is known as ILE-ITIS. The onset of *Crohn's disease* can be quick and brutal, the pains simulating appendicitis, but more often its onset is slow and insidious, with chronic abdominal pain and diarrhea. See INTESTINAL DISORDERS and DI-ARRHEA. The body is sending an important message that there is a profound need for self-acceptance. There has been an underlying fear of rejection and fear of not living up to the loved ones' expectations.

CROSS-EYE

See STRABISMUS

CROUP

Croup is the common name for *diptherial laryngitis*. It usually occurs in young children and is marked by a hoarse cough and difficulty in breathing. The first signs of croup are as follows: the voice becomes husky, then hoarse and after a few days, is lost. There is pressure on the chest, a barking cough sets in and a noticeable whistling sound on inhalation. See LARYNGITIS, ANGINA, and COUGH.

CUSHING'S SYNDROME

Cushing's Syndrome is linked to an increased concentration of glucocorticoid hormone in the bloodstream that is being produced by an adrenal gland tumor (adenoma). See ADRENAL GLAND PROBLEMS.

CUT

A *cut*, *lesion* or *abrasion* is the body's way of telling you that you are feeling cut off from someone or something that is of importance to you. You are blaming and punishing yourself for it. See ACCIDENT and ARTERIES.

CUTICLES

Cuticles are the fine skin that grows at the base of the nail bed on fingers and toes. See FINGER DISORDERS.

CYST

PHYSICAL BLOCK

A *cyst* is a sac made up of membranous tissue containing fluid. Its content has no vascular contact, thus is not fed by the bloodstream, and may be located anywhere on or in the body. Cysts can be either benign or malignant.

EMOTIONAL BLOCK

Cysts are manifestations of unresolved issues. The spherical shape of the cyst develops as an accumulation of emotional pain (sadness or sorrow) over a long period of time to cushion the blows received by the ego. The location of the cyst on the body gives a clear indication in what sphere of life the sadness is caused. Cysts on the breasts, for example, are linked to love or maternal issues. If the cyst is malignant, see CANCER.

MENTAL BLOCK

Your body is sending you a clear and urgent message that it is harmful to continue to feed this old psychological wound and it's time to learn about forgiveness. Although you may perceive that someone has hurt you or that they continue to hurt you, understand that your attitude is what's hurting you. It is unnecessary to develop unhealthy accumulations to act as armor against emotional pain. You can defend yourself. Your cyst is a reminder of your need to forgive. Learn to forgive yourself and others by referring to the steps to true forgiveness at the back of this book.

SPIRITUAL BLOCK AND CONCLUSION

To uncover the spiritual block that keeps you from responding to the needs of your BEING, refer to the "KEY QUESTIONS" at the back of this book. In answering these questions, you will come in touch more easily and accurately with the true cause of your physical problem.

CYSTIC FIBROSIS (MUCOVISCIDOSIS)

PHYSICAL BLOCK

Cystic fibrosis is a life-shortening, inherited disorder that affects the way that salt and water move into and out of the body's cells. The most important effects of this problem are in the lungs and the digestive system (especially the pancreas), where thick mucus blocks the small tubes and ducts. The lung problem can lead to progressive blockage, infection, and lung damage, and even death if there is too much damage, while the pancreatic blockage causes poor digestion and poor absorption of food, leading to poor growth and malnutrition. The sweat glands are also affected, in that they make a much saltier sweat than normal. Most parts of the body that make mucus are also affected including the reproductive tract in men and women with Cystic fibrosis.

If you have this disease, you are receiving an important message that it is time to take your life into your own hands and to recognize your enormous power to shape your own life, rather than believing that you cannot do so without others. This attitude is absolutely the opposite of your life plans because this disease, which is able to turn you into an invalid, makes it impossible to act in your life. Your soul is crying: *"Help! I want to live!"*

SPIRITUAL BLOCK AND CONCLUSION

To uncover the spiritual block that keeps you from responding to the needs of your BEING, refer to the "KEY QUESTIONS" at the back of this book. In answering these questions, you will come in touch more easily and accurately with the true cause of your physical problem.

CYSTITIS

PHYSICAL BLOCK

Cystitis or *bladder infection* is an inflammation of the urinary bladder and ureters. Symptoms include burning and

pain on urination, increased urinary urgency and frequency even though not much urine is expelled.

EMOTIONAL BLOCK

This indicates internal frustration over your emotional
state. You have difficulty going with the flow and you express your needs inordinately. You have grown accustomed to waiting after others and it burns you that others
seem oblivious to your feelings.

MENTAL BLOCK

Listen to your body; it is giving you a clear message that
it's time to take responsibility for your life. If you wait for
others to bring you happiness, you will have a long wait.
Only you can see to your happiness and express your
needs and frustrations to others. Remember: when you
feel anger towards others, there's an underlying accusation. If you stop accusing others for your unhappiness,
you will be less angry. See BLADDER DISORDERS and
SECTION 2.

SPIRITUAL BLOCK AND CONCLUSION

To uncover the spiritual block that keeps you from responding to the needs of your BEING, refer to the "KEY
QUESTIONS" at the back of this book. In answering
these questions, you will come in touch more easily and
accurately with the true cause of your physical problem.

DANDRUFF

Dandruff is a common scalp condition in which the dead skin is shed, producing white flakes. They can be fine and dry or coarse and oily. See HAIR and SKIN DISORDERS.

D

DEAFNESS

See EAR DISORDERS.

DEHYDRATION

PHYSICAL BLOCK

Dehydration occurs when there is excessive fluid loss in the body due to perspiration from overexertion or fever, or inadequate intake of fluids to maintain fluid balance in the cells. Symptoms of dehydration include loss of skin elasticity, sunken eyes, dark circles around the eyes and rapid pulse or lowered blood pressure.

EMOTIONAL BLOCK

Metaphysically, water is related to the emotional body. Dehydration means you have cut yourself off from feeling anything - more specifically, feeling good about yourself. You allow yourself to be depleted by what goes on around you and in many cases, by obsessive thinking.

MENTAL BLOCK

Water is one of the most important things in a person's life. Without it, one cannot live long (same as love). You must learn to feel love for yourself and when you achieve this, you'll want to drink more water. I suggest you also read the metaphysical description of OBSESSION.

SPIRITUAL BLOCK AND CONCLUSION

To uncover the spiritual block that keeps you from responding to the needs of your BEING, refer to the "KEY QUESTIONS" at the back of this book. In answering these questions, you will come in touch more easily and accurately with the true cause of your physical problem.

DELIRIUM

See INSANITY.

DENTAL DECAY

PHYSICAL BLOCK

Dental decay, which causes cavities, is the result of tooth enamel that has been ravaged by a diet of over-processed food and sugars and also by an acidic environment in the mouth that reflects systemic acidic body chemistry. Acids eat through tooth enamel, causing sensitivity and discomfort as the dentin is eroded. Once the root of the tooth has

168

been reached, there is swelling and inflammation of the nerve endings, causing intense pain.

EMOTIONAL BLOCK

D

Dental decay is an indication that there's a person or situation in your life that you can't accept because you are too angry. This is preventing you from sinking your teeth into your needs and desires.

It can also indicate that you undermine the laughter in your life. You are taking life too seriously. See TEETH to see in which part of your life your desires are blocked.

MENTAL BLOCK

You have developed a cavity as a signal from your body that your stubbornness and acidic disposition are harmful to you. Learn to laugh and remember that truth is all in your perception. Lighten up and you will be enlightened. Once you cultivate a sweeter disposition you will no longer have the desire for sweets that destroy your teeth.

SPIRITUAL BLOCK AND CONCLUSION

To uncover the spiritual block that keeps you from responding to the needs of your BEING, refer to the "KEY QUESTIONS" at the back of this book. In answering these questions, you will come in touch more easily and accurately with the true cause of your physical problem.

DENTAL TARTAR

Dental tartar is a hard, yellowish deposit on the teeth, consisting of organic secretions and food particles deposited in various salts, such as calcium carbonate. See TEETH PROBLEMS and add that this indicates an accumulation of negative thoughts to the point of becoming bone weary.

DEPRESSION

PHYSICAL BLOCK

I refer here to *clinical* or *chronic depression*. For depression that is short-lived or the result of reaction to sad or difficult situations, I suggest you refer to the sections on ANGUISH, ANXIETY or AGORAPHOBIA.

Common symptoms of depression include loss of interest and lack of pleasure in normal everyday activities, a feeling of hopelessness or despondency associated with exhaustion or loss of energy, loss of concentration, feelings of indifference, disinterest, discouragement, withdrawal and preoccupation. The depressive becomes completely self-absorbed and feels no need for help from others. They feel others should change, not themselves. Serious depression can lead to suicidal thoughts. Depression is often misdiagnosed as burnout, so read BURNOUT to know the difference.

EMOTIONAL BLOCK

If you are experiencing depression, realize that it is a state of mind to which you retreat in order to escape the feeling of pressure, especially emotional pressure. After many years of careful observation, I have determined that most depressive people carry unresolved issues with opposite-sex parents. This explains why it is very common to blame their spouses for their depression. The resulting torment the spouse goes through was meant for the parent. By refusing to get help, you continue to feed the monstrous frame of mind a steady diet of bitterness and hatred that builds and increases the weight of the depression. This cloud of accumulated destructive thoughts and emotions becomes heavier and heavier.

The depth of emotional wounding determines the depth of the depression. Wounds of rejection, abandonment, humiliation, betrayal, or injustice set the stage for tremendous mental upheaval, especially if experienced in isolation. As young children, depressives had no one to talk to, to hear their questions and to share their anguish. If they do not learn to trust others, they will continue to withdraw and deny their desires.

MENTAL BLOCK

Since a depressive person doesn't want to be helped, it's usually the people close to them that want to help. If you are one of these people and have someone close to you who is depressive, I suggest you be quite firm with them. Tell them they are the only one capable of digging them-

171

selves out of the pit they dug for themselves and, thereafter, stop trying to solve their problem.

Note to the depressive: The most important thing for you to realize is that the depression is a result of tremendous emotional wounding, when young, on the deepest level - the level of BEING. You refuse who you are. You reject yourself and believe you are unlovable and unworthy because of the profound rejection of someone you loved and trusted. We all need nurturing and need to trust someone completely. If those needs are violated through rejection or abandonment, we will naturally be bitter, as we feel intensely alone and afraid. If you can understand that the parent or loved one that you feel rejected you was coming from their own pain and rejection; if you can learn to see them as fellow human beings and have compassion for them, you will have taken the first step toward your own recovery. It wasn't a lack of love that caused them to reject you; it was their own wounded inner child that made them unable to express their love.

By connecting with the inner child of the person who hurt you, you will find that you are able to forgive them. The next important step is to get in touch with your own inner child and to forgive it for being angry and bitter. Love this child unconditionally to begin the healing process.

The final step is to talk openly with the person who hurt you about what you have felt. Tell them how you have carried all this pain inside, talk about the anger and the bitterness **without judgment or accusation**. (See the steps of forgiveness at the end of this book.) Once you have expressed your feelings, reconnect with your own

172

self-worth. If this is difficult for you, ask others close to you to show you your positive attributes. It may seem superficial at first, but you will slowly begin to feel validated.

If you have been having suicidal thoughts, there is a part of you that wants to die in order to make room for a healthier, more vital part of you - your true self. You are confusing the part of you that wants to die with yourself.

SPIRITUAL BLOCK AND CONCLUSION

To uncover the spiritual block that keeps you from responding to the needs of your BEING, refer to the "KEY QUESTIONS" at the back of this book. In answering these questions, you will come in touch more easily and accurately with the true cause of your physical problem.

DIABETES

PHYSICAL BLOCK

Diabetes is a disturbance in the metabolism from lack of insulin secreted by the pancreas, or from its inability to function normally. 85% of adults diagnosed with diabetes are overweight.

EMOTIONAL BLOCK

The pancreas is the gland linked with the solar plexus, which deals with emotions, desires and all intellectual activities. Pancreatic disorders indicate imbalance on the emotional level. If you are diabetic, you are often very emotional and have too many desires for yourself and others. You want everyone to have a slice of the pie. But you can also be envious if someone has more than you.

You are a devoted person but you expect too much from yourself and others. You tend to blame yourself readily for others' dissatisfaction. You also tend to expend excessive energy and mental activity researching the means necessary to respond to your needs. This behavior is caused by an inner sadness from an unmet desire to be loved.

Juvenile diabetes may manifest in children who feel insufficiently acknowledged. They are exhibiting an inner emptiness that seeks some form of compensation.

MENTAL BLOCK

Diabetes is a signal that you need to learn to let go and let things happen at their own pace. Stop trying to control the course of events. You need to realize that it is not your purpose to make everyone else happy. In addition, others may not necessarily want what *you* want for them, or they might not desire it as intensely. Acknowledge all the goodness that flows freely in your life, become mindful of the moment and taste each moment in all its delicious glory. Don't let yourself be distracted by what you may want tomorrow. Accept that, even though you may have been unable to fulfill a very important desire in the past, you still can enjoy smaller ones in the moment.

If you are a young child or adolescent with juvenile diabetes, stop thinking that you are the forgotten child. Find yourself and your place in the family.

SPIRITUAL BLOCK AND CONCLUSION

To uncover the spiritual block that keeps you from responding to the needs of your BEING, refer to the "KEY QUESTIONS" at the back of this book. In answering these questions, you will come in touch more easily and accurately with the true cause of your physical problem.

DIARRHEA

PHYSICAL BLOCK

Symptoms of *diarrhea* include the frequent passing of loose, watery stools, often with abdominal cramping. Diarrhea is a common symptom of a digestive disorder.

EMOTIONAL BLOCK

On a physical level, the body is rejecting unassimilated nutrients. This correlates on an emotional and mental level to the premature rejection of ideas and situations. Since you think that what is happening to you is difficult to assimilate, you can't see that's it's useful to you. Therefore, you expel anything that causes you emotional discomfort and don't enjoy life to its fullest.

You feel rejection and guilt more often than you feel recognition. The rejection you feel is more on the level of *having* and *doing* rather than *being*. You are afraid of not having something, doing too much or not doing enough. You are extremely sensitive emotionally and fearful of new situations.

MENTAL BLOCK

Frequent diarrhea is an indication that you have a poor self-image and don't feel you deserve good in your life. It is important that you learn to nourish your own soul and stop waiting for others to feed it for you. You could end up waiting an awfully long time. I speak from personal experience!

Many years ago, when I first began speaking to large audiences, I was terrified. I was sure that I wasn't good enough and that I would be rejected. I remember running to the washroom before the conference with an inopportune case of diarrhea! My body was telling me exactly what I thought of myself! I realized that I needed to believe in myself and in my ideas, without thinking I was arrogant. I am allowed to be good at what I do but I feared that if I thought that, I wouldn't want to better myself. Which was a very false belief because ever since I started, I've been constantly perfecting my teachings and myself.

SPIRITUAL BLOCK AND CONCLUSION

To uncover the spiritual block that keeps you from responding to the needs of your BEING, refer to the "KEY QUESTIONS" at the back of this book. In answering these questions, you will come in touch more easily and accurately with the true cause of your physical problem.

DIGESTIVE DISORDERS

The digestive tract includes all organs involved in the process of digestion. If you are suffering from digestive problems, see STOMACH and/or INDIGESTION. If the description does not fit your problem, see LIVER or INTESTINAL DISORDERS.

DIPHTHERIAL LARYNGITIS

See CROUP.

DIPHTHERIA

Diphtheria is characterized by formation of false membranes in the throat and other air passages, resulting in respiratory difficulty. See THROAT PROBLEMS and LARYNGITIS.

DISEASES (CHILDHOOD)

See CHILDHOOD DISEASES

DISK (SLIPPED)

PHYSICAL BLOCK

The vertebral column is composed of thirty-three vertebrae and its supple movement is attributed to the interposition, between each vertebra, of a disk in the shape of a double-convex lens, called an intervertebral disk. A disk that gets out of alignment, or "slips," immediately causes intense pain and immobilization of the spine.

EMOTIONAL BLOCK

If you are suffering from a *slipped disk*, determine what thoughts are blocking you and keeping you from doing what you had planned to do. You have difficulty making a decision and are putting it off until you feel you have more support from others.

MENTAL BLOCK

Make a habit of deciding more quickly. Become your own source of support instead of waiting for others and for all the right circumstances before going ahead. Go forward with confidence while remaining flexible when faced with your own limitations. Give yourself the right to experiment and to learn from these experiences. If your disk is out, maybe it's time to change your tune!

SPIRITUAL BLOCK AND CONCLUSION

To uncover the spiritual block that keeps you from responding to the needs of your BEING, refer to the "KEY QUESTIONS" at the back of this book. In answering these questions, you will come in touch more easily and accurately with the true cause of your physical problem.

DIVERTICULITIS

Diverticulitis is the inflammation of small sacs in the walls of an organ (such as the intestine) caused from the lodging of undigested food irritating the intestinal wall. See INTESTINAL DISORDERS and realize that inflammation indicates accumulated anger. Also see SECTION 2.

DIVERTICULOSIS

Diverticulosis is a condition in which a person has small sacs or pouches in the walls of a canal or organ, such as the intestine. These sacs can become inflamed to cause *diverticulitis*. See INTESTINAL DISORDERS.

DIZZINESS

PHYSICAL BLOCK

Dizziness is characterized by a short-lived sensation of faintness, distortion in hearing and visual disturbances, and unsteadiness with lightheadedness.

EMOTIONAL BLOCK

Dizziness may be experienced when you want to escape a situation that is causing you to re-live some old unhealed wound. Perhaps you accuse yourself of being a "dizzy broad" by acting without thinking, by being easily distracted and disorganized.

MENTAL BLOCK

When you have a dizzy spell, examine what was said or what happened in the moments just prior to each spell or what may happen right after. Know that these dizzy spells are the result of a surreal interpretation of events, of a fertile imagination and altered perception. You have unrealistic expectations of yourself. You have a tendency toward exaggerating events either due to tremendous fear or due to unresolved issues suffered as a child that have distorted your perception. The Universe has a way of giving you a second chance to look at past experiences so that you can come to terms with them once and for all through forgiveness (see the steps of forgiveness at the end of this book)

SPIRITUAL BLOCK AND CONCLUSION

To uncover the spiritual block that keeps you from responding to the needs of your BEING, refer to the "KEY QUESTIONS" at the back of this book. In answering these questions, you will come in touch more easily and accurately with the true cause of your physical problem.

DRY EYES

See TEARS (Lack of)

DRY SKIN

D

PHYSICAL BLOCK

Dry skin or *ichthyosis*, is characterized by scaly, flaking patches on the skin. See also SKIN DISORDERS.

EMOTIONAL BLOCK

When this condition is present at birth or early infancy, it indicates an attitude carried over from a previous life. All forms of dry skin are connected to an overly dry attitude (one that is not gentle or soft enough). As the skin represents the outer self, or what is displayed outwardly, it reflects what you want others to see of your personality. In this case, you are unwilling to expose your vulnerability or your softness.

MENTAL BLOCK

Your body is telling you that you need to be gentler with yourself and others. You don't need to control yourself any longer; let your softer self come forward. Observe those you admire who allow themselves to be gentle and you'll realize that they are not being taken advantage of. Shed your armor and show your soft side. You will find you are much more resilient and alive.

If you are reading this in reference to a child, read them this passage and know that they will assimilate the information on a soul level. Understand that it is up to the soul of the child to decide whether or not to respond.

SPIRITUAL BLOCK AND CONCLUSION

To uncover the spiritual block that keeps you from responding to the needs of your BEING, refer to the "KEY QUESTIONS" at the back of this book. In answering these questions, you will come in touch more easily and accurately with the true cause of your physical problem.

DUODENAL ULCER

The duodenum is the beginning portion of the small intestine. Secretions from the liver and pancreas drain into the duodenum for processing through the small intestine. An *ulcer* in this area occurs when the mucous lining has been eaten away by an over secretion of gastrointestinal juices from the stomach. Refer to STOMACH DISORDERS and add that accumulation of acidic thoughts towards a certain situation will eat away at you. These thoughts will irritate you until you let go of your powerless and rebellious feelings. You need to learn to express these feelings while acknowledging your difficulty to accept what *is*.

DUODENITIS

Duodenitis is defined as inflammation of the duodenum and is often misdiagnosed as gastroenteritis. See DUODENAL ULCER. Note that inflammation always indicates repressed anger. See also SECTION 2.

DYSLEXIA

PHYSICAL BLOCK

Dyslexia is defined as an impairment of the ability to read, characterized by the reversal of letters and words. Temporary symptoms of dyslexia may be present in stressful or emotional circumstances, but should not be misdiagnosed. A dyslexic child or adult often has difficulty organizing their space; the specific errors that they make while reading persist or worsen.

EMOTIONAL BLOCK

Dyslexia seems to occur more frequently in children who feel pushed or forced to perform intellectually. The two hemispheres of the brain do not interact simultaneously. In metaphysical terms, this is an indication that the dyslexic has difficulty merging the masculine and feminine aspects of their own psyche. Their souls remain undecided as to the sex they have chosen in this life. This is a profound and fundamental problem that is deep-seated in the subconscious. The mind has difficulty harmonizing the exchanges between the two hemispheres of the brain.

MENTAL BLOCK

If you are suffering from dyslexia, the first step I would advise you to take is to consult an educational kinesiology instructor (brain gym) who will have you perform certain exercises to help you re-establish the balance between the two hemispheres of your brain. Next, it is important that you decide once and for all that your chosen sex is the one you accept in this lifetime, so that you can move forward. This decision must be made firmly and with conviction, as it must be resolved to the core of your being. Understand that it is not necessary for you to subconsciously create a disability as an excuse for being what you consider imperfect. That does not prevent you from being an intelligent and talented individual.

SPIRITUAL BLOCK AND CONCLUSION

To uncover the spiritual block that keeps you from responding to the needs of your BEING, refer to the "KEY QUESTIONS" at the back of this book. In answering these questions, you will come in touch more easily and accurately with the true cause of your physical problem.

DYSPEPSIA

Dyspepsia is a blanket term used to describe imperfect or painful digestion and covers any number of minor digestive disorders, including indigestion or stomach upset (See STOMACH) or uncomfortable digestion in the intestinal tract (See INTESTINAL DISORDERS).

DYSPNEA

Difficulty in breathing, often associated with lung or heart disease and resulting in shortness of breath. Also called *air hunger*. See LUNG DISEASE.

EAR DISORDERS

PHYSICAL BLOCK

The *ear* is the organ of hearing, responsible for maintaining equilibrium as well as sensing sound. It allows us to open ourselves to the world around us. Therefore the ear represents our capacity to listen thus better understand our world.

Ear disorders affect every age group. Here are some of the most common: *deafness, otalgia* (or earache), *otitis,* MASTOIDITIS, ECZEMA, and any problem starting with OTO. TINNITUS and MENIERE'S DISEASE (loss of equilibrium) can also be a problem, refer to them in this book.

EMOTIONAL BLOCK

Any ear disorder that impedes the ability to hear indicates a judgmental attitude about what you are hearing. Infection or inflammation in the ear indicates internal anger and a desire to shut out whatever you don't want to hear. Ear infections are more common in today's children because they find it difficult to listen to the moralizing of the adults around them. Children will open their ears, instead, to intelligent reasoning that is presented coherently, as opposed to emotional reasoning. Babies and young children have a difficult time when spoken to harshly or emotionally about how to behave or not behave.

You can go "deaf" when you have difficulty listening to others and are too busy, instead, preparing what you want to say. In general, you feel you are easily vilified and thereby live constantly on the defensive. Listening to criticism of any kind is very painful. If you are stubborn and determined in your ways and closed to the advice of others, you might find yourself experiencing hearing loss that can be mild or even severe. If you have a fear of disobeying, you may also experience hearing loss, as you do not allow yourself to deviate from the straight and narrow. It may be that you are so sensitive that it is hard for you to listen to the problems of others as you fear you will be obligated to help and will have no time left for yourself.

Pain in the ear that does not affect hearing is a signal that you feel guilty and are punishing yourself over what you want or don't want to hear.

If the problem is purely esthetic, such as eczema, and prevents you from wearing earrings, for example, your body is telling you to simply acknowledge and accept your desire to adorn yourself and to enjoy the finer things without guilt.

MENTAL BLOCK

If you are refusing or simply unable to hear what is going on or being said around you, it may be that you've had it *up to your ears* with everything. Take the time to listen, instead, with your heart. Accept that those you refuse to hear are doing the best they can, even if you don't agree with them. Understand that it isn't what they are saying that is upsetting you, but your interpretation and your perception of what they are saying. In doing so, you will love yourself more and will become confident that no one is trying to hurt you. Regain your balance; open yourself to what others have to say.

If you believe that others will like or love you only when you obey them, it's time to change your belief system. You are living in such fear of being caught in the act that deafness becomes an excuse for not doing what others want you to do.

If you are the type who likes to help others, it would be a good idea to learn how to listen without feeling responsible for their happiness. Develop empathy and compassion; in doing so, you will open your heart rather than close your ears.

Instead of blaming yourself and manifesting pain in your ear, change your belief system. To do so, simply share with others what it is you feel guilty about so that you can determine whether or not what you believe is justified.

SPIRITUAL BLOCK AND CONCLUSION

To uncover the spiritual block that keeps you from responding to the needs of your BEING, refer to the "KEY QUESTIONS" at the back of this book. In answering these questions, you will come in touch more easily and accurately with the true cause of your physical problem.

EAR INFECTION

See OTITIS.

ECCHYMOSES

See BRUISE

ECTOPIC PREGNANCY

See TUBAL PREGNANCY.

ECZEMA

Eczema, or dermatitis, is an extremely common inflammation of the skin, usually with blisters, red bumps, swelling, oozing, scaling, crusting and itching. There are many types of eczema depending on the cause and where it occurs on the body.

See SKIN DISORDERS and add that eczema indicates a lack of confidence or inner balance. You experience a general feeling of anxiety and uncertainty in your life and about your future.

If certain products or chemicals cause your eczema, note that you are too easily influenced by what is going on around you.

If there is ITCHING, refer to it.

EDEMA

E

PHYSICAL BLOCK

Edema is the excessive accumulation of fluid in spaces between cells. It may be caused by lymphatic system disorder or a venous system disorder. Symptoms include bloating and swelling. *Mild edema* is referred to as *water retention*, but a minimum of 10% fluid accumulation is considered endemic; test simply by pressing with the finger. If your finger leaves an imprint, there is excess fluid present.

EMOTIONAL BLOCK

The degree of water retention corresponds with the degree of emotional retention. Your body is swelling in reaction to a desire to protect yourself emotionally. Edema may also occur once resolution of conflict has been experienced, followed by a conflict between the head and the heart. You are wrestling, in this case, with whether to maintain the conflict or resolve it. Determine what area of the body is affected by fluid retention; this will indicate what is being retained emotionally. For example, a swollen leg will indicate hesitation in moving forward toward a goal after having found a solution.

MENTAL BLOCK

Fluid retention is a signal from the body that you are holding yourself back due to a lack of confidence in your talent and abilities. You create obstacles and limitations for yourself. Your body is telling you to let go and to take more risks in the direction your heart is telling you to go. Choose your solution, rather than remaining mired in the conflict.

SPIRITUAL BLOCK AND CONCLUSION

To uncover the spiritual block that keeps you from responding to the needs of your BEING, refer to the "KEY QUESTIONS" at the back of this book. In answering these questions, you will come in touch more easily and accurately with the true cause of your physical problem.

ELBOW PROBLEMS

The movement of the *elbow* governs the flexibility of the arm and the direction and length of your reach thereby defining your personal space. It seems you need more "elbow room!" Pain in the elbow indicates that you are holding yourself back with your own inflexibility through fear of being stuck. Let go and take back your space! See ARM PROBLEMS and see FRACTURE if you suffer from a fractured elbow.

EMACIATION

Emaciation is the state of being emaciated or reduced to excessive leanness. For emotional and mental block, see THINNESS.

EMBOLISM (PULMONARY)

See PULMONARY EMBOLISM

EMPHYSEMA

E

Emphysema is a pathological condition of the lungs marked by an abnormal increase in the size of the air spaces, resulting in labored breathing and an increased susceptibility to infection. It can be caused by irreversible expansion of the alveoli (air cells of the lung) or by the destruction of alveolar walls. It's often associated with chronic bronchitis. See BRONCHITIS, but add that this oppressive suffocation of the physical body correlates to a psychological suffocation as your personal space is overwhelmed. It is urgent that you take control and reclaim your personal space.

ENDOCARDITIS

Endocarditis is an inflammatory disease of the endocardium (the membrane that lines the cavities of the heart). See HEART DISORDERS and SECTION 2.

ENDOMETRIOSIS

PHYSICAL BLOCK

Endometriosis is an all-too-common condition in which portions of the lining of the uterus (the endometrium) back up through the fallopian tubes and into the pelvic cavity. This tissue adheres to organs and/or to the pelvic wall and continues to function as uterine tissue.

EMOTIONAL BLOCK

Endometriosis may stem from a fear of bearing children. Although you may want to have children, you fear the possible consequences of childbirth, including the complications and discomfort that may occur in pregnancy or during the birth itself. You may even fear suffering or dying in the process. Perhaps your mother had difficulty in childbirth. I have seen cases where a profound fear of bearing children has come from a past life. A women who suffers from this is usually the type that runs things, that *create* in other fields.

MENTAL BLOCK

Whatever your fears regarding birth, whether timing or anticipated pain, they are substantial enough to create confusion in your reproductive organs. On a spiritual level, you have a strong desire to have a child - strong enough, in fact, that your body has responded by creating an extra uterus - yet you are holding yourself hostage to your own fear.

I have noticed that a great number of women who suffer from endometriosis are afraid of labor more than they are of the actual raising of the child. Acknowledge this fear and give yourself permission to be apprehensive. At the same time, acknowledge your deep desire for a child and your right as a woman to bring this desire to fruition. On a more material level, don't be self-critical when you are defeated by projects or when you want to give birth to new ones.

SPIRITUAL BLOCK AND CONCLUSION

To uncover the spiritual block that keeps you from responding to the needs of your BEING, refer to the "KEY QUESTIONS" at the back of this book. In answering these questions, you will come in touch more easily and accurately with the true cause of your physical problem.

E

ENTERIC FEVER

See TYPHOID FEVER.

ENURESIS

See BEDWETTING (for a child) or INCONTINENCE (for an adult)

EPIDEMICS

See SECTION 2.

EPILEPSY

PHYSICAL BLOCK

Epilepsy is a neurological disorder marked by periodic seizures, impaired consciousness and altered behavior, and involuntary and abnormal motor function and sensation caused by uncontrolled electrical discharges in the brain's nerve cells. Recurrent episodes of disturbances in brain electrical activity manifest as sudden brief attacks. *Grand mal* seizures are major episodes associated with loss of consciousness while *petit mal* seizures are milder, usually without loss of consciousness.

EMOTIONAL BLOCK

Epileptics are extremely self-critical, turning violent emotions inward and punishing themselves for the smallest error. They try to hide these perceived errors from others. Epilepsy is violence turned on themselves. Blame and self-loathing are internalized and they look for love in others, since they can't give it to themselves.

Often, the first epileptic seizure helped the child get more affection and attention from the parents. It may also have been used as a tool to distract attention from outside events or problems between the two parents and bring them back together to care for him.

MENTAL BLOCK

If you suffer from epilepsy, understand that you only need to sow love and affection to reap the benefits. It is unnecessary to endure such suffering to connect with others. I'm sure you receive more affection than you think. Talk openly with those you are close to about what you mean to each other so that you can clearly see your place in the world.

Be gentle with yourself, allow yourself to be human - with all human errors and frailties - without guilt or fear that you will be unloved. Your guilt and rage will disintegrate and you will no longer feel a need to express your violence inwardly or outwardly. A welcome, well-deserved and gentle calm will prevail. See CONVULSIONS.

SPIRITUAL BLOCK AND CONCLUSION

To uncover the spiritual block that keeps you from responding to the needs of your BEING, refer to the "KEY QUESTIONS" at the back of this book. In answering these questions, you will come in touch more easily and accurately with the true cause of your physical problem.

EPIPHYSIS

See PINEAL GLAND.

ESOPHAGUS

The *esophagus* is the muscular, membranous tube for the passage of food from the pharynx to the stomach. Esophageal disorders include *diverticula,* HERNIA and MALFORMATION. Pain can also be caused by a foreign object that becomes lodged in the esophagus or simply by having the sensation of a foreign object.

Since the esophagus is located near the beginning of the digestive tract, esophageal disorders indicate difficulty in accepting or welcoming something new. You refuse to digest new ideas more quickly than someone with stomach disorders. You may be self-critical; sometimes feeling easily hurt and "choked up" when your dreams are not realized. See MOUTH and STOMACH DISORDERS.

ESOPHAGITIS

Esophagitis is the inflammation of the esophagus, most commonly due to a gastro-esophageal reflux, or heartburn. Inflammation indicates repressed anger. In this case, the cause of your anger returns again and again, growing and preventing you from swallowing what has happened. See ESOPHAGUS and SECTION 2.

EXCRESCENCE

See SKIN TAGS.

EYE DISORDERS

PHYSICAL BLOCK

The *eye* is defined as an organ of sight or of light sensitivity. Eye disorders are numerous and varied but they all have one thing in common: they diminish or completely impede natural vision. Read the following explanation and refer also to the specific disorder for further corresponding metaphysical implications.

E

EMOTIONAL BLOCK

All eye disorders indicate a preference for closing your eyes to what is happening around you rather than to risk losing someone or something. It's a way to protect yourself. It's possible that you no longer want to *keep an eye* on things. There are many commonly used phrases pertaining to the eyes. Here are a few examples:

PHRASE	MEANING
"My eye"	In no way; not at all.
"Keep an eye out."	Keep constant watch over.
"I can do it with my eyes shut"	Being confident about one's ability.
"Quit eyeing me!"	"Stop looking at me!"

To see eye to eye   To share the same
                               opinion.

The repetitive use of any of these expressions can affect your eyesight. By examining what you were feeling when you said it, you may discover fear underlying your statement and, hopefully, relate it to the belief system that is affecting your vision.

When an eye disorder prevents you from seeing at close range, your body is telling you that you have difficulty seeing something that is going on in front of you, whether it's the aging of your own body, or circumstances or people in your present life. What you see scares you and causes a lack of clarity regarding what is actually going on. Reality becomes warped and indiscernible. Being unable to see details close up is comforting to you and allows you to live within the parameters of denial, resulting in a sense of undisturbed peace and detachment. See FAR-SIGHTEDNESS.

When an eye disorder prevents you from seeing well at a distance, your body is telling you that you have built unrealistic fears regarding your view of your own future or of the future of those close to you. You imagine situations and live in fear of watching them occur. You may not be inclined to look farther than your own nose due to laziness, complacency or because of life's deceptions. (See MYOPIA.)

The *left eye* represents your internal view, or your self-image. It is influenced by what you have learned from your mother, as the left side of the body reflects the feminine aspect.

The *right eye* represents your external, or world view. Your perception of life is influenced by what you have learned from your father, as the right side of the body reflects the masculine aspect.

MENTAL BLOCK

Understand that nothing will change in your life even if you refuse to see the truth. Rather than believing that you will lose something meaningful by seeing the truth, it is wiser and more beneficial in the long run to face up to it and address it as it happens.

If you harbor a belief that seeing things too clearly will result in your having to meet great expectations and leave no room for error, you are not seeing straight. This is an inappropriate and unhealthy perception. **There are no experiences without mistakes and there is no evolution without experiences.**

It is said that the eyes are mirrors of the soul. Every eye disorder, therefore, is an important message that clearly indicates you are not moving in the right direction, or in the direction of your soul's purpose. Accept the idea that it is neither normal nor hereditary to have poor eyesight. Only a stubborn belief has the power to influence your vision in such a way. Given the subtlety of the message from the eyes, it is often difficult to determine the basis of your belief. I recommend you refer to the list of KEY QUES-

201

TIONS at the back of the book to help you in determining what lies at the root of your problem.

SPIRITUAL BLOCK AND CONCLUSION

To uncover the spiritual block that keeps you from responding to the needs of your BEING, refer to the "KEY QUESTIONS" at the back of this book. In answering these questions, you will come in touch more easily and accurately with the true cause of your physical problem.

EYELID PROBLEMS

PHYSICAL BLOCK

Eyelids are defined as either of the two folds of skin and muscle that open and close over the eye. They serve to protect the eye from external dangers such as dust, particles, cold and light. Disorders of the eyelid include *irritation* and *eczema*. If you are suffering from ECZEMA, refer to it as well.

EMOTIONAL BLOCK

Disorders of the eyelid indicate that you are not protecting yourself effectively from external forces, allowing yourself to be easily and overly influenced by what you see. It may be, also, that you are so preoccupied with seeing everything that you do not allow yourself some necessary shut-eye, or time to rest and withdraw.

MENTAL BLOCK

If you are experiencing irritation of one or both eyelids, understand that it is your perception of what is going on around you that is irritating you, not what is actually going on. If you can't seem to tolerate what's happening, take time to withdraw and rest. Once you are rested, you will be re-energized and empowered to do what you need to do, without demanding or having expectations of others. You will see with fresh eyes, from a more tolerant perspective.

If you are suffering from ECZEMA, refer to it in this book.

SPIRITUAL BLOCK AND CONCLUSION

To uncover the spiritual block that keeps you from responding to the needs of your BEING, refer to the "KEY QUESTIONS" at the back of this book. In answering these questions, you will come in touch more easily and accurately with the true cause of your physical problem.

EYES (DRY)

See TEARS (Lack of)

203

FACIAL DISORDERS

PHYSICAL BLOCK

The *face* is the first part of the body that identifies a person. Facial disorders are numerous, from simple facial ACNE to total disfigurement through *disease* or *accident*.

EMOTIONAL BLOCK

If you find yourself susceptible to facial problems, it is likely you feel easily ashamed or humiliated at the least little thing. You tend to feel guilty frequently and push yourself in order to impress others and maintain the image they expect of you. You are afraid of losing face and, because of this, you always try to put on a good face, regardless of how you are feeling on the inside.

MENTAL BLOCK

Facial disorders exist to remind you that you worry too much about what others think of you, which prevents you from being yourself. Your body is telling you that the belief system you hold regarding your self-image is no longer appropriate or conducive to good health. Don't mask your true self any longer.

SPIRITUAL BLOCK AND CONCLUSION

To uncover the spiritual block that keeps you from responding to the needs of your BEING, refer to the "KEY QUESTIONS" at the back of this book. In answering

these questions, you will come in touch more easily and accurately with the true cause of your physical problem.

FACIAL PALSY

See BELL'S PALSY.

FAINTING

PHYSICAL BLOCK

Fainting is defined as a sudden and brief loss of consciousness. It is often characterized by dimming of vision, seeing spots of light, pale complexion and cold sweats prior to complete loss of consciousness.

EMOTIONAL BLOCK

Fainting is a form of escape in the face of a situation that's been going on for a while and that has caused you to feel discouraged, anguished and powerless.

MENTAL BLOCK

Your body is telling you that you want to be involved in this particular situation, but you need to learn to view it from a different perspective. Rather than surrendering to your fears and trying to escape, face them and discuss them openly. Your mind is telling you that you can't face them, but is that true? You have been presented with the situation as a growth and learning experience. Don't run from it or you will have to face it over and over again until you have dealt with it. Become conscious of what it is trying to teach you, rather than unconscious. Get in touch with your inner power.

SPIRITUAL BLOCK AND CONCLUSION

To uncover the spiritual block that keeps you from responding to the needs of your BEING, refer to the "KEY QUESTIONS" at the back of this book. In answering these questions, you will come in touch more easily and accurately with the true cause of your physical problem.

F

FALLOPIAN TUBE DISORDERS

PHYSICAL BLOCK

The *fallopian tubes* (or *oviduct*) normally transport the egg of the female from the ovary to the uterus. Normal tubes have small hair-like projections on the lining cells called cilia. These cilia are important to movement of the egg through the fallopian tube and into the uterus. If the tubal cilia are damaged by infection, the egg may not get 'pushed along' normally and can settle in the tube. Any process that narrows the tube and thus decreases the caliber of the passageway can increase the chance of a tubal pregnancy. Examples of these would be ENDOMETRIOSIS, TUMORS or SALPINGITIS.

EMOTIONAL BLOCK

Since the fallopian tubes are the channels through which the ova travels to meet the sperm in the process of procreation, disorders in this area indicate a psychological blockage between the feminine and masculine aspects. You, therefore, experience difficulty creating your own life as you would like it to be, and may also be experiencing difficulties in your relationships with men.

MENTAL BLOCK

Your body is telling you that it's time to open yourself up to new ideas and to get on with the business of creating your life without guilt. In doing so, you will also open up to the possibilities that men can bring into your life. These fears become obstacles and are causing you to close yourself off. See also UTERINE DISORDERS.

SPIRITUAL BLOCK AND CONCLUSION

To uncover the spiritual block that keeps you from responding to the needs of your BEING, refer to the "KEY QUESTIONS" at the back of this book. In answering these questions, you will come in touch more easily and accurately with the true cause of your physical problem

FARSIGHTEDNESS

PHYSICAL BLOCK

Farsightedness occurs when the visual image falls behind the retina, preventing proper focusing on nearby objects.

Refer to HYPEROPIA for farsightedness when young.

EMOTIONAL BLOCK

The medical profession believes that farsightedness is a natural occurrence aligned with aging and that it occurs normally around the age of 45. Statistically, more people over the age of 45 suffer from farsightedness than not. Medically, the eye is said to be "accommodating" when it adjusts its visual functions. Interestingly, *accommodation* also refers to adjusting easily to people and circumstances.

Metaphysically, farsightedness indicates difficulty adjusting to what is going on around you. You may find it difficult to look at yourself in the mirror and see your body as it ages, as it seems less desirable. You may also be having a hard time taking a good look at your current family or work situation.

MENTAL BLOCK

If your vision is blurred when images are near, it is a specific message from your body that you are letting yourself get upset about what you see close to you. It is telling you

209

that it's imperative that you change your belief system about aging - the one that says getting older renders you incapable or invalid. It may be that your body is becoming physically worn, which is completely natural, but emotionally and intellectually you are gathering your forces with age, acquiring the priceless gifts of wisdom and maturity.

Your body is telling you that you've been wasting far too much time and energy on the physical dimension, or in the material world. It clouds your inner vision and you lose sight of your true worth, the wealth of experiences you have gathered over the years. Remember that the way you look at life today will determine your future. Your ability to adjust easily to people and circumstances will clarify your vision and improve your quality of life immeasurably.

SPIRITUAL BLOCK AND CONCLUSION

To uncover the spiritual block that keeps you from responding to the needs of your BEING, refer to the "KEY QUESTIONS" at the back of this book. In answering these questions, you will come in touch more easily and accurately with the true cause of your physical problem.

FATIGUE

PHYSICAL BLOCK

Fatigue is a state of exhaustion, lack of energy or muscle strength. It is discussed here as fatigue that results without apparent physical cause.

EMOTIONAL BLOCK

If you feel listless, make a list! Nothing is more energizing than desire and a sense of purpose! The emotional body must be fed with goals, for there is no point *being* without a reason for *doing* or a desire for *having*. Emotional health is kept in balance with short-term, medium-term and long-term goals. You need a reason to get up in the morning - something that will light a fire under you. If you are feeling constantly fatigued, it is because you have misplaced your energy and imprisoned yourself with fear and worry, rather than putting your energy into achieving something concrete.

MENTAL BLOCK

Evaluate your self worth. Are you worthy? Are you taking life too seriously? Are you expending more mental energy than physical energy? Look around you and begin to appreciate what you have in your present life. Take the time to enjoy simple pleasures and make a list of what would make you happy in the short term and in the long term. Next, make a concrete plan and take the necessary steps to achieve your goals.

211

It doesn't matter how long it takes you to reach your goals; what is important is that you feel you achieve something every day in the direction of your goals. Your emotional body must be fed; your desires must be rekindled constantly, in order for you to feel alive and energetic. Note that extreme fatigue may be experienced after the resolution of conflict. Determine whether or not this is your situation. If so, realize that it will be short-lived and that once you have reestablished your goals, you will feel recharged.

It may also be the beginning of BURNOUT - refer to it.

SPIRITUAL BLOCK AND CONCLUSION

To uncover the spiritual block that keeps you from responding to the needs of your BEING, refer to the "KEY QUESTIONS" at the back of this book. In answering these questions, you will come in touch more easily and accurately with the true cause of your physical problem.

FELON

See WHITLOW.

FEVER

PHYSICAL BLOCK

Fever is an elevation of the body temperature. Higher than 38 degrees Celsius or 100.4 degrees Fahrenheit is considered pathological. Prior to the onset of fever, the body feels chilled. When the cause of the fever is eliminated, the body feels warm.

EMOTIONAL BLOCK

On an emotional level, fever is the result of repressed anger. The chills during a fever indicate that anger is still being repressed - once the chills are over, anger is released and the current conflict is in the process of resolution. For example: a school-aged girl, feeling rejected by her mother following some incident, awakens the following day with a high fever. She shivers and feels chilled, so her mother keeps her home from school and takes care of her. As the conflict is being resolved with the attention she receives from her mother, she begins to feel hot. At this point the body begins the process of recuperation.

Fever also refers to a burning passion about some situation you may feel is not playing out the way you would like it to.

MENTAL BLOCK

It's not enough to temporarily resolve the cause of a conflict. If you are subject to frequent fevers, get to the root of your anger. Realize that your reaction is based on your frame of reference, or belief system. This belief system has been built, brick by brick, from your experiences up to this point in time.

If you are feeling anger toward another person, talk openly with that person and determine whether or not

213

your anger is justified. Understand that it is your perception of the other person's attitude that causes you to be angry. Then ask forgiveness of this person (see the steps to true forgiveness at the back of this book). If you fail to do so, you will perpetually be over-reactive whenever confronted with a similar situation.

If you are burning up about something (a burning passion) and you become worked-up to the point that you overdo it, ask yourself what fear is making you feel that way. The more intense the fever, the more significant the message you are being given. The body is urging you in no uncertain terms to address this problem once and for all.

SPIRITUAL BLOCK AND CONCLUSION

To uncover the spiritual block that keeps you from responding to the needs of your BEING, refer to the "KEY QUESTIONS" at the back of this book. In answering these questions, you will come in touch more easily and accurately with the true cause of your physical problem.

FIBROID (UTERINE)

See UTERINE FIBROID.

FIBROMYALGIA

PHYSICAL BLOCK

Fibromyalgia is a disorder characterized by muscle pain, stiffness and easy fatigue. .

F

EMOTIONAL BLOCK

Fibromyalgia seems to occur more commonly in those who have felt chronic guilt from a very early age. They felt broken and guilty for being alive, for existing. For example, a sensitive little girl may imagine that her parents would be better off without her. As a result, she feels vulnerable and easily "broken." She usually becomes very rigid in life.

MENTAL BLOCK

Stop believing that others don't care about you and they would be better off without you. There is no need to make yourself sick to gain the attention that you seek. Look, instead, outside yourself and you will realize that you are welcome and that you are getting more attention than you believe. It is your mindset that is distancing you from others and distorting your perception of the situation. Let go of this perception and become more flexible. This will allow you to become aware of the love that others have for you, even if they don't seem to be expressing it in the way you had expected. See MUSCULAR DISORDERS.

SPIRITUAL BLOCK AND CONCLUSION

To uncover the spiritual block that keeps you from responding to the needs of your BEING, refer to the "KEY QUESTIONS" at the back of this book. In answering these questions, you will come in touch more easily and accurately with the true cause of your physical problem.

FINGER DISORDERS

PHYSICAL BLOCK

The *fingers* are designed to provide ultimate mobility and render movement with remarkable precision. The following conditions are considered problematic: *stiffness,* PAIN, or FRACTURE

EMOTIONAL BLOCK

Since fingers help us to be precise, when we have a problem with one or more fingers, the message the body is sending is that the reason for our search for precision is not a good reason. Why do you want to be so precise? By fear of being rejected, laughed at, etc.? This doesn't mean we should quit dealing with details, but perhaps we need to try a different approach to the situation.

Each finger has its own metaphysical significance as follows:

The THUMB is often referred to as the master finger, as it governs much of the function of the hand. It represents the voluntary and responsible part of us. It is the finger that helps us to push. Stiffness or injury in the thumb is an indication that you may be pushy, controlling and overly preoccupied with certain details. You are pushing yourself or someone else too much in order to accomplish something.

The INDEX finger represents authority, the strength of your character and your power to decide. It points things out (as the mistakes of others), makes decisions and is also called the pointer. It is used to threaten, to probe, to give orders, to single out and also to make people understand certain things. Injury of the index finger is a message that you might feel pointed at by some authoritative figure.

The MIDDLE finger relates to inner life and sexuality. Strain, pain, stiffness or fracture of this finger is a message that you feel easily rejected in intimacy due to your idealistic idea of what perfection should be.

The RING finger rarely moves independently from the other fingers. It represents the ideal in a coupling relationship and its dependence on others to achieve this ideal. Discomfort in the ring finger represents chagrin in your intimate relationship. It is a message that you need to take a look at the larger picture (instead of focusing on the details).

The LITTLE finger, or pinky, reflects mental agility and ease of communication. The ease with which it separates and moves independently from the other fingers indicates independence, innate curiosity and intuition. This is where the expression *"my little finger told me"* comes from. Injury to the little finger represents an undue con-

217

cern about what others might think and maybe guilt about not "raising your little finger" to help. It may also mean inhibiting your intuition and need for independence.

MENTAL BLOCK

Generally speaking, problems with the fingers are a message to let go of all non-essential details. Your perfectionism is getting the better of you. It's OK to search for perfection but you must concentrate on the things that will help your *be* in harmony with yourself and stop trying to *do* and *have* perfection. I suggest you also let go of all the details that concern other people.

See FRACTURE if necessary.

SPIRITUAL BLOCK AND CONCLUSION

To uncover the spiritual block that keeps you from responding to the needs of your BEING, refer to the "KEY QUESTIONS" at the back of this book. In answering these questions, you will come in touch more easily and accurately with the true cause of your physical problem.

FISHSKIN DISEASE

Fishskin disease is a congenital skin disease characterized by dry, thickened, scaly skin. Also called *Ichthyosis.* See DRY SKIN.

FISSURE

PHYSICAL BLOCK

A *fissure* is a narrow crack in the skin, usually in the anal area, but may occur elsewhere on the skin's surface. Read the following and also refer to the relevant location, i.e. ANUS.

EMOTIONAL BLOCK

A fissure can occur when you feel divided, split in two, or caught between two people or two situations. Perhaps you are uncertain about a particular decision. The fissure will burn uncomfortably to the degree you feel burned or frustrated about the situation.

MENTAL BLOCK

Instead of feeling divided over this situation, evaluate what you really want and then act accordingly. Learn to live according to your own principles, rather than doing what you believe others think you should do.

SPIRITUAL BLOCK AND CONCLUSION

To uncover the spiritual block that keeps you from responding to the needs of your BEING, refer to the "KEY QUESTIONS" at the back of this book. In answering these questions, you will come in touch more easily and accurately with the true cause of your physical problem.

FISTULA

PHYSICAL BLOCK

A *fistula* is defined as an abnormal passage leading from an abscess, cavity or hollow organ to the body surface or to another hollow organ. Drainage fluids are usually transferred through the fistula.

EMOTIONAL BLOCK

A fistula can occur as a physical manifestation of a mixed-up personality. You allow yourself to be easily influenced and find it difficult to make allowances. The result is confusion, aggression and, often, depression. Refer to the relevant location in the body where the fistula has developed to determine the basis of the contributing attitude.

MENTAL BLOCK

In developing a fistula, your body is sending you the message to shut yourself off from the influence of certain people around you so that you can make use of your own good judgment. The people influencing you don't necessarily mean you harm; on the contrary, they are probably well intended, but at this particular time you need to make your own decisions based on trust in your own intuition. Only you can know what you need and what you are feeling. Try it and see!

SPIRITUAL BLOCK AND CONCLUSION

To uncover the spiritual block that keeps you from responding to the needs of your BEING, refer to the "KEY QUESTIONS" at the back of this book. In answering these questions, you will come in touch more easily and accurately with the true cause of your physical problem.

F

FLATULENCE

PHYSICAL BLOCK

Flatulence is defined as the buildup and expulsion of intestinal gas. Symptoms include an uncomfortable distention of the abdomen, colic, or cramping.

EMOTIONAL BLOCK

Gas is trapped in the upper abdomen through the gulping of air when you are eating or talking, indicating fear of not having enough and being anxious about it.

MENTAL BLOCK

Flatulence is a sign of worry and unjustified fear. Assess your life as it is right now and you will begin to see the cup half full rather than half empty. Worry is an indication that you are living in the future rather than the present. Be here now and you will become more aware of your blessings. Let go and be less possessive of what you have. See also BELCHING if necessary.

221

SPIRITUAL BLOCK AND CONCLUSION

To uncover the spiritual block that keeps you from responding to the needs of your BEING, refer to the "KEY QUESTIONS" at the back of this book. In answering these questions, you will come in touch more easily and accurately with the true cause of your physical problem.

FLU

PHYSICAL BLOCK

The *flu*, or *influenza*, exhibits similar symptoms as the common cold as both are caused by the same family of respiratory viruses. The flu, however, is usually more severe, develops quickly and affects more of the body. Symptoms vary in severity and may include respiratory inflammation, headaches, coughing fits, moderate to high fever, aching muscles and acute fatigue. Regardless of the severity, bed-rest is usually needed.

EMOTIONAL BLOCK

The flu is the result of critical mass emotionally and physically. It will manifest frequently if it is difficult for you to express your desires or do what it takes to realize them. You feel easily smothered and overwhelmed. The body is saying, *"I've had it!"* The flu provides an obvious reason to get away from a situation. For example, a secretary who can no longer stand working with her boss may come down with a good case of the flu and stay home for a week. Her soul's desire is to be at work, but with a differ-

222

ent attitude. The flu is always linked to your relationship with someone specific.

MENTAL BLOCK

The severity of your flu is determined by the strength of your belief that's preventing your from fulfilling who you are and what you need to do. Rather than believing the flu is the only ticket out of an uncomfortable situation, examine your mindset and change it! Often, it's your own perspective, not the attitude of others that is the problem. Are you overly dramatic? Do you picture yourself as the victim? Instead of trying so hard to flee the situation, find a way to accomplish what you need with joy and acceptance. Let go and know you have all the tools you need to get the job done.

SPIRITUAL BLOCK AND CONCLUSION

To uncover the spiritual block that keeps you from responding to the needs of your BEING, refer to the "KEY QUESTIONS" at the back of this book. In answering these questions, you will come in touch more easily and accurately with the true cause of your physical problem.

FOOT PROBLEMS

PHYSICAL BLOCK

The feet are the extremities of the legs that have direct contact with the ground. There are so many *foot problems* that podiatry has become a medical specialty. The feet are comprised of a complicated network of small bones designed to allow optimal flexibility of the foot, facilitate movement in all directions while, amazingly, supporting the full weight of the body. If your problem affects the bone, see BONE DISORDERS also.

EMOTIONAL BLOCK

Foot disorders indicate difficulty in finding the means to go forward in life. Either fear is stopping you, or you are feeling impeded by others. You are uncertain which direction to take.

It may be that you feel stuck in one place or can't get your footing, or feel as if you're walking in place or in circles. Perhaps you would like to run away and are not sufficiently anchored on a physical level. This is known as not being grounded and is usually due to fear or refusal to deal with the material world.

Foot pain can also occur if you fear *getting the boot* at work.

If the pain in your foot is more pronounced in a resting position, rather than during activity, it indicates refusal to stop and rest when needed. You tend to be on the run all the time, doing too much too quickly in the pursuit of your goals. You tend to identify strongly with your external pursuits and base your self-worth on performance.

MENTAL BLOCK

The contribution that your feet make to the physical body is often underestimated. Feet play a vital role in the support and transportation of the body as a whole. You are receiving a message from your body that you must let go and move forward joyfully. Your feet are in direct and constant contact with the earth, which is, symbolically, the nurturing mother. They are telling you to remain firmly anchored in the reality of the here and now and have more confidence in the support of the Universe and in your intuition. Take the necessary leap on the path to your dreams and don't allow yourself to be *walked all over* by those who stand in your way. Trust that you are supported by life.

SPIRITUAL BLOCK AND CONCLUSION

To uncover the spiritual block that keeps you from responding to the needs of your BEING, refer to the "KEY QUESTIONS" at the back of this book. In answering these questions, you will come in touch more easily and accurately with the true cause of your physical problem.

FRACTURES

A *fracture* is the breaking or cracking of a bone, usually caused by violent trauma, with the exception of older individuals whose bones have become fragile and porous from osteoporosis. Note the location of the fracture in the body to determine its metaphysical significance and refer to it in this book. See also BONE DISORDERS and AC-

CIDENT and add that a fracture signifies a lack of acceptance concerning the break-up or impending break-up of some form of relationship.

FRIEDREICH'S ATAXIA

PHYSICAL BLOCK

Friedreich's Ataxia is a genetic brain disorder characterized by early symptoms of instability while standing and progressing to a general clumsiness, trembling in the hands, then in the arms, measured speech in which individual syllables are pronounced separately and jerky eye movements.

EMOTIONAL BLOCK

Development of Friedreich's Ataxia is a strong message from the body that you have allowed yourself to be overly influenced by your family. You have become so emotionally dependent on them that you would rather do nothing at all than be yourself and risk their displeasure.

MENTAL BLOCK

Rather than feeling completely powerless in the shadow of your parents' expectations (generally the mother) or from the expectations of your family, thereby surrendering to a slow and quiet death, listen to what your body is telling you: *"Find yourself. Give your parents permission to have their expectations and accept that they have them. They have simply transferred the fulfillment of their own dreams onto you. Have compassion for your parents and feel unconditional love for them. Let go of any bitterness toward them."*

Determine what it is you deeply desire and take the necessary steps to achieve it. Accept that your parents may be disappointed in your choices and realize that their disappointment is their choice and not your responsibility. Each of us is responsible for achieving our own potential. It was up to your parents to achieve theirs - and up to you to achieve your own.

SPIRITUAL BLOCK AND CONCLUSION

To uncover the spiritual block that keeps you from responding to the needs of your BEING, refer to the "KEY QUESTIONS" at the back of this book. In answering these questions, you will come in touch more easily and accurately with the true cause of your physical problem.

FRIGIDITY

PHYSICAL BLOCK

Frigidity is the common medical term for the absence of female sexual pleasure. It is not to be confused with the term *anorgasmic*, which is defined as the absence of orgasm, but not of sexual pleasure.

EMOTIONAL BLOCK

Frigidity is common in women who decided at a very early age to cut themselves off from pleasure of any kind, not just sexual enjoyment. In general, they are women of unyielding character who have disassociated themselves from their own feelings. They have an unconscious fear of being a warm person. Ironically, they need normal sexual bonding more than most women because their self-control eventually leads to a loss of control in other areas of their lives.

MENTAL BLOCK

If you suffer from sexual frigidity, you probably have an underlying belief that pleasure is synonymous with sin. Your mindset must be very powerful to be able to control yourself so well. It is important that you understand that every human being has emotional limits and that when you reach your own personal emotional critical mass, you will lose control. If this loss of control is not exhibited sexually, it may surface as overindulgence in other areas, such as substance abuse, uncontrollable crying, anxiety, overeating, or trembling in the body. Denying yourself healthy sexual pleasure punishes you more than it punishes your sexual partner. Let yourself become the warm person you desire to be. You are like a time bomb waiting to explode. Diffuse the situation by getting in touch with your true feelings; by granting yourself permission to feel pleasure in every area of your life, you will be reborn.

SPIRITUAL BLOCK AND CONCLUSION

To uncover the spiritual block that keeps you from responding to the needs of your BEING, refer to the "KEY QUESTIONS" at the back of this book. In answering these questions, you will come in touch more easily and accurately with the true cause of your physical problem.

F

FURUNCLE

See BOIL.

GALLBLADDER DISORDERS

The *gallbladder* is a sac located under the liver. It stores and concentrates the bile produced in the liver. Bile is released from the gallbladder in response to food, especially fats, in the upper small intestine (duodenum). Conditions that slow or obstruct the flow of bile out of the gall bladder result in gallbladder disease. The most common disorder of the gallbladder is the formation of small stones, or of the obstruction of the biliary canal by larger stones. Either of these disorders betrays an underlying fear that something is being taken from you. See STONES and LIVER DISORDERS.

6

GANGRENE

Gangrene, from the Greek word *gaggraina* means *rotting* or *decay*. Any number of circulatory problems can cause reduced blood flow to the extremities, in extreme cases resulting in death of the tissue, or gangrene. After putrefaction of the flesh (necrosis), gangrene begins to form as a small, painful blackish patch on the skin. Within several days, the necrotic tissue begins to fall away in pieces. See ARTERIES. It should also be stated that the message received from the body on a metaphysical level is urgent; the situation indicates a severely diminished *joie de vivre* and underlying psychological self-destruction derived from low self-worth.

231

GAS

See FLATULENCE.

GASTRITIS

Gastritis, more commonly known as *heartburn*, is symptomatic of anger and frustration. See HEARTBURN.

GASTROENTRITIS

Gastroenteritis is the simultaneous inflammation of both the stomach lining and the small intestine. It is characterized by vomiting, diarrhea and abdominal pain. This is a strong and urgent message from the body indicating a number of repressed fears are brewing from more than one belief system. See VOMITING, DIARRHEA, STOMACH DISORDERS and SECTION 2.

GENETIC DISORDERS

The word *genetic* is defined as relating to heredity. For further explanation about *hereditary diseases* in general, see SECTION 2.

GERMAN MEASLES

See RUBELLA.

GINGIVITIS

Gingivitis is localized inflammation of the gums that may be the early stages of periodontal disease. See GUM PROBLEMS. It should also be stated that inflammation always represents repressed anger. See SECTION 2

GLANDS (SWOLLEN)

G

PHYSICAL BLOCK

Swollen glands are the enlargement of one or more lymph nodes. Lymph nodes are small, glandular nodules distributed throughout the body's lymphatic system. They serve as filters for the lymphatic fluid that flushes out waste material from the tissues on a cellular level. Blood is released into the cellular tissue from the capillaries, cleansed by the lymph fluid and returned to the bloodstream. The nodes play a primary role in defending the body from invading organisms.

EMOTIONAL BLOCK

When a lymph node is swollen or inflamed, it indicates an accumulation of regret and anger concerning a specific person or situation. You want everything to flow smoothly and the way you want it to, but cannot communicate your feelings to the person/s in question. Consequently, the relationship is blocked as effectively as your lymph nodes.

233

This attitude slows you down. You do not give yourself credit and feel awkward in your relationship with others. Swollen lymph nodes in the left armpit indicate a lack of self-worth as a parent; in the right armpit, a lack of self-worth in other relationships (i.e. spouse, co-worker, etc.); in the groin, a lack of self-worth in sexual relationships.

MENTAL BLOCK

It is important that you accept that you cannot control the people and the situations around you. Believing that you can will cause nothing but regret. Thinking that you can establish better relationships by being and doing everything is too much to expect of yourself. Your body is telling you to respect your own limitations and to see things from another perspective. There must be a good side to this; maybe it's a good time to let go and love yourself. Quitting or slowing yourself down is not the solution.

SPIRITUAL BLOCK AND CONCLUSION

To uncover the spiritual block that keeps you from responding to the needs of your BEING, refer to the "KEY QUESTIONS" at the back of this book. In answering these questions, you will come in touch more easily and accurately with the true cause of your physical problem.

GLAUCOMA

PHYSICAL BLOCK

Glaucoma is an eye disorder characterized by loss of peripheral vision, accompanied by an increase in fluid pressure within the eyeball. It can result in the gradual degeneration of the optic nerve, due to compression.

6

EMOTIONAL BLOCK

The presence of glaucoma indicates difficulty in accepting what you are seeing and especially what you saw in your past emotional life. The emotional trauma has bred many years of distrust. Over time, some of this pent-up emotion has built up in the eyeball as optic hypertension, or glaucoma. Once emotional pressure has reached critical mass, the pressure in the eye also reaches its limit. You are refusing to look at what has reopened old emotional wounds.

MENTAL BLOCK

Your body is telling you to let go of the past. Free yourself through simple and complete forgiveness (see the steps to true forgiveness and the end of this book). Look inside your heart and learn to love and accept the differences in those you love and who love you. You are a deeply sensitive person who has misplaced your sensitivity in allowing it to hurt you. Your perception is depriving you of wonderful, fulfilling relationships. Accept that others also suffer and have their own limitations. In doing so you will

235

accept your own suffering and limitations. Be more trusting of others. See EYE DISORDERS.

SPIRITUAL BLOCK AND CONCLUSION

To uncover the spiritual block that keeps you from responding to the needs of your BEING, refer to the "KEY QUESTIONS" at the back of this book. In answering these questions, you will come in touch more easily and accurately with the true cause of your physical problem.

GOITER

A *goiter* is an abnormal enlargement of the thyroid gland, visible as a swelling in the front of the neck. See THYROID GLAND. It should also be stated that the problem is usually related to a relationship.

GOUT

PHYSICAL BLOCK

Gout is a painful inflammation of the big toe and foot caused by defects in uric acid metabolism resulting in deposits of the acid and its salts in the blood and joints. It can also affect other joints.

EMOTIONAL BLOCK

Gout in the big toe signifies a repressed desire to dominate. Although you may not seem like the dominant type, you are oblique about it. Gout also indicates a lack of flex-ibility, even stubbornness in the way you view your future. You also have suppressed a strong dislike of someone or some situation.

MENTAL BLOCK

As gout is a form of arthritis, the metaphysical implica-tions are similar. Your body is telling you to let go - accept and acknowledge that you may want to be in control once in awhile. Don't deny it and stop trying to hide it. Al-though you have concerns about the future, keeping them inside may magnify your fear. Open up to those close to you. Refer to the metaphysical definition of OSTEOARTHRITIS.

SPIRITUAL BLOCK AND CONCLUSION

To uncover the spiritual block that keeps you from re-sponding to the needs of your BEING, refer to the "KEY QUESTIONS" at the back of this book. In answering these questions, you will come in touch more easily and accurately with the true cause of your physical problem.

GRAVE'S DISEASE (or Basedow's disease)

Grave's disease is a disorder of the thyroid gland in which too much of the hormone thyroxin is produced. An excess of thyroxin causes a wide range of symptoms, including jitters or nervousness, heat intolerance, weight loss de-spite a healthy appetite, rapid and irregular pulse, and a fine tremor of the hands. *Exothalmism* (a combination of the protrusion of the eyeballs and a retraction of the upper eyelids) may also occur. See GOITER and HYPERTHYROIDISM.

GROIN

The *groin*, which is the point where the abdomen meets the thigh, is a region of the body where nerves, muscles, blood vessels, and underlying/deep-seated lymph nodes and lymph glands intersect. Refer to the specific problem that applies to you in the groin area, keeping in mind that inflexibility or sexual repression/inhibition are contributing factors. See also HERNIA, ANEURYSM, and especially swollen GLANDS (Adenitis).

GUM PROBLEMS

PHYSICAL BLOCK

The *gums* are comprised of the firm connective tissue at the base of the teeth. The following reference pertains only to pain in the gums. For bleeding gums, see BLEEDING.

EMOTIONAL BLOCK

Pain in the gums indicates an underlying fear of setting into motion a decision that has already been made. A sense of powerlessness and distress results from a fear of consequences if the decision is acted upon.

MENTAL BLOCK

Determine whether the fear is justified. Understand that, although you may have failed in the past, it has no bearing on your success or failure now. There is no right or wrong way to do things, only experiences that ultimately bring personal growth. Everything you have ever gone through and will go through is a learning experience. Dare to ask for help in order to carry out what you want, one step at a time. Don't try to do it all at once. You have the power and confidence you need to go forward. Believe it!

SPIRITUAL BLOCK AND CONCLUSION

To uncover the spiritual block that keeps you from responding to the needs of your BEING, refer to the "KEY QUESTIONS" at the back of this book. In answering these questions, you will come in touch more easily and accurately with the true cause of your physical problem.

HAIR LOSS (sudden)

PHYSICAL BLOCK

Hair loss is a natural condition so long as dead hair is re-placed by new. For gradual and permanent hair loss, see BALDNESS. For a sudden hair loss with no apparent rea-son, read the following.

EMOTIONAL BLOCK

H

Loss of hair is associated with the loss of something or someone, or the *fear* of losing that brings on a sense of powerlessness, weakness, or lack of material or psycho-logical control of one's life. Identifying with anything outside of your true self will result in misalignment of spirit and imbalance of the psyche.

You tend to dwell on the past and worry about the future, about material things, about the opinions of others. You fear that what you decide might cause someone else to lose something.

MENTAL BLOCK

You are a human *being*, not a human *having*. Don't con-tinue to identify yourself with what is outside of you. Doing so only perpetuates fear of loss, as ultimately you have no control of anything but your own consciousness. It is not degrading to lose someone or something. Become aware of who you are in the truest sense of the word. What is in your life or the way others see you must not deter-

241

mine who you are. Accept the idea that whatever your decisions might be, their consequences will be learning experiences for you. Stop trying to hang on to people or things that will naturally flow in and out of your life. Cultivate detachment in all areas of your life. Refer also to HAIR PROBLEMS and ALOPECIA (if it applies to your condition).

SPIRITUAL BLOCK AND CONCLUSION

To uncover the spiritual block that keeps you from responding to the needs of your BEING, refer to the "KEY QUESTIONS" at the back of this book. In answering these questions, you will come in touch more easily and accurately with the true cause of your physical problem.

HAIR PROBLEMS

PHYSICAL BLOCK

BALDNESS, ALOPECIA, DANDRUFF, *oily hair, gray hair,* and sudden HAIR LOSS are considered unhealthy hair conditions.

EMOTIONAL BLOCK

Psychological trauma to which there is overreaction can generate a sense of powerlessness, hopelessness or over-excitement that may manifest as an overdose of worry related to material matters. This occurs when there is an over-identification with the event itself and with the physical world. Symbolically speaking, the hair is the an-

242

tenna that links the head (our I AM) with the cosmic energy (the DIVINE). Problems with the scalp and hair indicate a weak link or lack of confidence in divine energy, the life source from which we gain the insight to shape our own lives. This lack of confidence strips us of our vital energy. Note that hair also provides a layer of protection for the head and a sense of security that we are protected from above and linked directly with our internal God.

MENTAL BLOCK

Through hair loss, graying or scalp problems, you are being reminded to get in touch with your true self and stop identifying with what is outside of you. Although the material world is important, it's not all there is in life and is therefore no measurement of your status as a human being. Activate your antenna and you will feel a resurgence of energy that will help solve what worries you. You will experience a sense of peace, balance and clarity.

SPIRITUAL BLOCK AND CONCLUSION

To uncover the spiritual block that keeps you from responding to the needs of your BEING, refer to the "KEY QUESTIONS" at the back of this book. In answering these questions, you will come in touch more easily and accurately with the true cause of your physical problem.

HALITOSIS

See BAD BREATH.

HALLUCINATIONS

See INSANITY.

HAND PROBLEMS

PHYSICAL BLOCK

The human *hand* is one of the most sensitive and mobile parts of the human body. Mechanically, it is as complex as any piece of new technology, yet it has the capacity to experience the most profound sense of touch. Problems related to the hand include PAIN, FRACTURE, ARTHRITIS, RHEUMATISM, and ECZEMA.

EMOTIONAL BLOCK

The hand performs a multitude of functions. To determine the metaphysical cause of the pain, examine what it prevents you from doing and what area of your life seems to be most affected. The hands, as well as the arms, are an extension of the heart region, therefore pain in the hands indicates that what is being done is not being done out of love, especially self-love. The hands must be used to express love for yourself as well as love for others.

The *left hand* is linked to receiving and the *right hand* to giving. Pain in the hands indicates that you are out of touch with your needs and heart's desires. You are holding back from doing what you really want to do with your hands.

244

MENTAL BLOCK

If pain is experienced in the *left hand*, examine what you feel about receiving. Are you afraid to receive a helping hand? Do you receive with love and gratitude or do you feel that you are obligated to return the favor in order to avoid looking ungrateful or selfish? Do you believe it is impossible for someone to give you something without wanting something from you in return? Your belief system is creating an obstacle to enjoyment. Learn to receive graciously and openly, with the understanding that you are a special person whom others like to give to and you deserve it.

H

If pain is experience in the *right hand*, examine what you feel in regard to giving. Do you give with strings attached or out of obligation? Are you apprehensive about giving a helping hand to others? Do you hold back because you feel others will take advantage of your generosity and because you find it difficult to say *no*? Do you feel that you need to do everything yourself? Learn to give simply for the pleasure of giving. If it is not well received, understand that the other person may simply not have the same tastes and desires you have and accept that for what it is.

Pain in the hands may be linked to your attitude about your work. The hands should always be used with love and pleasure; appreciate them openly and thank them for all they do for you. Allow yourself to take situations in hand without fear of being taken advantage of. You have all the necessary tools to face that situation if it arises.

If the pain in your hands is preventing you from doing something you like (playing the piano, painting a picture, holding someone you love, etc.) see which fear is behind that. Is it still justified considering who you have become? Get in touch with simple pleasures, perhaps childhood pleasures that you sense a longing for. Allow yourself to indulge them without fear of being judged.

SPIRITUAL BLOCK AND CONCLUSION

To uncover the spiritual block that keeps you from responding to the needs of your BEING, refer to the "KEY QUESTIONS" at the back of this book. In answering these questions, you will come in touch more easily and accurately with the true cause of your physical problem.

HAY FEVER

PHYSICAL BLOCK

Hay fever, or *allergic rhinitis*, is an allergic condition affecting the mucous membranes of the upper respiratory tract and the eyes, most often characterized by nasal discharge, sneezing, and itchy, watery eyes. It is usually caused by an abnormal sensitivity to airborne pollen.

EMOTIONAL BLOCK

Hay fever tends to recur annually, notably in spring, indicating the reawakening of an old wound that occurred during that season when the hay fever first began. Basically, you refused to address a difficult experience that occurred

246

at that time. The release of pollen every spring triggers the memory of the event and reopens the emotional wound.

MENTAL BLOCK

Your body is telling you that it's time to go through the process of forgiveness. The fact that you have the same physical symptoms in your body, year after year, indicates that you continue to sustain bitterness toward the person you hold responsible for your suffering.

Understand that you choose your reaction at any given time and that the other person is not responsible for your pain. Only true forgiveness will transform what you are experiencing. Follow the steps to true forgiveness at the back of the book.

SPIRITUAL BLOCK AND CONCLUSION

To uncover the spiritual block that keeps you from re-sponding to the needs of your BEING, refer to the "KEY QUESTIONS" at the back of this book. In answering these questions, you will come in touch more easily and accurately with the true cause of your physical problem.

HEADACHE

PHYSICAL BLOCK

The following explanation applies to a *normal headache*. For bigger problems linked to the head, such as migraines, refer to the description of the condition or illness in this book.

EMOTIONAL BLOCK

The head, as is explained under MIGRAINE, has a direct link with the I AM. If you have a headache (especially on the top of the head), it means that you hit yourself *over the head* with belittling I AM's. You accuse yourself of not being this or that and especially of not being intelligent enough; you ask a lot of yourself.

You belittle instead of appreciate yourself. If you feel as though your head is going to burst, the message is to stop accumulating so much within yourself through fear of other people's judgment of what you are or are not.

You may fear being ahead, in other words being in front, being first or leading the way.

Having a headache, especially in the area of the forehead, indicates that you try too hard to understand everything. You should give your intellect time to accumulate enough data in its memory for your intelligence to be able to make a synthesis and better understand.

MENTAL BLOCK

Because the head is the seat of four of the five senses, it is a very important part of the body. When it hurts, you are prevented from seeing, hearing, feeling and saying clearly what meets your needs; this distances you from what you want to *be*. You're being sent the message to get in contact with your real I AM, in other words with who you are at the moment. There's no point in forcing yourself to be what you believe others want you to be. No one in this world can be exactly what all those around them would like.

Your body is showing you that you should let go of your mental activity, stop wanting to understand everything mentally and just be yourself.

SPIRITUAL BLOCK AND CONCLUSION

H

To uncover the spiritual block that keeps you from responding to the needs of your BEING, refer to the "KEY QUESTIONS" at the back of this book. In answering these questions, you will come in touch more easily and accurately with the true cause of your physical problem

HEART ATTACK

See MYOCARDIAL INFARCTION.

HEARTBURN

Also known as *esophageal reflux, heartburn* occurs when acid-containing stomach contents are allowed to regurgitate back into the esophagus. Under normal conditions, the sphincter muscle of the esophagus prevents this, but if the muscle becomes lazy (relaxes) heartburn will occur. Heartburn is an indication that you have a burning desire for something or someone that you will not allow yourself. You are finding a situation "difficult to stomach" but, rather than dealing with it, internalize your anger. See STOMACH DISORDERS.

HEART DISORDERS

PHYSICAL BLOCK

The *heart* acts as a two-way pump for the circulatory system. Its life-giving rhythm regulates the flow of the life force throughout the body. *Coronary heart disease* is the most common cause of death in North America.

EMOTIONAL BLOCK

It's interesting to note that the heart is placed virtually at the center of the body. If you are centered, you are living from the heart in a balanced state of love and trust that is in synch with the natural flow of the Universe. Your perspective is one of balance and you tend to listen to the mutterings of your own heart when faced with decisions. A heart disorder is the manifestation of the opposite mindset. If you are having heart trouble, you probably tend to take everything to heart, or to take things far too seriously. You are not allowing for the proper flow in your life, whether it's the flow of ideas, of love or of your very lifeblood. You are fighting the current of life to the point of physical and emotional exhaustion. You tend to deny your own needs and fulfill other people's needs in order to be loved. You seek love through what you do for others. The main message associated with any heart condition is LOVE YOURSELF!

MENTAL BLOCK

Heart disease is an urgent message from your body to change your perception of yourself. There is a need for self-validation. Fill the wellspring of love within you by changing your belief that love can come only from others. Give yourself the love you seek and it will always be there; you won't have to search for it.

Get in touch with your self-worth step by step. Begin by giving yourself ten compliments a day until you begin to believe them. You are unique and very special, yet your low self-esteem does not allow you to keep some of your goodness to yourself. Become whole emotionally and spiritually and your heart will heal as you begin to nurture it.

A healthy heart no longer fears being unloved. It is able to cope with disappointment, as nothing can disturb its equilibrium. You will continue to nurture others because you want to, not because you need to prove to yourself and others that you are lovable.

SPIRITUAL BLOCK AND CONCLUSION

To uncover the spiritual block that keeps you from responding to the needs of your BEING, refer to the "KEY QUESTIONS" at the back of this book. In answering these questions, you will come in touch more easily and accurately with the true cause of your physical problem.

HEAVES

See NAUSEA.

HEEL PAIN

PHYSICAL BLOCK

The *heel* is the rounded back part of the foot that supports the body while walking. Most heel pain occurs for no apparent physical reason.

EMOTIONAL BLOCK

Pain in the heel indicates that you want to move in the direction of your goals, but hesitate because you don't feel sufficiently supported by others. You probably prefer to have the consent of others prior to making a move. You dare not admit to yourself that you need someone *on your heels* and feel guilty acting without the approval of others. Conversely, you suffer from the consequences of being stuck in one spot.

MENTAL BLOCK

Your heel is trying to tell you that you can move forward and *lean on yourself* when making major decisions. You are the best support you could possibly have. There's no longer any need for you to hold on to the belief that, in order to prove your love or to be loved, others must agree with you. It's impossible for everyone to agree. If we all had the same opinion on everything, life would be very uneventful. Remember that no one in the world is obliged to support you. The same thing goes for you; you do not always have to support those you love. Accept that you may be helped and supported by others while still moving forward on your own.

SPIRITUAL BLOCK AND CONCLUSION

To uncover the spiritual block that keeps you from responding to the needs of your BEING, refer to the "KEY QUESTIONS" at the back of this book. In answering these questions, you will come in touch more easily and accurately with the true cause of your physical problem

---

HEEL SPUR SYNDROME

PHYSICAL BLOCK

A *bone spur* is a condition where the sole becomes inflamed at the region of a bony spur or growth off the heel. Common symptoms include foot pain that is exacerbated by activity.

EMOTIONAL BLOCK

A bone spur that develops under the heel usually prevents you from standing for long periods of time. Symbolically, this indicates that you are uncomfortable standing up for yourself and in moving forward with your plans. You probably fear displeasing someone who represents authority and have a defeatist attitude about your own future.

MENTAL BLOCK

You need an attitude adjustment, because the one you have is hurting your inner-self as much as it's hurting your heel. Take some risks, take the leap - a little self-confidence will do a lot to spur you on to achieving what you want. Whatever happens, you'll be able to handle it. You have what it takes to face the consequences of your decisions.

Don't expect others to be in constant agreement with your plans and ideals. They all have their own agendas and limitations. Take that first step, and then the next. Each step will bring a new experience. Dare to take risks while moving forward.

SPIRITUAL BLOCK AND CONCLUSION

To uncover the spiritual block that keeps you from responding to the needs of your BEING, refer to the "KEY QUESTIONS" at the back of this book. In answering these questions, you will come in touch more easily and accurately with the true cause of your physical problem.

HEMATOMA

See BRUISES.

HEMOPHILIA

Hemophilia is an "inherited" blood disorder marked by severe, protracted, sometimes spontaneous bleeding. It is caused by a lack of coagulants, or platelets, in the blood and poses severe danger in the event of injury or hemorrhaging. Hemophilia affects only males, although the female passes on the gene. I suggest you refer to SECTION 2 where HEREDITARY DISEASES are treated. Also see HEMORRHAGE. It should be stated also that the hemophiliac generally has issues surrounding his mother, whom he allowed too much importance and influence in his life. I'm not saying that her influence was detrimental, only that he needs to learn to be happy with who he is and not live entirely according to her expectations. It would also be advantageous to get in touch with his feminine aspect and to let it express itself joyfully.

H

HEMORRHAGE

PHYSICAL BLOCK

A *hemorrhage* is an excessive discharge of blood from the blood vessels, internally or externally. The latter is more serious.

EMOTIONAL BLOCK

Metaphysically, blood represents the love of life. When there is a loss of blood, it indicates an attitude that's preventing *joie de vivre* in your life. Since a hemorrhage occurs suddenly, it is an indication that you've been holding back for some time; that you have hidden your anguish or listlessness.

Having reached critical mass emotionally, you can no longer hold back and suddenly, it seems, you've given in. In order to determine in which area you have lost your joy of life, examine the location of the hemorrhage on the body. This applies only to *external* hemorrhage.

If the hemorrhage is internal, it is an indication that you suffer in silence and don't want anyone to know what you are going through. You feel you have no one to confide in and that there is no one who can help you.

MENTAL BLOCK

A hemorrhage is an important message from your body that it's time to alter your perception of your life in the area in question. You are taking life too seriously and need to become more involved with activities that make you happy, rather than expending energy on things that drain the life out of you. Try to get more joy out of what you are doing at any given time through a simple change in attitude.

If hemorrhaging is caused by an ACCIDENT, I suggest you refer to it in this book.

SPIRITUAL BLOCK AND CONCLUSION

To uncover the spiritual block that keeps you from responding to the needs of your BEING, refer to the "KEY

QUESTIONS" at the back of this book. In answering these questions, you will come in touch more easily and accurately with the true cause of your physical problem.

HEMORRHOIDS

PHYSICAL BLOCK

Hemorrhoids are simply the uncomfortable swelling of a blood vessel in the rectum or anus. Constipation and the resulting strain during bowel movements are the primary cause.

EMOTIONAL BLOCK

Hemorrhoids reveal a build-up of emotional pressure caused by stress and fear that you would rather not discuss and show. The result is burdensome. Hemorrhoids may occur if you pressure or force yourself to *have* more; perhaps you are enduring a job that you do not like. Since hemorrhoids are located in the rectum (the terminal portion of the large intestine), you are constantly pushing yourself to finish things. Do you ask too much of yourself? Have you created undue tension trying to have something or someone because of material insecurity and difficulty in making decisions?

MENTAL BLOCK

The more pronounced your inner sense of insecurity, the more you may suffer from hemorrhoids. In order to mitigate this insecurity, you push yourself to *do* in order to

257

have. When you feel that things are not moving along as quickly as you want, do you *burn* with impatience? It is essential that you develop a consistent faith in the Universe, an unfailing trust that everything is as it should be and that all of God's children will be provided for. Learn to let go and to express your feelings openly and honestly while acknowledging your fear of material deprivation.

See CONSTIPATION or HEMORRHAGE, if applicable.

SPIRITUAL BLOCK AND CONCLUSION

To uncover the spiritual block that keeps you from responding to the needs of your BEING, refer to the "KEY QUESTIONS" at the back of this book. In answering these questions, you will come in touch more easily and accurately with the true cause of your physical problem.

HEPATITIS

Hepatitis is characterized by inflammation of the liver, with jaundice, appetite loss, discomfort and dark urine. See LIVER DISORDERS. *Infectious hepatitis* is contracted by virus or through a chemical agent. I suggest you refer to SECTION 2 where EPIDEMICS are treated.

HEREDITARY DISEASES

Refer to SECTION 2 where HEREDITARY DISEASES are treated.

Your Body is Telling You: Love Yourself!

HERNIA

PHYSICAL BLOCK

A *hernia* is defined as the rupture or protrusion of an organ, such as the stomach or large intestine, through its surrounding muscular wall.

EMOTIONAL BLOCK

A hernia indicates a feeling of being cornered. There is a desire to get out of a given situation through separation or a break-up, but there is also an underlying fear of missing out on a material level in doing so.

MENTAL BLOCK

Rather than imprisoning yourself in an undesirable situation, evaluate what it is you really want and need. Understand that it is only your belief system that imprisons you and leads you to believe you can't get out of this by yourself. Your body is telling you that you are self-contained and have what it takes to get what you want. Take one step at a time and you will achieve your desires.

SPIRITUAL BLOCK AND CONCLUSION

To uncover the spiritual block that keeps you from responding to the needs of your BEING, refer to the "KEY QUESTIONS" at the back of this book. In answering these questions, you will come in touch more easily and accurately with the true cause of your physical problem.

259

HERPES SIMPLEX TYPE 1

See COLD SORES.

HERPES SIMPLEX TYPE 2
GENITAL HERPES

PHYSICAL BLOCK

Genital herpes is a very common sexually transmitted disease. Genital ulcerations begin to occur four to seven days after contact with an infected partner. Blisters are painful and may burst. In women, blisters tend to accumulate on the external genitalia, cervix and around the anus. In men, lesions may occur on the head of the penis, the foreskin, the anus and rectum. It can take up to two weeks for the pustules to heal.

EMOTIONAL BLOCK

Genital herpes is the manifestation of sexual guilt. The infected person wants to punish him/herself (unconsciously) for a sexual act. They have judged this act according to their belief, and are full of self-depreciation and self-criticism. A deep-rooted moral code, based on your sexual education, governs your sexual behavior. In the name of that moral code, you are denying your sexual desires. There is a tendency to blame others rather than take responsibility for your own actions and hidden desires.

260

MENTAL BLOCK

The degree of physical pain from genital herpes coincides directly with the degree of condemnation you place on yourself regarding your sexual behavior. Get in touch with your true sexual desires and reappraise your sexual education. Your restraint is an obstacle to your fulfillment.

Understand that the small voice inside you telling you sex is bad is the voice of someone else's belief system. Decide once and for all if you really want to continue believing it. Sexual energy is the ultimate creative energy - REMEMBER: it is pro-creative energy. Harness it, don't deny it; and most of all don't feel guilty about it!

SPIRITUAL BLOCK AND CONCLUSION

To uncover the spiritual block that keeps you from responding to the needs of your BEING, refer to the "KEY QUESTIONS" at the back of this book. In answering these questions, you will come in touch more easily and accurately with the true cause of your physical problem.

HTT (Hereditary Hemorrhagic Telangiectasis)

See OSLER'S DISEASE.

HICCUPS

PHYSICAL BLOCK

A *hiccup* is defined as an involuntary spasm of the diaphragm that occurs on inhalation and closes the glottis, producing a sharp staccato sound every 15-30 seconds. The following definition is for a recurring problem and not for the occasional hiccup.

EMOTIONAL BLOCK

Hiccups usually occur when you are having difficulty stopping doing something, such as laughing or eating, or when you are feeling restless or agitated. It is an indication that you are emotionally expressive and generally find it difficult to remain calm.

MENTAL BLOCK

Determine what is difficult to stop. Your body is telling you that enough is enough for the moment, and that you should get back to whatever it was at a later time. Believe that you are capable of controlled and calm behavior and you will be able to relax.

SPIRITUAL BLOCK AND CONCLUSION

To uncover the spiritual block that keeps you from responding to the needs of your BEING, refer to the "KEY QUESTIONS" at the back of this book. In answering

these questions, you will come in touch more easily and accurately with the true cause of your physical problem.

HIGH BLOOD PRESSURE

PHYSICAL BLOCK

High blood pressure, or *hypertension*, takes two forms: *essential hypertension*, when the cause is unknown, and *secondary hypertension*, when damage to the kidneys or endocrine dysfunction cause blood pressure to rise. The symptoms of hypertension appear throughout the body and may include dizziness, headache, fatigue, restlessness, difficulty breathing, insomnia, intestinal complaints and emotional instability. In advanced stages, the hypertensive often experiences cardiovascular disease as well as damage to the heart, kidneys, eyes and brain in the form of vascular lesions.

EMOTIONAL BLOCK

The term *high blood pressure* indicates pressure that has built up from over-emotional behavior. It is caused when we continually re-live emotional situations from the past that stimulate unhealed and unresolved emotional wounds. There is a tendency to be melodramatic and to expend enormous mental energy, resulting in the resurgence of misaligned emotions. The hypertensive is usually deeply sensitive to the needs of others and creates a great deal of internal pressure in their search for ways to make others happy.

263

MENTAL BLOCK

High blood pressure is a message from the body to take care of yourself - before you burst. You are responsible for your own potential and were not put on this planet to make others happy, no matter how much you love them. There is a fine line between loving someone and being responsible for their happiness. Just as cutting back on salt is a proactive step toward your physical health, taking life with a grain of salt is a proactive step toward your psychological health. Liberate yourself from responsibility for the happiness of others and reclaim the joy and fulfillment in your own life. Live in the moment!

SPIRITUAL BLOCK AND CONCLUSION

To uncover the spiritual block that keeps you from responding to the needs of your BEING, refer to the "KEY QUESTIONS" at the back of this book. In answering these questions, you will come in touch more easily and accurately with the true cause of your physical problem.

HIP PROBLEMS

PHYSICAL BLOCK

The primary function of the hip is to support the lower limbs and to assure movement between the legs and the pelvis. If hip problems are caused by OSTEOARTHRITIS or by a FRACTURE, refer to the pertinent definition after reading the following.

EMOTIONAL BLOCK

As the hip joint initializes the walking process, pain in this joint signifies difficulty or resistance to going forward or taking steps toward your heart's desire. The underlying attitude *is "This isn't going to work!"* or *"Nothing will ever be right again if I do things this way!"* You hesitate to get involved with someone or something that pertains to your future, because you are afraid it will all be for naught.

You may be saying to yourself: *"This work is doing nothing for me anymore"* or *"I'm not getting anywhere in life."* If the pain is more pronounced in a standing position, you likely want to "stand your ground," but are actually immobilized by fear. If, on the other hand, the pain occurs while sitting or lying down, it is a message from your body that you will not allow yourself to relax and regenerate when you need to.

MENTAL BLOCK

Whether the pain is mild or intense will be determined by the degree of your defeatist attitude. Examine the situation you are facing and make a decision. Then take steps confidently in that direction. As you move forward, you will know whether it was a good decision for you. If you change your mind don't worry, you'll know what to do. You need to open yourself to new experiences in order to distinguish what you want from what is actually good for you. The belief *"It won't work!"* is not going to help you do that.

265

Rather than feel you aren't getting anywhere, try instead to be more aware of your own progress. If you still feel you're not making any headway, ask those close to you whether or not they see any advancement. Be more flexible in your thinking and approach change with confidence, rather than fear. Remember that there are no mistakes in life - only experiences!

SPIRITUAL BLOCK AND CONCLUSION

To uncover the spiritual block that keeps you from responding to the needs of your BEING, refer to the "KEY QUESTIONS" at the back of this book. In answering these questions, you will come in touch more easily and accurately with the true cause of your physical problem.

HISTIOCYTOSIS

Histiocytosis refers to a group of disorders *(pulmonary histiocytosis X, histiocytosis X, eosinophilic granuloma, nonlipid reticuloendotheliosis, Langerhans histiocytoses, Letterer-Siwe Disease, Hand-Schuller-Christian Disease, pulmonary Langerhans' granulomatosis)* in which there is an abnormal amount of scavenger cells, called histiocytes, in the blood. There are histiocytosis diseases that affect adults and those that affect children. In adults, the lungs are affected. There is inflammation of the small airways and small blood vessels (see LUNGS). In children the bones are affected (see BONE DISORDERS). In many cases the skull is involved (see HEADACHE). However, any other single site or multiple sites can be affected.

HIVES

Hives is a skin condition characterized by intensely itching welts and caused by an infection, a nervous condition, or an allergic reaction to internal or external agents. Also called *nettle rash* or *urticaria*, hives is triggered by strong emotions and fear when suddenly faced with a situation that is beyond your emotional limitations. See ITCHING and SKIN DISORDERS.

HOARSENESS

See LARYNGITIS.

HODGKIN'S DISEASE

Hodgkin's disease is a painless, progressive and malignant enlargement of lymph tissue. See CANCER and LYMPHATIC SYSTEM DISORDERS.

HOLLOW-BACK

See LORDOSIS

HOT FLASHES

A *hot flash* is characterized by a sensation of warmth that builds up around the face. Excessive perspiration and a feeling of suffocation can accompany it. The onset of a

267

hot flash can be rapid and usually disappears just as quickly. It may be caused by digestive problems and accompanied by a feeling of heaviness in the gastrointestinal region. Or it may be a common symptom of menopause. See INDIGESTION or MENOPAUSE as the case may be. Sudden reddening and overheating of the face can also indicate a release of energy that often follows the resolution of emotional conflict.

HUNCHBACK

PHYSICAL BLOCK

Hunchback is an abnormal rearward curvature of the spine, resulting in protuberance of the upper back. It usually affects adolescent boys.

EMOTIONAL BLOCK

If you suffer from this, you may feel like you have the world on your shoulders and that everybody's on your back. Your parents have expectations of you (for your future) that are weighing heavily on you.

MENTAL BLOCK

It's very important for you to decide what you want out of life. You must realize that your parents, in their own way, are excited about your potential and want the best for you. Instead of wanting them off your back, remember that all that goes on around you reflects what goes on inside you. When you become clear that you can achieve your goals yourself, your parents will be happy to let you handle your own future projects.

SPIRITUAL BLOCK AND CONCLUSION

To uncover the spiritual block that keeps you from responding to the needs of your BEING, refer to the "KEY QUESTIONS" at the back of this book. In answering these questions, you will come in touch more easily and accurately with the true cause of your physical problem.

H

HYDROCEPHALUS

PHYSICAL BLOCK

Hydrocephalus is usually a congenital condition in which an abnormal accumulation of fluid in the cerebral ventricles causes enlargement of the skull and compression of the brain, destroying much of the neural tissue. It is a condition that is commonly known as *water on the brain.*

EMOTIONAL BLOCK

Metaphysically, water symbolizes the emotional body. Hydrocephalus can occur when there is an over-accumulation of emotions. There is an over-identification with the emotional self to the point of believing you *are* your emotions. The result is a highly emotional individual who bases their decisions and everyday actions on emotional criteria. Having misplaced their identity, they have difficulty knowing who they really are and fear being laughed at.

269

MENTAL BLOCK

If you are experiencing hydrocephalus, your body is sending you an urgent message that you need to learn the difference between sensitivity and emotion so that you don't get caught up in and overwhelmed by your feelings. It is critical that you also learn how to express what you are feeling, rather than let it build up inside you. Refer to the steps to true forgiveness at the back of this book.

If you are reading this in reference to a child who is suffering with hydrocephalus, understand that the child's soul has carried this concept with them from a previous life and they are already over-identifying with their emotional self. Read this passage to them, knowing that the information will be assimilated on a soul level. Only the soul who has chosen this child's body is responsible (and thus able) to rectify the situation. You can only provide nurturing and guidance.

SPIRITUAL BLOCK AND CONCLUSION

To uncover the spiritual block that keeps you from responding to the needs of your BEING, refer to the "KEY QUESTIONS" at the back of this book. In answering these questions, you will come in touch more easily and accurately with the true cause of your physical problem.

HYPERCHOLESTEROLEMIA

See CHOLESTEROL.

HYPERGLYCEMIA

See DIABETES.

HYPERMETROPIA

See HYPEROPIA.

HYPEROPIA

H

PHYSICAL BLOCK

Hyperopia or *farsightedness* occurs when the visual image falls behind the retina, preventing proper focusing on nearby objects. Causes stem from the eye being shorter than normal, the cornea too flat, and lack of muscle tone in the ciliary muscle that controls the lens, or from a combination of these.

EMOTIONAL BLOCK

Farsightedness is an indication that you are afraid to examine your life too closely. You need a lot of time to think before you act and have difficulty seeing all the details in any given situation because you don't feel confident enough in your ability to manage them.

MENTAL BLOCK

Your body is telling you to overcome your fear of getting closer to people and situations. You can handle it, what-

271

ever the outcome. Fear is keeping you from enjoying many of life's most rewarding and enriching experiences. Don't watch your life go by - live it to the fullest.

Refer to FARSIGHTEDNESS also.

SPIRITUAL BLOCK AND CONCLUSION

To uncover the spiritual block that keeps you from responding to the needs of your BEING, refer to the "KEY QUESTIONS" at the back of this book. In answering these questions, you will come in touch more easily and accurately with the true cause of your physical problem.

HYPERTENSION

See HIGH BLOOD PRESSURE.

HYPERTHYROIDISM

Hyperthyroidism is an over-secretion of hormones by the thyroid gland. See THYROID GLAND DISORDERS.

HYPERVENTILATION

PHYSICAL BLOCK

Hyperventilation is an abnormally fast or deep respiration, which results in the loss of carbon dioxide from the blood, thereby causing a fall in blood pressure, tingling of the extremities, and sometimes fainting.

EMOTIONAL BLOCK

Hyperventilation can result from fear of losing control. Rather than going with the flow and fully experiencing what you are doing or feeling, you keep it all inside. You fear the unknown and lack confidence.

MENTAL BLOCK

If you find that you hyperventilate frequently, try to avoid situations that are overwhelming for you until you are emotionally able to expand your boundaries. For now, accept your fears and limitations in all their humanness and move gradually toward the unknown. Don't write off new experiences completely or you'll inhibit your personal growth and miss out on what you truly desire. Just as oxygen must be taken in at a comfortable rate, so must life be experienced at a comfortable rate.

SPIRITUAL BLOCK AND CONCLUSION

To uncover the spiritual block that keeps you from responding to the needs of your BEING, refer to the "KEY QUESTIONS" at the back of this book. In answering these questions, you will come in touch more easily and accurately with the true cause of your physical problem.

HYPOGLYCEMIA

PHYSICAL BLOCK

Hypoglycemia is often referred to as *low blood sugar*, but also applies to abnormal fluctuations of blood sugar (glucose) levels, secondary to an over-secretion of insulin by the pancreas. Symptoms of hypoglycemia may vary from mild to severe, from occasionally to after every meal. They include: anxiety, weakness, cold sweat, rapid heart rate, dizziness, cramps and hunger.

EMOTIONAL BLOCK

Metaphysically, the pancreas is closely linked with emotion, desire and intellect. If you are hypoglycemic, you probably have a very sweet disposition to place the needs and desires of others above your own. Consequently, you may feel trapped. You need to indulge yourself more without feeling guilty about it. You are much too busy serving others. I have observed over the years that hypoglycemics are often agoraphobic as well. See AGORAPHOBIA.

MENTAL BLOCK

Your body is clearly telling you that it's time to partake in what you've been dishing out for others. Save some of that wonderful energy for yourself! You don't have to parent everyone. Play a little, enjoy yourself and befriend the small, sweet child inside you. You probably experienced a childhood in which you were told that self-love is selfish;

because you've never loved yourself, you always sought love outside yourself. Even though you may have been well loved, it probably wasn't enough for you. In your mind, therefore, you came to the conclusion that love equals suffering. Circumstances in your life may have forced you to grow up too quickly. It's time to let go, live a little, love a lot and have some fun! It's never too late to enjoy your life!

Taking care of yourself is not selfish. A selfish person is one who uses others for their own gain - someone who thinks *"what's in it for me?"* People who love themselves consider their own needs before responding to the needs of others, but from a balanced, win/win perspective. Learn to love yourself honestly and you will radiate and attract love. Remember that you reap what you sow.

SPIRITUAL BLOCK AND CONCLUSION

To uncover the spiritual block that keeps you from responding to the needs of your BEING, refer to the "KEY QUESTIONS" at the back of this book. In answering these questions, you will come in touch more easily and accurately with the true cause of your physical problem.

HYPOTENSION

See LOW BLOOD PRESSURE.

HYPOTHYROIDISM

Hypothyroidsim is a glandular disorder resulting from in-sufficient production of thyroid hormones. See THY-ROID GLAND DISORDERS.

ICHTHYOSIS

Ichthyosis is a congenital skin disease characterized by dry, thickened, scaly skin. Also called *fishskin disease.* See DRY SKIN.

ICTERUS

See JAUNDICE.

ILEITIS or ILEOCOLITIS

See CROHN'S DISEASE.

IMPETIGO

PHYSICAL BLOCK

Impetigo is a bacterial skin infection, usually of children, that is characterized by the eruption of superficial pustules and the formation of thick yellow crusts, commonly on the face. See also SKIN DISORDERS.

EMOTIONAL BLOCK

Impetigo reflects a personality that dislikes being touched on an emotional level. There is an underlying fear of being influenced by others and a desire to create a false barrier of rigid insensitivity.

277

MENTAL BLOCK

Impetigo is a message from your body that says you no longer need to protect yourself against others and that it is perfectly natural to need other people. It's far healthier to be touched emotionally by others than to create a barrier in order to shut yourself away. Understand that sensitivity is not a sign of weakness and stop believing that you are incapable of defending yourself when necessary.

SPIRITUAL BLOCK AND CONCLUSION

To uncover the spiritual block that keeps you from responding to the needs of your BEING, refer to the "KEY QUESTIONS" at the back of this book. In answering these questions, you will come in touch more easily and accurately with the true cause of your physical problem.

IMPOTENCE

PHYSICAL BLOCK

Impotence is defined as the inability to sustain a satisfactory erection to perform intercourse and ejaculation. Although impotence is common, the cause is rarely pathological. See PENILE DISORDERS.

EMOTIONAL BLOCK

Every man will experience impotence at some time or another in his life. An erection is a very fragile phenomenon. When impotence occurs, it should never be dramatized or ridiculed. On the contrary, simply ascertain what situation rendered you psychologically impotent or powerless prior to the sexual impotence.

Chronic impotence experienced with the same sexual partner is usually an indication that you have changed your perception of the partner or of the relationship. Either you feel you don't want to defile her, or perhaps the relationship has become platonic and you see her more as a maternal figure or as a friend. Perhaps you are subconsciously refusing to satisfy her and want to deprive her of pleasure.

MENTAL BLOCK

If you are experiencing sexual impotence, it is an indication that you are feeling powerless in some other area of your life. Obviously, this is an unhealthy attitude that carries over into your physical life. Determine whether there is a specific situation in another area of your life causing this feeling of powerlessness and if so, put it in perspective. Let others solve their own problems and don't let these issues preoccupy you.

If you are experiencing impotence because of a previous negative sexual experience, distance yourself from that and understand that it is your belief system that is the obstacle to your satisfaction. Remember: you are what you think you are.

If you are subconsciously using your sexual impotence to deprive your partner, keep in mind that you are also depriving yourself and blocking a healthy creative energy.

279

The destructive attitude you are exhibiting will only feed your ego, not your relationship.

If you are experiencing sexual impotence because you see your partner more as a mother figure, you are having a mother/father relationship. This happens when each partner is trying to have power over the other. This type of relationship is very unhealthy. Your sexual impotence is telling you to get back in touch with your internal strength and stop believing that you are powerful only when you have power over the opposite sex.

SPIRITUAL BLOCK AND CONCLUSION

To uncover the spiritual block that keeps you from responding to the needs of your BEING, refer to the "KEY QUESTIONS" at the back of this book. In answering these questions, you will come in touch more easily and accurately with the true cause of your physical problem.

INCONTINENCE

If you are reading this concerning a child, refer to BEDWETTING, as *incontinence* is fairly rare in children.

Incontinence is the inability to control urination. If the problem is an occasional leakage of urine see BLADDER DISORDERS. If you suffer from a complete inability to hold your urine, you may be reliving similar situations from childhood. You feel like a child instead of an equal when you are with a certain person. It's never a good thing to have a parent-child relationship between two adults.

Take charge of your life and feel like an equal! Also see BEDWETTING.

INDIGESTION

Indigestion is defined as difficulty or discomfort in digesting food. Causes include dietary and nutritional factors, food allergies, viral and bacterial infections or parasites. Refer to the pertinent listing of the area of the digestive system most obviously affected for corresponding metaphysical implications. See STOMACH DISORDERS. If the indigestion is caused by POISONING, refer to that section.

If indigestion is caused from over consumption of food or alcohol, you may be "fed up" with someone or some situation that is weighing on you. Be cognizant of the fact that your perception is what has created your reality; your indigestion stems from your own attitude, not from outside of you.

INFARCTION

An *infarction* (or *infarct*) is a localized necrosis resulting from obstruction of the blood supply. See pertinent listing of the area affected for corresponding metaphysical implications. See HEART DISORDERS and ARTERIES.

INFECTION

PHYSICAL BLOCK

An *infection* is defined as an invasion of the body or of a specific bodily part by disease-causing microorganisms. Whether caused by bacteria, viruses or fungus, infection can occur anywhere in the body. Symptoms include: redness, inflammation, pain, swelling and formation of pus-filled pockets, or abscess, is at the site of the infection.

EMOTIONAL BLOCK

Infection at a specific site in the body is a sign of fragility in that area on a psychological level. You have allowed yourself to be invaded by the thoughts, words and deeds of others. This has affected and infected you. You are allowing it to eat away at you. You are out of touch with your psychological immunity and your physical immune system responds accordingly.

An infection can also occur if you have a defeatist attitude or are overly pessimistic. If you find yourself saying, *"What's the point?"* you are giving up and losing the fight.

It is sometimes said that an infected person is repulsive; if you believe this, you must feel repulsive to others in some way, or perhaps to yourself.

MENTAL BLOCK

Don't allow yourself to be psychologically assaulted by others. Remember: *you choose your reaction.* Your fear of aggression attracts the aggression of others. The Universe has a way of presenting you with what you fear most. Understand that your perception has created your reality. The truth is, others probably don't see themselves as aggressive toward you at all. You are more powerful than you realize - get in touch with that power and take control of your life.

The meek do not inherit the earth; there is no nobility in trying to appear weak and fragile in order to receive the nurturing you need. Others will love you to the degree you love and respect yourself.

For your own well being, I suggest you reappraise how you define being "repulsive" or vile.

SPIRITUAL BLOCK AND CONCLUSION

To uncover the spiritual block that keeps you from responding to the needs of your BEING, refer to the "KEY QUESTIONS" at the back of this book. In answering these questions, you will come in touch more easily and accurately with the true cause of your physical problem.

INFLAMMATION

Inflammation is characterized by redness, swelling, pain and heat in localized areas of the body (internal or external). See SECTION 2, which explains that inflammation is the body's first step in regenerating and rebuilding following the resolution of conflict. Although inflammation is a natural process, anti-inflammatory drugs are not contraindicated, if your doctor recommends them. Rather than interpreting inflammation as illness, thank your body for coming to your defense and together you can heal quickly.

INFLUENZA

See FLU.

INJURY

See ACCIDENT.

INSANITY

PHYSICAL BLOCK

Insanity is defined as a serious mental disorder impairing a person's ability to function mentally. Listed by increasing degree of severity: ALIENATION, DELIRIUM, DEMENTIA, HALLUCINATIONS, MANIA, NEUROSIS, PARANOIA, PSYCHOSIS, and SCHIZOPHRENIA.

EMOTIONAL BLOCK

Mental illness is always closely linked with a severed connection with the I AM, or a loss of identity. You have become out of touch with your *self*. To compensate, you obsess about understanding situations and other people, instead of opening yourself up to *feel* them. In my observation, in the vast majority of cases those suffering from varying degrees of mental illness are carrying with them a deep-seated bitterness toward a parent of the opposite sex.

To unearth the cause of mental illness, it must be traced back to infancy and childhood. During your most impressionable years, someone kept you from being yourself and as a consequence, you reacted by creating your own private world, where you could take refuge. As an adult, you have remained cloistered in that world and have been unable to find your way back to the reality of everyday existence.

It is often the case that someone who is mentally ill is vulnerable to obsessions of all kinds. They tend to throw their lot in with other persons or things, thereby avoiding taking a closer look at their inner selves and escaping any confrontation with their true being. The day comes when they are no longer able to flee into obsession and escape instead into insanity, as others escape into alcohol, prescription medications, or illicit drugs.

MENTAL BLOCK

In my experience, the only process that works completely and permanently to deal with any degree of insanity is true forgiveness. The most frequent problem, however, is that the person has no intention of getting better. They have chosen insanity as an escape. Caring individuals that want to help them must exhibit a great deal of love and patience to help them forgive their parent and themselves.

Those suffering from mental illness generally believe in God and in the Devil as *beings* of judgment and condemnation. They are consumed by fear of retribution and often become obsessed with religion and live in fear of Satan, just as they lived their lives in fear of one of their parents. In order to heal and to regain some semblance of sanity, it must be understood that God and Satan are purely symbolic of the love and hate inside themselves - energies of creation and destruction, or states of being. No more, no less. (See the steps to true forgiveness at the back of this book.)

SPIRITUAL BLOCK AND CONCLUSION

To uncover the spiritual block that keeps you from responding to the needs of your BEING, refer to the "KEY QUESTIONS" at the back of this book. In answering these questions, you will come in touch more easily and accurately with the true cause of your physical problem.

INSECT BITE

A *bite*, whether from an insect or as referring to a needle or other sharp object, often results in localized burning or itching from the body's reaction either to the quick attack

or to subsequent injection of foreign substance. See
BURN and ITCHING.

INSOMNIA

Insomnia is defined as *chronic sleeplessness*, or sleep deficient in either quantity or quality. Psychological studies have proven that insomniacs are generally emotional and anxiety-ridden. If you suffer from frequent insomnia, your sleeplessness probably reflects restlessness in your waking life. You are trying to stay awake so that you will resolve the issues that are preoccupying you. Once you understand that sleep brings comfort and solutions, you will find you are determined to settle the unrest in your life. See ANXIETY.

INTESTINAL DISORDERS

PHYSICAL BLOCK

The *intestines* are part of the alimentary canal and consist of the small and large intestine. The small intestine plays an essential role in the absorption of nutrients by the body and the large intestine, or colon, breaks down the residue and reabsorbs enough water to provide the proper consistency for the stool to pass from the body. The colon also acts as a reservoir for food waste the body no longer requires. Refer to specific disorders for further information.

Disorders of the small intestine include: TUMORS, CANCER, DIVERTICULITIS, CROHN'S DISEASE and sometimes DIARRHEA.

Disorders of the colon include: CONSTIPATION, DIARRHEA, COLIC, COLITIS, INTESTINAL GAS, TUMOR, CANCER, CRAMPS, GASTROENTERITIS, and WORMS.

EMOTIONAL BLOCK

Disorders of the *small intestine* are linked with an inability to retain and absorb that which is beneficial and contributes to your homeostasis. You tend to get hung up on details and can't see the forest for the trees. If a particular issue irks you, you will reject the entire situation. You have a fear of missing something that may be essential.

Disorders of the *large intestine* are linked with your inability to let go of old ideas or belief systems that are no longer of use (constipation). In the case of diarrhea, you reject ideas too quickly. You are often perturbed and find it impossible to digest disagreeable concepts. You don't take the time to be objective or look for the upside of a person or situation that has reawakened your fear of loss before placing judgment.

MENTAL BLOCK

Your body is telling you to re-educate yourself about feeding or nourishing yourself. There is no spiritual nutrition in fear and self-deprecating thoughts. You don't have to fear a lack of money or anything else. Have faith in your

288

material abundance and the divine presence within you. The Universal Divinity housed within you watches over you as it watches over all living things. Let go of your old belief system - it no longer nourishes you - and let in the new. See also STOMACH DISORDERS.

SPIRITUAL BLOCK AND CONCLUSION

To uncover the spiritual block that keeps you from responding to the needs of your BEING, refer to the "KEY QUESTIONS" at the back of this book. In answering these questions, you will come in touch more easily and accurately with the true cause of your physical problem.

I

INTESTINAL WORMS

See PARASITES.

ITCHING

PHYSICAL BLOCK

Itching is a skin sensation prompting a desire to scratch. It can be more or less irritating.

EMOTIONAL BLOCK

A physical itch can appear when you want something but you won't let yourself have it. You believe someone is in your way or life circumstances make it impossible for you to fulfill your desire. This preoccupies and exasperates you.

MENTAL BLOCK

Pay attention to what part of your body is itchy and what that part is used for. The location of the itch will have a direct metaphysical correlation. As the skin is representative of the outer self, or personality, you may be afraid of what people might think of you if you take what you want. Or maybe you're afraid of hurting someone's feelings.

Make sure that what you're itching to do is not simply a whim and that it's something you desperately want. If it's just a whim, let go without wanting to control everything and put it off for a while. If you really want this, identify your fears and take action to face them.

SPIRITUAL BLOCK AND CONCLUSION

To uncover the spiritual block that keeps you from responding to the needs of your BEING, refer to the "KEY QUESTIONS" at the back of this book. In answering these questions, you will come in touch more easily and accurately with the true cause of your physical problem.

JAUNDICE

Jaundice (also called *icterus*) is characterized by yellowing of the skin and the whites of the eyes caused by an accumulation of bile pigment (bilirubin) in the blood. It can be a symptom of gallstones, liver infection or anemia. See ANEMIA, STONES or LIVER DISORDERS.

JAW DISORDERS

J

PHYSICAL BLOCK

Jaw refers to either of the two bony structures that hold the teeth and frame the mouth. The upper and lower jaws are hinged and joined directly to the skull. Jaw disorders can range from PAIN, FRACTURE, or LOCKJAW.

EMOTIONAL BLOCK

Proper jaw action is essential to the movement of the mouth in eating or speaking. It is important to know whether the problem prevents you from chewing or from speaking. If it impedes speech, it indicates repressed anger, which prevents you from expressing yourself. If this mindset persists, your jaw will lock, indicating a tendency towards self-control. Ironically, in demanding this self-control, you have lost control of your jaw. You have an urgent need to express yourself.

If it impedes chewing or biting into something, this indicates difficulty in taking a good bite out of life or in biting into a situation you desire.

MENTAL BLOCK

Your body is telling you to ascertain what fears are causing you to be so restrained and self-controlling. Are these fears justified? Face up to them; you have the strength to do so. If appropriate, refer to FRACTURE.

SPIRITUAL BLOCK AND CONCLUSION

To uncover the spiritual block that keeps you from responding to the needs of your BEING, refer to the "KEY QUESTIONS" at the back of this book. In answering these questions, you will come in touch more easily and accurately with the true cause of your physical problem.

JOINT DISORDERS

Joints are composed not only of moveable bone, but also of connective tissue that controls the movement. *Joint disorders* include pain or a difficulty in bending or flexing the joint. See RHEUMATOID ARTHRITIS because the metaphysical definition is the same but add that joint disorders are an indication that you are weary and have difficulty expressing your opinion or making decisions. You don't feel like doing anything anymore. If you remain inactive, you will block your joints and you will be able to move less and less.

JOINT STIFFNESS

Joint stiffness refers to the decrease in joint mobility that can result in *anchylosis*. This indicates a lack of flexibility on a psychological level, especially toward yourself. Refer to the pertinent listing of the area of the body most obviously affected by joint stiffness for corresponding metaphysical implications. Also see JOINT DISORDERS.

J

KERATITIS

Keratitis is an inflammation of the cornea causing watery painful eyes and blurred vision. Development of keratitis is an indication that you need to get in touch with your emotions, mainly anger and sadness. Express them and stop holding back your tears. See EYE DISORDERS and SECTION 2.

KERATOSIS

Keratosis is a skin condition marked by an overgrowth of layers of horny skin mainly found on the palm of the hands and at the sole of the foot. See SKIN DISORDERS and HAND or FOOT PROBLEMS.

K

KIDNEY DISORDERS AND STONES

PHYSICAL BLOCK

The *kidneys* are a pair of organs located in the right and left side of the abdomen; they are complex structures whose disorders are numerous and varied. As blood passes through the kidneys, it is "cleaned" - the body's waste products and excess fluid are removed. These waste products, along with the excess fluid, are then sent through the ureters to the bladder and passed out of the body as urine. Kidneys also balance the blood chemicals and produce hormones that control blood pressure and maintain healthy blood cells and bones.

EMOTIONAL BLOCK

Since the kidney helps to maintain the balance of volume and pressure of fluids in the body, kidney disorders are a clear message from the body that there is an imbalance on the emotional level. You tend to demonstrate poor judgment or are incapable of making decisions regarding your own needs. You are sensitive and often over-emotional, worrying a great deal about others.

A diseased kidney can also indicate a perceived lack of inner resources, even a sense of powerlessness in a relationship or a situation you have undertaken. When confronted with difficult situations, you perceive them as being unfair. You allow yourself to be easily influenced by others. Your desire to help others is remarkable; however, it tends to get in the way of your own judgment of what's good and not good for *you*.

You are often moved to idealize a person or situation and suffer disillusionment and frustration when your ideals are not lived up to or your expectations are not met. You tend to be quick to criticize others or situations, judging them as unfair. In the long run, your expectations and dissatisfaction will grow and you will always remain the victim.

MENTAL BLOCK

The more serious your kidney disorder, the more urgent the message. Your body wants you to get back in touch with your inner strength and to change your belief system; you can face difficult situations as well as anyone else.

Your belief that life is unfair is blinding you to your own inner strength. The energy you expend criticizing and comparing yourself to others is wasted.

Your tremendous sensitivity is being misplaced. Your intense brain activity causes you to experience the full gamut of emotions, undermining your clarity and clouding your good judgment, resulting in an emotional imbalance that impedes your ability to cope. Learn to see people and things as they really are, rather than imaging an unrealistic ideal. By maintaining a more balanced perspective, your sense of injustice and unfairness will diminish.

SPIRITUAL BLOCK AND CONCLUSION

K

To uncover the spiritual block that keeps you from responding to the needs of your BEING, refer to the "KEY QUESTIONS" at the back of this book. In answering these questions, you will come in touch more easily and accurately with the true cause of your physical problem.

KNEE PROBLEMS

PHYSICAL BLOCK

The *knee* is the articulation point of the leg, responsible for mobility and flexibility. It carries the full weight of the body when standing, walking, running and bending; it plays a primary role in standing from a sitting position, going up and down stairs or simply lifting. The following reference pertains to any problems inhibiting the natural movement of the knee and to pain in the knee joint.

EMOTIONAL BLOCK

Knee pain, stiffness or inflexibility reflects inflexibility in your perception of the future. It occurs more often in those with an arrogant or stubborn personality, who are unable to bend to new ideas or to the ideas of others. An inflexible attitude keeps you from finding easier ways to face your future and guarantees dis-ease in going forward physically and psychologically. Refer to OSTEOARTHRITIS or RHEUMATOID ARTHRITIS as appropriate.

MENTAL BLOCK

Your body is providing a painful reminder that you are not as flexible as you want to believe. Remember that your body will warn you of things you are not conscious of. You don't have to fear losing control by bending to the will of others or accepting new ideas. Allow yourself the flexibility to see things from another perspective. You have misinterpreted *bending* to mean *"on your knees in submission."* You may have some latent fear of being too *flexible* related to one of your parents. Address this and realize that you are distinctly different from either of them and, although the apple may not fall far from the tree, your life is your own. It doesn't hurt, however, to be a little flexible and accept some help once in awhile from those who care.

SPIRITUAL BLOCK AND CONCLUSION

To uncover the spiritual block that keeps you from responding to the needs of your BEING, refer to the "KEY QUESTIONS" at the back of this book. In answering

these questions, you will come in touch more easily and accurately with the true cause of your physical problem.

KNEE MISALIGNMENT

Misalignment of the knee can be exhibited either as an inward turning of the joint that causes the axis of the leg to turn outward, or as an outward turning of the joint that causes the axis of the leg to turn inward, resulting in bent legs. See LEG problems and it should also be stated that on a psychological level, misalignment of the knee indicates difficulty in standing up straight and in moving in a straightforward direction toward goals or future endeavors.

KYPHOSIS

See HUNCHBACK

K

LARYNGITIS

PHYSICAL BLOCK

Laryngitis is an inflammation of the larynx, which is the organ that facilitates speech. It may also include swelling of the vocal chords, hoarseness, loss of voice and, sometimes a harsh cough. For *dipthereal laryngitis*, see CROUP.

EMOTIONAL BLOCK

Since laryngitis usually results in partial or total loss of voice, it is a message from the body that you fear communicating vocally. You want to say something, but you're afraid you won't be heard or will displease someone. Instead, you choke back your words and they remain stuck in your throat (which can lead to a sore throat!). These words are struggling to get out.

Perhaps you are afraid you won't live up to someone's expectations if you allow these words to come out; or you may fear being judged as inept by others who are more well-versed on the subject at hand. It may be that you've already said something you regret, or have spoken out-of-turn and are determined to shut up in case something else inappropriate slips out.

Is there some important request you are afraid to make because you think it will be rejected? Are you avoiding speaking to someone specific for some reason?

303

MENTAL BLOCK

Whatever your fear, it is counter-productive when it causes you to stifle self-expression. If you persist in believing it is better that you don't express yourself, what you repress will build up and surface elsewhere in your body. The throat is the energy center relating to creativity and it must be kept open for creativity to flow through every area of your life.

Accept that not everyone will agree or even be pleased with everything you have to say. Acknowledge your right to freedom of speech and others will acknowledge it as well. Your opinion is valid and important and you have as much right to express it as any one else. When you have a request to make of someone, understand that the worst that can happen is that they will say no. If they respond with a no, don't take it personally - it is no reflection on who you *are*, but simply a refusal of your particular request. See SECTION 2.

SPIRITUAL BLOCK AND CONCLUSION

To uncover the spiritual block that keeps you from responding to the needs of your BEING, refer to the "KEY QUESTIONS" at the back of this book. In answering these questions, you will come in touch more easily and accurately with the true cause of your physical problem.

LAZY EYE

See STRABISMUS

LEG PAIN

PHYSICAL BLOCK

The *legs* are the lower extremities of the body designed to provide support and mobility for the rest of the body. The following metaphysical definition is for pain in the lower leg (from knee to ankle). If the problem concerns the THIGH area, refer to it.

EMOTIONAL BLOCK

Without legs, we cannot advance. Therefore, *leg pain* indicates fear of the future and lack of confidence in the ability to go forward. You are apprehensive about taking steps in a new direction or toward a specific goal. This may refer to a new job or a loved one.

On the other hand, if the leg is especially painful in a resting position, your body is telling you that you do not allow enough time to recharge yourself so that you are better prepared to embark on a journey toward a new destination.

Refer to ACCIDENT if appropriate.

MENTAL BLOCK

If you experience leg pain while mobile, your body is sending you the following message: you are spending far too much time thinking things over before taking steps toward your goal. This indecision is based on fear. Although

305

your fear has developed to keep you from making mistakes, it is preventing you from fully experiencing life. Develop more confidence in your innate ability and trust in a Universal Intelligence. It will give you the necessary impetus to move forward and take the steps you need toward a plan of action.

If pain is experienced only while resting, you want to take steps prematurely and do too much. Your body is telling you that you will not be judged as lazy or unproductive if you rest.

SPIRITUAL BLOCK AND CONCLUSION

To uncover the spiritual block that keeps you from responding to the needs of your BEING, refer to the "KEY QUESTIONS" at the back of this book. In answering these questions, you will come in touch more easily and accurately with the true cause of your physical problem.

LEPROSY

PHYSICAL BLOCK

Leprosy is a chronic, highly infectious bacterial disease marked by the progressive destruction of tissue. Early symptoms include small, brownish spots on the skin, accompanying numbness, growing into circular lesions, or rings of discoloration and further loss of feeling in the area. As the disease progresses and the bacteria further invade the body, nerve tissue dies, resulting in local paralysis and deformation, possibly atrophy and gnarling of the extremities, and there may be an accompanying loss of facial hair, including eyelashes.

EMOTIONAL BLOCK

Leprosy is often viewed as repulsive and is generally feared because of its contagion. Victims of leprosy often feel defiled, considering themselves not good enough, clean enough and pure enough to deserve other people's interest. They are inwardly clawing at themselves. They abandon their life's plans, as they feel powerless in the face of their circumstances.

MENTAL BLOCK

Although this disease has finally been controlled throughout Europe and America, it is still prevalent in third world countries. Victims of leprosy harbor a feeling of shame that is accompanied by a self-generated sense of powerlessness. If you have contracted leprosy, understand that your sense of shame and invalidation, your perception of rejection and loss of power are generated in your own mind. You have allowed your ego to rob you of your self-worth and to convince you that you are worthless in the eyes of others. Only you can change this way of thinking.

Your body is sending you an urgent message that you need to reconnect with your essence - with the extraordinary being you really are. Begin by making a list of your talents and abilities, acknowledge your achievements and your gifts and become in tune with your own usefulness and place in the world. Cultivate your inner life and your outer life will begin to reflect it. Take your rightful place in the Universe.

SPIRITUAL BLOCK AND CONCLUSION

To uncover the spiritual block that keeps you from responding to the needs of your BEING, refer to the "KEY QUESTIONS" at the back of this book. In answering these questions, you will come in touch more easily and accurately with the true cause of your physical problem.

LEUKEMIA

Leukemia is a malignancy of the blood-forming tissues, especially bone marrow, with uncontrolled excess of white blood cells, or leukocytes. Aside from the increase in white blood cells, symptoms include a decrease in red blood cells resulting in anemia, and a decrease in platelets resulting in hemorrhaging. Enlargement of the spleen or lymph nodes are other indications of the presence of leukemia. See BLOOD CELL DISORDERS, SPLEEN DISORDERS and CANCER.

LEUKODERMA

See VITILIGO.

LEUKOPENIA

Leukopenia is a deficiency of the white blood cells. See BLOOD CELL DISORDERS.

LEUKORRHEA

PHYSICAL BLOCK

Leukorrhea is the medical term used to describe a thick, whitish vaginal discharge. Under normal circumstances, beneficial bacteria that serve to maintain a specific balanced chemistry in the vagina occupy the vaginal environment. When this chemistry is altered through the introduction of invasive bacteria, the use of antibiotics, or through the invasion of parasites or fungus in the body (such as *candida*), the vaginal discharge can become thick and odorous, resembling curdled milk. It may be accompanied by mild to severe itching or burning of the vaginal area.

EMOTIONAL BLOCK

Excessive and odorous vaginal discharge indicates anger surrounding your sex life. You feel violated and accuse your partner of wanting sex too frequently. You also tend to be self-critical, feeling that you allow yourself to be easily seduced, or of being unable to say "no." Perhaps you feel you are not in control, sexually, or you feel sex is dirty and you would prefer to be pure or innocent.

MENTAL BLOCK

Your body is indicating a need to alter your perception about your sexual relations. You've devised a physical barrier, even though your body naturally desires your partner. Understand that it is your belief system that is the real barrier to your pleasure. Let go of those beliefs and let yourself go. I'm not suggesting that you always say *yes* to your partner, but give yourself permission to enjoy sex and let go of the fear that your partner might take advantage of you or might control you. It's not "dirty" to want to make love; it is an act of communication, so don't barricade yourself from it.

See also YEAST INFECTION and VAGINAL DISORDERS.

SPIRITUAL BLOCK AND CONCLUSION

To uncover the spiritual block that keeps you from responding to the needs of your BEING, refer to the "KEY QUESTIONS" at the back of this book. In answering these questions, you will come in touch more easily and accurately with the true cause of your physical problem.

LICE

Head lice are a common infestation among school-aged children. Symptoms include a persistently itchy scalp that reveals tiny, Grey-colored insects crawling among the hairs. These are the adult lice. The eggs, or nits, are white and adhere to the hair shafts. Various other types of lice tend to appear in pubic hair and on the body. See PARA-SITES.

LIGAMENT

A *ligament* is defined as a band of tough, fibrous tissue joining bones or cartilage. Ligaments play a pivotal role in optimal joint mobility, which is dependent on their elasticity and resistance. When their physical limitations are exceeded, they will tear (See SPRAIN). Refer to the pertinent listing of the area of the body affected for corresponding metaphysical implications.

LIP PROBLEMS

L

The *lips* perform a multitude of functions, from grasping food to protecting the teeth, but they are also extensions of your true self in that they allow you to speak, whistle, smile, and to kiss.

Metaphysically, the upper lip is linked with your innermost desires and the lower lip is linked with your surroundings, or the environment with which you interact and through which you evolve. Biting your lip indicates pent up rage as a consequence of what has just been said.

Disorders affecting the lips are: *cracks* (see FISSURE), *dryness* (see DRY SKIN), SWELLING, NUMBNESS, COLD SORE, CLEFT LIP, PARALYSIS and CANCER. Refer to the specific disorder.

311

LIPOMAS

Lipomas are benign sub-cutaneous tumors consisting of contained accumulations of fatty tissue. They are soft, round formations that vary from the size of a hazelnut to the size of a grapefruit. Only one lipoma may develop, or many, anywhere on the body. Refer to the pertinent listing of the area of the body most affected by lipomas for corresponding metaphysical implications. See CYSTS.

LIVER DISORDERS

PHYSICAL BLOCK

The *liver* is the largest and one of the most complex organs of the body. It performs a number of critical functions, including active intervention in the metabolism of glucides (sugars), proteins, and lipids (fats) and the management of bile secretions and their diversion to the intestines. It aids in blood coagulation and is one of the major filtering and detoxifying organs. Symptoms of dysfunction in any of these areas may indicate the following liver problems: ABSCESS, STONES, CIRRHOSIS, LIVER FAILURE, HEPATITIS, JAUNDICE and TUMOR.

EMOTIONAL BLOCK

In metaphysical terms, the liver is the portal of repressed anger. Repression results in depression, even when you may not be consciously aware of it. If you suffer from a liver disorder, you probably seldom seem offended or get outwardly angry. This is because you keep everything inside. You feel powerless in the face of an offense. You don't get along well with people who are easily shocked, or those who "fly off the handle" because you value self-control above all. Inwardly, you feel sad and bitter. Rather than expose yourself or express yourself, you store your emotions in your liver. Instead of letting it all out in a fit of anger, you experience liver failure.

MENTAL BLOCK

Since the liver plays a primary role in the coordination of a number of vital body functions, liver disease indicates neglect in the coordination of what is going on in your life. Rather than adjusting to various situations and to the ebb and flow that is natural in human relations, you are judgmental and demand others to change according to your own belief system. Each internalized bout of anger is a reflection of your own self-righteous indignation. You refuse to put yourself in someone else's shoes and are determined to be right. If others don't see things your way, you are easily hurt and believe you are very sensitive. Your liver is giving you a stern message that it's time you digest what's going on around you; don't jump so quickly to conclusions. It's also telling you that you have all the necessary tools to defend yourself.

SPIRITUAL BLOCK AND CONCLUSION

To uncover the spiritual block that keeps you from responding to the needs of your BEING, refer to the "KEY QUESTIONS" at the back of this book. In answering

313

these questions, you will come in touch more easily and accurately with the true cause of your physical problem.

LOCKJAW

See JAW DISORDERS.

LONG-SIGHTEDNESS

See FARSIGHTEDNESS.

LORDOSIS

PHYSICAL BLOCK

Lordosis is a spinal disorder that exhibits an abnormal inward curvature of the vertebral column creating a hollow in the lumbar region. It is the opposite of *scoliosis*.

EMOTIONAL BLOCK

The posture that results from lordosis gives the impression of pulling back the upper body when facing other people. This indicates psychological difficulty receiving from others. You tend to want to do everything yourself and have a hard time accepting support. Perhaps you felt pushed when you were younger.

MENTAL BLOCK

Let go of the misconception that you couldn't possibly allow yourself to accept anything from others because you would feel obligated to them or because you don't deserve it. Your body is telling you that you need to accept things graciously and simply say thank you in return. Feel the pleasure that others derive from giving or helping you. Your new attitude will allow you to be more flexible, to stand up for yourself and stand tall. See BACK PAIN also.

SPIRITUAL BLOCK AND CONCLUSION

To uncover the spiritual block that keeps you from responding to the needs of your BEING, refer to the "KEY QUESTIONS" at the back of this book. In answering these questions, you will come in touch more easily and accurately with the true cause of your physical problem.

L

LOW BLOOD PRESSURE

PHYSICAL BLOCK

Low blood pressure is also known as *hypotension. Chronic low blood pressure* (your blood pressure is below average but not hazardously so) is not uncommon. Aside from causing a tendency to faint, low blood pressure can cause *poor circulation* in the extremities, *exhaustion* and *vertigo.* Correct blood pressure may vary from person to person. If no symptoms are exhibited, the blood pressure may be adequate.

EMOTIONAL BLOCK

If you suffer from *low blood pressure*, you probably feel easily discouraged or defeated before you even get started. Your life force is depleted and your energy level is low from carrying the perceived weight of the world on your shoulders or even the weight of the events of every-day life. You tend to give up easily and lack the courage to take life by the horns.

MENTAL BLOCK

The fact that you suffer from low blood pressure indicates that you don't feel you have the power to create your own life. You spend your time listening to your mind telling you that you aren't capable and that you're doomed from the start. The only way to break the cycle is to focus on concrete goals. Start simply and with clarity. You will gather the energy gently at first, but it will build as you build momentum and reach each goal with confidence and courage. Get in touch with your dreams and plant them firmly in your mind and your heart. Simply, you need to have something to aspire to - a reason to live! Look inside yourself and uncover what it is you really want in your life.

SPIRITUAL BLOCK AND CONCLUSION

To uncover the spiritual block that keeps you from re-sponding to the needs of your BEING, refer to the "KEY QUESTIONS" at the back of this book. In answering these questions, you will come in touch more easily and accurately with the true cause of your physical problem.

LOW BLOOD SUGAR

See HYPOGLYCEMIA.

LUMBAGO

Lumbago is a backache affecting the lumbar region or lower back that can be caused by muscle strain, arthritis, vascular insufficiency, or a ruptured intervertebral disc.

See BACK PAIN and add to that metaphysical definition that lumbago reveals repressed anger brought on by guilt. You believe that you are no longer able to stand up to your material responsibilities. Your inflexibility is caused by an inability to let go and move on without the need to control everything around you. You need to back off - allow others to lend their support while accepting their way of doing things.

L

LUNG DISORDERS

PHYSICAL BLOCK

The *lungs* are the principle respiratory organs. It is in the lungs that the gaseous exchanges between air and blood take place. This exchange transforms the blood from the veins, which is full of waste products, to the clean blood of the arteries, for distribution throughout the body. Acting as a carburetor for the cells, the lungs provide the body with oxygen and eliminate carbon dioxide, which is

317

the waste generated from cell combustion. Lung disorders are numerous and include all respiratory problems.

EMOTIONAL BLOCK

As lungs are the managers of air, which is the primary life force, they are directly linked with the desire to live and the quality of life. The lungs carry the life force to every cell in the body. Lung disorders of any kind are an indication that you are feeling depressed. There is an underlying sadness, a feeling of being suffocated by someone or a situation that is keeping you from taking in the life force you need.

You may have a feeling of discomfort, as though you don't have enough room to maneuver in order to get out of a situation. There may be a fear of suffering or death or of seeing someone else suffer or die. When you harbor thoughts of being better off dead, you lose your desire, or your will to live, an essential ingredient to a healthy emotional body. Fear of dying usually reflects a fear of letting something die away, thus keeping out anything new. Change is always a death of sorts; it can be overwhelming to the point that the fear of change steals any enthusiasm necessary for moving on to something else.

MENTAL BLOCK

Because the lungs play such a primary role in the physical body, disorders of the lungs are a vital and urgent message. The more serious the problem, the more critical the message. Your body is telling you to take a deep breath of life - to fill your lungs and fulfill your life.

Begin to experience with reverence and gratitude the wonder and passion that is your life. Realize that only you have the power to smother the fire within you or to allow your surroundings to smother you. Fire needs oxygen, and only you can ignite your private fire. Rather than being melodramatic about what goes on around you, detach enough to see the good side of your life - all the potential and all the possibilities for happiness. You alone can grasp this happiness and bring it to fruition with *joie de vivre*. Establish a more active social life and take the time to practice taking deep and deliberate breaths into your solar plexus each day, preferably outside in the fresh air. Not only will it aid in the oxygenation of all of your body cells, clearing your mind and activating the body processes, it will clear you emotionally, too.

SPIRITUAL BLOCK AND CONCLUSION

To uncover the spiritual block that keeps you from responding to the needs of your BEING, refer to the "KEY QUESTIONS" at the back of this book. In answering these questions, you will come in touch more easily and accurately with the true cause of your physical problem.

LUPUS

PHYSICAL BLOCK

Disseminated Lupus is a serious inflammatory autoimmune disease, primarily affecting women. It is known to damage the kidneys, skin, blood vessels, nervous system and heart. Symptoms include joint pain, headaches, rashes, sleeplessness, anorexia, fever and fatigue. *Chronic Lupus* is tenacious and recurring, and character- ized by red blotches on the skin that flake off and relocate around the face.

EMOTIONAL BLOCK

Disseminated Lupus indicates an underlying psychologi- cal self-destruction. You feel you have no purpose and would prefer to die, but have not made the decision to do so. Deep down, however, you want to live and have a good reason to, but find yourself easily and frequently overshadowed by others. You are easily dominated and tend not to stick up for yourself. For *Chronic Lupus* see SKIN DISORDERS.

MENTAL BLOCK

Interestingly, *Lupus* is the Latin word for *wolf*. Is it possi- ble you picture yourself as a wolf? Do you tend to believe that you are too vicious toward others and hate yourself all the while? Such a self-destructive attitude has probably resulted from a difficult start in life, but it's never too late to change your perspective and realize that life is worth living. Look inside yourself and determine what would make your life worthwhile. Then make the decision to go after it! Take one step at a time in the direction of your dreams and you will begin to feel renewed. You'll find the reason for living that you've been searching for.

SPIRITUAL BLOCK AND CONCLUSION

To uncover the spiritual block that keeps you from responding to the needs of your BEING, refer to the "KEY QUESTIONS" at the back of this book. In answering these questions, you will come in touch more easily and accurately with the true cause of your physical problem.

LYMPHATIC SYSTEM DISORDERS

The *lymphatic system* is made up of an intricate network of vessels, valves and nodes throughout the body that carry the lymph fluid and help to remove toxins from the body. Lymph fluid is a clear, transparent liquid that circulates through the lymphatic system to bathe the tissues. It also feeds the cells, carrying nutritional elements from the blood and returning waste to the bloodstream. Lymph nodes purify the lymph fluid and also serve as filters for toxins throughout the body, trapping poisons and invading bacteria, preventing them from circulating in the body's tissues and through the bloodstream. An over-accumulation of toxins in the lymph nodes can result in swollen GLANDS and/or lymphatic CANCER. Refer to them.

L

321

MALARIA

Malaria is an infectious parasitic disease transmitted by the bite of the infected female anopheles mosquito and marked by cycles of chills, fever, anemia and sweating. It is also called *paludism* or *swamp fever*. See FEVER and PARASITES.

MALFORMATIONS

PHYSICAL BLOCK

Malformations are congenital anomalies that can affect any organ or tissue. If this malformation is labeled hereditary, see the metaphysical explanation of HEREDITARY DISEASE in SECTION 2.

EMOTIONAL BLOCK

Finding the exact cause of a congenital malformation may prove to be difficult because in a majority of cases, the cause comes from a previous life. It is critical, however, that the parents not hold themselves responsible. In general, a malformation from birth is experienced in order to learn unconditional love, as much for the person who has the malformation as for those close to them. The purpose of the malformation is to teach us to look beyond the superficial and experience the extraordinary person within.

M

323

MENTAL BLOCK

If you are afflicted with a congenital malformation, understand that you chose this state prior to your birth. Nothing is preventing you from *being* happy. Wholeness and harmony come from within and nothing in this world is impossible if you choose to achieve it.

Although modern medical technology allows that many malformations may be altered, it is important for you to understand that the primary message your body is sending you is one of self-love and acceptance. Remember that your body is only the packaging - the gift is inside!

Refer to the listing that pertains to the part of the body affected by malformation for further information on the corresponding metaphysical implications.

SPIRITUAL BLOCK AND CONCLUSION

To uncover the spiritual block that keeps you from responding to the needs of your BEING, refer to the "KEY QUESTIONS" at the back of this book. In answering these questions, you will come in touch more easily and accurately with the true cause of your physical problem.

MANIA

See INSANITY.

MANIC DEPRESSION

See PSYCHOSIS, DEPRESSION, and INSANITY.

MARFAN'S SYNDROME

PHYSICAL BLOCK

Marfan's syndrome is a hereditary condition of the connective tissue. Symptoms and signs include a tall lean body type, irregular or unsteady gait, long extremities (including fingers and toes), abnormal joint flexibility, flat feet, stooped shoulders, dislocation of the optic lens, and aneurysms of the aorta. Affects 1 in 50,000 people. See MALFORMATIONS.

M

MASTITIS

Mastitis is an inflammation of the breast or udder. As inflammation always indicates repressed anger, mastitis is connected with the way you are feeling about new motherhood. See ABSCESS, BREAST PROBLEMS, and SECTION 2.

MASTOIDITIS

PHYSICAL BLOCK

Mastoiditis is an inflammation in the mastoid process of the temporal bone (situated behind the external ear canal).

This condition is most often secondary to acute *otitis media*. See EAR DISORDERS and SECTION 2.

MEASLES

Rubeola, or *red measles*, is more severe in those with a compromised immune system. It begins with a slight fever and dry cough that accelerates over five days, a rash that begins at the head and spreads to the feet within 24 hours. Once the fever disappears, the rash fades. See FEVER, SKIN DISORDERS and CHILDHOOD DISEASES.

MELANOMA

Melanoma is a malignant tumor that arises from the pigment-producing cells of the deeper layers of the skin. Refer to the pertinent listing of the area of the body affected by melanoma for corresponding metaphysical implications. See CANCER and SKIN DISORDERS.

MÉNIÈRE'S DISEASE

Ménière's disease is a pathological condition of the inner ear characterized by dizziness, ringing in the ears, and progressive loss of hearing. Also called Ménière's Syndrome. It is a serious dysfunction characterized by a buildup of fluid pressure of the inner ear, which ultimately upsets the balance mechanism and can cause bouts of intense vertigo accompanied by anguish, nausea, vomiting, sensory hearing loss and an imminent fainting sensation. Buzzing in the ears often precedes an attack, but actual loss of consciousness is rare. This disorder is an urgent message from the body that there is tremendous, but unfounded, guilt and fear. Agoraphobia may also be present. See AGORAPHOBIA, EAR DISORDERS and VERTIGO.

MENINGITIS

PHYSICAL BLOCK

Meningitis is an inflammation of the meninges (membranes surrounding and protecting the brain and spinal cord) characterized by fever, vomiting, intense headache, and stiff neck.

M

EMOTIONAL BLOCK

Since meningitis can be fatal, the body's message is critical and urgent, an issue of life and death. It occurs when you are suddenly faced with a situation that angers you and is very difficult to accept. The trauma of this event causes emotional shock and, because you are generally cerebral and over-analytical, you rack your brains to try to understand this situation!

MENTAL BLOCK

Your body is sending you an urgent message that one of your beliefs is not helping you. Your anger and perhaps a profound sense of guilt, brought on by the fact that you're

327

robbing yourself of happiness, are killing you. Listen to your body - it's time to do what you came for in this life: let yourself be happy and grab your dreams with both hands! You have as much right to be on this planet as any one else. See SECTION 2.

SPIRITUAL BLOCK AND CONCLUSION

To uncover the spiritual block that keeps you from responding to the needs of your BEING, refer to the "KEY QUESTIONS" at the back of this book. In answering these questions, you will come in touch more easily and accurately with the true cause of your physical problem.

MENOPAUSE

PHYSICAL BLOCK

Menopause is simply the cessation of all menstrual bleeding. It can trigger a variety of symptoms, such as hot flashes, fatigue, vaginal dryness, insomnia, anxiety and depression. It can be as complicated and difficult, emotionally, as puberty.

Men may experience similar phenomena around the age of 60, called ANDROPAUSE.

EMOTIONAL BLOCK

Menopause is a natural transition in a woman's life. The ease of this transition is dependent on your acceptance and your attitude about getting older. You're having a hard time accepting the fact that your "motherhood" days are over. The waning of your procreative forces must give way to creative forces that you can finally direct toward yourself. To do this, it will be necessary to come in touch with your masculine aspect to get through this phase with ease.

MENTAL BLOCK

The more difficult your menopause, the more your body is telling you to let go of the fear of growing old. Just because your body is not in the shape it used to be does not mean that you're becoming powerless. Getting old does not mean being disabled or dying, If you feel you will become undesirable, lonely or useless, you must realize that your perception is out of whack. Maturity can be equated to a fine wine or a great book that's been many years in the writing - full-bodied and full of wonderful experiences. The wealth of experiences you've amassed will help you face anything and can help you mold your life into anything you desire.

Creating for yourself, using your masculine aspect, means taking time for introspection, making your decisions calmly and allowing yourself more time to be alone. Your masculine aspect will help you organize and structure your new life. Menopause is a wonderful opportunity to put your family obligations behind you and create your own life.

M

329

SPIRITUAL BLOCK AND CONCLUSION

To uncover the spiritual block that keeps you from responding to the needs of your BEING, refer to the "KEY QUESTIONS" at the back of this book. In answering these questions, you will come in touch more easily and accurately with the true cause of your physical problem.

MENORRHAGIA

PHYSICAL BLOCK

Menorrhagia is defined as abnormally heavy or prolonged menstruation. It is common among women who have an IUD (a contraceptive device that is placed within the uterus).

EMOTIONAL BLOCK

Blood symbolizes the life force or *joie de vivre;* therefore excessive loss of blood is linked to the loss of joy in your life, or loss of vitality. If menorrhagia is experienced in conjunction with the insertion of an IUD, your body is sending you a clear message that the conscious decision to prevent pregnancy is causing you sadness. Deep down, you want a child, but are preventing yourself from doing so due to fear or to outside influences. If menorrhagia is not linked to the use of an IUD, see MENSTRUAL DISORDERS.

MENTAL BLOCK

Take a moment to look inside and see what you're afraid of. What could happen that might make having a child so unpleasant or difficult? Ask yourself whether your concerns are justified, or whether you may simply have an over-active imagination. Are you allowing yourself to be unduly influenced by someone else? If you have evaluated this issue from every angle and conclude that prevention at this time is the right decision, do so with joy.

SPIRITUAL BLOCK AND CONCLUSION

To uncover the spiritual block that keeps you from responding to the needs of your BEING, refer to the "KEY QUESTIONS" at the back of this book. In answering these questions, you will come in touch more easily and accurately with the true cause of your physical problem.

M

MENSTRUAL CRAMPS or DISORDERS

PHYSICAL BLOCK

Menstruation is defined as discharging of the *menses*, or blood and dead cell debris from the uterus. Non-pregnant women release menses through the vagina at approximately monthly intervals (every 25 to 32 days) between puberty and menopause. Problems may include: *amenorrhea* (absence of monthly period), *swelling, breast tenderness, pelvic pain,* menorrhagia (heavy or prolonged menstruation) and *metorrhagia* (uterine bleeding that occurs outside of the menstrual cycle).

EMOTIONAL BLOCK

Menstrual disorders are an indication that you are having difficulty accepting your femaleness. Probably since adolescence you've been reacting negatively toward your mother, who was your first female role model. Because of your perception of your mother's life, you may have decided that the female role is an unenviable role. It may be that, subconsciously, you would have preferred to be a man, to the point of feeling resentment toward men, because in your view, they can do things you can't. You strive to lead your life according to the male's model, but unconsciously feel guilty about it.

MENTAL BLOCK

Through menstrual disorders, your body is telling you that your belief system concerning women in general is inaccurate. This is a prime example of what can happen in the body when you refuse to go with the flow. Your perception is unhealthy and is a stumbling block to your own happiness. You find that you are frequently emotionally reactive, which is disrupting your peace of mind. Understand that your femaleness is not the obstacle that you make it out to be. More women than ever are making choices in their lives that were previously reserved for men.

Society's rules that once defined the roles of men and women are now considered archaic and no longer apply. Rather than envying men, enjoy them and allow yourself to want them as a complement to your own femininity. In this way you will achieve a healthy masculine/feminine balance. You may choose to adopt a man's role; however, allow yourself the right to need men without becoming dependent. Relax, be yourself and this will make room for the right man to come into your life.

It is possible that your belief system has been culled from your own family. When you were younger, was there someone close to you who believed that menstruation was shameful, sinful, dirty, or simply an illness? Did you learn that it was normal to have menstrual problems (or pain) and thus come to expect them? Take responsibility now for your own mindset regarding menstruation and change those beliefs. Understand that menstruation is a necessary, natural, painless and healthy reproductive function.

SPIRITUAL BLOCK AND CONCLUSION

M

To uncover the spiritual block that keeps you from responding to the needs of your BEING, refer to the "KEY QUESTIONS" at the back of this book. In answering these questions, you will come in touch more easily and accurately with the true cause of your physical problem.

METORRHAGIA

Metorrhagia is defined as uterine bleeding that occurs outside of the menstrual cycle. See HEMORRHAGE. If the origin is *endometrial*, see ENDOMETRIOSIS.

333

MIGRAINE

PHYSICAL BLOCK

A *common migraine* is a severe, recurring headache, usually affecting only one side of the head, characterized by sharp pain and often accompanied by nausea, vomiting, and visual disturbances.

A *classic migraine* is a common migraine with aura. The auras consist of blurred vision, muddled thinking, exhaustion, worry and numbness or tingling on one side of the body.

EMOTIONAL BLOCK

Migraines are directly linked with the I AM. They are most common in those who will not allow themselves to live according to their true nature. If a teenager, for example, dreams of being an artist, but allows himself to be influenced by his parents into another line of work, he can suffer from migraines as long as he does not allow himself to be what he wants TO BE.

Migraines can occur when you feel guilty for daring to question those who influence you. You may not even be fully conscious of what it is you truly desire, to the point of living in someone else's shadow. How often do you find yourself saying, *"I can't be what I want"?* If you suffer from migraines, take a look at your sexual relationship. You most likely are having difficulties in that area also, because you are out of touch with your power to create your life, which is reflected in the sexual organs.

MENTAL BLOCK

Ask yourself the following question: *"If every circumstance around me had been perfect, what would I have wanted to BE, or what do I want to BE now if circumstances would allow?"* Determine what it is that has proven to be the greatest obstacle to your dreams. If you take a close and honest look, you will discover that it's your belief system that is creating the greatest barrier to the fulfillment of your potential. There is no reason to believe that you will be more loved when dependent on others. Acknowledge and accept your fears and then go forward in the direction of your dreams by taking your time to reach your goal.

SPIRITUAL BLOCK AND CONCLUSION

To uncover the spiritual block that keeps you from responding to the needs of your BEING, refer to the "KEY QUESTIONS" at the back of this book. In answering these questions, you will come in touch more easily and accurately with the true cause of your physical problem.

MISCARRIAGE

See ABORTION.

335

MONONUCLEOSIS

Mononucleosis is an acute systemic infectious disease marked by the presence of an abnormally large number of white blood cells in the bloodstream, which indicates a triggering of the immune system. The disease is often referred to as *mono* or the *kissing disease*.

Mono affects the lymph tissue, the respiratory tract, and sometimes the liver, spleen, heart or kidneys. Symptoms include severe fatigue, headache, chills and high fever, sore throat and enlargement of lymph nodes, especially in the neck. The symptoms are varied and often confusing because of the reaction of some of the organs involved. For example, if the liver is affected, mild jaundice may occur.

Mono occurs most commonly at the age when the immune system is at its peak function, which is between fifteen and seventeen years of age. Because it is caused by a virus, it is resistant to antibiotics and difficult to treat. The appearance of this disease is an indication that there is a great deal of resistance, a refusal to let go. It occurs frequently among adolescents who believe they fell in love too quickly.

Refer also to the pertinent listing of the area of the body most obviously affected for corresponding metaphysical implications: ANGINA, BLOOD CELL DISORDERS, SPLEEN and LIVER DISORDERS.

MOTION SICKNESS

PHYSICAL BLOCK

Motion sickness manifests in some individuals while traveling or acceleration and deceleration by car, train, sea and air. Symptoms may include headache, nausea, vomiting, weakness, cold sweat, pallor, and torpor.

EMOTIONAL BLOCK

Often, motion sickness is caused by an underlying fear of death or loss of control. Symptoms parallel those of mild panic or anxiety. You want to take control in order to avoid being caught in a new situation from which you wouldn't know how to escape. This keeps you from fully experiencing the joy and exhilaration of the present moment. Motion sickness is very common in agoraphobics. See AGORAPHOBIA.

MENTAL BLOCK

If you experience motion sickness, your body is telling you to let go and stop trying to control everything. Allow yourself to openly express your fears. It's interesting to note that motion sickness is rarely experienced when traveling alone. Determine what is going on in your head prior to the motion sickness. In whom do you lack confidence? Are they not capable of having the answers and solutions you need? Your body is telling you to let go and trust others, especially to trust in the Universe. You'll find that,

337

once you do, the Universe will take care of you and you'll be able to go with the flow.

Refer also to NAUSEA, VOMITING, WEAKNESS, and HEADACHE if applicable.

SPIRITUAL BLOCK AND CONCLUSION

To uncover the spiritual block that keeps you from responding to the needs of your BEING, refer to the "KEY QUESTIONS" at the back of this book. In answering these questions, you will come in touch more easily and accurately with the true cause of your physical problem.

MOUTH PROBLEMS

PHYSICAL BLOCK

The *mouth* is the body's first passage to the digestive and respiratory tracts. There are a number of problems that can occur in the mouth including CANKER SORES, oral THRUSH, PAIN, etc.

EMOTIONAL BLOCK

Problems in the mouth indicate that you find something hard to swallow; new ideas are difficult to accept and you experience an instinctive and unexamined reaction. These situations and ideas may come from you or from others. Your mouth is telling you to be more open to new ideas and situations that could prove beneficial to you.

If you have a tendency to chew the inside of your mouth, you will find you also have a tendency to avoid saying things that you want to hide from others, things that cause you anguish.

MENTAL BLOCK

Release these unhealthy thoughts and the fear that keeps them prisoner in your mouth. Also, allow yourself to change your mind about decisions you may have made too quickly. Remember that being your best by being open and honest with others is also what is best for those around you. You need to believe that new ideas may be good for you.

SPIRITUAL BLOCK AND CONCLUSION

To uncover the spiritual block that keeps you from responding to the needs of your BEING, refer to the "KEY QUESTIONS" at the back of this book. In answering these questions, you will come in touch more easily and accurately with the true cause of your physical problem.

M

MUCOVISCIDOSIS

See CYSTIC FIBROSIS.

MUMPS

PHYSICAL BLOCK

Mumps, also called *parotitis*, is an infectious disease characterized by weakness, fever, sore throat, puffiness to the cheeks and swelling of the parotid glands (the largest of the salivary glands). The glands situated just in front of or below the ear are those most often affected. Mumps can also inhibit chewing.

EMOTIONAL BLOCK

As mumps manifests in the salivary glands, its metaphysical implications are linked with saliva. Mumps usually occurs in children, indicating that the affected child feels "spat upon." Being spat upon psychologically refers to the feeling of being criticized or ignored, or not being allowed to have what we want. We have an underlying desire to spit on the offender but hold back, turn a deaf ear, and allow accumulated resentment to swell up inside of us.

MENTAL BLOCK

If you are an adult with mumps, your body is sending a clear message that you are currently experiencing a situation that causes you to relive a painful childhood experience. You continue to behave as a child. Your mumps are telling you that if you feel someone has spat on you, it's because you've allowed it to happen. Use this awareness to gather your inner strength and stop feeling inferior. Have compassion for the other person, admit to them what you are feeling, and recognize that they are as fearful as you are. They are there as a mirror to reflect your belief system; that you tend to spit on yourself also. See also SECTION 2.

If a child has mumps, you can help them by reading the above and explaining to them that they have as much power to heal as they have in creating their illness. See CHILDHOOD DISEASES.

SPIRITUAL BLOCK AND CONCLUSION

To uncover the spiritual block that keeps you from responding to the needs of your BEING, refer to the "KEY QUESTIONS" at the back of this book. In answering these questions, you will come in touch more easily and accurately with the true cause of your physical problem.

M

MULTIPLE SCLEROSIS

PHYSICAL BLOCK

Sclerosis is the hardening of an organ or tissue. *Multiple sclerosis* is the progressive degeneration of the protective covering of nerve fibers in the brain and spinal cord.

EMOTIONAL BLOCK

Multiple sclerosis indicates a desire to become hardened or desensitized in order to avoid emotional suffering. All suppleness is lost, both physically and psychologically, preventing you from adapting to the people and situations

341

around you. Someone has really *jangled your nerves* and an inner revolt has ensued. This war going on within you finally reaches critical mass and you don't know which way to turn.

Generally, this disease indicates that you are set in your ways and no longer capable of change. You wish to be completely dependent on someone but you push yourself so that you don't want to appear or admit to being dependent. You are probably somewhat idealistic and a perfectionist who expects a great deal of yourself. You want to please at any price. Since it's impossible to attain this unrealistic ideal all by yourself, becoming handicapped provides all the excuse you need for not achieving your dreams. It's also hard for you to accept that others who work less than you might *have* more.

MENTAL BLOCK

The more serious the disease, the more urgent the message from your body. It's telling you to reveal your natural gentleness and to stop being so hard on yourself. Learn to let go of any hard feelings you may have toward others and allow yourself to be emotionally dependent - before you become completely physically dependent.

Let go. Stop demanding so much of yourself - you have nothing to prove to anyone. Examine the idealized personality you've been trying so hard to achieve and realize and accept that it may be beyond your limitations. Let go of your underlying fear that you may displease someone; it is stifling the expression of your true self and blocking any progress you will make toward your own evolution.

342

It may be that you were so utterly disappointed in your same-sex parent that you are now doing everything you can to avoid being like them. The result is that you expect far too much of yourself. Accept your parent unconditionally and forgive yourself for being so judgmental. This can have a profound effect on your recovery. Refer to the steps to true forgiveness at the back of the book.

SPIRITUAL BLOCK AND CONCLUSION

To uncover the spiritual block that keeps you from responding to the needs of your BEING, refer to the "KEY QUESTIONS" at the back of this book. In answering these questions, you will come in touch more easily and accurately with the true cause of your physical problem.

M

MUSCULAR DISORDERS

PHYSICAL BLOCK

Muscles are bodily tissues comprised of fibers that contract and relax to facilitate movement or exert force. I am referring here to muscles that are controlled voluntarily not the involuntary muscles that are controlled by the body itself, such as the cardiac or intestinal muscles. The most common muscular disorders are muscular PAIN or WEAKNESS. Also see CRAMP, if applicable.

EMOTIONAL BLOCK

Since muscles facilitate movement, muscular disorders indicate a lack of motivation or will power to fulfill your desires.

MENTAL BLOCK

It isn't muscular weakness or pain keeping you from moving, but an internal weakness that reflects your fear of actually achieving your goal. Your body is telling you to move ahead, to connect with your will power and put some muscle into it! You have what it takes! All that's required is that you become conscious of your internal power. Unearth whatever it is that will motivate you in the direction of your dreams!

SPIRITUAL BLOCK AND CONCLUSION

To uncover the spiritual block that keeps you from responding to the needs of your BEING, refer to the "KEY QUESTIONS" at the back of this book. In answering these questions, you will come in touch more easily and accurately with the true cause of your physical problem.

MUSCULAR DYSTROPHY

PHYSICAL BLOCK

Muscular dystrophy is a chronic disease marked by gradual muscular deterioration. Dystrophy occurs due to mal-nourishment of the cells of the muscle and results in atrophy, which is a notable diminution of the normal volume and weight of the muscle itself.

EMOTIONAL BLOCK

The loss of muscle control inherent in muscular dystrophy signifies that you have constantly controlled yourself and have now reached your emotional and physical limits.

There is an unconscious self-destruction underlying this disease. You are self-critical and quick to "knock" yourself - to the point of playing the victim in order to get attention - but you have tried hard to hide this side of you. It has been difficult for you to love yourself and because of this, you have become dependent on others to make you happy.

M

MENTAL BLOCK

If you suffer from muscular dystrophy, you are receiving an urgent message from your subconscious: *learn to love yourself and let go of your expectations*. True love and happiness come from within, not from having a serious illness. You have falsely believed that you needed the attention of others to fulfill you and your physical dependence on them would bring you this attention. Are you really ready to pay the price for this attention - total dependence on others and on the system? Wouldn't it be much wiser to tune in to your own abilities and strengths and validate yourself rather than becoming invalid? See MUSCULAR DISORDERS.

SPIRITUAL BLOCK AND CONCLUSION

To uncover the spiritual block that keeps you from responding to the needs of your BEING, refer to the "KEY QUESTIONS" at the back of this book. In answering these questions, you will come in touch more easily and accurately with the true cause of your physical problem.

MYALGIA

Myalgia is muscular pain that may be experienced while resting, but is intensified during exertion. See MUSCULAR DISORDERS and realize that if it occurs while you rest, it is a signal from the body that you are not indulging your need to rest and rejuvenate. Refer to the pertinent listing regarding the part of the body involved for more information on the metaphysical implications.

MYOCARDIA

Myocardia is characterized by insufficient cardiac activity, specifically of the heart muscle itself, or the *myocardium*, and subsequent increased volume of the heart. It generally affects young males. Whether myocardia is mild or more severe, it is an urgent message from the body that you need to love yourself. See HEART DISORDERS.

MYOCARDIAL INFARCTION

A *myocardial infarction* is the destruction of heart tissue resulting from obstruction of the blood supply to the heart muscle. It is commonly known as a *heart attack*. Usual symptoms include crushing chest pain that may radiate to the jaw or arms. Chest pains may be associated with nausea, sweating and shortness of breath.

In metaphysical terms, myocardial infarction indicates a desire to stop the emotions that have become overwhelming and that block your enjoyment of life. Blood represents the life force and blockage in any form is an expression of an obstructed *joie de vivre*. See HEART DISORDERS and ARTERIES.

M

MYOPIA

PHYSICAL BLOCK

Myopia, or *nearsightedness*, is a visual defect in which distant objects appear blurred because their images are focused in front of the retina rather than on it.

EMOTIONAL BLOCK

On an emotional level, you are afraid of the future and what it may hold for you. In order to fully understand the cause, it is necessary to look back to the point in time when your nearsightedness began and try to pinpoint what it was that you were afraid of.

347

Nearsightedness often sets in at the beginning of puberty, when many young adolescents are afraid of becoming adults. What they perceive about the adult world is unsettling for them. Myopia also indicates that you may be overly concerned with yourself in comparison with your concern for others. You have a difficult time seeing things from anything but your own perspective and lack a generosity of spirit.

MENTAL BLOCK

If you suffer from nearsightedness, understand that whatever frightened you in the past no longer has a hold on you. Open yourself to new ideas and experiences that are generated from outside of you, and recognize that you are not the same person you were. Stop anticipating the worst and face new situations with open eyes and an open mind. Your imagination is causing you to be afraid, not reality. Look to the future with vitality and learn to see others' viewpoints, even if they don't mesh with your own.

SPIRITUAL BLOCK AND CONCLUSION

To uncover the spiritual block that keeps you from responding to the needs of your BEING, refer to the "KEY QUESTIONS" at the back of this book. In answering these questions, you will come in touch more easily and accurately with the true cause of your physical problem.

NAIL DISORDERS

PHYSICAL BLOCK

A *nail* is the natural thickening of fibrous protein, or keratin, that grows on the upper side of the tips of the fingers and toes. Nails serve several purposes: to protect soft tissue, to grasp with precision, and to scratch, among others. Nail disorders include: *biting the nails, broken nails, ingrown nails* and ONYXITIS.

EMOTIONAL BLOCK

Biting the nails disrupts all three nail functions and betrays an internal gnawing that is the result of feeling vulnerable, especially about the details of everyday life. You may feel bitterness toward a parent that, in your perception, was not protective enough. Each time you relive this insecurity with that parent or indirectly through someone else, you are driven to biting your fingernails. This habit gives you a sense of security and calms your distress.

Nails that tend to break easily indicate guilt for perceived imperfections in daily performance. You probably feel you are not precise enough or are inaccurate about necessary details. This search for perfection drains all of your energy.

For *ingrown nails*, see TOE PROBLEMS.

351

MENTAL BLOCK

Disorders that affect the nails are a signal from your body that you believe you are alone and unprotected to deal with the details of your life. This is an unhealthy and extremely stressful mindset. Let go, also, of your need for perfection regarding details.

If you bite your nails, this is an indication that you believe that others will come to your aid if you create stressful situations. Such expectations will only result in magnifying your emotions. Focus, instead, on getting things done, knowing that you are fully capable. When you do ask for help and begin to trust others, you'll realize that they are there to protect and support you when needed.

SPIRITUAL BLOCK AND CONCLUSION

To uncover the spiritual block that keeps you from responding to the needs of your BEING, refer to the "KEY QUESTIONS" at the back of this book. In answering these questions, you will come in touch more easily and accurately with the true cause of your physical problem.

NARCOLEPSY

PHYSICAL BLOCK

Narcolepsy is a disorder characterized by sudden and uncontrollable, though often brief, attacks of deep sleep, sometimes accompanied by paralysis and hallucinations.

This can happen at any time, and may be accompanied by a loss of muscle tone or partial paralysis.

EMOTIONAL BLOCK

This affliction appears in people who, when awake, are always busy. Unfortunately, these people don't take the time to ask themselves what they really want out of life. They are often cut off from their ability to know how they feel. They also find it hard to live in the present, and constantly anticipate what's going to happen.

MENTAL BLOCK

If you suffer from this illness, your body is telling you that it is important for you to be awake to life, but because you feel little pleasure or joy in accomplishing the tasks you impose on yourself, you regularly escape into sleep. See if what you decide to do is really taking you towards what you want in your life. It will then be easier for you to fully live in the present.

SPIRITUAL BLOCK AND CONCLUSION

To uncover the spiritual block that keeps you from responding to the needs of your BEING, refer to the "KEY QUESTIONS" at the back of this book. In answering these questions, you will come in touch more easily and accurately with the true cause of your physical problem.

NAUSEA

PHYSICAL BLOCK

Nausea is a feeling of sickness in the stomach characterized by an urge to vomit. If accompanied by VOMITING,
refer to it in addition to the following description.

EMOTIONAL BLOCK

A bout of nausea indicates that you feel threatened at that
particular moment by someone or some event. You may
have a marked aversion to someone or something, or are
disgusted by what is going on, as it is not what you expected. Perhaps you are simply sick of someone or something around you.

It's interesting to note that many pregnant women suffer
from nausea. They may find it "hard to swallow" the
changes that their pregnancy is making in their lives and
in their future plans. They either have a subconscious
aversion to what they consider the malformation of their
own bodies during pregnancy, or to watching themselves
grow more physically cumbersome. They may be afraid
of losing their freedom, which is something they can't
stomach, or of not having the support of the child's father,
or any number of fears associated with the pregnancy or
the birth of the child and its impact on their own lives.

354

MENTAL BLOCK

Nausea is a signal from your body that you need to change your perception of what is going on in your life at that particular moment. Instead of rejecting yourself or someone or something that you are feeling an aversion toward, determine what is frightening you about the situation and address it. Are you being melodramatic? Do you believe that you won't be able to face up to something? Take control of the situation and access your own potential and ability to face up to what is going on. Love and accept yourself and regain a balanced perspective.

SPIRITUAL BLOCK AND CONCLUSION

To uncover the spiritual block that keeps you from responding to the needs of your BEING, refer to the "KEY QUESTIONS" at the back of this book. In answering these questions, you will come in touch more easily and accurately with the true cause of your physical problem.

N

NEARSIGHTEDNESS

See MYOPIA.

NECK PAIN

PHYSICAL BLOCK

Because the *neck* is the link between the head and body in a physical sense, metaphysically it joins the spiritual

355

world to the material world. Neck pain is usually felt when moving the neck in a certain direction.

EMOTIONAL BLOCK

Pain and stiffness in the neck denote inflexibility in thinking. You may be in a situation that you feel you can't control as you wish. You may feel someone or something around you has become a *pain in the neck.* Perhaps you are uncomfortable with what you feel is going on behind your back. Whatever the issue, you pretend it does not bother you, but in fact you feel as if stuck in an emotional roller coaster.

MENTAL BLOCK

Remember that your reality is based on your perception and is therefore completely within your control. If your fear is related to what's going on behind your back, become aware that this is the result of your imagination working overtime. I suggest you check with the people concerned and express your beliefs and fears.

As a test, note whether the stiffness and pain in your neck is more predominant when you nod your head *yes* or shake your head from side to side as in *no.* Then ask yourself what it is you need to make a decision about at this time. Is it more difficult to say yes or no? If yes is more painful, the reason you are refusing to say yes to a situation or to a person is not valid. Ask yourself what it is you are afraid of and evaluate this fear. Check with the person to see if your fear is justified. Simply, if you feel pain in your neck when you nod *yes*, your body is telling you that your decision should be yes and that your stubbornness and inflexibility are the obstacles you face in making the appropriate decision. The same applies if the pain occurs when shaking your head *no*.

For acute stiffness in the neck area, see TORTICOLLIS.

SPIRITUAL BLOCK AND CONCLUSION

To uncover the spiritual block that keeps you from responding to the needs of your BEING, refer to the "KEY QUESTIONS" at the back of this book. In answering these questions, you will come in touch more easily and accurately with the true cause of your physical problem.

NEPHRITIS

N

Nephritis is the inflammation of the kidneys. Inflammation invariably indicates repressed anger. See KIDNEY DISORDERS and SECTION 2.

NEPHROSIS

See KIDNEY DISORDERS.

NERVOUS TIC

See TWITCH.

357

NETTLE RASH

See HIVES.

NEURALGIA

PHYSICAL BLOCK

Neuralgia is defined as a sharp and severe paroxysmal pain extending along a nerve or group of nerves. For further information on the metaphysical implications, refer to the pertinent listing that corresponds to the physical location in the body.

EMOTIONAL BLOCK

Neuralgia is a signal from the body that some past emotional pain that you are trying to escape has struck a nerve in you. When you are reminded of this emotional trauma in some way, you relive the fear and guilt associated with it. Some current event or situation triggers the bitterness and strife and you subconsciously attempt to cut yourself off from feeling it.

MENTAL BLOCK

Attempting to repress the pain only serves to magnify it without your being aware of it. Address the issue instead of avoiding it. Even if this past trauma was extremely painful for you, know that you are not the same person you were then and can now face it. Acknowledge the limi-

358

tations you had at the time and stop blaming yourself or anyone else. We all have limitations.

SPIRITUAL BLOCK AND CONCLUSION

To uncover the spiritual block that keeps you from responding to the needs of your BEING, refer to the "KEY QUESTIONS" at the back of this book. In answering these questions, you will come in touch more easily and accurately with the true cause of your physical problem.

NEUROSIS

PHYSICAL BLOCK

Neurosis is defined as any of various mental or emotional disorders, such as *hypochondria*, arising from no apparent organic lesion or change and involving symptoms such as insecurity, anxiety, depression, and irrational fears. Neurosis tends to alter the personality less severely than psychosis. Neurotics are usually aware of their disorder, sometimes acutely and painfully so. They may, however, feel powerless to stop it, therefore they ask for help.

EMOTIONAL BLOCK

Most neurotics exhibit characteristics of obsessive-compulsive disorder, indicating a fissure within their ethereal bodies. This is created by an unsettled grudge toward one or both parents.

N

359

Neurotics tend to have a tremendous appetite for attention and, in their perception, have suffered since childhood from its lack. The operative word is *perception* as, regardless of the amount of attention bestowed upon them, it was and continues to be not enough. This unmet need snowballs into excessive dependence. If neurotics are unable to depend on those close to them in order to meet their needs, they become *obsessive*, or controlling of specific areas of their environment, leading to compulsive behaviors such as obsessive cleanliness.

MENTAL BLOCK

Neurosis is a signal from your body that you need a paradigm shift or a major change in your belief system. Your thoughts are rendering you powerless to end the psychological pain. Take an objective look at your past and remember all the good things that have happened to you. Begin to see your parents as fellow human beings that did their best with the knowledge they had. Take responsibility for your own life, for your own happiness. You must now focus on your abilities and your self-sufficiency. You have all the tools you need to build yourself the marvelous, rewarding life you desire.

If you decide to enlist a therapist to help you through this transformation, remember to choose a therapist who will simply support and guide you, but understand that you alone can pull yourself out of this and stop depending on others to do it for you. Forgiving yourself is the best way to go forward with a clean slate. See the steps to true forgiveness at the end of this book.

SPIRITUAL BLOCK AND CONCLUSION

To uncover the spiritual block that keeps you from responding to the needs of your BEING, refer to the "KEY QUESTIONS" at the back of this book. In answering these questions, you will come in touch more easily and accurately with the true cause of your physical problem.

NIGHTMARES

PHYSICAL BLOCK

One out of ten people suffer frequent *nightmares*. A *nightmare* is more or less distressing, ends abruptly, and generally leaves us fraught with anxiety in our waking hours.

EMOTIONAL BLOCK

N

Dreams are an extension of the state of consciousness experienced when we are awake. Fears and anguish that you don't want to face up to and repress during waking hours are given free reign in sleep. Pay attention to the messages provided in your dreams and address the issues that your subconscious is showing you. Be thankful that you are being made aware of these fears and face them while you are awake. Your dreams are communicating with you about issues that need to be dealt with, just like illnesses and diseases do.

MENTAL BLOCK

Thank your subconscious for showing you your fears and use your nightmares as a training ground for developing the strength and courage to face these fears in your waking life. Allow your psyche to take you by the hand and guide you to resolution of the issues that confront you or that you are running away from. Before you fall asleep, program yourself to participate consciously in your dream. If, for example, something or someone is chasing you in your dream, you will be able to turn and face them. Look them in the eye and ask them what it is they want from you. This is even more imperative if you are experiencing a recurring nightmare, as the issue being repressed is of great importance to your well being. Understand that in your dreams, as in your waking hours, you are not alone in facing these fears. You have the help and guidance of a higher consciousness to support you. Remind yourself that it is safe to do this in your dreams because the danger is not real. Befriend your subconscious, face your demons together and find the peace of mind that you deserve.

SPIRITUAL BLOCK AND CONCLUSION

To uncover the spiritual block that keeps you from responding to the needs of your BEING, refer to the "KEY QUESTIONS" at the back of this book. In answering these questions, you will come in touch more easily and accurately with the true cause of your physical problem.

NODULES

Nodules are small, painless and benign nodes of body tissue that form in knob-like lumps under the skin. When palpated, they appear hard, elastic and moveable. See CYST or SKIN TAGS.

NOSEBLEED

PHYSICAL BLOCK

The following definition refers to intermittent or infrequent *nosebleeds*. If the bleeding is significant and cannot be stopped, see HEMORRHAGE.

EMOTIONAL BLOCK

N

A nosebleed without apparent reason indicates a temporary loss of joy. A nosebleed often represents the desire to cry, and serves as an emotional release when you refuse to allow yourself to do so. It may give you an excuse to withdraw from an activity you are not enjoying.

MENTAL BLOCK

Rather than seek attention or stop what you are doing, take a look at the positive side of the activity. When you feel like crying, acknowledge your emotions and wash away your stress with real tears.

363

SPIRITUAL BLOCK AND CONCLUSION

To uncover the spiritual block that keeps you from responding to the needs of your BEING, refer to the "KEY QUESTIONS" at the back of this book. In answering these questions, you will come in touch more easily and accurately with the true cause of your physical problem.

NOSE PROBLEMS

PHYSICAL BLOCK

The *nose* has three principle functions: 1) mucous membranes lining the nasal passages assure warming and moistening of incoming air, which is essential for the efficient gaseous exchange. 2) These mucous membranes are also the first line of defense of the respiratory system; in conjunction with hairs that line the nasal passages, they prevent bacteria and foreign particles from entering the respiratory tract. 3) Finally, the nose is the organ of the sense of smell.

The most common problem associated with the nose is *nasal congestion*, or simply a stuffy nose. Swelling of nasal tissues due to allergies or trauma is also very common. Both swelling and congestion impede oxygen intake, resulting in headache and fatigue.

Although a large or misshapen nose contributes to disharmony of the face and may be of aesthetic concern, it rarely has physical ramifications. Preoccupation with how the nose looks indicates misplaced emphasis on *appearing* to the detriment of *being*.

Refer to ADENOIDS (lymphoid tissue growths in the upper part of the throat, behind the nose) if a child has *adenoids* that are overdeveloped and cause nasal obstruction, causing the child to breathe through the mouth.

EMOTIONAL BLOCK

As air is a symbol of the life force and fundamental to life on a physical level, difficulty in taking in breath through the nose is directly linked with taking in life. You tend to cut yourself off on a sensory level for fear of feeling your own suffering or the suffering of someone you love. On the other hand, it might be because you can't stand someone, something or a situation in your life.

Maybe you feel that something *doesn't smell good*, indicating distrust and fear.

It is interesting that nose problems often occur during those seasons when we have to rub shoulders with others (in cold weather). This indicates difficulty in social adjustments.

MENTAL BLOCK

If, for whatever reason, you've lost or have a diminished sense of smell or a stuffy nose, ask yourself the following question: *"Who or what am I unable to stand at the moment?"* It will get you nowhere to tell yourself that you feel nothing in order to avoid facing a situation. Determine what is frightening you. In my observation, those who refuse to acknowledge their feelings usually fear injustice. Take a more loving look at the situation from an accepting and compassionate point of view, rather than from the critical standpoint that your ego occupies. The ego tends to want to change other people to justify its own need to be right.

Frequent nasal congestion occurs in those who are very sensitive, but who block their sensitivity for fear of being flooded emotionally. Embrace your sensitivity with gratitude and enjoy the love that will flow into your life. Understand that there is a difference between emotion and sensitivity; you can be sensitive without becoming emotionally involved. In doing so, you will release the life force that has been stifled and be able to love and support others more freely. Take a deep, satisfying breath - it will open the blocks to your own wholeness and the achievement of your full potential.

SPIRITUAL BLOCK AND CONCLUSION

To uncover the spiritual block that keeps you from responding to the needs of your BEING, refer to the "KEY QUESTIONS" at the back of this book. In answering these questions, you will come in touch more easily and accurately with the true cause of your physical problem.

NUMBNESS

PHYSICAL BLOCK

Numbness refers to a tingling feeling of fleeting paralysis. It is seldom painful, usually experienced in the extremities.

EMOTIONAL BLOCK

Since numbness is usually felt in the legs, hands, or arms, it is emotionally linked with *doing*. You may experience numbness if you are anxious about something and refuse to acknowledge it, or if you are trying to hide your sensitivity. Numbness can be a physical manifestation of this suppression. You're preventing yourself from being the sensitive person that you are and are letting your anxiety get the better of you.

MENTAL BLOCK

Numbness is a direct and simple message from the body to acknowledge what you are feeling. It is telling you to stop deluding yourself, to confront your fears about admitting your feelings whether to yourself or someone else. Also, examine whether or not your anxiety is justified. Pay attention to the part of the body that is numb. If, for example, you experience numbness in your feet or legs, what is keeping you from moving forward, taking a step or taking a stand on a particular issue? If the numbness is in your hands or arms, what is it you are afraid to reach for? What is it you refuse to grasp? If the numbness occurs in another area of the body, determine what that particular area of the body is used for in order to understand the corresponding psychological blockage. Acknowledge your right to make decisions about what you need to do now (hands or arms) or what you are planning to do (feet or legs).

SPIRITUAL BLOCK AND CONCLUSION

To uncover the spiritual block that keeps you from responding to the needs of your BEING, refer to the "KEY QUESTIONS" at the back of this book. In answering these questions, you will come in touch more easily and accurately with the true cause of your physical problem.

OBESITY

PHYSICAL BLOCK

Obesity is an increase in body weight as a result of an excessive accumulation of fat in the body beyond skeletal and physical limitations.

EMOTIONAL BLOCK

Although obesity can be caused by a number of physiological factors, the psychological implications are related to a situation or person that humiliated you when you were young and you felt ashamed. You now live in a state of perpetual fear of feeling ashamed, making someone else feel ashamed or being ashamed by someone else.

You have built a psychological wall around you - a barrier of fat to shield you from the demands and expectations of others. You probably have difficulty saying no and have a tendency to take on too much because you would be ashamed to say no.

You may feel sandwiched between two people; doing everything you can to satisfy both. You want to make others happy to prove that you are not ashamed of them. While doing this, you're completely out of touch with your own needs.

It is also common to gain weight as a protective psychological barrier against the opposite sex. You may believe that your obesity will not be attractive to the opposite sex

371

and you will therefore avoid being hurt, humiliated or emotionally abused by them.

Frequently, obese people want to take their rightful place in life but are uncomfortable doing so. Little do they know that they are already taking a lot of space in life, not only physically.

MENTAL BLOCK

In my observation, those with problems with obesity are often deeply sensitive; they are unable to take a long, hard, honest look at themselves in a mirror. Are you able to really look at each part of your body in a mirror? It's very important if you want to address your obesity and fully understand it. The ability to look honestly at your physical body is linked with your capacity to look beyond the physical to the real cause of this problem.

Experiencing the humiliation you did as a child has caused you to build a protective barrier to prevent you from being taken advantage of. You thought you could achieve your goals by being a "nice" person and by taking on other people's burdens. It is important for you to learn how to receive instead of always giving. Realize that receiving takes nothing away from others.

I suggest that, at the end of each day you recount any incident that humiliated you or made you feel ashamed, and determine whether or not the shame was really justified. Ask someone you trust what they think.

Also, make it a habit to ask yourself *"What do I really want?"* before agreeing to others' requests or before offering your services. The love and esteem that others have for you will not diminish. On the contrary, they will appreciate the fact that you respect yourself and that you are taking a stand. Although you will always be an obliging person, as is your nature, you also need to learn to feed your own soul. It is your birthright to be happy and to take your place in the lives of those close to you. Believe in your own self-worth!

SPIRITUAL BLOCK AND CONCLUSION

To uncover the spiritual block that keeps you from responding to the needs of your BEING, refer to the "KEY QUESTIONS" at the back of this book. In answering these questions, you will come in touch more easily and accurately with the true cause of your physical problem.

OBSESSION

An *obsession* is a persistent and compulsive preoccupation with an idea or emotion. It intrudes on your thoughts and invades the consciousness to the point where it becomes virtually impossible to keep at bay. Common obsessions involve religious or moral ideals, thoughts of order or precision, or a preoccupation with danger, founded or unfounded. An obsessive personality is fraught with anxiety. See NEUROSIS and ANXIETY.

OLIGURIA

Oliguria is the diminishing of the volume of urine, resulting in the insufficient elimination of waste from the body and ultimate toxemia. See DEHYDRATION and KIDNEY DISORDERS.

ONYXITIS

Onyxitis is an inflammation of the nail bed, indicating repressed anger. See NAILS and SECTION 2.

ORGASM (absence of)

PHYSICAL BLOCK

The inability to reach *orgasm* is known as *anorgasmia*, meaning an absence of orgasm. An orgasm is the highest point of sexual excitement, characterized by strong feelings of pleasure and marked normally by ejaculation in the male and by vaginal contractions in the female.

EMOTIONAL BLOCK

The body experiences orgasm as a simultaneous opening of all of the energy centers, or chakras, of the body. Absence of orgasm indicates rejection of what you're receiving from your partner and a refusal to surrender to that partner or to the sexual experience itself. As the sharing of one's whole self is a precious gift, lack of orgasm is a refusal of this gift, indicating difficulty in accepting what is

374

offered by the opposite sex. You generally tend to be controlling. You need to control yourself rather than abandon yourself fully to the enjoyment of the experience. Also, as an orgasm is synonymous with pleasure, you probably don't allow yourself much pleasure in everyday life.

MENTAL BLOCK

If you believe that holding back and blocking your orgasm is punishing your partner, you'd best realize that you're only punishing and depriving yourself. Orgasm is the ultimate intimate act, transcending physical levels and fusing your feminine and masculine aspects on a spiritual level. The pro-creative energy experienced during sex is experienced with love and sharing of the whole self. The physical orgasm signifies the fusion of mind and spirit, which is the ultimate human experience.

Learn to be more loving toward yourself and accept the idea that you deserve some pleasure in your life. It's your responsibility to allow pleasure into your life, not the responsibility of others to give it to you. No one can give you what you cannot give yourself. This is one of the fundamental spiritual laws of cause and effect. Learn to let go; let yourself go. There is no truth in the belief that if you don't control yourself, others will control you.

SPIRITUAL BLOCK AND CONCLUSION

To uncover the spiritual block that keeps you from responding to the needs of your BEING, refer to the "KEY QUESTIONS" at the back of this book. In answering

375

these questions, you will come in touch more easily and accurately with the true cause of your physical problem.

OSLER'S DISEASE (or Hereditary Hemor-rhagic Telangiectasis or HHT)

Hereditary Hemorrhagic Telangiectasia (HHT) is a ge-netic disorder of the blood vessels that affects about one in 10,000 people. This disorder is also referred to as *Osler-Weber-Rendu* (OWR). It is a rare hereditary condi-tion in which the patient's capillaries dilate to produce red skin spots and mucous membranes. It is marked by in-flammation of the lining of the heart and fever due to viral infection. The symptoms can usually be found on the fin-gertips, face, lips, and mouth, inside the nose and in the di-gestive tract. The condition can cause serious breathing difficulties, bleeding in the lungs and, potentially, blood clots on the brain. Please refer to the parts of the body the most affected by this disease.

OSTEOARTHRITIS

PHYSICAL BLOCK

Osteoarthritis is one of the most common disorders known to humankind, affecting tens of millions of North Americans. It has been recognized for centuries. Wear and tear on the joints is the principle cause; the cartilage that cushions the impact on the joint gradually deterio-rates. Its smooth surface roughens and eventually disinte-grates, resulting in painful bone-on-bone contact that

376

restricts movement. Unlike rheumatoid arthritis, the joint is not inflamed. People suffering from osteoarthritis are usually in pain when they get up in the morning and it takes time before they can move the part of the body that's affected.

EMOTIONAL BLOCK

Both *rheumatoid* and *osteoarthritis* exhibit similar emotional blocks, although osteoarthritis indicates a calcified, bitter personality that projects toward others, while the rheumatoid arthritic is more self-critical and self-destructive. If you are suffering from osteoarthritis, you probably have a tendency to feel victimized, blaming others for your own unhappiness. Rather than internalizing your sense of injustice, develop more compassion for others and work on a more positive outlook. See RHEUMATOID ARTHRITIS for the MENTAL and SPIRITUAL BLOCK.

O

OSTEOPOROSIS

Osteoporosis is a disabling disease affecting one-third of postmenopausal women. It is characterized by excessive reduction in bone mass, generally affecting the spinal column, wrist and hip and often results in fracture that is difficult to heal. Refer to BONE DISORDERS.

377

OTALGIA

Otaligia is the term used for pain felt in the ear. See PAIN and EAR DISORDERS.

OTITIS

Otitis is an inflammation/infection of the ear. See EAR DISORDERS and SECTION 2.

OVARIAN DISORDERS

PHYSICAL BLOCK

The *ovary* is one of two organs that produce ova and secrete estrogen and progesterone. Disorders include: PAIN, INFLAMMATION and CANCER.

EMOTIONAL BLOCK

Metaphysically, the ovaries link the physical body to the *sacral chakra*. This energy center is related to the power of creation. The ovaries perform two specific functions: reproduction or the creation of new life, and the secretion of female hormones that determine femininity. Ovarian disorders are strong messages from the body that you are not in contact with your creative ability. You subconsciously feel you are at a disadvantage as a woman and have little faith in your ability to create something on your own to the point of often telling yourself *"I can't do it."*

378

MENTAL BLOCK

Your body is telling you that you need to start believing in yourself. Being a woman diminishes neither your ability nor your worth. Underestimating and undervaluing yourself in this manner will manifest in menstrual disorders. Stop trying to prove to men that you can do as much as they because, down deep, you don't believe it!

Remember that it takes a man and a woman to create a baby. It also takes a balance of masculine and feminine in your own life to create a successful life. Take the confident assertiveness of your inner male and pair it with the instinctive and creative inner female to tap into the strength and power of this synergy. To achieve this optimal balance, learn to have confidence not only in your own masculine aspect, but also in the men in your life. At the same time, acknowledge the tremendous value of your intuition and inherent creativity.

SPIRITUAL BLOCK AND CONCLUSION

To uncover the spiritual block that keeps you from responding to the needs of your BEING, refer to the "KEY QUESTIONS" at the back of this book. In answering these questions, you will come in touch more easily and accurately with the true cause of your physical problem.

OVERWEIGHT

See OBESITY.

OXYURIASIS

See PINWORMS.

PAGET'S DISEASE

Paget's disease occurs chiefly in old age. The bones become enlarged and weakened, often resulting in fracture or deformation. See BONE DISORDERS.

PAGET'S DISEASE OF THE BREAST

Paget's disease of the breast is a form of breast cancer affecting the areola and nipple. See BREAST PROBLEMS.

PAIN (SUDDEN)

PHYSICAL BLOCK

Sudden pain is referred to as sharp or shooting discomfort anywhere in the body that comes on without warning and without reasonable explanation.

EMOTIONAL BLOCK

Once our justice system has decided that an accused is guilty, it deems punishment justified. As an individual, once your subconscious decides you are guilty, it does the same. Pain is the time-honored method of punishment. Sudden, inexplicable pain therefore indicates an unconscious sense of guilt that manifests as pain in a corresponding area of the body. By looking into which part of your body is affected, you will discover the area of your life in which you have pronounced yourself guilty.

381

MENTAL BLOCK

If you are generally judgmental and self-critical, you will find yourself guilty and punish yourself accordingly. Pain as a form of punishment is not very useful; you need to start all over again the next time you feel guilt. Pain doesn't solve anything.

Pain is more likely to disappear if you stop to assess whether you really are guilty. Did you intentionally want to harm someone (or yourself)? Feeling guilty when your intentions were good means that you are plugged into a belief system that is haywire! It was probably broadcast long ago by someone (probably your parents) and remains as an echo in your head. Punishment usually follows. What you need is not punishment; it's a paradigm shift. Think about this and stop punishing yourself.

SPIRITUAL BLOCK AND CONCLUSION

To uncover the spiritual block that keeps you from responding to the needs of your BEING, refer to the "KEY QUESTIONS" at the back of this book. In answering these questions, you will come in touch more easily and accurately with the true cause of your physical problem.

PALPITATIONS

Palpitations are unpleasant sensations of irregular and/or forceful beating of the heart. They may occur due to difficulty in dealing with something that you find emotional or poignant. You want to skip with joy or jump from fear, but will not allow yourself to do so. Your heart responds by doing it for you. See HEART DISORDERS.

PALUDISM

See MALARIA.

PANCARDITIS

Pancarditis is an inflammation of the lining of the heart that may be experienced during an acute bout of articular rheumatism. It can result in lesions on the heart valves and insufficient cardiac activity. See HEART DISORDERS, RHEUMATISM and SECTION 2.

PANCREATITIS

Pancreatitis is the inflammation of the pancreas. *Acute pancreatitis* is a short-lived episode that resolves completely. *Chronic pancreatitis*, on the other hand, is a dramatic and on-going inflammation of pancreatic tissue and related blood vessels. Refer to DIABETES and add the following to EMOTIONAL BLOCK: In general, pancreatitis occurs in someone who tends to worry too much about others and who has over-dramatized events, causing them to feel intense emotion, usually anger, over unmet expectations. Refer also to SECTION 2.

P

PARALYSIS

PHYSICAL BLOCK

Paralysis is defined as total loss or partial impairment of motor function or voluntary movement of a part of the body because one or more muscles cannot be properly contracted. It can involve a wide range of muscles and can be permanent or temporary. The affected body part manifests loss of controlled motion, rigid, spastic or flaccid muscle. Paralysis may be caused by spinal cord problems, brain disorders affecting the spine and brain, traumatic injury to the spine and brain, diseases that affect these organs, peripheral nerve disorders, or muscle diseases.

When all four limbs and the trunk of the body are paralyzed, it is called quadriplegia. Paraplegia is when both legs and possibly part of the trunk is involved. Hemiplegia is when one half of the body is paralyzed.

EMOTIONAL BLOCK

Paralysis can occur when you've deemed a situation so difficult that you want to extricate yourself from it. It may be that you want to flee from someone specific. The thought of the person or situation in question is paralyzing in itself. Paralysis allows you to retreat into your body and results in having someone else take charge. They'll take care of you so that you don't have to face whatever it is alone. The part of the body affected by paralysis will give you a clue as to the psychological implications.

MENTAL BLOCK

Paralysis is a clear message that you create your own limitations. You believe that you can't face what is going on in your life. Your body is telling you that you can run away if you really want to, but the problem will still be there. At some point you'll have to address it - in another lifetime, if necessary.

You need to understand that we are always presented with the solution at the same time we are presented with the problem. If you consciously take some of your energy and your focus off of the problem, you'll see that the answer was there all the time. It's up to you to decide whether to bury your creative power or to unearth it and live your life fully.

SPIRITUAL BLOCK AND CONCLUSION

To uncover the spiritual block that keeps you from responding to the needs of your BEING, refer to the "KEY QUESTIONS" at the back of this book. In answering these questions, you will come in touch more easily and accurately with the true cause of your physical problem.

P

PARANOIA

See OBSESSION and INSANITY.

PARASITES

PHYSICAL BLOCK

Any organism that lives off another host organism can be defined as parasitic. The term *parasite* refers specifically to those organisms, insects and worms that invade and feed off host organisms. Research has indicated that three out of five people will be infected with parasites at some point in their lives.

EMOTIONAL BLOCK

Just as a parasite lives off a body without contributing positively to it, so is *parasite* a term often used to define someone who is dependent on others to meet their own needs, without providing adequate return. If your physical body is suffering with parasites, it is likely that, on a psychological level, you allow other people to infest you with their thoughts and demands.

It is common for children to suffer from parasites because they are easy targets for invasion by the adult world. Children tend to feel obliged to avoid being themselves in exchange for doing whatever is necessary to be loved by adults.

If you have parasites because you traveled to a foreign country, this indicates that you attached too much importance to minor details, thereby allowing them (the details) to take over and overwhelm you.

386

MENTAL BLOCK

With a parasitic invasion, your body is telling you that no one has the power to infest you unless you allow it to happen.

To be liked, you have no need to BE someone other than yourself; you are complete and lovable just as you are. Others will respect you when you respect yourself. Just as you are particular about whom you let into your home, be selective about the thoughts and beliefs you let in.

SPIRITUAL BLOCK AND CONCLUSION

To uncover the spiritual block that keeps you from responding to the needs of your BEING, refer to the "KEY QUESTIONS" at the back of this book. In answering these questions, you will come in touch more easily and accurately with the true cause of your physical problem.

P

PARESIS

Paresis is a slight or incomplete paralysis, appearing as a diminution of muscular strength. See PARALYSIS and WEAKNESS.

PARINAUD SYNDROME

Parinaud syndrome is characterized by the inability to move the eyes in an upward direction. The muscles of the eyes are paralyzed. See PARALYSIS and add that you don't want to see what's happening in reference to a particular person or situation, and the way you see it is paralyzing.

PARKINSON'S DISEASE

PHYSICAL BLOCK

Parkinson's disease is a slowly progressing neurological disease of the central nervous system, with disorders in gait, posture and movement coordination. Men are more often affected than women. Symptoms include slow movement, muscular rigidity, resting tremor and postural instability. Handwriting becomes indecipherable, facial expression may become set, the head inclined forward, words become muffled and the voice hollow, dull and increasingly feeble.

EMOTIONAL BLOCK

On a metaphysical level, Parkinson's indicates fear of being unable to hold on to something or someone. This is why symptoms are first exhibited in the hands. Generally, you are an unyielding person who has suppressed themselves on an emotional level for a long time; you have held back in order to hide your sensitivity and vulnerability. You've probably always kept your fears and anxieties to yourself, especially when they were linked to indecision or uncertainty. You've tried for so long to remain in control of everything around you that you've reached your limits. Your nervous system is on overload from the inner tension that you've hidden for so many years.

MENTAL BLOCK

Because Parkinson's progresses slowly, you have the opportunity to reverse it. Learn to have confidence in the Universe and to trust others. Revise your belief that letting go means loss of control. Your concept of perfection is misplaced and simply incorrect. Believing that self-control leads to perfection stifles growth and full expression on every level. Give yourself permission to be human, to be indecisive and to make mistakes. It will then be easier for you to grant others the same rights. Acknowledge your fears and limitations and, most of all, your humanness. You are simply and beautifully human after all, not the bionic man or woman you've strived to be.

SPIRITUAL BLOCK AND CONCLUSION

To uncover the spiritual block that keeps you from responding to the needs of your BEING, refer to the "KEY QUESTIONS" at the back of this book. In answering these questions, you will come in touch more easily and accurately with the true cause of your physical problem.

P

PAROTIDITIS

See MUMPS.

PELLAGRA

Pellagra is a niacin deficiency disease characterized by skin lesions, gastrointestinal disturbances and nervous-

389

ness. Depression, dermatitis, dementia and diarrhea are common symptoms. See SKIN DISORDERS and realize there is repressed anger.

PENILE DISORDERS

PHYSICAL BLOCK

The *penis* is to a man what the vagina is to a woman: the organ of copulation through which you can reach an orgasm. Penile disorders include *premature ejaculation*, ITCHING, GENITAL HERPES, IMPOTENCE, TUMOR, CYST and MALFORMATION. Refer to the pertinent disorder for corresponding metaphysical implications and to URETHRITIS if appropriate.

EMOTIONAL BLOCK

Penile disorders that prevent you from engaging in sexual intercourse are usually the result of subconscious blocking due to guilt or fear. It may be that you feel you don't deserve pleasure. Sexual energy is the energy called upon to create new life - whether a baby or your own pro-creative energy. You are stopping yourself not only from actively procreating but also from creating your life proactively. Sexual dysfunction indicates guilt or fear of creating life the way you want it.

MENTAL BLOCK

Your belief system is keeping you down in more ways than one. Your body is telling you that you need to give yourself permission to make love and to enjoy it fully. Don't let guilt and fear get in the way! Whatever you learned about sexuality early in life may not apply to you at all. It was likely based on someone else's belief system. Sexual intercourse is the ultimate means of communication and expression of love toward your partner. Learn to use your penis to let go and express this love and it will be happy to help!

It's time you learned to appreciate yourself and to know that you deserve pleasure, not only sexually, but in all areas of your life. You have everything you need to create a satisfying and fulfilling life; it's up to you to take control of your creative power.

SPIRITUAL BLOCK AND CONCLUSION

To uncover the spiritual block that keeps you from responding to the needs of your BEING, refer to the "KEY QUESTIONS" at the back of this book. In answering these questions, you will come in touch more easily and accurately with the true cause of your physical problem.

P

PENIS

See PENILE DISORDERS

PERICARDITIS

Pericarditis is an acute or chronic inflammation of the pericardium, or the lining of the heart. Inflammation indicates repressed anger. See HEART DISORDERS and SECTION 2.

PERITONITIS

PHYSICAL BLOCK

Peritonitis is an inflammation of the peritoneum, the membrane that lines the walls of the abdominal cavity and encloses the internal organs. Symptoms of peritonitis include persistent, intense, even stabbing abdominal pain that is initially localized but rapidly radiates throughout the abdomen. Vomiting, intestinal dysfunction, abdominal distension and rigidity, fever, and rapid pulse may also accompany peritonitis.

EMOTIONAL BLOCK

Inflammation that occurs anywhere in the body reveals repressed anger, frustration and guilt. If you suffer from peritonitis, it is likely that you are experiencing a situation in your life that feels like a knife wound to you, an unprovoked assault. You keep everything inside, especially your anger, and because of your rigid attitude you are most likely out of touch with your feelings. You prefer, instead, to refuse to acknowledge that the situation is affecting you and delude yourself into believing that everything will work out.

Your bravado masks a great deal of fear and you don't want to know about it. The anger and guilt that you have suppressed is self-directed. You are bitter about your perceived powerlessness to alter what you consider to be an unbearable situation.

MENTAL BLOCK

Your body is telling you that you need to become more tolerant with yourself, to acknowledge and accept your own limitations. Stop believing that exposing your feelings will cause others to judge you as weak. It is time to give yourself permission to be vulnerable, be gentle and stop building unrealistic expectations for yourself. There is no longer any need to punish and hurt yourself by pretending you can do anything. You are simply a human being, with all the human limitations and weaknesses.

Love and accept yourself as such and accept help from others. In doing so you will approach the situation you are going through from a new, gentler and more rational perspective. See SECTION 2 also.

SPIRITUAL BLOCK AND CONCLUSION

P

To uncover the spiritual block that keeps you from responding to the needs of your BEING, refer to the "KEY QUESTIONS" at the back of this book. In answering these questions, you will come in touch more easily and accurately with the true cause of your physical problem.

PERSPIRATION DISORDERS

PHYSICAL BLOCK

Perspiration is the salty moisture secreted by the sweat glands through the pores of the skin. The purpose of perspiration is to maintain a stable body temperature of approximately 37° Celsius or 98.6 ° Fahrenheit. Excessive perspiration in everyday situations can be extremely unhealthy and embarrassing. Inability to perspire adequately or at all is also abnormal and not conducive to good overall health.

EMOTIONAL BLOCK

Perspiration is comprised of 95% water, which is directly linked to the emotional body. Perspiration disorders, therefore, indicate emotional imbalance. If you are unable to perspire adequately, you are likely to be very emotional but suppress your emotions for fear of hurting others. You may also exhibit skin problems. Refer to SKIN DISORDERS.

Excessive perspiration indicates that your repressed feelings have accumulated to the point that you've reached the boundaries of your emotional limitations. Sweating profusely is like letting a dam of emotion burst forth. Your body is sending you a signal that you must express yourself, whether or not others agree with you, or even if they find it distasteful.

You may feel awkward expressing your feelings at first because you're out of practice. Just warn those around you in advance, so that you can prepare them psychologically.

If your perspiration has an *offensive odor*, you've likely been harboring thoughts of self-loathing. You have become bitter from the toxic soup of negative thoughts that has stewed over a period of years. It is urgent that you forgive those toward whom you have directed these emotions. Especially, forgive yourself. Love and accept yourself as you are. Refer to the steps to true forgiveness at the back of the book.

MENTAL BLOCK

The message you are receiving from your body is very clear. It's showing you that you harbor an unhealthy belief system regarding the expression of your emotions. Your pent-up feelings serve no purpose. By learning to express them, you will let go of the belief that being emotional is wrong and you will find you will rediscover your sensitivity. Blocking your emotions blocks access to your sensitivity. Ideally, you can enjoy your sensitivity without becoming emotionally involved.

SPIRITUAL BLOCK AND CONCLUSION

To uncover the spiritual block that keeps you from responding to the needs of your BEING, refer to the "KEY QUESTIONS" at the back of this book. In answering these questions, you will come in touch more easily and accurately with the true cause of your physical problem

PERTUSSIS

See WHOOPING COUGH.

PHARYNGITIS

Pharyngitis is an inflammation of the pharynx, the passage between the nasal cavities and the larynx. Its muscular walls are responsible for the progression of food, from the mouth toward the esophagus. The pharynx plays an equally important role in communication, both through the facilitation of speech and hearing. Inflammation indicates repressed anger. See THROAT PROBLEMS and SECTION 2.

PHLEBITIS

Phlebitis is the localized inflammation of a vein, often associated with the formation of a clot. Generally, the onset of phlebitis is exhibited in the lower extremities - the veins of the feet, calf or thigh. Phlebitis indicates a strong tendency to worry, to feel anxiety in the midst of uncertainty while waiting for something. Inflammation indicates repressed anger See LEG, THROMBOSIS and SECTION 2.

PHOBIA

See NEUROSIS.

PIERCING (by accident)

PHYSICAL BLOCK

Piercing creates a perforation, or hole, in the body where it has been impaled, whether through accident or injury.

EMOTIONAL BLOCK

Piercing reflects a subconscious perception of being impaled by a situation, incident or another person. You feel that someone or something is determined to take a piece out of you or threatens to take a part of you away.

MENTAL BLOCK

Piercing indicates a need to look at reality from another perspective and to see if what you perceive around you is real. Your belief system has holes in it. You are probably deeply sensitive and take everything to heart. Others are not invading you, but you are allowing yourself to feel invaded. By changing your perception, you'll begin to realize that others do not have the intentions you thought they did.

SPIRITUAL BLOCK AND CONCLUSION

To uncover the spiritual block that keeps you from responding to the needs of your BEING, refer to the "KEY QUESTIONS" at the back of this book. In answering these questions, you will come in touch more easily and accurately with the true cause of your physical problem.

PILES

See HEMORRHOIDS.

PIMPLES

PHYSICAL BLOCK

A *pimple* is a small inflamed elevation of the skin.

EMOTIONAL BLOCK

The appearance of the occasional pimple denotes impatience and unexpressed frustration at the lack of control concerning a change in plans. The size and severity of the pustules will be relative to the degree of frustration and their location on the body will be indicative of the psychological source.

MENTAL BLOCK

If you are an impatient person, you must learn to control less and be more flexible when things don't go as planned. Remember that the only certainty is change. Understand that the unexpected often holds valuable lessons and rewards that you may not have anticipated. Trust your intuition to guide you by getting your ego out of the way (the part of you that is afraid of losing face). Go with the flow and clear the way for new experiences to unfold in your life. Clear up your self-image and your skin will clear up in the process!

If you have more than an occasional pimple, see ACNE or SKIN DISORDERS.

SPIRITUAL BLOCK AND CONCLUSION

To uncover the spiritual block that keeps you from responding to the needs of your BEING, refer to the "KEY QUESTIONS" at the back of this book. In answering these questions, you will come in touch more easily and accurately with the true cause of your physical problem.

PINEAL GLAND

PHYSICAL BLOCK

The *Pineal Gland* is a small, rudimentary gland, the size of a pea, situated in the frontal lobe of the brain which appears to secrete the hormone melatonin (hormone that normalizes *circadian rhythm*, relating to biological processes occurring at 24-hour intervals). In some animals it is connected with a rudimentary eye, the so-called pineal eye, and in other animals it is supposed to be the remnant of a dorsal median eye. In humans, it is known as the "Third Eye." The exact role of the pineal gland remains obscure. A TUMOR seems to be the only problem that can affect this gland.

EMOTIONAL BLOCK

You will experience problems in the pineal gland when you are either misusing your psychic ability or unsure or afraid to use it. It may be that you had a traumatic psychic

P

experience when you were younger, or even in a past life, that left you afraid to fully express this ability. Your body is drawing your attention to the fact that this ability must be used with love to help yourself and others and not take advantage of others. Problems in the pineal gland will also occur if you are forcing the opening of the third eye and causing an imbalance.

MENTAL BLOCK

Your body is saying that you must allow yourself to see beyond what the average person can see. Learn to use it for the betterment of a common humanity. Let go of any past fear and deal with the present. If, on the other hand, you suffer from problems in the pineal gland because you are pushing too hard to develop your psychic ability, your subconscious is protecting you from energies that you are yet unable to deal with. Forcing psychic development can be very dangerous. It is imperative that you allow this ability to develop naturally and freely from a foundation of love, simplicity and balance.

SPIRITUAL BLOCK AND CONCLUSION

To uncover the spiritual block that keeps you from responding to the needs of your BEING, refer to the "KEY QUESTIONS" at the back of this book. In answering these questions, you will come in touch more easily and accurately with the true cause of your physical problem.

PINK EYE

See CONJUNCTIVITIS.

PINWORMS

Pinworms are an infestation of the intestine by small white worms, or parasites, known as oxyuris. Pinworms are more common in children. See PARASITES.

PITUITARY GLAND MALFUNCTION

PHYSICAL BLOCK

The *pituitary gland* is a small, oval endocrine gland attached to the base of the vertebrate brain and consisting of an anterior and a posterior lobe, the secretions of which control the other endocrine glands and influence growth, metabolism, and maturation. A short stature can result from an under-performance of the pituitary gland.

P

EMOTIONAL BLOCK

As the master gland, the pituitary links the intellect with the I AM. It is through this connection that we establish our spiritual depth and touch our very essence. Disturbance in the pituitary gland indicates a blockage between the material world and the spiritual world. This can occur when you refuse to accept the divinity of the human family and, especially, your personal divinity. You do not acknowledge your place in the Universe; you feel smaller than you really are.

MENTAL BLOCK

Regardless of the fear that is preventing you from seeing clearly what an extraordinary person you are, it is unjustified and unhealthy. Your body is sending you a powerful message that you need to shift your belief about yourself. Because the pituitary functions on a more subtle level than the scientific and medical communities acknowledge, it is virtually impossible to determine the cause of any malfunction. Expand your awareness beyond the physical realm and regain your balance.

SPIRITUAL BLOCK AND CONCLUSION

To uncover the spiritual block that keeps you from responding to the needs of your BEING, refer to the "KEY QUESTIONS" at the back of this book. In answering these questions, you will come in touch more easily and accurately with the true cause of your physical problem.

PLANTAR WART

See FOOT PROBLEMS.

PLATELETS (reduction)

Platelets are microscopic oval cells that measure from two to three microns in diameter, without a nucleus. They circulate throughout the blood stream and play an important role in the coagulation of the blood. A reduction in platelets can result in excessive bleeding. See HEMORRHAGE.

PLEURISY

Pleurisy is an acute inflammation of the pleura, or the membranes lining the lungs and thoracic cavity, which are constantly moist to facilitate lung movement within the chest. Symptoms include sudden pain when breathing or coughing, varying from mild discomfort to a severe, stabbing sensation, fever and rapid pulse. The pain may refer to the shoulder. Breathing becomes rapid and shallow. Pleurisy indicates discontent and repression of emotion. It would be beneficial to allow yourself to cry and to express your emotions. See LUNG DISORDERS.

PNEUMONIA

P

Pneumonia is defined as a severe inflammation of the lungs. It can be caused by viral or bacterial invasion. Symptoms are abrupt and include chest pain, coughing, difficulty in breathing, shortness of breath, fever, fatigue, muscular pain, headaches and single episodes of shaking chills. Metaphysically, pneumonia indicates the appearance of a sudden, traumatic event that is having an impact on your personal space. See LUNG DISORDERS.

POISONING

PHYSICAL BLOCK

Poisoning is the result of the accumulation and absorption by the body of toxic chemicals and/or pollutants in the earth's atmosphere, water, food and soil. *Toxemia* (also called *blood poisoning*) is a condition in which the blood contains toxins produced by body cells at a local source of infection or derived from the growth of microorganisms.

EMOTIONAL BLOCK

When poisoning results from an accumulation of external toxins originating from the earth's atmosphere, water, food, and soil, the body is telling you that you are so influenced by outside forces that you actually feel poisoned by some person or situation. This outlook is not only physically toxic, but psychologically as well.

When the body produces toxins, they are the reflection of toxic thoughts. The body is warning you that those thoughts are not conducive to the fulfillment of your needs. A toxic outlook will block anything positive from coming into your life.

MENTAL BLOCK

It's time you realized that no one on earth but yourself has the power to poison your life. You choose your reaction based on your belief system. Compassion for yourself, or the person you feel is poisoning your life, is the only antidote.

SPIRITUAL BLOCK AND CONCLUSION

To uncover the spiritual block that keeps you from responding to the needs of your BEING, refer to the "KEY QUESTIONS" at the back of this book. In answering these questions, you will come in touch more easily and accurately with the true cause of your physical problem.

POLIO

Polio, or *poliomyelitis*, is a childhood viral infection with a wide range of manifestations from general mild illness to paralysis. Symptoms vary widely from sore throat, fatigue, fever, headache and vomiting, to muscular paralysis. The central nervous system may be affected, with deep muscle pain, hypersensitivity and tingling of the skin, meningitis, stiff neck and back pain and eventual lung paralysis. As polio signifies pollution, it indicates that you perceive yourself as being polluted or soiled on an inner level, which causes you a great deal of despair. Refer to PARALYSIS or LUNG DISORDERS.

P

POLIOMYELITIS

See POLIO.

405

POLYP

A *polyp* is usually a nonmalignant growth or tumor protruding from the mucous lining of an organ such as the nose, bladder, or intestine, often causing obstruction. See CYST.

POTT'S DISEASE

Pott's disease is a partial destruction of the vertebral bones, usually caused by a tuberculous infection and often producing curvature of the spine. See TUBERCULOSIS and BACK PAIN.

PREGNANCY DISORDERS

The most common complaints during pregnancy are NAUSEA and BLEEDING. Refer to them for more information, adding that both represent fear linked to the impending arrival of the baby.

For a TUBAL PREGNANCY refer to it in this book.

PREMENSTRUAL SYNDROME

See MENSTRUAL DISORDERS.

PROSTATE GLAND PROBLEMS

PHYSICAL BLOCK

The *prostate* is a gland attached to the male genital apparatus, situated around the base of the urethra, under the bladder. It secretes a milky liquid that constitutes the majority of the ejaculatory fluid. Its role is to dilute the thick spermatic fluid, to nourish and protect the spermatozoids and to ensure their activation. Most common problems are INFLAMMATION, TUMORS and CANCER.

EMOTIONAL BLOCK

The prostate links the physical body with the *sacral chakra*, the center of creativity or pro-creative energy. Prostate disorders occur most often after the age of 50 and indicate a sense of powerlessness in a given situation, with an underlying weariness.

The body is telling you that there is a need to let go of the reins, to surrender control to the Universe, which is sending you opportunities in the form of certain situations that will allow you to let go. In letting go, you will be able to re-channel your creative energies in other areas. When a man feels a sense of powerlessness, his libido (procreative drive) becomes diminished, reflecting his inner feelings.

MENTAL BLOCK

Prostate disorders are manifested to help you regain contact with the power to create your own life. Your belief

P

system no longer applies; just because your physical body is aging, you are no less powerful or capable of harnessing the energy to create new possibilities. Now is the time in your life when you can make all your dreams come to fruition, harvest the fruits of your labors, and delegate to younger people some of the practical tasks. This in no way negates your worth; on the contrary, it denotes wisdom and effective management.

SPIRITUAL BLOCK AND CONCLUSION

To uncover the spiritual block that keeps you from responding to the needs of your BEING, refer to the "KEY QUESTIONS" at the back of this book. In answering these questions, you will come in touch more easily and accurately with the true cause of your physical problem.

PRURITUS

See ITCHING.

PSORIASIS

Psoriasis is a very common skin condition at any age and is prone to reoccurrences. Symptoms include patches of skin that may be thickened and reddened and covered with silvery scales. It is not usually itchy, but does cause discomfort and cosmetic embarrassment and may rub off in contact with clothing, causing a powder-like residue. Areas of the body most commonly affected are the ones over bony prominences, such as the arms, elbows, palms, soles, scalp, behind the ears and knees. Occasionally, it will spread to the rest of the body.

See SKIN DISORDERS and note also that psoriasis is an indication that you are uncomfortable in your own skin and have a desire to turn over a new leaf. You don't feel recognized or acknowledged for who you really are and suffer from a degree of identity disorder, wanting to take on a personality other than your own. You are having difficulty accepting who you are in this life. The message your body is sending you is that you need to love and accept yourself in all your humanness, with all the flaws, weaknesses, and fears as well as the talents, abilities and tremendous potential you were given. Let go of your fear of rejection and stop being ashamed of yourself.

PSYCHOSIS

PHYSICAL BLOCK

P

Psychosis is a severe mental disorder, with or without organic damage, characterized by derangement of personality and loss of contact with reality and causing deterioration of normal social functioning. It is characterized by obvious symptoms that manifest in behavioral problems. Psychotics are prisoners of a universe accessible only to them; they suffer from a severe state of depersonalization. Hallucinations or delirium may accompany psychosis.

EMOTIONAL BLOCK

Psychosis occurs when you are no longer in touch with your essence, your I AM. I have observed several cases of psychosis in which the common denominator was a hatred of the opposite sex parent. In every case, they have suffered since childhood from not having been recognized by this parent for what they were. Over the years, they learned to compensate by becoming someone else in order to gain the recognition they craved. Psychosis manifests once the mental limitations of this person have been reached, when being someone else is just too much to take. The desire to become like other personalities has made them lose touch with their own BEING. Generally, there is a refusal by the psychotic to accept help because they would rather hold others responsible for their misery, especially those of the opposite sex.

MENTAL BLOCK

If you suffer from psychosis or psychotic tendencies, you must realize once and for all that only you can regain contact with who and what you are. It is never too late to get past the suffering you endured as a child. The most effective way to do so is through true forgiveness of yourself, as described at the end of this book. This method has extraordinary and permanent results.

If you are reading in reference to someone else, know that you cannot solve such a serious problem on their behalf, even with the best of intentions. Suggest, but don't insist, that they read this passage. Speak to them lovingly and with encouragement in the direction of forgiveness. Help

410

them through the steps to true forgiveness (see back of the book) toward their parent. It is best, especially in advanced cases, to have someone of their same-sex to help them. Refer also to INSANITY.

SPIRITUAL BLOCK AND CONCLUSION

To uncover the spiritual block that keeps you from responding to the needs of your BEING, refer to the "KEY QUESTIONS" at the back of this book. In answering these questions, you will come in touch more easily and accurately with the true cause of your physical problem.

PTOSIS

PHYSICAL BLOCK

Ptosis is a condition in which a particular organ has dropped out of its normal position, even slightly. Normal position is a variable and ptosis only becomes a problem when it causes difficulties in function of the organ or surrounding tissue. If this is causing you physical problems, read the following.

P

EMOTIONAL BLOCK

Generally speaking, settling or sagging in any area of the body indicates feeling "low" as pertains to that area. You have settled for less. For example, the sagging of the breasts indicates disappointment in the quality of mothering one has exhibited. It indicates a falling short of one's ideals or of the expectations of others. Refer to the perti-

411

nent listing of the organ affected for corresponding meta-physical implications. Generally, any body part that is sagging or drooping indicates a person that needs the attention of others in order to feel loved and important.

MENTAL BLOCK

The body is helping you become more aware of your level of self-worth and telling you to stop comparing yourself to others, stop trying to live up to self-generated ideals, and stop expecting so much of yourself. Acknowledge and accept your limitations and develop reverence and gratitude for both your body and your abilities. If you have difficulty finding your qualities, don't hesitate to ask for the help of others. Understand that you alone have the power to elevate your self-esteem. In seeking validation from others, understand that they can only offer their opinions; the work required on a deeper level can be done only by you. It is inner work. Don't forget that what is manifesting in your physical body is a reflection of what is going on psychologically.

SPIRITUAL BLOCK AND CONCLUSION

To uncover the spiritual block that keeps you from responding to the needs of your BEING, refer to the "KEY QUESTIONS" at the back of this book. In answering these questions, you will come in touch more easily and accurately with the true cause of your physical problem.

PULMONARY EMBOLISM

PHYSICAL BLOCK

A *pulmonary embolism* is an obstruction of the pulmonary artery to the lung. The blockage may be caused by a foreign body, but is usually the result of a blood clot or PHLEBITIS (an inflammation of the blood vessel itself).

EMOTIONAL BLOCK

An embolism is characterized by a brutal, stabbing pain at the specific site of the embolism; indicative of a strong sense of guilt related to something you did or should have done. The feeling of guilt is so strong, even to the point where you want to die.

MENTAL BLOCK

Your body is telling you that you must stop believing that you can be that guilty. No one, including yourself, is responsible for somebody's life (or death) or for other people's decisions. Understand that you did what you thought best according to your level of awareness at the time.

SPIRITUAL BLOCK AND CONCLUSION

To uncover the spiritual block that keeps you from responding to the needs of your BEING, refer to the "KEY QUESTIONS" at the back of this book. In answering these questions, you will come in touch more easily and accurately with the true cause of your physical problem.

413

PYORRHEA

See GUM PROBLEMS.

RABIES

PHYSICAL BLOCK

Rabies is an acute, infectious, often fatal viral disease of the central nervous system transmitted by the bite of an infected animal. Symptoms progress from irritability and nervous excitement to aggression and paralysis.

EMOTIONAL BLOCK

A person who's been bitten by an animal suffering from rabies is someone who has been experiencing tremendous internal rage following an irritating, even paralyzing event. They have repressed this rage to a point that they have become paralyzed by it and can no longer function in everyday life.

MENTAL BLOCK

By contracting rabies, your body is telling you that it is urgent to express and experience the rage that you've suppressed within yourself. You can now express it openly and no longer have to deal with it alone. Some great fear has been keeping you from releasing this rage up till now. You probably value self-control, especially when it concerns the expression of your anger and you were probably taught as you were growing up that it was inappropriate to throw tantrums or to display your anger openly. Consequently, you've internalized pain and bitterness toward someone who bothers you and whom you find to be aggressive.

R

415

Your body is telling you that you've reached the boundaries of your limitation and can no longer contain yourself. Show yourself a little compassion and forgive yourself. Acknowledge your suffering. I strongly suggest you follow the stages of true forgiveness outlined at the end of this book.

SPIRITUAL BLOCK AND CONCLUSION

To uncover the spiritual block that keeps you from responding to the needs of your BEING, refer to the "KEY QUESTIONS" at the back of this book. In answering these questions, you will come in touch more easily and accurately with the true cause of your physical problem.

RACHITIS

See RICKETS.

RECTAL DISORDERS

The *rectum* is the final segment of the large intestine and therefore of the digestive tract. Rectal disorders or discomfort indicate that you are someone who puts undue pressure on yourself to bring something to completion. You tend to have unrealistic expectations of yourself. See HEMORRHOIDS, POLYP, HEMORRHAGE, TUMOR and CANCER.

RED SPOTS ON THE SKIN

PHYSICAL BLOCK

Red spots on the skin refer to mild rashes that cause no pain or itching and are of unknown origin.

EMOTIONAL BLOCK

These red areas indicate inner control: wanting so much to be a certain way that you can feel trapped in that role to the point of frustration. You are pressuring yourself to assume that role because you are fearful and ashamed of not living up to the ideal personality you outwardly project. This will all have to surface eventually. Refer to the pertinent listing of the area of the body most obviously affected for corresponding metaphysical implications. By identifying the location on the body, you will begin to understand in which area of your life you are fighting to maintain control of yourself.

If you find red spots recurring frequently or easily on the neck and face area, a sudden feeling of fear is often what has triggered it. The most common fear, in this case, is of not meeting the expectations of others, or not living up to who they think you are. You tend to find it difficult to accept yourself just as you are.

R

MENTAL BLOCK

Your body is telling you that you have created an unrealistic ideal that is impossible to live up to. Others certainly

417

don't have the same expectations of you that you have of yourself. Talk openly and honestly with them about it.

SPIRITUAL BLOCK AND CONCLUSION

To uncover the spiritual block that keeps you from responding to the needs of your BEING, refer to the "KEY QUESTIONS" at the back of this book. In answering these questions, you will come in touch more easily and accurately with the true cause of your physical problem.

REGURGITATION

PHYSICAL BLOCK

Regurgitation is the involuntary rejection of the contents of the esophagus or the stomach, from the esophagus into the mouth.

EMOTIONAL BLOCK

Regurgitation may simply be a sign that the body did not require what it was just given. On the other hand, it's possible that regurgitation may occur at the same time you are rejecting what you've just seen or heard around you.

MENTAL BLOCK

If the regurgitation is an expression of rejection of what is going on outside of you, your body is telling you to address the fear of rejection that was reawakened by this incident. This fear is probably linked to your mother

418

because physical nourishment symbolically represents the mother. Is this fear still an issue for you?

SPIRITUAL BLOCK AND CONCLUSION

To uncover the spiritual block that keeps you from responding to the needs of your BEING, refer to the "KEY QUESTIONS" at the back of this book. In answering these questions, you will come in touch more easily and accurately with the true cause of your physical problem.

RESPIRATORY PROBLEMS

See LUNG DISORDERS.

RETINITIS

See EYE DISORDERS and SECTION 2.

RETT'S SYNDROME

R

PHYSICAL BLOCK

Rett's syndrome is a serious neurological disorder distinguished by mental handicap. It is characterized by a progressive degeneration of motor skills, and to date seems to affect only girls between the ages of six months and two years.

419

EMOTIONAL BLOCK

Since this is a progressive disease and the baby seems normal at birth, this little girl, for an unknown reason, has made the decision that she cannot face life. She becomes increasingly handicapped in the hands and legs, rendering her entirely dependent in a short period of time. It's possible that her soul, prior to birth, had high expectations for this incarnation and decides she cannot fulfill them. She doubts herself and experiences tremendous insecurity, especially regarding material things.

MENTAL BLOCK

Share what you are about to read with the child. She will pick up on your vibration, even though she cannot share this with you intellectually. Tell her that she must accept the fact that she has chosen to return to this planet for a reason. There are experiences waiting for her that are essential for her growth on a soul level. *She does have what it takes and need not be afraid.* Only by living through these experiences will she come to realize her full potential and utilize her capabilities. If she doesn't do it in this lifetime, she will have to come back and do it.

Parents should not feel guilty in this situation. This condition is a choice the child has made, a part of her life experience. The role of the parent is to love and nurture her unconditionally and give her the right to decide whether or not she wants to pull through this. However, the parents can share openly and honestly with the child what they are experiencing as a result of her choice. They must respect their own limitations. Understand that everyone whose life is touched by this child has something to learn on a soul level from the experience.

SPIRITUAL BLOCK AND CONCLUSION

To uncover the spiritual block that keeps you from responding to the needs of your BEING, refer to the "KEY QUESTIONS" at the back of this book. In answering these questions, you will come in touch more easily and accurately with the true cause of your physical problem.

RHEUMATISM

Rheumatism is a painful and disabling autoimmune disorder of the muscles, tendons, joints, bones or nerves and serves as a blanket term used in reference to various forms of rheumatic disease. Symptoms include pain and stiffness. The most common forms of rheumatism are *degenerative rheumatism* (see OSTEOARTHRITIS) and *inflammatory rheumatism* (see RHEUMATOID ARTHRITIS).

R

RHEUMATOID ARTHRITIS

PHYSICAL BLOCK

Rheumatoid arthritis, unlike the more common osteoarthritis, is not the natural result of time and normal wear and tear or due to a build-up of calcification in the joint. Rather, it is an autoimmune disease in which your body's immune system attacks itself, causing painful joint inflammation and swelling even during sleep.

EMOTIONAL BLOCK

The degree of seriousness is relative to the degree of emotional, mental, and spiritual blockage. Generally, if you suffer from *rheumatoid arthritis*, you are very self-critical; you have difficulty doing what you enjoy and asking others for help. Although you seem amenable enough, you let resentment build up while you wait for others to figure out telepathically what you need. You may even have thoughts of vengeance when others don't figure it out. Just as this disease is paralyzing physically, it also indicates emotional paralysis.

Pay attention to the location of your symptoms. If the inflammation is in your hands, for example, you need to examine your attitude while working with your hands. Do you need help with the work you are doing? Then say so.

MENTAL BLOCK

Why do you think it is so difficult for you to express your needs to others? Do you feel that you will be viewed as selfish if you do what you enjoy? Is that really true? What is "being selfish" for you? Listen to your own body and learn to say no when you are asked to do something that you do not feel like doing. But if you decide to say yes, experience greater enjoyment of the things you are doing without criticizing yourself.

Heaping responsibility on yourself simply to gain the recognition of others is OK, if you accept the fact that you're doing it only for yourself and not because someone is forcing you. If you want and need recognition, acknowledge and accept this in yourself without judgment or criticism. Also see SECTION 2.

See JOINT DISORDERS and OSTEOARTHRITIS.

SPIRITUAL BLOCK AND CONCLUSION

To uncover the spiritual block that keeps you from responding to the needs of your BEING, refer to the "KEY QUESTIONS" at the back of this book. In answering these questions, you will come in touch more easily and accurately with the true cause of your physical problem.

RHINITIS

Rhinitis is an inflammation of the mucous membrane of the nostrils. Refer to NOSE PROBLEMS and remember that inflammation indicates repressed anger. See also SECTION 2.

R

RIB (FRACTURED)

See FRACTURE, noting that the person feels as if he has lost his armor, that he is unprotected and unable to defend himself.

423

RICKETS

PHYSICAL BLOCK

Rickets is a disorder involving softening and weakening of the bones of children, primarily caused by lack of vitamin D and/or lack of calcium or phosphate.

EMOTIONAL BLOCK

The baby suffering from rickets is a child who suffers from an emotional deficiency. They are not necessarily neglected, but have a great need for affection. They are resisting normal growth in order to receive the ongoing care and attention that a baby receives.

MENTAL BLOCK

If you have a baby suffering from rickets, aside from increasing their intake of vitamin D, it is important to communicate lovingly and openly with them. Don't hesitate to communicate as you would with another adult. Babies pick up on your vibration. Tell them simply that they will have to learn to become self-sufficient at some point and that doing so indicates a healthy and normal progression. Help them to understand that a life of dependency won't bring them the love they seek; they'll only be disappointed and unfulfilled. They need to learn to accept the way their parents (or any adult acting as a parent) are taking care of them; they are doing so according to their limitations and capabilities.

SPIRITUAL BLOCK AND CONCLUSION

To uncover the spiritual block that keeps you from responding to the needs of your BEING, refer to the "KEY QUESTIONS" at the back of this book. In answering these questions, you will come in touch more easily and accurately with the true cause of your physical problem.

RINGING IN THE EARS

See TINNITUS.

RINGWORM

Ringworm is an affliction of the skin due to the presence of a vegetable parasite. It forms ring-shaped discolored patches covered with vesicles or powdery scales. It occurs either on the body, the face, or the scalp. See SKIN DISORDERS and PARASITES.

R

ROGER'S DISEASE

Roger's Disease is a congenital cardiac malformation, characterized by a weak flow of blood from the left to the right ventricle. See HEART DISORDERS, and the section on CONGENITAL DISEASE in SECTION 2.

ROSACEA

Rosacea is a benign skin condition characterized by superficial reddening of the surface layer due to dilation of small, underlying blood vessels. It most commonly occurs on the face. When it occurs on the leg, it is called *varicosity*. This condition indicates a slight loss of *joie de vivre*. See SKIN DISORDERS.

ROSEOLA

Roseola, also called *baby measles*, is a non-serious but common childhood viral infection that starts with a high fever and swollen lymph glands. After 24 hours, the fever breaks and a red rash develops on the child's neck and trunk. See CHILDHOOD DISEASES and SKIN DISORDERS.

RUBELLA (or GERMAN MEASLES)

Rubella, or *German measles*, is a mild viral infection that lasts approximately three days and is characterized by low-grade fever, red cheeks, and a fine rash all over the body. The lymph glands located behind the ears will usually be swollen. See FEVER, SKIN DISORDERS and CHILDHOOD DISEASES.

RUBEOLA

See MEASLES.

S.A.D.
(SEASONAL AFFECTIVE DISORDER)

PHYSICAL BLOCK

Symptoms of this disorder include fatigue, sleepiness and depression during seasons of shortened daylight hours and diminished sunlight.

EMOTIONAL BLOCK

If you suffer from *Seasonal Affective Disorder*, note that you feel vitalized at the first sign of sunlight. Considering that the degree of outside brightness affects you, your message is that you are not in touch with your Inner Light. You feel depressed because you see yourself as a bad person, instead of seeing your inner beauty.

MENTAL BLOCK

You may have felt guilty about some incident that happened before you showed signs of this disorder and began to believe that you were not a good person. The message you are receiving is very clear: this false guilt is smothering you. You must give yourself the right to have limitations and to reacquaint yourself with the beautiful, luminous person that you are.

SPIRITUAL BLOCK AND CONCLUSION

To uncover the spiritual block that keeps you from responding to the needs of your BEING, refer to the "KEY

QUESTIONS" at the back of this book. In answering these questions, you will come in touch more easily and accurately with the true cause of your physical problem.

SALIVARY GLAND DISORDERS

PHYSICAL BLOCK

The *salivary glands* are located under the tongue and along the walls of the mouth. They produce and secrete saliva, which initiates the digestion of carbohydrates and moistens food for easier swallowing. They also serve to moisten the walls of the mouth and maintain bacterial balance in the environment of the mouth. The most common problems associated with the salivary glands are the overproduction or underproduction of saliva. Painful swelling of the glands may occur due to MUMPS.

EMOTIONAL BLOCK

When you want something enough, it makes your *mouth water*. Therefore, over-salivation indicates excessive desire and impatience to achieve gratification when trying to please others. You want to "swallow" swiftly new ideas without taking the time to digest them properly and discover whether they correspond to a real need. Your desire to please others may be excessive.

You may also be over-salivating because of an unconscious desire to spit on someone. You hold back, causing the saliva to accumulate in your mouth.

On the other hand, under-salivation betrays a suspicious personality, someone who isn't about to swallow any-thing from others. You are afraid of being "had" so de-prive yourself of a lot of new experiences. You have a *dry* personality that makes you seem indifferent, even though that may not be the case. You may, however, be blocking your own desires.

MENTAL BLOCK

If you tend to over-salivate, your body is telling you that you don't have to swallow everything that other people present to you. Happiness is a personal choice and no one can make anyone else happy. You are expending far too much energy trying to make others happy and need to keep some in reserve to address your own needs. In doing so, you will be able to minimize your aggression and will no longer experience the unconscious desire to spit on a situation or on someone else. It's important that you get in touch with your own needs, be realistic about them and find a happy medium.

If you tend to under-salivate, suffering, as a result, from a dry mouth, your body is telling you to become more open-minded toward other people and new ideas. Open up, express your sensitivity, and learn to trust and to un-derstand that everyone reaps what they have sown. Allow yourself to reap the good things coming into your life.

SPIRITUAL BLOCK AND CONCLUSION

To uncover the spiritual block that keeps you from re-sponding to the needs of your BEING, refer to the "KEY

QUESTIONS" at the back of this book. In answering these questions, you will come in touch more easily and accurately with the true cause of your physical problem.

SALPINGITIS

Salpingitis is an inflammation of the fallopian or eustachian tube. See FALLOPIAN TUBE DISORDERS or EAR DISORDERS. Remember that inflammation indicates repressed anger. See also SECTION 2.

SCABIES

Scabies, commonly known as *the itch* is a benign itchy skin disorder. If left untreated, it can result in chronic eczema. See SKIN DISORDERS and note that scabies reveals a personality that is too easily affected by others, easily annoyed, nervous and edgy. Since scabies tend to make you itch, also see ITCHING.

SCALP PROBLEMS

See HAIR PROBLEMS.

SCAPULA

See SHOULDER BLADE PROBLEMS.

SCARLET FEVER

Scarlet fever, also called *scarlatina,* occurs predominantly among children and characterized by a scarlet skin eruption and high fever. The onset is quick and brutal and usually follows an infection. On a metaphysical level, it indicates a great deal of anger experienced following a sudden and unexpected situation. See FEVER, ANGINA, SKIN DISORDERS, and RED SPOTS OF THE SKIN.

SCARS

PHYSICAL BLOCK

When body tissue has been traumatized, whether cut or burned, the body normally regenerates *scar* tissue to replace it. A problem occurs when a wound doesn't heal.

EMOTIONAL BLOCK

If you have this problem, you don't want to learn the lesson this incident has to offer. You feel a need to gain attention from your wounding. The wound will stay open as long as you continue to dwell on the issue.

MENTAL BLOCK

Examine the situation, whether a disease or accident, that resulted in the wound and determine what message your body is sending you. Physical *scars* correspond to psychological and emotional scars and heal accordingly.

433

Scarring is an indication that you feel a need to hold on to something that should be left in the past. Use your energy to build your future, rather than building unnecessary tissue around an old injury, physical or psychological.

SPIRITUAL BLOCK AND CONCLUSION

To uncover the spiritual block that keeps you from responding to the needs of your BEING, refer to the "KEY QUESTIONS" at the back of this book. In answering these questions, you will come in touch more easily and accurately with the true cause of your physical problem.

SCHEUERMANN DISEASE

Scheuermann disease is a painful condition that is more common in adolescence. It appears, initially, as dorsal and lumbar pain. After several months, the shoulders become rounded, the back curved and distorted in a slouching position. There is a noticeable stiffness in the spine. On a metaphysical level, this indicates a perceived need to *brace yourself* because you have the impression there is someone *on your back.* It would be beneficial to become more assertive and to realize that you are allowing others to *climb all over you.* See BACK PAIN.

SCHIZOPHRENIA

Schizophrenia is usually characterized by withdrawal from reality, illogical patterns of thinking, delusions, and hallucinations, and accompanied in varying degrees by other emotional, behavioral, or intellectual disturbances. See PSYCHOSIS.

SCIATICA

PHYSICAL BLOCK

Sciatica is an acute condition that manifests as radiating pain from the back, either into the buttock and/or the lower extremities. The sciatic nerve is the largest nerve in the human body, extending from the lumbar region of the spine, crossing the buttock, thigh and leg and ending in the foot. Sciatica is caused by inflammation of the sciatic nerve, and its onset is brutal, marked by burning, tingling, or stabbing pain anywhere along the path of the nerve. Most sciatic pain occurs down one side of the body, but it's possible to be affected in both legs.

EMOTIONAL BLOCK

Sciatica may be experienced if you are insecure about your future or have an unconscious fear of lack of material abundance. I emphasize unconscious because, in my observation, sciatica is especially common in those who are materially and financially comfortable, but would have a difficult time if that were lost.

Sciatica, therefore, is located in the body at the level of *having*. You are probably not consciously aware of your fear of lack because you don't think of yourself as attached to material things. Acknowledging your attachment would make you feel guilty because you believe it is

435

not spiritual to love earthly possessions. Your guilt, however, impedes your progress and prevents you from taking a leap, plunging into life head-on and taking risks. Your life has become too dull, unlike the pain in your leg.

Sciatica also indicates that you are carrying a grudge, repressing aggression, or refusing to submit to someone or to an idea in relation to the material aspect of your life.

MENTAL BLOCK

If you are experiencing sciatica, your body is giving you a signal that your way of thinking is *a pain* and is causing you distress; it's really *getting on your nerves*. Pain always indicates guilt; therefore what are you punishing yourself for? What do you feel guilty about? The degree of intensity of the pain reflects the degree of punishment you feel you deserve. Acknowledge and accept that you are attached to material things and do it without guilt or self-depreciation. Be honest with yourself and admit your fear of losing these things. If risk taking is beyond your limitations, acknowledge that too, and accept it as your current state of affairs. Make a personal decision to move forward when you feel ready to do so.

It's critical that you stop believing it's ignoble to love earthly possessions. At some point, you'll be confident enough in your ability to create all that you need when you need it, that you'll no longer be afraid of losing your things and will be able to allow yourself to love them while remaining detached from them. Regarding any grudge or bitterness you may be harboring, refer to the steps to true forgiveness at the back of the book. By following these steps, you will liberate yourself from the impression that you must submit to others.

SPIRITUAL BLOCK AND CONCLUSION

To uncover the spiritual block that keeps you from responding to the needs of your BEING, refer to the "KEY QUESTIONS" at the back of this book. In answering these questions, you will come in touch more easily and accurately with the true cause of your physical problem.

SCLERODERMA

Scleroderma is a widespread connective tissue disease. It causes the skin and other body parts to slowly degenerate, thicken, and stiffen, hampering flexibility. Skin may appear shiny on the hands and forearms. When it occurs on the face, the eyelids are retracted and the mouth is reduced to a thin line. As it spreads throughout the body, it encloses it in an armor-like casing. *Sclera* means hardening, *derma* means skin.

Your body is telling you to stop wanting to withdraw and hide. On a psychological level, you have become so hardened and desensitized that you cut yourself off from your own feelings. You want to give the impression that you're a hard person, but the soft and gentle part of you wants to be expressed. Stop being so hard on yourself and let go of your need to control yourself. See SKIN DISORDERS and MULTIPLE SCLEROSIS.

437

SCOLIOSIS

Scoliosis is a condition in which the spine is bent to one side. It can occur in infants and children, but typically develops during adolescence. The curve of the spine may vary from a C-shaped to an S-shaped pattern.

Metaphysically, scoliosis indicates a lack of faith in your own inner strength and ability to make decisions. You lean too much to one side. See BACK PAIN.

SCURVY

PHYSICAL BLOCK

Scurvy is a disease resulting from a vitamin C deficiency and is marked by spongy and bleeding gums, bleeding under the skin, muscular pain, skin lesions, cold sores, spontaneous tooth loss and extreme weakness and fatigue. The immune system is severely compromised.

EMOTIONAL BLOCK

Any physical deficiency has an underlying emotional deficiency. Scurvy is a message from the body that you've become too emotionally dependent on others. In order to feel loved, you need others' attention, care and love. It's rare for you to do what needs to be done in order to realize your own dreams. Learn, instead, to plant your own garden, to shower yourself with love, to treat yourself like someone you care about. Any love you receive from others is icing on the cake.

MENTAL BLOCK

Scurvy indicates that it is vital for you to change your belief system. You have all the tools you need to build a satisfying life. First of all, get back in touch with what you want out of life and make the decision to go after it. Take concrete steps, one at a time, in the direction of your heart's desire. This doesn't prevent you from asking help from others, but learn to make your own decisions. A self-sufficient person is not necessarily someone who does everything themselves; they are, however, able to make up their own minds and when someone refuses to help, they do not collapse. Instead, they take another route to their destination.

SPIRITUAL BLOCK AND CONCLUSION

To uncover the spiritual block that keeps you from responding to the needs of your BEING, refer to the "KEY QUESTIONS" at the back of this book. In answering these questions, you will come in touch more easily and accurately with the true cause of your physical problem.

SEASICKNESS

See MOTION SICKNESS.

SENILE DEMENTIA

A number of different factors can contribute to the development of *dementia*. Dementia means a loss of mental functioning. Alzheimer's disease is only one type of dementia. It is, however, the most common cause of dementia. Dementia and Alzheimer's disease are not the same as 'senility.' Senility is really just the term used to refer to the mild slowing down of mental functioning, decreased memory and reduced concentration that happens to most of us as we get older. See ALZHEIMER'S.

SEPSIS

Sepsis can occur when we have a severe infection. The infection may start in any part of the body, but usually starts with *pneumonia*, or a *urinary infection*. Sepsis can also occur after an abdominal infection such as *appendicitis*. As the infection worsens, bacteria may enter the bloodstream. When this happens, toxins produced by the bacteria can affect the blood vessels, causing severe low blood pressure. This is known as septic shock, and is a medical emergency. If not treated, septic shock will lead to death.

Metaphysically, sepsis indicates an obsession about something that is poisoning you psychologically. The body is sending an urgent message that you follow the steps to true forgiveness at the back of the book. Refer to FEVER and BLOOD DISORDERS.

440

SEXUALLY TRANSMITTED DISEASES

See VENEREAL DISEASE.

SHINGLES

PHYSICAL BLOCK

Shingles, or *herpes zoster*, is an acute viral infection of the central nervous system that affects certain areas of the skin. It is the same virus that causes chicken pox. It is characterized by inflammation of the sensory ganglia; the skin area becomes very sensitive and small blisters begin to erupt that crust and hurt along the path of a nerve so that the reddened outbreak affects a strip of skin, forming a line. It occurs most often over the ribs in the thoracic area and is usually limited to one side.

EMOTIONAL AND MENTAL BLOCK

See SKIN DISORDERS and add that *shingles* indicates a great deal of anger about a current situation or a specific individual. You feel you need to grovel and that you cannot live as you wish. There is an underlying bitterness and what is going on really burns you, but your fear surrounding this issue is stopping you from facing it.

As this disease is affecting your central nervous system, it is an urgent message from your body that you are being increasingly affected by your perception of this situation. Forgiveness is appropriate and fundamental to your healing. Refer to the steps to true forgiveness at the back of the book.

SHOULDER BLADE PROBLEMS

The *shoulder blade* or *scapula* is a large flat bone linking the SHOULDER, the COLLARBONE and the ARM. Since pain in the shoulder blade affects all three, refer to the pertinent listing of the area most affected for corresponding metaphysical implications. See also BONE DISORDERS.

SHOULDER PROBLEMS

PHYSICAL BLOCK

The *shoulder* joint links the arm to the trunk and is a complex structure designed for ultimate motility and flexibility. It is capable of moving in all directions with great precision. Pain in the shoulder joint can vary from mild discomfort to intense, correlating with its degree of metaphysical manifestation. For a fracture, see ACCIDENT.

EMOTIONAL BLOCK

Shoulder pain signifies a feeling of being emotionally burdened. You have "the weight of the world on your shoulders." You want to do too much for others, so prevent yourself from doing what *you* want because of that inner obligation to them. In focusing on keeping others happy, you fail to reach out and grasp your own happiness. You have tremendous capacity for working hard. Your body isn't telling you to stop doing so much, but to do it out of love instead of obligation. If you have difficulty moving your arms, you may be apprehensive about embracing a person or a new situation.

MENTAL BLOCK

Shoulder pain is a message that you are overburdening yourself for no real reason; you are taking on burdens that do not belong to you. Liberate yourself by allowing others to live their own lives and make their own mistakes - they'll learn something! Did you ever promise them that you would do all this for them? Or do you believe that it all falls on your shoulders automatically?

It is time to establish your limitations and personal needs and take on your shoulders only what corresponds to what you want for yourself. Take care of yourself as if you were someone you cared about. Understand that you alone put pressure on yourself; others will respect your needs when you learn to respect them yourself. Allow yourself to be flexible, embrace anyone or anything you want, and let go of your belief that the consequences will be harsh.

SPIRITUAL BLOCK AND CONCLUSION

To uncover the spiritual block that keeps you from responding to the needs of your BEING, refer to the "KEY QUESTIONS" at the back of this book. In answering these questions, you will come in touch more easily and accurately with the true cause of your physical problem.

SILICOSIS

Silicosis is the chronic fibrosing disease of the lungs produced by the prolonged and extensive exposure to free crystalline silica. When workers inhale crystalline silica (dust), the lung tissue reacts by developing fibrotic nodules and scarring around the trapped silica particles. If the nodules grow too large, breathing becomes difficult and death may result. Silicosis victims are also at high risk of developing active tuberculosis. Silicosis continues to evolve, even after exposure has long been discontinued. It is directly linked to the mindset you have regarding your work. It's interesting to note that not all workers exposed to the same dust contract the disease.

See LUNG DISORDERS and realize that the ego always engages a physical agent of some sort on which to place the blame for the cause of a disease. Silicon dioxide, in this case, is the perfect scapegoat, as science has "verified" it as the cause of silicosis. People, in general, must be cautious about allowing themselves to be duped by their personal and collective egos and by physical appearances and learn to take responsibility for their quality of life.

SINUSITIS

Sinusitis is an unpleasant and often painful aggravation of the common cold or hay fever, resulting from the inflammation or infection of the air-filled bony cavities that surround the nasal passages and sinus openings of the face.

444

Sinusitis indicates repressed anger and an underlying feeling that someone or some situation is resistant to or provoking you. See NOSE problems and SECTION 2.

SKIN CANCER

See MELANOMA

SKIN DISORDERS

PHYSICAL BLOCK

The *skin* is the tough, membranous tissue that forms the external covering of the body. It is comprised of an outer layer called the *epidermis* and a deeper, inner layer called the *dermis*. Refer to the pertinent listing of your skin problem for corresponding metaphysical implications, as well as the following.

See also RED SPOTS ON THE SKIN.

EMOTIONAL BLOCK

The skin is linked closely to self-image and reflects this to the outside world. If you are a soft and gentle person, your skin will say so. If you are tough, yielding, transparent or resilient, your skin will be, too. A person who wants to know how he sees himself can simply take a look at his skin.

445

All skin disorders are manifestations of shame and self-depreciation. You pay too much attention to how others see you and to their judgment of you. You tend to identify with what is outside of you, rather than simply being yourself.

Generally, you are very sensitive to what goes on around you and are easily touched by situations involving others, although you have difficulty loving and accepting *yourself* as you are.

Serious skin disorders succeed in keeping others at a distance. Through the skin, you make contact with others so can justify avoiding contact once you've developed a skin problem. You may be feeling such a sense of shame over what you are or what you could be, that you refuse to get close to others and make yourself untouchable. Subconsciously, you'd like to try on a new skin, or change completely.

When you've tried without success to get close to someone and harbor tremendous bitterness as a result, it can manifest as skin CANCER.

If your skin problem is itchy, refer to ITCHING but if your disorder includes RED SPOTS on your skin, refer to it.

If your skin disorder is superficial, affecting only the epidermis, as in the case of VITILIGO, it indicates difficulty in getting through a separation, a loss of contact or communication. Such loss is interpreted as rejection and is viewed as final. You tend to be a rescuer or protector, especially of the opposite sex.

The part of the body affected by skin disorders of any kind will give you a clue as to the psychological implications. For example, if the skin on your face is affected, you may fear "losing face."

MENTAL BLOCK

The skin is the part of you that is most visible to the outside world. The degree to which disorders of the skin affect or upset you reflects the degree to which your belief system regarding a particular issue is affecting or upsetting you. Your perception of the skin disorder directly reflects your self-image. Revamp your self-image by making a list of your good qualities. When completed, add one quality each day. If you find you can't be objective, talk openly with someone you trust and get their input.

Your body is sending you an important message to be more gentle and accepting of yourself. Allow yourself to be human and learn to love yourself in all your humanness, with all its fears and limitations, weaknesses and insecurities. Let go of the belief that says you are worth nothing. You have the right to make a decision, without guilt, that would help you *save your own skin* - even if it means displeasing those you love. Your worth is determined by the quality of your own heart, from the person you are in the innermost recesses of your soul, not by what goes on in the physical world.

447

SPIRITUAL BLOCK AND CONCLUSION

To uncover the spiritual block that keeps you from responding to the needs of your BEING, refer to the "KEY QUESTIONS" at the back of this book. In answering these questions, you will come in touch more easily and accurately with the true cause of your physical problem.

SKIN TAGS (or EXCRESCENCE)

PHYSICAL BLOCK

An *excrescence*, commonly known as a *skin tag,* is an abnormal, benign outgrowth of skin anywhere on the surface of the body.

EMOTIONAL BLOCK

All forms of excrescence are a fabrication of superfluous tissues on the body. These tags of skin indicate sorrow you have held onto for too long that prevents you from living in the here and now. As an overabundance of skin tags can be esthetically displeasing, there is an underlying poor self-image, a distinct lack of connection with your own inner beauty. The location of the tags on the body will correlate directly to the psychological implications.

MENTAL BLOCK

Your body is telling you that it's time to see your inner beauty. Instead of living in the past, decide now to grow within according to your true needs. Let go of the belief

448

that says you wouldn't be a good person if you lived your life the way you wanted to live it. Turn the page, forgive yourself and others and go forward. See the steps of forgiveness at the end of this book. Also, see SKIN DISORDERS and WARTS (if necessary).

SPIRITUAL BLOCK AND CONCLUSION

To uncover the spiritual block that keeps you from responding to the needs of your BEING, refer to the "KEY QUESTIONS" at the back of this book. In answering these questions, you will come in touch more easily and accurately with the true cause of your physical problem.

SLEEP DISORDERS

A *sleep disorder* is considered to be any condition that consistently or frequently affects the quality or quantity of sleep. The most common sleep disorders are: NIGHTMARES, BEDWETTING, INSOMNIA, SLEEPWALKING and APNEA. Refer to them in this book for the metaphysical definitions.

SLEEPWALKING

Sleepwalking, or *somnambulism*, is more common in children and adolescents. It is often characterized by full physical mobility, normal coordination and even the pronunciation of well-constructed sentences during sleep. A sleepwalker may seem fully conscious, with eyes open, even carrying on a conversation. Once returning to bed, sleep continues without further disturbance. The next day, there is no waking memory of the incident.

Sleepwalking usually occurs during a period of intense dreaming when there is no differentiation made between the physical world and the dream world. Somnambulism occurs more often in children who possess a fertile imagination that is suppressed when awake. Unattainable desires that are glimpsed when fully conscious are recaptured by the subconscious in the dream state. In my opinion, sleepwalking isn't a problem for those who are doing it, but for those who live with the sleepwalker who are usually afraid for them.

SMALLPOX

Smallpox, or *variola*, is characterized by fever, weakness and skin eruptions. The skin eruptions, or pustules, form scabs that leave scars as they slough off. The rash begins on the forehead and temples then within three days encompasses the head, the arms, trunk, and entire body. See CHILDHOOD DISEASES. In reference to an adult, see FEVER and SKIN DISORDERS.

SNEEZING

PHYSICAL BLOCK

A *sneeze* is the expulsion of air and often accompanying liquids forcibly through the nose and mouth by an involuntary convulsive action. The purpose of a sneeze is to move along an over-secretion of the nasal mucous membranes that results from a reaction to dust, odors or abrupt changes in temperature. Frequent and violent sneezing can become a frustrating problem.

EMOTIONAL BLOCK

As the purpose of a sneeze is to expel something, frequent or repetitive sneezing indicates a need to get rid of something or someone that is irritating, thwarting, or boring you. You may or may not be aware of your feelings at the time.

MENTAL BLOCK

When you have a sneezing fit, take a second to find the thought you were having just before. You'll discover that there was something annoying you and that you were probably feeling critical of it. Rather than stifling your criticism and forcing your body to drive away who or what is bothering you, assess the situation and accept what is positive about it. If, for example, you are among a group of people who are gossiping about another person and you find this uncomfortable, boring, or simply irritating, express yourself verbally and then you may choose to leave.

SPIRITUAL BLOCK AND CONCLUSION

To uncover the spiritual block that keeps you from responding to the needs of your BEING, refer to the "KEY QUESTIONS" at the back of this book. In answering

451

these questions, you will come in touch more easily and accurately with the true cause of your physical problem.

SNORING

PHYSICAL BLOCK

Snoring is the act of breathing through the open mouth during sleep so that the currents of inspired and expired air cause a vibration of the uvula and soft palate, thus giving rise to a more or less harsh sound.

EMOTIONAL BLOCK

During sleep, you are liberating yourself from the events of your waking hours. This explains why everyone dreams. If you snore, it is likely that you would have liked to make more noise during the day and repressed it. You may feel that you don't make yourself heard enough so make up for it at night. If you dare not speak up during the day for fear of rejection, you will experience rejection anyway because your snoring effectively keeps others away.

MENTAL BLOCK

It's important that you determine what is upsetting you most about snoring. If it's because it keeps others at a distance, the message your body is giving you is that you are the one actually rejecting yourself. Others are there to mirror what you are doing to yourself.

If what bothers you about snoring is that it makes a lot of noise, acknowledge that you crave attention and want to be heard. If you think others aren't listening, you may believe that you aren't important enough to be heard. If others really are not listening to you, they are reflecting your own inability to listen. Your body is telling you: *"Listen to others and others will listen to you. They'll even enjoy listening to you."*

SPIRITUAL BLOCK AND CONCLUSION

To uncover the spiritual block that keeps you from responding to the needs of your BEING, refer to the "KEY QUESTIONS" at the back of this book. In answering these questions, you will come in touch more easily and accurately with the true cause of your physical problem.

SOMNAMBULISM

See SLEEPWALKING.

SORE THROAT

See THROAT PROBLEMS.

SPINAL DISORDERS

See BACK PAIN.

453

SPITTING

PHYSICAL BLOCK

Spitting is referred to as the intentional act of projecting saliva and mucous from the mouth.

EMOTIONAL BLOCK

A person who spits too often shows contempt and rejection for someone or something. They want to spit on this person or situation. They spit out what is good for them instead of using it to better themselves.

MENTAL BLOCK

Contempt is a harmful mindset that will undermine your own health while having no effect whatsoever on the person or situation for which you feel contempt. Examine your feelings and look deeper at your fears regarding the situation. It's time for you to let go and open your heart to feel compassion and understanding. Accept that the person or situation in question has not come into your life by accident. Let go of your anger and allow the proper message to emerge. Your rejection is unnecessary and unproductive.

SPIRITUAL BLOCK AND CONCLUSION

To uncover the spiritual block that keeps you from responding to the needs of your BEING, refer to the "KEY QUESTIONS" at the back of this book. In answering

454

these questions, you will come in touch more easily and accurately with the true cause of your physical problem.

SPLEEN DISORDERS

PHYSICAL BLOCK

The *spleen* is a large organ located on the left side of the abdomen near the stomach. Its primary function is to store, filter and purify the blood and disintegrate old blood cells. It produces white blood cells, thereby playing an important role in strengthening the immune system in its battle against infection. It also constitutes an important reserve of blood and can, when needed, rapidly dispense red blood cells throughout the bloodstream to compensate for a loss of blood. The spleen is susceptible to CONTUSIONS, rupture, enlargement, TUMORS and CANCER.

EMOTIONAL BLOCK

Disorders of the spleen indicate exaggerated concern or worry to the point of obsession, which impedes joy in your life. You're keeping yourself from seeking what would make you happy. You are discouraged, overwhelmed, and have lost your will to fight. You feel emotionally empty; the reserves needed to face up to life's daily challenges are diminished. Paradoxically, you may find yourself laughing yourself sick, but you are laughing on the outside, crying on the inside.

S

MENTAL BLOCK

Any malfunction or disorder of the spleen is the body's attempt to tell you to regain contact with your inner strength and your capacity to face life with joy. To do this, you need to see life less melodramatically and more objectively - and stop worrying so much! Let it flow!

The job of your spleen is to battle the invasion of foreign bacteria, or infection, and to maintain the integrity of the blood. Thus, illness involving the spleen is a message that you must do the same: address your own integrity and combat external influences.

Allow yourself to have desires and to use the tools in your possession to build your dreams. All that remains is for you to make the decision to tap into your own inner resources. Stop believing you are not strong enough.

SPIRITUAL BLOCK AND CONCLUSION

To uncover the spiritual block that keeps you from responding to the needs of your BEING, refer to the "KEY QUESTIONS" at the back of this book. In answering these questions, you will come in touch more easily and accurately with the true cause of your physical problem.

SPLENITIS

Splenitis is an inflammation of the spleen. Remember, inflammation indicates repressed anger. See SPLEEN DISORDERS and SECTION 2.

SPRAIN

PHYSICAL BLOCK

A *sprain* is defined as an injury and laceration of the ligaments of a muscle or joint caused by the over-stretching of the ligaments beyond their capacity. The capsule of fibrous tissue that surrounds the joint may also be injured. Sprains may be mild, with tenderness and swelling but without torn ligaments. There may be partial tearing of a ligament with obvious swelling, bruising and difficulty using the joint (especially if it is weight bearing). A bad sprain is comprised of a completely torn ligament with much swelling, extreme bruising with hemorrhaging under the skin, joint instability and inability to use the joint at all. Joints affected most frequently are the ankles, knees, wrists and fingers.

EMOTIONAL BLOCK

A sprain, especially if it involves the knees or ankles, indicates you may feel obligated to go in a certain direction that you are not comfortable in going. If it involves the wrists or fingers, you probably feel obligated to *do* something you really don't want to do. You loathe taking a stand and saying *no* to others. Instead, you exceed the limits of your own comfort and sprain yourself, transferring the emotional strain to your physical body. In doing so, you have the excuse you need to get out of going where you don't want to go, doing what you don't want to do.

457

MENTAL BLOCK

Your physical suffering indicates the degree of inner suffering you're creating by insisting on seeing things your own way, i.e. according to your own rules. I suggest you exercise a little more flexibility. Instead of believing that others impose something opposite of what you want, take a closer look at their reasoning by asking them why they want you to do this thing. If you cannot respond to their expectations because you are unable to do so, talk to them about it.

Perhaps no one else is involved and you are simply overextending yourself in a direction you are really not comfortable in going. Examine your motives, acknowledge your limitations and either restrict or expand them as they apply to your true needs. Determine whether you can justify a fear that may be restricting you. When you become more flexible towards yourself and others, it will be easier for you to have your needs met.

SPIRITUAL BLOCK AND CONCLUSION

To uncover the spiritual block that keeps you from responding to the needs of your BEING, refer to the "KEY QUESTIONS" at the back of this book. In answering these questions, you will come in touch more easily and accurately with the true cause of your physical problem.

SQUINTING

See STRABISMUS.

STERILITY

PHYSICAL BLOCK

Sterility may affect the male or female and renders either incapable of reproduction, or procreation. In the female, it is characterized by a lack of ovulation or an inability to produce fertilizable eggs. In the male, it can result from inadequate or infertile sperm production or poor motility of sperm. It is not to be confused with *impotence*, which is simply the inability to achieve erection.

EMOTIONAL BLOCK

On several occasions, I have seen couples that were diagnosed as infertile having one or more babies. I have also witnessed couples, unable to conceive, that were deemed to have no physical obstacles to conception.

For some people, sterility is a lesson they were meant to experience in this lifetime. It may be that their desire for a child is misguided by a belief system that says it is "normal" to have children, or perhaps their parents are anxious to become grandparents. Many women with difficulty accepting their femininity feel that having children will validate their femininity. In this case, sterility may be a lesson in learning to love themselves completely and wholeheartedly, without having a child.

For other couples, although the desire may be strong to have a child, there is fear about some aspect of the experience that is overriding the desire. Sterility becomes, there-

459

fore, a subconscious birth control method. In this case, the desire to have a child must not be abandoned, but the fear, which is the real block, must be addressed.

Sterility often seems to occur in people who feel useless or see themselves as unproductive in other areas as well.

MENTAL BLOCK

To determine whether or not your sterility is due to a life lesson or whether it is due to unconscious fear, ask yourself the KEY QUESTIONS you will find at the end of the book. If you are a woman, have you known someone who had a difficult time in childbirth? What did you learn from your own parents regarding having children? Are you afraid of losing someone or something by having a child? Your trim figure, perhaps?

Fear that has grown from some past experience or belief system probably doesn't apply at this time and may not apply at any time for some people. You must decide which will win - your fear or your desire. Your life is your own to live as you like, thus the decision you make must be your own and not influenced by outside forces. You need only to be ready to accept the consequences of your decision.

Also, talk with those who know you well and ask them whether or not they feel you are an unproductive person. I'm sure you'll discover that your perception of your own productivity is not the way others see it.

SPIRITUAL BLOCK AND CONCLUSION

To uncover the spiritual block that keeps you from responding to the needs of your BEING, refer to the "KEY QUESTIONS" at the back of this book. In answering these questions, you will come in touch more easily and accurately with the true cause of your physical problem.

STOMACH ACHE

See UPSET STOMACH.

STOMACH DISORDERS

PHYSICAL BLOCK

The *stomach* is one of the most important organs of digestion. Stomach acid breaks down ingested food and liquefies it so that its nutrients can be assimilated by the body. Some gastrointestinal disorders involving the stomach include INDIGESTION, VOMITING, STOMACH ULCER, HEARTBURN, GASTRITIS, HEMORRHAGE, and CANCER. Refer to your specific problem in this book and read the following paragraphs.

EMOTIONAL BLOCK

All stomach disorders are the manifestation of a failure or refusal to "stomach" a person or situation you fear or cannot tolerate. You resist new ideas, especially those of others. It is also difficult for you to deal with someone or

461

something that contradicts your plans, habits or way of doing things. You criticize easily (inwardly) and this prevents you from letting go.

MENTAL BLOCK

Your stomach is telling you to let go and allow things to unfold as they should. Accept that you cannot control others and stop resisting their ideas. Rather than wallowing in a sense of powerlessness because you can't manipulate the people and situations around you, use your energies to create the life you want. Become more aware of your power to change your own life and have confidence in others to do the same. In doing so, you will understand that your body also knows what it is capable of and you will allow your stomach to do the job it was meant to do.

It is not necessary for you to instruct your body - it knows how to digest your food. The same holds true for your friends and family; they each have their own agenda and their own perspective on life. Note that the stomach is situated in close proximity to the heart. A heart that is lovingly accepting of others and of their differences will have a calming affect on the stomach, in turn facilitating healthy digestion, On the other hand, thoughts such as *"it's not fair...it's wrong...what an idiot"* and so on will block your spiritual growth, as your stomach blocks the digestion of your food. By becoming more tolerant of others and going with the flow, you will become more physically tolerant of the foods you ingest.

SPIRITUAL BLOCK AND CONCLUSION

To uncover the spiritual block that keeps you from responding to the needs of your BEING, refer to the "KEY QUESTIONS" at the back of this book. In answering these questions, you will come in touch more easily and accurately with the true cause of your physical problem.

STOMACH ULCER

An *ulcer* is defined as a festering lesion in skin or mucous membrane resulting in destruction of the tissue. It is also defined as something that corrupts. An ulcer that results in a hole in the gastric lining (the wall of the stomach) indicates a weakening of the natural defenses of the lining against powerful digestive acids. The physical cause is a lack of sufficient mucous on the stomach lining that prevents the stomach from digesting itself. Symptoms include localized and painful cramping. See STOMACH DISORDERS and realize that stomach ulcers can develop when you feel defenseless and intimidated by others. You have an underlying feeling of powerlessness that can only be resolved by reacquainting yourself with your innate defenses. Know that in altering your perception of others and of events, you will know how to defend yourself.

S

STONES (CALCULUS)

PHYSICAL BLOCK

Stones are crystalline structures made of calcium salts and organic matter. They can be as small as a grain of sand or larger than a golf ball, and are found in the kidneys or gall bladder. They may produce no symptoms or they may result in intense and sudden pain in the upper abdomen that may last several hours and be accompanied by NAUSEA and VOMITING.

EMOTIONAL BLOCK

Depending on the whereabouts of the stone, the metaphysical cause can differ. I suggest you refer to KIDNEY or GALLBLADDER DISORDERS for better accuracy. Metaphysically speaking, an accumulation of bile that crystallizes, forming stones, is the result of noxious and bitter thoughts that are usually rooted in jealousy and envy. These thoughts are carried around, unresolved and unexpressed, over a period of years. A rigid person, one who doesn't let himself feel what he feels, will be apt to have stones.

MENTAL BLOCK

A stone formed in the body is also known as a *calculus*. By thinking one way and acting another, you are making a grave *error in calculation*. For example: you want to go ahead but you don't listen to your own inner voice, you listen to others or to your fear, calculating the outcome of any given situation without taking into consideration that your intuition knows best. Your failure to listen to your self results in dissatisfaction. You must listen to your inner voice and do what you want to do.

SPIRITUAL BLOCK AND CONCLUSION

To uncover the spiritual block that keeps you from responding to the needs of your BEING, refer to the "KEY QUESTIONS" at the back of this book. In answering these questions, you will come in touch more easily and accurately with the true cause of your physical problem.

STRABISMUS

PHYSICAL BLOCK

Strabismus, also known as *lazy eye*, *walleye*, *cross-eye*, or *squint* is caused by a lack of muscle coordination between the eyes, causing the eyes to point in different directions. The eyes are unable to focus simultaneously on a single point.

EMOTIONAL BLOCK

Research has indicated that strabismus is often associated with difficulty in balancing the two hemispheres of the brain and having them function collaboratively. There is an imbalance that results in a personality that is either overly rational or overly sensitive, causing you to be unable to see things as they really are. You misread what's going on around you because you either *feel* things based

465

on the simplest feelings, or you *rationalize* based on information in your memory banks.

Variations on strabismus have various implications as follows:

The *left eye wandering upward* denotes an extremely sentimental and emotional personality.

The *right eye wandering upward* denotes an emotional intellect, someone who easily lets their thoughts wander.

The *left eye wandering outward* denotes a purely instinctive activity. Your great sensitivity commands your actions, which end up contradicting what you had said you would do. This is unintentional (not ill intended).

The *right eye wandering outward* denotes an awkward or clumsy relationship between the mental aspect and the object being viewed. This translates as an intellectual effort to compensate for what would otherwise be normal eye movement. The intellectual mind tends to go in circles and there is a predisposition to depression.

The *left eye wandering inward* denotes an inferiority complex due to fear. You rely too heavily on your sensitivity, forgetting a large part of yourself.

The *right eye wandering inward* denotes great susceptibility. Thoughts and attention are directed too much toward yourself. Generally, you tend to be combative and vindictive.

The *left eye wandering upward and outward* denotes an irrational personality, a daydreamer, who has lost all concept of time and tends to be ungrounded.

The *right eye wandering upward and outward* denotes an irrational, undisciplined and even amoral mind.

MENTAL BLOCK

As strabismus develops during childhood or adolescence, it is easily deduced that the psychological block results from childhood or adolescent experiences. If the wandering is in the right eye, it's likely the problem is connected with your studies, thereby influenced by your school life or the way someone wants you to learn. If it's in the left eye, the problem is linked more closely with your emotional life, therefore relating to your parents or other family members.

It is important to undertake an exercise program through *Brain Gym*[1] in order to help realign the functioning of the two hemispheres of your brain. It is also vital to carefully examine the decisions you made during your childhood in regard to the emotional blocks above. Accept the idea that you alone made the decision to refuse to see things as they really were. Understand, however, that you are no longer that same person and you are free to make new decisions that will help you see things more accurately, both inside and outside of you.

---

[1]   Book on Educational Kinesiology *Brain Gym* by Paul E. Dennison, Gail E. Dennison

SPIRITUAL BLOCK AND CONCLUSION

To uncover the spiritual block that keeps you from responding to the needs of your BEING, refer to the "KEY QUESTIONS" at the back of this book. In answering these questions, you will come in touch more easily and accurately with the true cause of your physical problem.

STRETCH MARKS

PHYSICAL BLOCK

A *stretch mark* is a shiny line on the skin of the abdomen, breasts, thighs, or buttocks caused by the stretching and weakening of elastic tissues as a result of pregnancy or obesity, for example.

EMOTIONAL BLOCK

As stretch marks are the result of rupture in the elastic tissue of the skin, the message your body is sending you is that you need to be more flexible, less rigid in your dealings with others. You need not create a rigid armor to protect yourself. If you are pregnant and are developing stretch marks, you probably tend to impose rigid expectations upon yourself. Learn to be yourself and honor your weaknesses and limitations.

MENTAL BLOCK

Your stretch marks most likely appeared at a time when you thought you had to put up a good front, be strong. It

468

was important to you at the time to mask your fears and your feelings, so you adopted an inflexibility that you thought would show your strength. Your body is telling you to let go of your rigidity; your way of thinking is not helping you. To find out in what part of your life your rigidity takes over, refer to the area of the body most affected by stretch marks and discover that area's purpose. I also suggest you read the explanation in SKIN DISORDERS.

SPIRITUAL BLOCK AND CONCLUSION

To uncover the spiritual block that keeps you from responding to the needs of your BEING, refer to the "KEY QUESTIONS" at the back of this book. In answering these questions, you will come in touch more easily and accurately with the true cause of your physical problem.

STUPOR

A *stupor* is marked by cessation or great decrease of mental activity or feeling; it suggests a benumbed or dazed state. See NUMBNESS but realize that this is more serious than a simple numbness and that the cessation of physical and intellectual activity can happen when you feel the urge to vacate your body.

STUTTERING

PHYSICAL BLOCK

Stuttering is a speech disorder characterized by involuntary hesitation, prolongation or repetition of sounds. Typically it begins between ages two and five, while a child is mastering the basics of speech. It can appear in older children but often disappears by adolescence.

EMOTIONAL BLOCK

Stuttering is a manifestation of fear of expressing one's wishes and needs, especially when it comes to expressing them to an authority figure.

MENTAL BLOCK

If you suffer from stuttering, it's high time you realized that it is your birthright to have needs and desires and to be happy. Listen to your heart, not your head and know that you are worthy. It is not necessary to justify your needs and desires to others. You can have what you want; besides, you and only you will live with the consequences of your choices. Accept responsibility for your life and for the choices you make.

If you find others overbearing when they speak up for themselves, realize that you are misinterpreting their behavior. IT'S OKAY TO EXPRESS YOURSELF! Stand up for yourself. Be clear about your needs and express them freely and openly. Accept that they are valid and you will become more comfortable in sharing your thoughts and feelings with others.

SPIRITUAL BLOCK AND CONCLUSION

To uncover the spiritual block that keeps you from responding to the needs of your BEING, refer to the "KEY QUESTIONS" at the back of this book. In answering these questions, you will come in touch more easily and accurately with the true cause of your physical problem.

STYE

PHYSICAL BLOCK

A *stye* is an infection of the gland at the base of the eyelash. Symptoms include initial pain and redness, followed by a small, swollen roundish area on the margin of the eyelid. Once the abscess breaks open, pus is discharged. Sties have a tendency to reoccur secondary to digestive disorders.

EMOTIONAL BLOCK

Sties occur frequently if you tend to be emotional, indicating that you have difficulty getting past what you see in front of you. You block what you are seeing and would prefer to observe only what you like. You tend to want to control what goes on around you and feel angry, often accusing others of not seeing things the way you do.

471

MENTAL BLOCK

The presence of a stye is a signal from the body for you to develop more tolerance for what you see around you. Although you may not agree with what you see, understand that it is impossible to control everything; you can only master yourself. If you allow yourself to let go and to look at others through the eyes of love, you will begin to see and to accept their differences and become a warmer person.

SPIRITUAL BLOCK AND CONCLUSION

To uncover the spiritual block that keeps you from responding to the needs of your BEING, refer to the "KEY QUESTIONS" at the back of this book. In answering these questions, you will come in touch more easily and accurately with the true cause of your physical problem.

SUFFOCATION

The term suffocation is sometimes employed synonymously with *asphyxia*. It signifies asphyxia induced by obstruction of the respiration. See ASPHYXIA.

SUICIDE

PHYSICAL BLOCK

Suicide is the act of voluntarily causing one's own death in order to be done with living.

EMOTIONAL BLOCK

It's obvious that a person who decides to commit suicide believes it is the only option remaining to them. It is their last resort. Most people who attempt suicide, however, do not succeed. What follows concerns these people.

Those with suicidal tendencies are looking for attention or someone to take care of them. They often play the role of the victim and thrive on the pity of others, as they pity themselves and their lot in life. Because they strongly believe they are victims, their lives reflect victimization and they are constantly running into difficulties that give credence to their views.

If you have a tendency to be suicidal, it is imperative that you go through the process of forgiveness. You are experiencing deep-seated bitterness and, often, hatred toward those you feel did not take adequate care of you in your childhood. You have no respect for your own limitations and want everything right now. A tremendous lack of patience, trust and courage underly your personality. You need to learn to reach your goals gradually, one step at a time.

MENTAL BLOCK

If you find you often entertain suicidal thoughts, or if you've already made attempts and find yourself still here, the message is clear that **you want to live**. Your view of life, however, is not healthy and balanced. I suggest you devise a new game plan. Get some help from someone who can be objective; that is, someone who does not feel responsible for your happiness and who can shed some light on a new path through your dark world.

Live one day at a time and learn to respect your limitations. You must get back in touch with your ability to create your life. Know that it is **your life** and you can do with it what you wish. Know also that life is eternal and the soul immortal. If you choose to end your life before fulfilling your purpose here, understand that you will have to return and start all over again. **You alone** will have to assume the consequences of your decision. Human beings devise various methods of escape in order to sidestep taking responsibility for their own lives. Suicide is the ultimate escape from responsibility.

If you are reading this because you have lost a loved one to suicide, understand that you must not judge them. They felt they had reached the boundaries of their own limitations and chose their own methods of escape. Millions of people find other means of escape - in alcohol, food, illegal or prescription drugs, work, etc. and the end result is the same.

Accept that, although your loved one's physical body is no longer here, their soul lives on. When it decides to re-enter the physical world and reincarnate, the suicide they experienced in this lifetime may help them in some way. There is something to be learned from everything. As for you, your lesson is to let go and realize that no one belongs to anyone else.

SPIRITUAL BLOCK AND CONCLUSION

To uncover the spiritual block that keeps you from responding to the needs of your BEING, refer to the "KEY QUESTIONS" at the back of this book. In answering these questions, you will come in touch more easily and accurately with the true cause of your physical problem

SUPRARENAL GLANDS

See ADRENAL GLAND PROBLEMS.

SWAMP FEVER

See MALARIA.

SWELLING

See EDEMA.

SYNCOPE

See FAINTING.

SYPHILIS

Syphilis is a chronic infectious bacterial disease that is usually transmitted by sexual contact. See VENEREAL DISEASE.

TACHYCARDIA

Tachycardia is a rapid heart rate, especially one above 100 beats per minute in an adult. See ANXIETY and AGORAPHOBIA (which can trigger tachycardia).

TAENIASIS

Taeniasis is marked by the infestation of a parasite known as a *taenia* or *tapeworm*, which typically takes over the digestive system. It indicates that what has infested you on a psychological level has taken over. You have become full of yourself, and in doing so, become even more lonely. There is ultimately no room for anyone else in your life. See PARASITES.

TAILBONE

See COCCYX.

TAPEWORM

See PARASITES.

T

TEARS (Lack of)

PHYSICAL BLOCK

Tears are drops of clear, salty fluid that lubricate the eye and eyelid. They also protect and supply nutrients to the cornea. Dryness, irritation, burning, and varying degrees of discomfort are caused by a failure to produce adequate tearing. Infrequent blinking aggravates the condition.

EMOTIONAL BLOCK

If you suffer from inadequate tearing, it may be an indication that you are trying to hide your sensitivity. You fear being thought of as weak if you are too polite or gentle. You may also be keeping an eye out for danger and refuse to blink in case you are caught off guard and taken advantage of. You try to see everything around you in order to know what others need.

MENTAL BLOCK

This condition is a signal from your body that you need to redefine the words *gentle* and *polite.* Gentle does not mean weak. You need not fear that gentleness will cause you to overstep your boundaries or those by which you protect your loved ones. Determine whether or not the fears that keep you on the lookout are justified and still relevant.

SPIRITUAL BLOCK AND CONCLUSION

To uncover the spiritual block that keeps you from responding to the needs of your BEING, refer to the "KEY QUESTIONS" at the back of this book. In answering these questions, you will come in touch more easily and accurately with the true cause of your physical problem.

TEETH PROBLEMS

PHYSICAL BLOCK

The following conditions are considered problematic: pain that comes from decayed or broken teeth, grinding of the teeth or crooked teeth.

EMOTIONAL BLOCK

As teeth are used to pulverize and pound food, *teeth problems* indicate difficulty pondering new information, ideas or situations. Hence, problems with the teeth indicate fear of making incorrect decisions. Teeth are also used to bite; therefore, a person with a tooth problem might feel incapable of defending himself.

According to Dr. Michèle Caffin, a prominent French oral surgeon: *The eight teeth of the upper right side are linked with the desire to express one's self outwardly*; a problem with one of these teeth indicates difficulty in finding one's place in the outside world. *The eight teeth in the upper left side are linked with the desire to show what a person carries inside*; a problem with one of these teeth therefore expresses difficulty in fulfilling one's desire to be. *The eight teeth on the lower right side are tied in with the solidification of something, such as work;* a problem with one of these teeth therefore indicates a problem with making concrete plans or getting one's self on solid ground. *The eight teeth on the lower left side are linked with the realization of a person's emotional sensitivity;* a problem with one of these teeth indicates lack of emotional recognition within the family. The message from *misaligned teeth* is also related to the above mentioned.

MENTAL BLOCK

The right side of the body controls the male aspect and is linked to our relationship with our father. Dental problems on the right side indicate unresolved father issues. Start to see your father in a different light—interact differently with him. Dental problems on the left side, however, are an indication of unresolved issues with your mother.

The upper incisors (four front teeth) represent the spot you want to occupy in relation to your parents, whose position is represented by the lower incisors. Dental problems in this area indicate an inability to sink your teeth into what you are doing in order to achieve the outcomes you desire. Learn to look at events as they are. If need be, accept the help of others to sharpen your discernment. Instead of having a grudge on someone, focus on what you want and reconnect with your power that will help you defend yourself more efficiently.

If the incisors are worn or eroded, you are letting people close to you wear you down. If you can identify with this, it is because you have low self-worth and difficulty expressing yourself. Don't be so critical of yourself. You also want others to change. The best way to stop *wearing yourself out* is to love and accept yourself and those close to you.

Bruxism, or grinding of the teeth, generally occurs during sleep as the mind ruminates about all the anger and tension that you kept inside during your waking hours. But this is only a temporary release. You must decide to handle this anger before it becomes a bigger problem than simple bruxism. To keep this pent-up rage from progressing to more serious physical problems, refer to the back of this book and follow the recommended steps of forgiveness.

SPIRITUAL BLOCK AND CONCLUSION

To uncover the spiritual block that keeps you from responding to the needs of your BEING, refer to the "KEY QUESTIONS" at the back of this book. In answering these questions, you will come in touch more easily and accurately with the true cause of your physical problem.

T

TENDONITIS

PHYSICAL BLOCK

Tendonitis is the inflammation of a tendon (which connects muscle to bone). Tendons can be overextended to the point of tearing, which causes acute pain and a sharp

481

cracking sound. Tendonitis may progress to degeneration of the tendon.

EMOTIONAL BLOCK

Tendonitis indicates that you have recently repressed your anger. You tend to avoid a certain situation out of fear of a *break-up*. Refer to the pertinent listing of the area of the body affected by tendonitis for corresponding metaphysical implications. For example, if tendonitis is experienced in the hand, determine what it is that you are avoiding doing with that hand that could cause disruption or break-up for which you would feel guilty.

MENTAL BLOCK

Your body is telling you that it's no longer necessary to believe that you can do what you want *only* when it pleases others, especially someone in particular. Your fear of separation or break-up is possibly the fruit of your imagination. Talk openly and honestly with this person and determine whether or not your fear is justified. Share with them what you want and what would meet your needs.

If your suppressed anger is directed at yourself, it's because you are not listening to your heart and not addressing your own needs. Although anger seems to be caused by external sources, often, on inspection, the reality is quite different. You discover that you are really only angry with yourself. See SECTION 2.

SPIRITUAL BLOCK AND CONCLUSION

To uncover the spiritual block that keeps you from responding to the needs of your BEING, refer to the "KEY QUESTIONS" at the back of this book. In answering these questions, you will come in touch more easily and accurately with the true cause of your physical problem

TESTICULAR PROBLEMS

The *testicles* are the two sperm-producing glands suspended in a protective pouch of skin beneath the penis. The left testicle generally lies lower than the right. As their function mirrors that of the ovaries in the female, refer to OVARIAN DISORDERS and replace the word *woman* with *man*.

TETANUS

Tetanus is a serious infectious disease that is transferred by toxins released in the body from invasion by a ground-dwelling bacteriam (bacillus *Clostridium tetani)*. This bacterium enters the body through an open wound, usually a puncture wound (for example those caused by metal nails, wood splinters, etc). Tetanus can cause convulsions and serious brain damage and can be lethal in children. Symptoms include lockjaw and a facial expression that causes you to look possessed.

It is possible that the physical wound has opened up a deeper psychological wound, reawakening sorrow or a re-

483

pressed hatred concerning another person. See the steps to true forgiveness at the back of the book. Only forgiveness will have a lasting and effective result. See CONVUL-SIONS.

THIGH PROBLEMS

PHYSICAL BLOCK

Generally, it is hard to give a diagnostic concerning discomfort in the *thigh*. There can be several physical causes. Discomfort is usually the result of muscle spasm; if so, refer to CRAMPS.

EMOTIONAL BLOCK

As the thigh is the powerful moving force of the leg and is also connected to the pelvic area, its metaphysical significance corresponds to passion and desire. The thighs also contain major arteries and veins that directly feed the extremities and return blood to the heart with tremendous force. Symbolically, blood circulation is related to the circulation of joy, therefore pain in the thigh indicates restraining of the life force and blocking of vitality and joy. Fear of going forward, of enjoying life to its fullest is the underlying psychological cause.

MENTAL BLOCK

Don't take life so seriously. Get in touch with your inner child and take a stand concerning your own needs. Pain in the thigh is your body's way to bring attention to your need to play and have fun with a simplicity that integrates the needs of your childlike and adult selves. Your body is urging you to go forward in the knowledge that you are the master of your own destiny and no longer the echo of your father's or your mother's voice.

SPIRITUAL BLOCK AND CONCLUSION

To uncover the spiritual block that keeps you from responding to the needs of your BEING, refer to the "KEY QUESTIONS" at the back of this book. In answering these questions, you will come in touch more easily and accurately with the true cause of your physical problem.

THINNESS

PHYSICAL BLOCK

As opposed to extreme weight loss or emaciation, which are pathological, *thinness* is neither an illness nor a disease. Many people complain about their slenderness from an aesthetic point of view. Just as obesity is often the outcome of psychological pain, so thinness can develop as the result of emotional and mental disharmony.

EMOTIONAL BLOCK

If you are very thin, you will probably find that you reject yourself, feel insignificant compared to others, and are afraid of rejection. You often want to disappear and tend to be *delicate* and self-effacing with others. Your fear of rejection has become an obstacle in terms of your behav-

485

ior, in that you act in ways contrary to your own needs or may not act at all. You may tend to become dependent on others or live vicariously through them. You are in a perpetual state of need and feel you never receive enough care and attention.

MENTAL BLOCK

If you've been overly thin since early childhood, it indicates a deep-seated belief that you can be abandoned or rejected. It may be that you developed this mindset at birth because you were unwanted by one or both of your parents or that they would have preferred a child of the opposite sex. Determine whether or not it was you they were rejecting or if it may have been the life they were living at the time that they were at odds with.

Even if your sense of rejection was justified and others were actually inattentive, understand that they were simply expressing their own limitations and that it is not a personal affront to you. Remember that the word *ignore* stems from the word *ignorance* and those who ignored you knew no better at the time. Begin NOW to treat yourself like someone you care about. Allow love to flow from within you and nurture yourself. You need only to change your belief system; you have all the tools necessary to build a substantial and fulfilling life. Experiencing the rejection of others in the past is simply that: rejection that you experienced *in the past*. Only you can decide whether you want to keep reliving that experience to the detriment of your own future or whether you'd rather get on with your life with balance and confidence, putting the past where it belongs. Your choice is your responsibility and the results your reward.

SPIRITUAL BLOCK AND CONCLUSION

To uncover the spiritual block that keeps you from responding to the needs of your BEING, refer to the "KEY QUESTIONS" at the back of this book. In answering these questions, you will come in touch more easily and accurately with the true cause of your physical problem.

THROAT PROBLEMS

PHYSICAL BLOCK

The *throat* is the section of the digestive tract forming a passage between the back of the mouth and the esophagus. It is also an aero-digestive crossroads in the form of a chimney, connecting the nasal opening with the larynx. The throat plays a number of essential roles during speaking, breathing and swallowing.

EMOTIONAL BLOCK

As mentioned, the throat is a psychologically multi-functional part of the body, as it is physically multi-functional. If you have pain in your throat, accompanied by difficulty in breathing, it is symbolic of having trouble breathing life in. See LUNG DISORDERS.

If pain in the throat causes you to lose your voice, see LARYNGITIS.

487

Tightening or constriction of the throat indicates you may be feeling restricted, under pressure, or grabbed by the throat to say or do something.

Pain upon swallowing is the body's way of asking you outright, *"What person or situation can't you swallow?"* Perhaps there is some specific emotional trauma that you are having difficulty in getting past or are simply unable to swallow an attitude of a certain person or the outcome of a situation. Inflammation of the tissues of the throat indicates repressed anger and self-directed aggression. Do you find yourself playing the part of the victim?

MENTAL BLOCK

As the throat is the center of creativity, it is imperative that you give yourself permission to design your own life the way you need to live it. Experience life without guilt, retribution, or fear you are a trouble to others. Learn to accept openly and with love all that you create, including any decisions you generate. You will then be able to connect with your individuality.

Here is an example taken from my own life. I developed a sore throat at the most inopportune time: I was just beginning a series of public appearances that was to last for five days. This was quite a workload, considering that it was over and above my other engagements. I assumed my body was telling me that I had taken on too much and that I was simply feeling sorry for myself. In reality, my body was reminding me that I was the one who had planned this itinerary and that I had to take full responsibility. I decided to forge ahead to conduct the seminars from a perspective of love and acceptance. Even though there were a lot of them in a short period of time, I had no further problem. The sore throat disappeared.

It is interesting to note that the throat forms a passage between the heart and the head. In metaphysical terms, between self-love and the I AM. When you create your life in accordance with your true needs, you connect with your I AM and open the channel for abundance. Giving yourself permission to live your life in alignment with your true nature lights a fire under your creativity. Disregard what you consider "abnormal" when you decide something that might be inconvenient to others.

If you feel *strangled*, it is only by your own perception. Detach yourself from the influence of others and from your need to control them. Save your energy for creating a delicious life for yourself. You'll find it easy to swallow!

SPIRITUAL BLOCK AND CONCLUSION

To uncover the spiritual block that keeps you from responding to the needs of your BEING, refer to the "KEY QUESTIONS" at the back of this book. In answering these questions, you will come in touch more easily and accurately with the true cause of your physical problem.

THROMBOSIS

Thrombosis is the formation of a clot anywhere in the circulatory system, whether the veins, arteries or in the chambers of the heart itself.

489

Thrombosis indicates that there is something in your life blocking your life force, or your *joie de vivre*. The need to let your life flow as it should is critical. Determine whether a person or situation is blocking you; do not blame the person or situation for your troubles, but alter your perception. See ARTERIES and BLOOD DISORDERS.

THRUSH

Thrush is the common name for *oral candidiasis*, or yeast infection of the mouth. It occurs most often in infants and children, characterized by small whitish eruptions on the mouth, throat, and tongue, and usually accompanied by fever, colic, and diarrhea. See MOUTH PROBLEMS.

THUMB PROBLEMS

See FINGER DISORDERS.

THYMUS GLAND DISORDERS

PHYSICAL BLOCK

The *thymus gland* is comprised of largely lymphoid tissue that functions in the development of the body's immune system. It is located in the upper chest, at the base of the neck.

490

EMOTIONAL AND MENTAL BLOCK

See HEART DISORDERS but also the following:

This gland is the link between the physical body and the *heart chakra*. Disorders in the thymus gland indicate a blockage of energy, or closure, of love. It's interesting to note that the thymus reaches its maximum development at about puberty and then undergoes a gradual process of in-volution resulting in a slow decline of immune function throughout adulthood. This atrophy corresponds closely with the inability to love ourselves as adults.

I am convinced that a few generations hence, science will be able to confirm that this gland has finally stopped atro-phying in adults, resulting in a greater immunity against auto-immune diseases such as AIDS. The word immunity means *sheltered from* or *free of*.

Autoimmune disorders, therefore, indicate an inability, from lack of self-love, to defend or protect yourself from the barrage of daily life. When human beings are finally able to love themselves unconditionally, great immunity will emerge on the level of collective humanity. This has been the lesson taught by all the great masters over the centuries.

T

491

THYROID GLAND DISORDERS

PHYSICAL BLOCK

The *thyroid gland* is a butterfly-shaped endocrine gland in the neck that is found on both sides of the trachea windpipe. It secretes the hormone thyroxin that controls the rate of metabolism. Disorders are usually HYPERTHYROIDISM (excessive functional activity of the thyroid gland) or HYPOTHYROIDISM (a deficiency of thyroid activity).

EMOTIONAL BLOCK

The thyroid gland links the physical body to the *throat chakra*. This chakra is linked to the will, the ability to make decisions based upon needs and, therefore, creating a lifestyle true to those needs. This is the thrust of psychological and spiritual growth. This center of energy is also directly linked with the *sacral chakra* (associated with creativity located in the genitals area). Disorders in either chakra will disrupt the functioning of the other. See OVARIAN DISORDERS (if you're a woman) or TESTICULAR PROBLEMS (if you're a man).

Over-activity of the thyroid gland, or *hyperthyroidism*, is your body's way of telling you that you are too busy expending energy outward. Although you want to slow down and modify your life, you will not allow yourself to do so because you feel obliged to engineer the lives of those you love. You don't take the time to determine your own needs prior to taking action. You seem to feel you always have something to prove and need the validation of others in order to feel loved. You have high expectations of yourself and of others. You live in constant fear of not being able to act fast enough, or of having your hands tied. Everything must be done right away. Your actions are often based on poor judgment or misplaced motivation, in other words, not according to your true needs. You will say whatever it takes, even lie, to get things moving.

Under-activity of the thyroid gland, or *hypothyroidism*, is your body's way of telling you that you want to be more active but that you don't make enough requests in order to get what you deeply want. You are afraid before even getting started. You are certain that you will not be quick enough to get what you want and, as such, have lost contact with your I WANT. These two small words harness a tremendous creative force. They are the fuel necessary to propel you toward what you want.

It is said that the throat chakra is the chakra of *abundance*. Why? Because by listening to the voice of your true needs, you honor your I AM, and from this point of balance and harmony, there can only be abundance on all levels: happiness, health, love and prosperity.

MENTAL BLOCK

If your thyroid gland is *overactive*, you are receiving an important message to live in moderation, to take the time to discover your true needs so that you can take the steps to create the life you deeply desire. There is no need to be continually doing in order to validate yourself, to feel important, recognized or loved. Let go a little and stop approaching every situation as an emergency. I'm sure that, once you return to your natural rhythm and acknowledge and fulfill your own needs, life will become not only more pleasant for you, but for those around you. As the thyroid manages physical growth, once you've learned to use your I WANT only in reference to your own needs, you will grow on a soul level. You will begin to realize what you were born to do.

If your thyroid gland is *under-active*, you must realize that you alone can bring it back to its natural, fully functioning state. Let go of the detrimental belief that you are unable to engineer your own life and must not make any requests. It's time you acknowledged your right to a full and satisfying life. If you had trouble asking for anything as a child, it's time to change. You now need only answer to yourself.

It's possible that you also need to go through a process of forgiveness concerning those who made you feel insecure about achieving your goals. They may have led you to believe you weren't capable or that your dreams were unreachable. Understand that these people were in your life to teach you a lesson about overcoming fear, to strengthen your resolve and actually *fuel* your determination to create. Refer to the steps to true forgiveness outlined at the back of the book.

SPIRITUAL BLOCK AND CONCLUSION

To uncover the spiritual block that keeps you from responding to the needs of your BEING, refer to the "KEY QUESTIONS" at the back of this book. In answering

these questions, you will come in touch more easily and accurately with the true cause of your physical problem

---
TINEA

See RINGWORM.

TINNITUS

PHYSICAL BLOCK

Tinnitus is a ringing, whistling or buzzing inside the ear that is not audible to anyone else. The sounds are not a hallucination, but are directly linked to one's center of balance.

EMOTIONAL BLOCK

Tinnitus occurs when there is too much noise going on in your mind. Have you allowed yourself to become so distracted with what is rattling around in your head that you are unable to hear what is really going on around you? Those suffering from tinnitus often feel a loss of balance and fear losing self-control. They are capable of hiding their fears and want to give the impression that they are well balanced. Tinnitus often occurs in people who berate themselves for not "walking their talk" or "practicing what they preach."

495

MENTAL BLOCK

It is imperative that you realize that you are confused between your intellect and your intuition. What you believe to be your intuition is merely a trick being played on you by your ego. You want so much to present yourself as courageous and well balanced that you fool yourself into thinking you are in control, rather than trusting enough to surrender to your intuitive self. Instead, you lose your balance, tripping through the cacophony of your tangled thoughts. Allow yourself to listen to criticism about yourself, knowing you have the freedom to do with them as you wish.

Make a conscious effort to listen to what is coming from outside, even the opinions of others, so that you can make informed decisions and communicate effectively. Remember, you don't always have to practice what you preach, but if you want to, you'll find a way that will suit you.

SPIRITUAL BLOCK AND CONCLUSION

To uncover the spiritual block that keeps you from responding to the needs of your BEING, refer to the "KEY QUESTIONS" at the back of this book. In answering these questions, you will come in touch more easily and accurately with the true cause of your physical problem.

TIREDNESS

See FATIGUE

TOE PROBLEMS

PHYSICAL BLOCK

The *toes* are vertebral extensions of the foot. Common problems experienced in the toes include *injury* (ACCIDENT), *deformation, calluses, ingrown toenail,* FRACTURE, CRAMPS, and CORNS.

EMOTIONAL BLOCK

As feet facilitate movement through life, the toes represent your perception of the details of this progression. Most problems experienced with the toes prevent you from walking freely and with ease, indicating a manifestation of fear linked to moving forward, or of the future. You are overly concerned with details that prevent you from seeing the larger picture in a given situation. You can't see the forest for the trees. As a result, you become out of touch with your desires and bit by bit, lose momentum.

The big toe is the one most often affected, as it takes the brunt of abuse. Since the big toe gives direction to the others, problems with it represent regret or guilt about the direction taken or the direction you want to take. Such guilt will impact on your future.

Refer to FRACTURE, CRAMP, CORNS, or ACCIDENT.

MENTAL BLOCK

The discomfort in your toe is a message that you need to get back in touch with what you want for your future and not allow yourself to become mired in details. Understand that it is perfectly normal to be afraid of the unknown and that only through action will you be able to determine what is beneficial to you. When you are tangled up in details, you impede your progress and block yourself from achieving your goals, usually out of fear. Whatever your goals, any regret or guilt you are carrying will serve only to magnify your fears. Remember: there are no mistakes; there are only experiences that will be useful in your future.

SPIRITUAL BLOCK AND CONCLUSION

To uncover the spiritual block that keeps you from responding to the needs of your BEING, refer to the "KEY QUESTIONS" at the back of this book. In answering these questions, you will come in touch more easily and accurately with the true cause of your physical problem.

TONGUE DISORDERS

PHYSICAL BLOCK

The *tongue* is the fleshy, muscular organ attached to the bottom of the mouth that is the main interpreter of taste; it moves to facilitate chewing, swallowing and the formation of speech. Taste buds on the tongue allow the differentiation between sweet and salty, sour and acidic.

Disorders of the tongue include: *biting the tongue, lesions, burning, swelling* (EDEMA), NUMBNESS, ULCERS, and CANCER.

EMOTIONAL BLOCK

The majority of tongue disorders are connected with guilt about what you've been eating. It may also be that you are punishing yourself for not holding your tongue when you feel you should have been more discreet. Since the tongue serves a number of purposes, refer to the questions listed at the end of this book for better understanding.

If biting the tongue has become a chronic habit or even if you find yourself doing it occasionally, as you become aware of it, see if you are feeling guilty about what has just been said or about what you are about to say.

MENTAL BLOCK

If you are often self-critical about your eating patterns or berate yourself for overindulgence, digest this: *"It isn't what goes into the mouth that is truly harmful, but rather that which comes out."* No matter what form your guilt is taking, your discomfort is a warning that your belief system is doing you harm. Your perception of right and wrong is no longer valid or applicable. Rather than relying on an outdated or invalid belief system, learn to live through your experiences; in doing so, you will develop an unconditional self-love that will allow you to express yourself freely.

T

SPIRITUAL BLOCK AND CONCLUSION

To uncover the spiritual block that keeps you from responding to the needs of your BEING, refer to the "KEY QUESTIONS" at the back of this book. In answering these questions, you will come in touch more easily and accurately with the true cause of your physical problem.

TONSILLITIS

PHYSICAL BLOCK

The tonsils are organs of defense for the body, providing a microbe barrier that is one of the first lines of defense. They are located in the upper part of the throat - the sentinel spot of the entrance to the breathing and digestive tracts. *Tonsillitis* is an inflammation of the tonsils, an uncomfortable infection that can make swallowing especially difficult.

EMOTIONAL BLOCK

Tonsillitis indicates anger or frustration at a situation that you just can't swallow. Determine what or whom you can't accept. What is it you're finding too much to swallow?

MENTAL BLOCK

If you are finding it difficult to swallow, there is a subconscious rebellion going on inside you (coming from your ego). You are being controlling or judgmental regarding someone else or regarding a specific situation. You are probably convinced you are right. (Judgment may also be directed toward yourself.) To resolve this, put some love and acceptance in the situation at hand. You will find everything much easier to swallow. See also THROAT problems and SECTION 2.

SPIRITUAL BLOCK AND CONCLUSION

To uncover the spiritual block that keeps you from responding to the needs of your BEING, refer to the "KEY QUESTIONS" at the back of this book. In answering these questions, you will come in touch more easily and accurately with the true cause of your physical

TORPOR

Torpor is a state of motor and mental inactivity with a partial suspension of sensibility. Subconsciously, you feel dispirited, but your body is telling you to be more active. See NUMBNESS.

TORTICOLLIS

T

Torticollis is an unnatural condition in which the head leans to one side because the neck muscles on that side are contracted.

You have leaned toward a certain decision that you must *straighten out* by altering your belief system. See NECK PAIN.

501

TOURETTE'S SYNDROME

PHYSICAL BLOCK

Tourette's syndrome is a severe neurological disorder characterized by multiple facial and other body tics, usually beginning in childhood or adolescence and often accompanied by grunts and compulsive utterances, as of interjections and obscenities.

EMOTIONAL BLOCK

Tourette's syndrome develops if you feel perpetually controlled and invaded; at the same time have a tremendous fear of losing control and being overwhelmed. It's highly probable that, in your childhood, you felt that one of your parents (generally of the opposite sex) was very controlling while the other parent was trapped and controlled. You may have experienced losing control of yourself, which turned out to be a traumatizing event for you. You are probably often angry and critical. You hide your vulnerability because you want to give the impression that you are strong.

MENTAL BLOCK

It's important that you acknowledge and honor the fact that you are a gentle, vulnerable person. Even if you lost control in your childhood, it doesn't necessarily have to reoccur. Refer to the steps to true forgiveness at the back of the book so that you can work on the issues concerning your parents, as this would be very beneficial to your peace of mind.

SPIRITUAL BLOCK AND CONCLUSION

To uncover the spiritual block that keeps you from responding to the needs of your BEING, refer to the "KEY QUESTIONS" at the back of this book. In answering these questions, you will come in touch more easily and accurately with the true cause of your physical problem

TOXEMIA

See POISONING.

TREMORS

A *tremor* is an involuntary trembling or quivering, as from nervous agitation or weakness.

See PARKINSON'S DISEASE but keep in mind that if the tremor is slight, the implications are less deeply rooted than if the tremor were more pronounced. If only one part of the body is trembling, refer to that part (in this book) to know in what area of your life you are having difficulty letting go.

T

TUBAL PREGNANCY

PHYSICAL BLOCK

A *tubal pregnancy* is a pregnancy in which the fertilized egg implants in tissue outside of the uterus and the placenta and fetus begin to develop there. The most common site is within a Fallopian tube; however, ectopic pregnancies can occur in the ovary, the abdomen, and in the lower portion of the uterus.

EMOTIONAL BLOCK

A tubal pregnancy signifies indecision on the part of the soul of the child, or on the part of the mother-to-be. It is quite possible also that this is a mutual indecision. The mother probably feels guilty about hesitating to the point of punishing herself (unconsciously) by creating very serious complications. She may have been trying to conceive in order to please her partner or someone else close to her in order to be loved, regardless of the fact that a pregnancy is beyond her limits right now.

MENTAL BLOCK

Acknowledge and accept your fears and limitations. If you decide that it's too much for you to have a baby right now, speak to the soul of this baby, tell him/her what you are going through while acknowledging the fact that it is your body, your life and also, that you have the right to decide what suits you best. You're the one who will have to take the consequences.

SPIRITUAL BLOCK AND CONCLUSION

To uncover the spiritual block that keeps you from responding to the needs of your BEING, refer to the "KEY QUESTIONS" at the back of this book. In answering these questions, you will come in touch more easily and accurately with the true cause of your physical problem.

TUBERCULOSIS

Tuberculosis, or *TB* occurs as pulmonary tuberculosis in the lungs, or extrapulmonary tuberculosis in other areas of the body. It is a disease that can be either acute or chronic. Early symptoms include coughing, chest pain, difficulty breathing, coughing up blood, decreased appetite, fever, night sweats and weight loss. See LUNG DISORDERS and keep in mind that the body's message is urgent, given the seriousness of the disease if it is left unattended. If tuberculosis has attacked another area of the body, refer to the pertinent listing of the area affected for corresponding metaphysical implications.

TUMOR

A *tumor* is an abnormal growth in or on the body. For a *benign tumor*, see CYST and for a *malignant tumor*, see CANCER.

TWITCH

PHYSICAL BLOCK

A *twitch* or *nervous tic* is a sudden spasm, especially one caused by a nervous condition. Twitches occur most often in the facial muscles.

EMOTIONAL BLOCK

A twitch indicates restraint that has reached critical mass and a subsequent loss of control. You want to show your sadness, fear, worries or limitations but don't allow it because you fear what others will think of you. This is why a twitch usually occurs in the face; it's the first part of you that others see. If the twitch is experienced in other muscles, refer to the pertinent listing of the area of the body most obviously affected for corresponding metaphysical implications.

MENTAL BLOCK

Your body is telling you that, although you've been able to control your feelings up to now, you can no longer do so. It's not necessary to put on a good face, presenting an image that was drummed into you in your childhood. Acknowledge to others your feelings, fears, needs, and aspirations knowing full well that they might not agree or may even judge you. You need only answer to yourself. Acknowledge others' right to disagree even before you express yourself. Do it out of love for yourself.

SPIRITUAL BLOCK AND CONCLUSION

To uncover the spiritual block that keeps you from responding to the needs of your BEING, refer to the "KEY QUESTIONS" at the back of this book. In answering these questions, you will come in touch more easily and accurately with the true cause of your physical problem

TYPHOID FEVER

Typhoid fever is an acute, highly infectious bacterial disease transmitted by contaminated water or food characterized by high fever, headache, coughing, intestinal hemorrhaging, and rose-colored spots on the skin. Also called *enteric fever.*

Because typhoid fever can be fatal, the message from your body is extremely urgent. You are experiencing so much anger that you are prostrated by it, dejected and indifferent toward those around you. You must immediately undertake a process of forgiveness with the person who has unleashed this anger in you and not let your pride keep you from doing so. Refer to the steps to true forgiveness at the back of the book. See FEVER.

T

507

ULCER

An *ulcer* is a lesion of the skin or a mucous membrane such as the one lining the stomach or duodenum that is accompanied by formation of pus and necrosis of surrounding tissue.

Ulcers indicate that you are experiencing bitterness that is eating you up inside. You are having a hard time healing. Only forgiveness, as explained at the end of the book, will help. Refer to the pertinent listing of the area of the body most obviously affected by the ulcer for corresponding metaphysical implications.

If the ulcer is situated in the stomach, refer to STOMACH ULCER.

UPSET STOMACH

PHYSICAL BLOCK

The *stomach* or *abdomen* refers to the part of the body that lies between the thorax and the pelvis and encloses the stomach, intestines, liver, spleen, and pancreas. Abdominal pain, in this case, refers to discomfort experienced that is not related to any specific cause. See NAUSEA, if applicable.

U

509

EMOTIONAL BLOCK

If you are experiencing pain in the upper abdominal area, or solar plexus, your body is sending you a signal that you are worrying too much for others. You fear for them.

For example, when the lower abdomen is involved (below the navel), your body is telling you that you are worrying too much about a situation that is going on in your life. You fear for yourself.

MENTAL BLOCK

Pain in the *upper abdominal* area is a message from your body that you need to understand you are not on the planet to cater to others and ensure their happiness on an ongoing basis. It's all right to feel compassion for others, but inappropriate to worry yourself sick. Ultimately, you are not doing them any favors. Allow them to learn through their own experiences and help them only when they ask, while respecting your own personal limitations.

Pain in the *lower abdominal* area is a message from your body that your excessive worry will not dissipate the circumstances or people whom you fear. If you let go and detach yourself from the situation, you can remain centered and more easily see solutions. Anxiousness only serves to knock you off balance psychologically, and any decisions you make will be based on fear rather than on your true needs.

SPIRITUAL BLOCK AND CONCLUSION

To uncover the spiritual block that keeps you from responding to the needs of your BEING, refer to the "KEY QUESTIONS" at the back of this book. In answering these questions, you will come in touch more easily and accurately with the true cause of your physical problem.

UREMIA

Uremia is a toxic condition resulting from the abnormal accumulation of urea in the blood, caused by renal insufficiency. It is the consequence of the majority of kidney disorders and can be fatal. See KIDNEY DISORDERS.

URETERITIS

Ureteritis is the inflammation of the ureter, the duct that allows urine to pass from the kidney to the bladder. (It is not to be confused with *urethritis*.) This disorder generally occurs when you have moved from one situation to another and you have not been able to cope with the change because of an inability to let go of your old ways. This causes you to experience anger. See KIDNEY DISORDERS and SECTION 2.

U

511

URETHRITIS

Urethritis is the inflammation of the urethra, the duct that drains urine from the bladder. (It is not to be confused with *ureteritis*.) See BLADDER and SECTION 2.

URINARY INCONTINENCE

See INCONTINENCE.

URINARY TRACT INFECTION

See URETHRITIS.

URTICARIA

See HIVES.

UTERINE DISORDERS

PHYSICAL BLOCK

The *uterus,* also called *womb*, is a hollow muscular organ located in the pelvic cavity of the female in which the fertilized egg implants and develops. Its strength and durability allow it to both protect and nurture the baby and to expel it with powerful muscular contractions during the birth process. Common uterine disorders include *retroversion, functional disorders,* INFECTION, UTERINE

FIBROID, TUMOR and CANCER (both of the uterus and of the opening, or *cervix*). In some cases, the uterus may drop, obstructing the vagina. See VAGINAL DISORDERS. Read the following then refer to the specific disorder for corresponding metaphysical implications.

EMOTIONAL BLOCK

The uterus is the first home of a new human being. All uterine disorders, therefore, are linked with the reception and the sheltering that are implied. If you are unable to give birth because of a uterine disorder, your body is telling you that you dearly want a child, but fear that looms larger than desire is affecting you so deeply that you've created a physical barrier to procreation. It may be that you harbor regrets about not properly welcoming a child you have already borne and have since developed a uterine disorder out of guilt.

Uterine disorders also indicate that you tend to act prematurely, not allowing the proper gestation time required for new ideas to take shape and become fully formed. These disorders may also indicate some degree of guilt over not creating a proper home for those you love.

MENTAL BLOCK

U

Your body is telling you that you need to deal with the fear you have surrounding birth or new beginnings, whether directly related to childbirth or the conception and nurturing of ideas and projects. Determine whether the fear is justified in the moment. Decide whether to face your fear or be controlled by it. You alone will face the consequences. Realize that you answer, ultimately, to no one but yourself. Your life and the decisions you make regarding that life, belong only to you.

Your body is also telling you that it would be beneficial all around for you to take more time before acting on impulse. You don't have to stop being spontaneous, but show more judgment in your decisions. Acknowledge and honor your limitations. Do you find yourself saying *"I can't conceive of that"* meaning *"I don't understand"*? That may be enough to prevent you from conception in any given area.

SPIRITUAL BLOCK AND CONCLUSION

To uncover the spiritual block that keeps you from responding to the needs of your BEING, refer to the "KEY QUESTIONS" at the back of this book. In answering these questions, you will come in touch more easily and accurately with the true cause of your physical problem

UTERINE FIBROID

PHYSICAL BLOCK

Fibroids are benign tumors of smooth, fibrous muscle tissue. When they occur in the uterus, they are not usually painful but can cause a heavy sensation in the pelvic region. They may also obstruct the bladder and the subsequent flow of urine. Fibroids may be present for many years without detection or may develop quickly to several centimeters.

EMOTIONAL BLOCK

A *uterine fibroid* mass is symbolic of a psychological or pseudo-baby. As all superfluous growths in the body indicate holding onto sorrow of the past, fibroids located in the uterus are usually an indication of regret regarding the loss or absence of a baby. This sense of loss can be felt after an abortion, a miscarriage or after a decision has been made to place a child for adoption or in an institution (in the event of a physically or mentally handicapped child). There may be guilt or self-reproach regarding a decision to exercise the right not to have children. There may be a subconscious desire to have children, but no desire to become involved with a man. Any of these scenarios can result in the development of a pseudo-baby, or uterine fibroid.

MENTAL BLOCK

Do not believe you are a better person if you feel guilt and regret. Get in touch with your sorrow and the pain you are experiencing over a child who isn't there and stop worrying about what others think - you will not be perceived as heartless.

If you have chosen not to have children, acknowledge your right to make that decision. Let go of the belief system that allows a woman to be validated only through motherhood. In this enlightened Age of Aquarius this is antiquated thinking. All women must live at least one lifetime solely for themselves in order to be able to love themselves as women, not only as mothers. If your desire in this lifetime is to have a child, but you are afraid of be-

515

coming involved with men, the first step you must take is to acknowledge and accept this fear and then deal with it before you have children.

SPIRITUAL BLOCK AND CONCLUSION

To uncover the spiritual block that keeps you from responding to the needs of your BEING, refer to the "KEY QUESTIONS" at the back of this book. In answering these questions, you will come in touch more easily and accurately with the true cause of your physical problem.

VAGINAL DISORDERS

PHYSICAL BLOCK

The *vagina* serves as a passageway extending from the mouth of the uterus to the vulva, or genitalia. It functions as the female organ of copulation and functions as the birth canal during childbirth. Common vaginal disorders include: *vaginitis*, HERPES SIMPLEX TYPE II *(genital herpes),* TUMORS and CANCER. Refer to the pertinent listing for further metaphysical implications.

EMOTIONAL BLOCK

The majority of vaginal problems are linked with your sexual life, as most disorders impede sexual activity. Your body is telling you that your beliefs regarding sexuality need to be revised. Although you want more satisfying sexual relations, you may feel used, manipulated or undervalued. The anger you feel results from not giving yourself the right to want sex (or intercourse).

MENTAL BLOCK

Your body is telling you that the belief you harbor regarding your sexuality no longer applies and is not good for your health, though it may have been so at some point in your life. Perhaps you are a controlling woman who feels taken advantage of when you are not the one who initiated sex. Your body would prefer that you feel *desired* at that moment, rather than invaded or abused. If you are feeling manipulated, remember that you also manipulate in other

V

517

areas of your life. Neither you nor your partner has malicious intentions.

If your sex life is unsatisfactory because of sexual abuse experienced in your childhood, your body is now telling you that it's unhealthy to block yourself sexually. Doing so will only prolong the fear of these past experiences. Learn to let go of the fear that serves as an obstacle to your sexual fulfillment. The process of forgiveness is the quickest and most efficient way to do so. Refer to the steps to true forgiveness at the back of the book.

SPIRITUAL BLOCK AND CONCLUSION

To uncover the spiritual block that keeps you from responding to the needs of your BEING, refer to the "KEY QUESTIONS" at the back of this book. In answering these questions, you will come in touch more easily and accurately with the true cause of your physical problem.

VAGINITIS

See YEAST INFECTION.

VARICELLA

See CHICKEN POX.

VARICOSE VEINS

PHYSICAL BLOCK

Varicose veins are caused by excessive and permanent dilatation of one or several veins, usually in the legs, accompanied by a weakening of the wall of the blood vessel and malfunctioning of the valves.

EMOTIONAL BLOCK

Varicose veins indicate a desire for more personal freedom and time, but you don't know how to go about it. You tend to take on a lot of work even though you find the load too heavy. It's heavy because you exaggerate the importance of small problems; you worry too much. You find it difficult to do your work for the sheer enjoyment of doing it and tend to remain in situations you find quite uncomfortable. To help you understand in what part of your life this applies, refer to the part of your body affected by the varicose veins.

MENTAL BLOCK

Because of the poor circulation caused in the area of the varicose veins, the blood tends to pool in the vein and surrounding tissues, causing a feeling of heaviness. The heavier this feeling, the stronger the message from your body that you are finding life *weighty* and *unwieldy*. The little voice inside you that continually says, *"You have to..."* that pushes you to do more, is not the voice of your heart. You can choose not to be pushed around by that

V

voice. Let it be *your choice* to do something (or not do it), instead of an obligation. Allow yourself a little time to *put your feet up* and relax without guilt and without feeling that you're not *pulling your weight*. Resting does not mean you are a bad person. Learn to listen to your heart, as it will guide you in the direction toward what you really want.

SPIRITUAL BLOCK AND CONCLUSION

To uncover the spiritual block that keeps you from responding to the needs of your BEING, refer to the "KEY QUESTIONS" at the back of this book. In answering these questions, you will come in touch more easily and accurately with the true cause of your physical problem.

VARIOLA

See SMALLPOX.

VEIN DISORDERS

The *veins* are the blood vessels that carry blood to the heart after receiving it from the capillaries. The arteries, on the other hand, carry the blood from the heart throughout the body. See ARTERIES with the difference that vein disorders indicate an inability to cope with what's coming from outside you. Conversely, when arteries are involved, the difficulties come from within.

VENEREAL DISEASE

PHYSICAL BLOCK

Venereal diseases are sexually transmitted diseases (commonly called VD or STD).

EMOTIONAL BLOCK

Since all venereal diseases carry a stigma, we feel ashamed of the disease, thus indicating that shame regarding our sexuality is the cause. Interestingly, you are probably not aware of your own shame. This is what your body is forcing you to acknowledge. Part of you wants to have an active sex life, but another part of you wants to prevent it. You are mostly ashamed of being easily influenced by others. You don't allow yourself to enjoy sex or be sexually addicted. You also doubt your choice of sexual partner.

MENTAL BLOCK

It's interesting to note that the incidence of venereal disease is increasing dramatically, in spite of the progress being made by the scientific community to combat it.

You contracted a venereal disease to help you evaluate the belief system that surrounds your sexuality. You are being told to live your sexual life the way you want to; your body belongs to you and you don't have to answer to anyone.

521

Acknowledge and honor your right to experience your sexuality without feeling guilty about it. Know that the more you want to maintain control, the more potential there will be for loss of that control somewhere down the line. It's wiser to experience something fully now with joy and acceptance. Giving you permission to live an experience in the moment does not mean you will be forever out of control.

Rather than being preoccupied by shame and guilt, trying to suppress your desires and hiding your behavior, find someone with whom you can talk openly about the subject, so that shame doesn't hover over you like a dark cloud.

SPIRITUAL BLOCK AND CONCLUSION

To uncover the spiritual block that keeps you from responding to the needs of your BEING, refer to the "KEY QUESTIONS" at the back of this book. In answering these questions, you will come in touch more easily and accurately with the true cause of your physical problem.

VERTIGO

PHYSICAL BLOCK

Vertigo is an abnormal sensation that causes you to feel as though you or your environment is moving or spinning (this is an actual sensation of movement and is different than dizziness). It occurs when there is a problem in the vestibular labyrinth, the portion of the inner ear that controls balance.

EMOTIONAL BLOCK

Vertigo indicates that you perceive a loss in your psychological balance. You feel you've lost your footing or your grasp on what you thought was a balanced life, even though it wasn't meeting your true needs. You may feel anguished about making a decision regarding a new direction and, as a result, your dreams remain unfulfilled. It's possible that you have just experienced a dramatic change in some area of your life that appears not quite balanced and causes you either to feel a temporary imbalance or to have others judge you as unbalanced. You have a difficult time dealing with the judgment of others, even if you refuse to acknowledge it.

MENTAL BLOCK

You are receiving an important message from your body to acknowledge and honor your true needs and alter your notion of what comprises a balanced person and a balanced life. The longer you cling to the fear of being unbalanced, the more likely your life will become so. I suggest you refer to AGORAPHOBIA or HYPOGLYCEMIA.

V

SPIRITUAL BLOCK AND CONCLUSION

To uncover the spiritual block that keeps you from responding to the needs of your BEING, refer to the "KEY QUESTIONS" at the back of this book. In answering

523

these questions, you will come in touch more easily and accurately with the true cause of your physical problem.

VIRUS

PHYSICAL BLOCK

A *virus* is any of various simple submicroscopic parasites that consist essentially of a core of RNA or DNA surrounded by a protein coat, and often causes disease. Unable to replicate without a host cell, viruses are typically not considered living organisms.

EMOTIONAL BLOCK

When a virus has caused a disease to develop in the body, it indicates a willingness to be invaded by a self-devised thought process that keeps you from being yourself. Allowing an invasion of this kind means that there must be a crack or an opening in your emotional or mental body. These cracks occur when bitterness or resentment have been allowed to fester. The virus has appeared to help you become aware of these unhealthy thoughts. Refer to the pertinent listing of the area of the body most obviously affected by the virus for corresponding metaphysical implications.

MENTAL BLOCK

I suggest you communicate with the virus as if you were doing so with another person. Examine the process that continues to entertain the bitterness and resentment. Next, pretend that those thoughts are another person who is communicating with you and encouraging you to harbor your resentment. Now, explain that you no longer want to harbor a grudge, which is making you sick, and that you want to learn to forgive instead.

Although forgiveness may seem impossible for you at the moment, at least you have good intentions and, once the sickness diminishes, you'll be able to forgive more easily. From now on, you have increased your awareness of the part you play in viral invasion and your body will no longer need to bring it to your attention by housing a virus. The virus, then, will no longer have a reason to become active. Refer to the steps to true forgiveness at the back of the book.

SPIRITUAL BLOCK AND CONCLUSION

To uncover the spiritual block that keeps you from responding to the needs of your BEING, refer to the "KEY QUESTIONS" at the back of this book. In answering these questions, you will come in touch more easily and accurately with the true cause of your physical problem.

VITILIGO

V

Vitiligo is a skin disease marked by development of smooth, milk-white spots (of varied sizes) upon various parts of the body, often symmetrically distributed and usually surrounded by a heavily pigmented border. Hair in the affected areas is usually, but not always, white. See SKIN DISORDERS.

VOICE LOSS

See LARYNGITIS.

VOMITING

Vomiting is the rejection through the mouth of the contents of the stomach, in a generally brutal and involuntary manner. See INDIGESTION and add the following:

Vomiting may be the result of accusation of another to the point of being "sick of" this person. This merits a process of acceptance and forgiveness. Remember that you can accept someone wholly and completely without having to agree with him or her. Acceptance is simply acknowledging and maintaining an objective empathy or compassion. Refer to the steps to true forgiveness at the back of the book.

VOMITING BLOOD

Vomiting blood indicates that you have reached the boarders of your emotional limitations. You can no longer control yourself and keep it in. See HEMORRHAGE.

WARTS

A *wart* is a firm abnormal elevated blemish on the skin. See SKIN TAGS but keep in mind that as warts are considered to be flaws, esthetically, you may feel a sense of ugliness in relation to what that part of the body does. For example, if the wart is on your hand, what do you do with that hand? Do you believe that what you do is ugly?

WATER RETENTION

See EDEMA.

WEAKNESS

PHYSICAL BLOCK

Weakness is defined here as a lack of physical strength.

EMOTIONAL BLOCK

General weakness can result when we refuse to be strong and take a good bite out of life. While we are spending time comparing ourselves to others, we are missing out on some of life's more interesting experiences. If your weakness is localized, affecting a specific part of your body, refer to that part of the body to understand the metaphysical cause and its ramifications in specific areas of your life.

W

MENTAL BLOCK

Evaluate your belief system and ask yourself why you feel you don't have the strength to live your life fully and completely. Your body is crying out, *"Believe in your own strength!"* It is warning you that the forces you are suppressing will surface as disease - the unchanneled energies will erupt like a time bomb inside you.

It is possible your general weakness is the result of psychological exhaustion. See BURNOUT.

SPIRITUAL BLOCK AND CONCLUSION

To uncover the spiritual block that keeps you from responding to the needs of your BEING, refer to the "KEY QUESTIONS" at the back of this book. In answering these questions, you will come in touch more easily and accurately with the true cause of your physical problem.

WHITLOW

Whitlow is a purulent infection at the end of a finger or toe in the area surrounding the nail. This infection indicates emotional repression, a weariness of spirit and lack of desire to lend a hand to others. See ABSCESS and FINGER DISORDERS.

WHOOPING COUGH

Also called *pertussis*, *whooping cough* is an infection producing severe throat inflammation and a strong cough that
is characterized by a specific high-pitched and very noticeable "whoop" sound. The whole respiratory tract may
be affected. Symptoms include mucous, fatigue, sneezing, and spasmodic coughing fits. See CHILDHOOD
DISEASES. Whooping cough is more common in young
children who think that they are no longer the center of attention and are quick to realize that the distinctive cough
attracts this much-needed attention.

WRIST PROBLEMS

PHYSICAL BLOCK

The *wrist* is the joint that unites the forearm with the hand,
facilitating optimal mobility and flexibility. Traumas to
the wrist are frequent and dangerous for a joint so sensitive and complex. See PAIN, SPRAINS, FRACTURE,
and CARPAL TUNNEL SYNDROME.

EMOTIONAL BLOCK

As all joints symbolize and reflect psychological flexibility, problems in the wrist indicate a lack of flexibility or
difficulty in deciding what your hands should be doing.
You don't acknowledge the right to use your hands to do
something that gives you pleasure, for fear of making a
mistake or of not being capable. Therefore, you choose to

W

531

use your hands for activities you feel are "worthwhile" - activities that will prove your worth.

You probably ask too much of yourself and may even believe you don't deserve to have a job that is enjoyable and fun, and so feel guilty about it. You generally do things your own way, *work your fingers to the bone*, and give your utmost.

MENTAL BLOCK

Your body is telling you that you are inflexible in your thinking. It's harmful for you to believe that you are not up to a task, especially when that task is something you really want to do. On the other hand, if you think someone else has been abusing you through what you are doing, your body is sending you the message that this is not so. Every task must be undertaken and executed without guilt, fear, or expectation.

If your *right wrist* is being affected, it is connected with your ability to give. If your *left wrist* is affected, it is connected with your ability to receive. The message you are receiving is to let go, to act out of love, acceptance and acknowledgment. Allow yourself to be helped and guided.

SPIRITUAL BLOCK AND CONCLUSION

To uncover the spiritual block that keeps you from responding to the needs of your BEING, refer to the "KEY QUESTIONS" at the back of this book. In answering these questions, you will come in touch more easily and accurately with the true cause of your physical problem.

WRYNECK

See NECK PAIN.

W

YEAST INFECTION

A *yeast infection* (or *vaginitis*) is an inflammation of the vagina. Symptoms include vaginal itching; inflammation; thick, curd-like discharge; pain during intercourse; pain in the lower abdomen and, occasionally, vaginal bleeding. It indicates repressed anger regarding sexual issues. See VAGINAL DISORDERS and SECTION 2.

Key questions

In order to pinpoint the cause of your physical illness more accurately, ask yourself the following questions:

PHYSICAL BLOCK

"What are the words that best describe what I am experiencing inside or on my body and how do I feel about it?"

The answer to the above question reflects what you are experiencing regarding the person or situation that is at the root of your illness.

EMOTIONAL BLOCK

a) "What is this illness preventing me from doing and/or having"?

The answers to this question represent one or more desires that are being blocked.

b) "If I allowed myself to achieve these desires, what would I be?"

MENTAL BLOCK

"If I allowed myself to be_____ (fill in the blank with the answer from the previous question) *what*

unpleasant situation could happen to me AND what would people think of me (or what would I think of myself?)"

Your answers will correspond with the harmful belief that is blocking you from meeting your own needs and achieving your dreams. This belief manifests as a physical block.

SPIRITUAL BLOCK

Refer to answer (b) under emotional block. Your response indicates a deep and profound need that is being blocked by an inappropriate belief system.

CONCLUSION TO KEY QUESTION EXERCISE

Once you are able to unearth the belief that blocks you from being what you really want and need, you will have to work on it. The first step is to acknowledge that at some point in your life, you *decided to believe* this. You thought that this belief would prevent you from suffering the same pain over and over. The next step is to ask yourself if you still need to believe this in order to be happy. If you answer *yes*, you've determined that your belief is still of use to you - by all means continue to believe it and behave as you always have. *But don't expect any change in your life.* As you are the architect of your own life, the choice is yours. Just know that by refusing to go towards what you want in life, your life will remain the same.

If you've determined that your belief is still partly true but that it makes you unhappy, determine whether or not it has diminished in strength in the last couple of years. If it has, it will be easier to let go of. By doing so, you will be on the road to recovery.

When you know deep inside that you want to change this belief, all that remains is to take steps to achieve your desires in order to let yourself to BE WHAT YOU WANT TO BE.

Conclusion

The only path to complete and permanent healing is through **self-forgiveness**. This is the only step powerful enough to let go of your illness on every level, as it addresses not only your self-love but also the very heart and blood in your physical body.

As you become reacquainted with this profound love, your blood stream is recharged and revitalized, bringing new life on a sub-molecular level. As it soothes the soul, so it acts as a salve on the physical body. Self-forgiveness and self-love have the power to transform your energy field, reharmonizing the body's cells as they move through you. If you find this difficult to believe on an intellectual level, consider what you have to lose and give it a try.

THE STEPS OF FORGIVENESS

Here are the steps of forgiveness that have been tried by thousands of people with extraordinary results:

1) **Identify your emotions** (there is often more than one). Become fully conscious of the accusations carried by you or against you and allow any emotions surrounding them to come to the surface. What does this makes you feel?

2) **Take responsibility.** Taking responsibility simply means acknowledging that you are choosing to react out of fear. Determine what it is you are afraid of and understand that you may also be concerned that you will be accused of the same thing. Accept that something inside of you is attracting this person or situation in your life to help you get over the hurt that has been present since childhood.

3) **Accept the other person and let go.** You will only be able to let go and get on with your life once you've *accepted* the other person. To do so, all you have to do is put yourself in their shoes; you will begin to see things from their perspective and better understand their intentions. Understand that they probably accuse you (and themselves) of the same thing you are accusing them of. For them to accuse you of the same thing, what could you have done?

4) **Forgive yourself.** This is the most important step to forgiveness. It helps you make peace with yourself. *Forgive yourself* for having judged, criticized or accused the other person. Know that only a part of you did these things... the part that suffered.

Forgive yourself for having done whatever you did to the other person. To do so, you must give yourself the right to have fears, beliefs, and limits that cause you to suffer and react. Accept yourself just as you are, and stop being so hard on yourself. Know you are simply a work in progress.

5) **Have the desire to express forgiveness.** In preparation for step 6, imagine yourself face to face with the person concerned, telling them that because you were hurting, you have judged, criticized or condemned them. If you can visualize sharing this with them and it arouses feelings of peace and liberation, you are ready to go on to step 6. (It is important to remember that your objective is not to tell them *you forgive them*.)

6) **See the person involved.** Express your thoughts and feelings (identified in step 1) to that person, saying you regret your accusation, judgment or resentment. (Only if they ask for your forgiveness do you say that *you forgive them*). I strongly suggest that you ask the person when he/she accused you of the same thing and in which situation.

7) **Make the connection with the past.** Look back at the events of your life and find a similar circumstance that relates to an authority figure: a father, mother, grandparent, teacher, etc. This person is usually of the same sex as the person you were accusing. Then, to liberate yourself, go over these six steps with this person from the past.

(Follow only steps 1,2,4 and 7 when the accusation is towards yourself and no one else is involved)

IF YOU FIND THESE STEPS DIFFICULT, PLEASE READ THE FOLLOWING.

Take as much time as you need to go through the *steps of forgiveness* effectively. It may take a day, a month, or up to a year between each step. The most impor-

543

tant thing to remember is that you go through the steps with sincerity and the desire to achieve true forgiveness. If the emotional pain is deep and long-standing, or if your ego resists, the process may take longer, but your persistence will pay off.

If you find step 6 especially difficult, it is because your ego is resisting. You may find yourself thinking: *"Why should I be the one doing all the work when they hurt me? I have every reason in the world to feel bitter toward them!"* you are hearing the voice of your ego, not your heart. Your heart's greatest wish is to make peace with and feel compassion for the other person.

When you've expressed yourself (at step 6), don't be upset by the other person's initial reaction. They may be surprised, say nothing, change the subject and refuse to discuss it, cry, ask forgiveness, or throw themselves in your arms. There is no way to know what will happen ahead of time. Respect their reaction and your own as well.

In step 6, I mentioned that it is important you do not offer to forgive another person unless they ask for your forgiveness. There are three good reasons for this:

It often happens that we feel offended by someone when that person never intended offense. Reality is often very different from our perception. Perhaps this person was not even aware that we felt wounded!

Realize that the process of forgiveness is there, first and foremost, for *your own liberation.* The act of forgiving someone else is only one step toward those necessary to forgive yourself.

Know that you don't have the power to truly forgive someone else. Only they can forgive themselves.

If another person is having difficulty responding to you, it may be because they can't forgive themselves. Even if you have forgiven them, you cannot do it for them; only they can reach the point of forgiveness. You are not responsible for another's reaction, only for your own. The act of forgiving yourself will be a good example to allow them to do so as well.

If others take offence or try to justify their actions when you discuss your perception of an experience or your feelings about it, ask if they feel you are accusing them. If so, look inside yourself to see if you still feel they are somewhat to blame and see if you are harboring the hope they will change.

If you are approaching another expecting them to apologize and hoping that they'll see how they've made you suffer, you are still laying blame on them. You may need more time to work through steps 2 and 3 of the forgiveness process. You are not yet at the point where you can walk in with an open mind and an open heart. Don't be too hard on yourself; you have reached the stage where you are forgiving with your head, on an intellectual level, but not yet with your *heart.* You'll know this is the case if you still don't feel peace or relief. This is very common. Your intentions are good and you are on the right track.

Letting go through forgiveness doesn't mean that you agree with the offense; rather, you see beyond the offense. You are able to look into the other person with the eyes of love, compassion, and understanding.

Thanks to this forgiveness, you'll be able to get on with your life and be who you are with all your human feelings.

Let's take a look at the three most unpleasant emotions: fear, anger and sadness. These feelings are to some extent suppressed, controlled, hidden and sidestepped because we don't want to reawaken the pain that we experienced when we were younger. These emotions are usually the result of psychological wounds such as *rejection, abandonment, humiliation, betrayal* and *injustice.*[1]

Rather than allow ourselves to be human and simply acknowledge our wounded feelings, most of us would rather lay the blame on others for what we feel. As we haven't yet forgiven ourselves, we are convinced it's someone else's fault if we are afraid, angry or sad. That's the reason we accuse others and why our bodies talk to us so often.

These emotions have a purpose and, in acknowledging them, we can learn to put them to good use:

---

[1]   For more information on the five wounds, read Lise Bourbeau's book *Heal Your Wounds and Find Your True Self!*

Fear exists as a reminder that we are attempting to protect ourselves. However, the only true protection lies within.

Anger exists to help us realize that we need to assert ourselves, to clearly express our requests and pay close attention to our needs.

Sadness exists to help us get in touch with our fear of loss. Acknowledging sadness will help us learn to let go.

That's what LOVING YOURSELF means - taking charge of your own life by acknowledging and accepting who you are and giving yourself the right to go through your life experiences while striving to reach your goal. In doing so, you will be nurturing a healthy body - a body full of the energy needed to engineer the life you want.

I hope this book will be a welcome companion, helping you increase your awareness and discover the keys to improve the quality of your life through love. Never lose touch with your own *divinity,* and listen to your body as it communicates the message:

"LOVE YOURSELF!"

Suggested reading

- Dychtwald, Ken, Ph.D., *Bodymind,* Jeremy P. Tarcher Inc. 1986

- Harrison, John, M. D., *Love Your Disease,* Angus & Robertson

- Hay, Louise L., *You Can Heal Your Life,* Hay House 1987

- Siegel, Bernie, M.D., *Love, Medicine & Miracles,* Harper & Row 1990

- Steadman, Alice, *Who's the Matter with Me?,* De Vorss & Company 1977

ÉCOUTE TON CORPS
International

Improving the quality of life!

The
LISTEN TO YOUR BODY
workshop

improves the quality
of your life!

Start enjoying life!

The dynamic and powerful teachings of the *"Listen to Your Body"* workshop are aimed at all people who are interested in their personal growth.

For the past twenty years, this workshop has provided people with a vital source of knowledge as well as a solid foundation in order to be more in harmony with themselves. Year after year, the startling results and enriching transformations achieved by over 25,000 people who attended this workshop are truly astounding.

Thanks to this workshop, thousands of people are no longer putting up with life; they are living it! They have regained control over their lives and are using the wealth of personal power within them to create the lives they really want for themselves. The rewards are far greater than could be imagined.

The *"Listen to Your Body"* workshop is a unique and comprehensive teaching which has tangible effects at all levels: physical, emotional, mental and spiritual.

Benefits of this workshop according to previous participants are:

- ✓ greater self-confidence;
- ✓ better communication with others;
- ✓ better judgement enabling a conscious choice between love and fear;
- ✓ an ability to forgive and let go of the past;
- ✓ a direct contact with your personal power and creativity;
- ✓ a revolutionary but simple technique to discover the real causes of illnesses and health problems;
- ✓ greater physical vitality;
- ✓ and much more!

If you would like to organize a workshop in your town/city, contact us for further information.

1102 La Sallette Blv, Saint-Jerome (Quebec) J5L 2J7 CANADA
Tel: 450-431-5336 or 514-875-1930, Toll free: 1-800-361-3834
Fax: 450-431-0991; E-MAIL: info@ecoutetoncorps.com
www.ecoutetoncorps.com

Books from the same author

Listen to your best friend on Earth, your body

LISE BOURBEAU takes you by the hand and, step by step, leads you beyond "packing your own parachute", to taking that step back into the clear, refreshing stream of life that flows from the Universal Source. She gives you the tools, not only to fix what is wrong in your life, but to build a solid foundation for your inner house - a foundation that extends as far as the global village. In this book, she helps you build an intimate, rewarding and powerful relationship with the most important person in your life - yourself.

Your body's telling you: Love yourself!

Lise Bourbeau has compiled 20 years of research in the field of metaphysics and it's physical manifestations in the body and brought it all to the forefront in this user-friendly reference guide, Your body's telling you: Love yourself! Since 1982, she has worked successfully with over 15,000 people, helping them to unearth the underlying causes of specific illnesses and diseases.

"I am certain that any physical problem is simply the outward manifestation of dis-ease on psychological and/or emotional levels. The physical body is responding to this imbalance and warning of the need to return to the path of love and harmony."

Cover to cover, the reader discovers a most powerful tool, as he becomes his own healer. The reference material, a comprehensive guide to the causes of over 500 illnesses and diseases, is a succinct and visionary work that is truly and literally a labor of love.

Heal your wounds and find your true self

Do you sometimes feel that you are going around in circles in your personal growth? Do you occasionally see a problem re-emerge, thinking you had solved it? Perhaps it's because you're not looking in the right place.

This new book by Lise Bourbeau, as concrete as her others, demonstrates that all problems, whether physical, emotional or mental, stem from five important wounds: *rejection, abandonment, humiliation, betrayal* and *injustice*. This book contains detailed descriptions of these wounds and of the masks we've developed to hide them.

This book will allow you to set off on the path that leads to complete healing, the path that leads to your ultimate goal: your true self.

Index

A

B

C

M

N

T

How to Buy and Raise a
GOOD
HEALTHY
DOG

How to Buy and Raise a

GOOD

HEALTHY

DOG

Terri Shumsky

Published by Doral Publishing, Sun City, Arizona
Printed in the United States of America.

Copyedited by Sagebrush Publications
Interior Design by The Printed Page
Cover by Masterpiece Publishing

Library of Congress Card Number: 2001086803
ISBN: 0-944875-67-X

Publisher's Cataloging-in-Publication
(*Provided by Quality Books, Inc.*)

Shumsky, Terri.
   How to buy and raise a good healthy dog / by Terri Shumsky ; [edited by] Lisa Liddy. -- 1st ed.
    p. cm.
   Includes bibliographical references and index.
   LCCN: 2001086803
   ISBN: 0-944875-67-X

   1. Dogs. I. Liddy, Lisa. II. Title.

SF426.S58 2001   636.7
                   QBI01-200324

Dedication

Dedicated to a few EXTRAORDINARY veterinarians who have seen the wisdom of working with this breeder and sharing information on the care of my dogs. My deepest appreciation and gratitude to all of them for their patience and guidance through all the years of my involvement in dogs.

Dr. Kenneth Davis, Bayview Animal Hospital, Atlantic City, NJ
Dr. Grant Patrick, Montecito Veterinary Clinic, Santa Rosa, CA
Dr. Steve Robinson, El Camino Veterinary Clinic, Atascadero, CA
Dr. Renee Leton, El Camino Veterinary Clinic, Atascadero, CA
Dr. Dale A. Heisler, D.V.M., Rockingham Animal Hospital, Reidsville, NC
Dr. Karen M. Tobias, D.V.M., M.S., Diplomate ACVS, University of Tennessee, College of Veterinary Medicine, Knoxville, TN

This book is a collection of information that I have gathered and saved over the years, written by people I've respected and admired, namely, Dr. Harvey Keyes, Dr. D.H. Lein, Dr. J. Mosier, Dr. Michael Lorenz, Mark Silveus, Aileen Martello, Beverly Berman, and Joanne Leyh, vet technician. I will be eternally grateful to the veterinarians that have edited, advised, and critiqued my writings and to whom I have dedicated this book. I have included many articles that were the result of my own efforts and some information I've collected over the years. Some of my articles have been published from time to time, while other information has been experienced and has not been published previously. I have been encouraged to take the time to compile this information by many dear friends, and it is my hope that the beginner and the professional alike will find the help they are seeking at their fingertips in this book. A special thanks to four wonderful veterinarians who put up with my constant questioning to help make this book as complete as possible for the general health of our four-footed friends! Thank heavens for e-mail.

Terri Shumsky

Contents

Chapter 1

How to Find A Breeder

Basically, breeders fit into six categories. Like every business, there are levels of desirability. The first three are: Well Known, High Profile Professionals; Well Known Professionals Who Exhibit and Advertise regularly; and Dedicated Fanciers, who do little advertising and are totally unconcerned about statistics, but regularly show up at specialty shows and regularly exhibit and finish dogs to their championships generation after generation. Also there are the OKs, Not–So-Hots, and "I'll do or say anything to sell a puppy" breeders. It is imperative to stick with the first three groups and to avoid the others.

First, it is important to distinguish between professional breeders and "backyard" breeders or so called "kitchen" breeders. The professionals, whether full- or part-time, make at least part of their living by raising, showing, and selling dogs, and they sometimes break even with expenses. They usually have many years of study and experience in the art and science of creating the best qualities in the breed they are selling. The "kitchen" breeder or "backyard" breeders may breed their female once to show the kids how puppies are born or may mate little "Fifi" with the dog down the street with no research or knowledge about whether the animals or their pedigrees are compatible. They just "make puppies" and usually offer no replacement guarantee.

Like the professionals, the dedicated *fanciers* also consider their reputation very important, have been in the same breed for ten years or more and are probably into their third generation of the breed. Fanciers are not so much concerned about the price of the dog as they are about the "placement" of the dog, regardless of the price. However, make no mistake about it, dogs from the fancier will not be cheap either, considering

It's amazing what these dogs will pose for!

Photos courtesy of Joan Gordon, Wildweir Kennels

*More Wildweir dogs
enjoying life!*

*Photos courtesy of Joan Gordon,
Wildweir Kennels*

the high cost of veterinary care and consultation these days, as well as the high cost of quality food and other supplies. The fancier doesn't care about making a profit, but would like to meet the expenses of raising the dogs or at least come close.

All living things mature differently. Therefore, the age of the puppy you are buying and the knowledge that the breeder can give you about the ancestors of the puppy will assure you that your pet will turn out more or less as the breeder suspects. It should turn out much better than buying from a "kitchen breeder" who has never bred before or an amateur who has no idea what is behind your pup temperamentally or genetically.

You will have to do your homework to find a good breeder or fancier. A good place to start is the American Kennel Club (AKC) or the Kennel Club in your country, which is a registry for purebred dogs. The number for AKC is 919-233-9767, extension 215. Many of the dog magazines like *Dog Fancy* and *Dog World* list shows and the dates they are held. Breeders and fanciers will attend them.

Ask questions, visit kennels, "surf" the World Wide Web, and make a lot of phone calls. Starting out with a well bred pup, even if it's not show quality, will save you a lot of money in the long run. All breeders, no matter how carefully they breed their dogs, do not have one hundred percent show dogs born in their kennel. Long term, you will not be paying more buying from a reputable breeder than you will from a "kitchen" or "backyard breeder" or "pet shop." In addition, you will obtain lots of information and establish a contact that you can call regarding how to take care of your puppy.

If a breeder is "trying" too hard to sell you a puppy, it is time for you to leave; simply tell the breeder that you want to give it more thought. Most legitimate breeders are too busy trying to find out if you are a good home for their precious puppy to which they have already devoted so much time raising, that they will not "pressure" you to buy the pup.

Most serious breeders have no expectations to "make money" raising dogs. They are allowing you to "adopt" someone they love. Their pups have been named, and health records are available. They can tell you the personality of each of the pups.

Some breeders breed for show champions and have no interest in a dog unless they can add to the prestige and price of their breeding lines. They have been known to practically kick dogs out of their facilities and have too many dogs for individual handling and attention; however, they may sell cheap just to "get rid" of their breeding excess. I strongly advise against buying a puppy or older dog from this kind of breeder because they are not really interested in *you*, either.

These people will try to wow you with a list of titles and awards a mile long. Their prices may be higher than average if they want to prove to you that their dogs are something special. The price may be really cheap if the animal is undesirable to them and they want to "get it out" of there.

Not all dogs who are champions will necessarily fit in to family life as a pet. Very often, these dogs' training has been neglected regarding household living, like paper training. They could have been abused by handlers who have no business being handlers and *might be* temperamental nightmares.

The most important thing for prospective owners to do is to learn everything they can about the breed in which they are interested and then go out "shopping." The more dog shows you attend and breeders you visit, the more you will appreciate the real thing when you find it. Also be honest with the breeders about your intentions. Don't insist you only want a "pet," because you think that will be cheaper, and then complain later because you did not get a dog that you can "show and breed." AKC does offer the breeder an avenue of escape in the "limited" registration of the pure bred dog. You can register the dog, but no puppies from this dog can be registered with AKC unless the breeder applies to AKC to reverse the "limited" registration when the dog reaches maturity.

Important things for you to look for as you visit breeders are: that the pups and their surroundings are clean and that the parents are on the site. The bill of sale should spell out the guarantee in writing including a full refund if genetic problems arise. You are looking for a member of your family, so take your time. Trust your gut feelings. If it doesn't feel right, then don't buy the pup.

Don't take home a puppy younger than twelve weeks of age, especially in the smaller breeds. Let the breeder get a couple of immunization shots in that pup before you bring it home. Reputable breeders will be happy to take a deposit on a pup and keep it for you until twelve weeks. It will give your pup a better start. Don't meet your breeder at a local parking lot, restaurant, or other meeting place. Insist on seeing where your puppy lives. Remember that "one time" or so-called "kitchen" pet breeders may not ever breed their dog again, so your chances of getting your money back or a replacement puppy should something happen to your puppy are limited when you deal with this kind of breeder. Don't buy a puppy just to save it from a filthy life. You are better off turning the breeders in and letting the authorities deal with them! The right dog and breeder for you are out there if you take the time to find them.

Breeders are responsible for each puppy that they have bred. A responsible breeder will give each puppy the socialization that it needs. This requires a great deal of devotion and patience. (The puppy's new owner will reap these benefits.)

Breeders' dogs are their number one concern as they understand that puppies are completely dependent on them for their care, training, and medical attention. Their dogs are "special" to them.

How Much is that Puppy in the Window? Buying From a Pet Shop

If you are going to go shopping in the pet shop for your puppy, you will probably be paying as much as or more than you would pay from a reputable breeder, and there is always the possibility that the papers that you get with your puppy are not correct. Most breeders who sell to pet shops care little where their puppies end up. They usually never meet the buyers, and the pups are sold in litter lots, like "stock" on a farm. Haven't we all heard of the truckload of puppies in the East found frozen to death?

Breeders who raise their pups with gentle loving care want to know the final home of their pups. They care whether the pups are well taken care of and healthy, would never place them in a pet shop or sell litter lots, and would be happy for you to see the parents and siblings on the premises. In this way, you will have some idea of what your pup will look like as an adult. Also, pet shops know very little about each specific breed and its care, whereas the breeder should be able to guide you in the grooming and care of your puppy for the first few years of its life and even thereafter.

The pet shops rely on impulse buys to sell their "item." If your pet shop puppy develops a health problem later in life, the pet shop owner would have no idea why it is sick, but a caring breeder could and would help you determine what is wrong with the puppy. The breeder is the best person to guide you in the care of the dog they bred.

AKC Papers

AKC papers do not assure you that the dog will look like the breed it is registered to represent. AKC papers simply mean that a breeder registered this puppy as a particular breed. AKC relies on the honesty of the person filling out the papers. I have personally seen dogs in my own breed that didn't even resemble the breed they were supposed to represent and still they had "papers" that said they were purebred.

AKC is a registry for pure bred dogs and does not have the staff it would take to "police" the honesty of breeders or of pet shops that sell puppies. There may be health defects in your puppy of which you may not be aware for a few years, only to learn too late—after you have become "bonded" to the puppy or, worse yet, have bred him/her.

A Guarantee

The pet store puppy usually comes with a guarantee for money back. After you have bonded with your puppy and cared for it through an illness, you go back to the pet store for a refund and the store will offer to give you another puppy, who may also be sick, and euthanize the one to which you and your family have become attached. Or they may tell you that the puppy will "outgrow" the problem. So the buyer usually opts to keep the puppy. On the other hand, a reputable breeder will offer you a guarantee for genetic problems and spell it out in writing on a bill of sale, before the puppy leaves home. In some cases where you are unable to keep your puppy, the breeder will resell or place your puppy for you in a suitable home. The responsible breeders "care" where their puppies end up and spell this out in the bill of sale.

Housebreaking

Puppies that are raised in a home situation are usually easier to housebreak. Puppies that you buy from the pet shop have spent most of their lives in a cage and, therefore, training has probably not even been started in potty habits. Depending on how long this puppy has been sitting in a cage at the pet shop, it may be almost impossible to housebreak. A pet store puppy may never have seen grass or run on a carpet.

Most pet store puppies come from parents that are only selected because they can make "more" puppies, not for their temperament or genetically sound pedigree, whereas reputable breeders do selective breeding to improve the breed according to the standard for their breed. Breeders try to select a puppy for each buyer that "fits" the ideal new home for each animal. The puppies have been introduced to a family situation, whereas pet store pups may never have left their cage and can be frightened of each new room or each sound they hear.

Pedigrees

Unless you are familiar with the names on the pedigree, it doesn't really mean anything. It really doesn't tell you anything about the quality of the dogs on the pedigree. The pet store can't tell you anything about the ancestors of the dogs in their shop, but the breeder can and will, particularly if he or she has been breeding for more than five years.

Puppy Mills

Don't think that everybody that has more than one breed or even three or four breeds is a puppy mill. I've heard these accusations many times in the past, and they are very hurtful to serious fanciers. Many breeders start out perfecting a breed long before they show it or settle on the breed that they feel comfortable showing and satisfied with the breeding results.

A puppy mill is a mass dog-breeding establishment that produces puppies for profit by selling them wholesale to the pet industry. Many puppy mills are characterized by overcrowding, filth, inadequate shelter, and insufficient food, water, and veterinary care. Most puppy mill owners sell their dogs wholesale to brokers who, in turn, sell them primarily to pet stores. Because profit, not quality dogs, is the ultimate goal of the puppy mill owner, breeding practices are often shoddy. The breeding dogs are kept under the most inexpensive possible conditions that will keep them alive and producing.

Most puppies sold in pet stores come from puppy mills. They mass produce puppies that they have obtained through auctions or "free dog" ads, or they will buy from the "pedigree" with the most champions in it, regardless of whether they are quality dogs or not. Selling champion-sired is all they care about, and some dogs that have finished their championships are not good representatives of the breed.

The females in a puppy mill situation are generally bred every time they come in heat, and then when they are too old to be productive, they are dumped at shelters or at pet shops to be sold "cheap" to someone who takes pity on them. Every time you buy a puppy from a pet shop you are encouraging puppy mills to breed more dogs and "dump" more dogs when they get old. Some puppy mill breeders even put their older breeding dogs to sleep because they are no longer productive.

In contrast, there are hundreds of responsible and reputable kennels and breeding establishments throughout the country whose owners make a profit, but not at the expense of their dogs. Whether these breeders are full-time professionals making an entire living from a kennel, or hobby breeders with five or ten animals, the responsible breeder is as concerned with improving the quality of the breed and showing at AKC shows, as he or she is about making money. Customers wishing to buy puppies from these breeders are welcome to inspect the premises and, in most cases, to meet the puppies' parents.

In between the puppy mill operators and the responsible kennel owners are the so-called " backyard breeders" whose newspaper ads dot Sunday classifieds each week. These are people who own one or two pure-bred dogs and produce a litter of puppies once a year or so for extra money or "because I want my dog to have the experience of being a mother before I get her spayed," or "Aunt Tillie would like to have a puppy just like my mine." Like puppy mill puppies, these animals are often haphazardly bred with no regard to the consequences, and their offspring will most often suffer the same consequences.

Please pass up the next puppy you see in the pet store and contact your local kennel club. Don't assume that you have found good breeders just because they are members of *any club.* Paying dues to a national or local breed club does not make someone an ethical and responsible breeder. Buyers must do their homework and visit with breeders and check out their reputation. All breed and breed clubs do not have the manpower to "police" breeders who happen to pay dues. In many cases, no officer of the club has ever been in the breeder's home or kennel where the dogs are kept.

Most kennel clubs have rescue people for each breed within the club, and you just might be able to find a pet of the breed of your choice in this way. Get in touch with your local All Breed Kennel Club and find out who is the rescue person for the breed in which you are interested. If all you are looking for is a pet, this is a wonderful alternative, and you are not help-ing the pet shops and puppy mills to condemn some little female dog to having more and more puppies. Other alternatives for rescue that are making a difference, one dog at a time, one day at a time, are www.puppymillrescue.com and http://members.tripod.com/~rescues/. Take a look through your Internet connection or a friend's Internet connection.

There are really too many mass breeding kennels in this country, and their arrivals usually go to the pet shops. When you buy a puppy, you are adding a member to your family, so plan on carefully researching this new member who will receive your long-term commitment.

Cute little Yorkshire puppies owned by Alice Ruiz,
Alta Loma, California

Chapter 2

Your First Show and Breeding Dog

The same information applies to shopping for your show dog as appeared in the previous chapter, "How to Find a Good Breeder," except that:

You do not want to co own a show dog. This is probably the most foolish way to purchase any dog, particularly a show and breeding dog. I could probably count on one hand the number of co-ownerships that reached an amicable ending, even fewer if you're looking for co-ownerships that reached an ending with all parties still admiring and respecting each other.

You do not want to buy a show dog until after the second teething (six to seven months) and preferably not until ten months of age.

There are "fanciers" who breed to perfect the breed and do not go to shows but are devoted to breeding better dogs. These people will be more likely to sell their "best." Some of these breeders do not show their dogs until they have perfected their line. Some of the true fanciers, like Joan Gordon and Janet Bennett of Wildweir fame bred and showed several different breeds before settling on the one for which they become really famous, and they never showed their dogs until they felt they were top quality. Too often today, handlers are "enhancing" and "building" show dogs instead of "breeding" to perfect their breed. *Building* a show dog never comes through in the whelping box, but breeding for quality always shows!

Dogs in all shapes and sizes
Clockwise from top left: Onyx, Chinese Crested;
Ofie, Japanese Chin; Jacquie, Bichon Frise;
Zack, Afghan; Sugar, Poodle; Bud, Doberman

Photos courtesy of Vicki and Dale Heisler, DVM, Rockingham Animal
Hospital, Reidsville, NC

Clockwise from top left:
Corky, Scottish Terrier; Luke and JR,
Rhodesian Ridgebacks; Zoika, Belgian
Tervern; Ariel, Belgium Malimon; Jewel,
Border Collie;

Photos courtesy of Vicki and Dale Heisler,
DVM, Rockingham Animal Hospital,

All dogs are born "show potential" so don't let this description fool you. It is only as they mature and "fall apart" that they are no longer "show potentials." A "show dog" is just that, old enough to be sure that it is a show dog.

You should be sure that your bill of sale has a guarantee in writing of how things will be handled if your dog develops liver shunt disease, Legg Perthes, hip dysplasia, or any other disease that makes it impossible for you to show or breed.

You are better off starting out with a sound female from free whelping lines, preferably linebred. However, it is perfectly all right to find a good sound breeding or show bitch that is the result of an outcross breeding (where the ancestors are not related) and breed her back into the lines that have the characteristics you like in the breed. It is almost always to your advantage to take the breeder's advice about how she should be bred.

The very best bloodlines have some problems that must be weeded out. In order to do an intelligent job of breeding, you must know where these problems exist. Be very direct with the breeder from whom you buy your foundation bitch and let him or her know that you want to know any problems up front so you can form a healthy relationship and a good future in healthy, beautiful, and sound foundation dogs.

Be wary of breeders who tell you they *never had any problems of any kind in their line.* These people are probably not being truthful or haven't been breeding long enough to learn how to cull (select the best for breeding and sell the others as pets) their litters, do test breedings, and thus perfect their line.

Make notes of the breeder's experience with problems encountered with different dogs in the breed. After purchasing your bitch, you may find other breeders who are willing to give their opinion on your bitch, but don't expect them all to be perfectly honest with you. They may very well be too intimidated to give their honest opinion, or envy may cloud their judgment.

The best way to get an honest opinion is to approach an AKC judge approved for judging your selected breed at a point show and ask the judge whether he or she believes your bitch to be good enough to be bred or shown. Whether the answer is "yes" or "no," ask what the good points of your bitch are as well as the flaws. Bear in mind that this doesn't mean you have to search forever for the "perfect" dog. Believe me, perfection doesn't exist. If you can know the faults or eliminate them, and thereby finish your dogs easily, you are better off financially, whether you take the dogs to show after show yourself or hire a handler to do it.

It is my opinion that every breeder should know just as much as any judge *before* they breed two animals. Doesn't it make sense that you cannot eliminate faults if you don't know what they are? Learn what a good front and a good rear is, and the reasons they develop that way, and the faults within your breed so that you don't double up on them. A very good book and video available on movement, by Rachel Page Elliott, are available through the American Kennel Club.

Most professional handlers, who have ten or more years experience, are very good at helping you to understand what is good and what is bad about your dog. After all, if you do breed good dogs, the handler may get lucky and be the one you select to show your dogs. All handlers really want good dogs to show!

Some of the problems that have been coming up in dogs, are: Legg Perthes, Liver shunt, PRA, hip dysplasia, bad bites, luxation of the patellas, poor rear angulation, poor shoulder layback and lay-on, incorrect tail sets, tubular bodies with no rib spring in a breed that should be compact, no neck (usually because of a poor lay-on of shoulders), or the other extreme "too much neck and leg," which in some breeds ruins the appearance and "type." Study the Standard for your breed and learn this word.

If any of these terms is a mystery to you, then you are not yet ready to breed a male to a female. You cannot breed good quality dogs if you do not know how to recognize problems. Do research and find out what the problems are so that you can recognize them and not propagate them. Some breeds, i.e. toys and bulldogs, are not easy whelpers, so if you are going to go to the trouble of breeding them, you might as well start off with a chance of producing some enviable dogs, from free-whelping lines. Intensive and selective breeding and culling is used by wise breeders to eliminate problems within any breed. *Culling means making selections and keeping only the best for breeding.* Anybody can "make puppies," but it takes serious planning and knowledge to improve a breed and leave it better than you found it. You, and generations after you, will reap the rewards of your efforts.

Correct Bite, Undershot Bite, and Overshot Bite

An illustration of a scissors bite, a level bite, an undershot bite, and an overbite follows.

A scissors bite in some toy dogs is acceptable all over, and a level bite is acceptable by AKC standards for Yorkies. The standard for each breed clearly states what is acceptable. You should become familiar with the standard for your breed.

In some breeds, an undershot bite is acceptable, like the Shih Tzus and Japanese Spaniels.

1) Scissors

2) Level

3) Undershot

4) Overshot

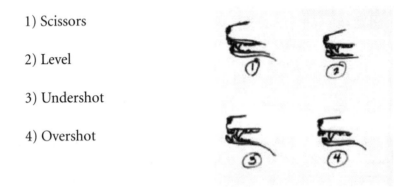

Other Resources

Some very good books, written by dog judges, will assist you in learning about movement and structure:

- *The Nicholas Guide to Dog Judging*, by A. K. Nicholas
- *Dog Judges Handbook* by Sari B. Tietjen
- *Winning with Pure Bred Dogs: Success by Design* by Dr. Alvin Grossman and Beverly Grossman.

Chapter 3 🐾

Breeding

Who Is The Best Stud For My Bitch?

Most breeders prefer that you breed your bitch back to one of their studs, and this may be the best approach for you to take as a novice with a first time litter. If you respect and admire the person from whom you purchased your foundation bitch, it is reasonable to have them guide you in the selection of the stud for your bitch. Remember, this breeder's reputation is at stake also. Some breeders will make the first stud fee a part of the purchase of your bitch to encourage you to come back to their stud. In most cases, they honestly feel that the stud they have in mind will start you off in the right direction and provide you with quality pups from the beginning. It would seem unlikely for breeders to encourage this if they have something to hide, because there would be no one to blame but themselves if the breeding produced any serious problems.

An old timer once told me that you should breed to a stud dog you like, preferably line-bred or in-bred to the same lines as your bitch. If all goes well, breed the get back to the parent to condense the genetic pool, and you'll find out just what good stuff or *garbage* you may have bought! After twenty-five years, I consider this good advice, if not a necessity, provided you have the know-how, determination, and *guts* to seriously *pet out* the results (putting down the serious problems, if necessary, due to a poor quality of life), rather than kidding yourself and keeping any of the siblings for further breeding. As long as they are healthy, it is possible that they can be placed in pet homes, provided the problems would not interfere with the quality of life and with the understanding that they are not to be bred. If, after this intensive test breeding, there are NO serious problems, you're on your way to bypass most of the pitfalls!

Inbreeding and Linebreeding

Inbreeding is the intermating of relatives, and it is virtually impossible to breed pedigree stock of any kind without the animals having some relationship somewhere. Once a breed is established, it is impossible to breed a male and female within this breed without finding some ancestors in common. The relationship may be so far back that you can't trace it, but by inbreeding these common ancestors, your animal's breed was formed.

Most breeders consider "outcrossing" as breeding animals that are completely unrelated in the last six generations. This is as far as most breeders trace their stock's ancestry, unless they have personally linebred for a longer period of time.

"Linebreeding" is considered to be a mild or less intense form of inbreeding. It includes mating of distant cousins or mating dogs who come from the same kennel and same strain but have no common ancestors closer than four or five generations behind them.

"Inbreeding" condenses the genetic pool. Because the sire and dam are the most closely related genetically the chances of the results being very good or VERY BAD are strong. Inbreeding should not be attempted by an amateur.

Inbreeding, which I also consider "test breeding," is the only way to sort out faults and virtues. Whether the results are good or bad will depend on the type of stock you start with, because inbreeding cannot create good or bad points. It merely uncovers them. When results of inbreeding are disappointing, don't run to an outcross to try to solve your problems, since you will only bring in more covered-up problems. Stick it out and keep culling (removing from the gene pool) the bad results. Don't overlook a fault, because inbreeding merely intensifies a fault and makes it worse. For instance, an outcross gives you a one to one thousand ratio

*Beautiful Shih Tzus from
Joi Rush, Sullivan, Missouri*

of finding the good or bad, and inbreeding brings the chances down to one to thirty.

You must start with good sound stock and learn as much as possible about it. The offspring are the only proof of what you can learn. The longer you linebreed, the more alike the offspring will become, *but don't hesitate to eliminate from your breeding program those dogs or bitches that throw serious faults.*

This latter problem is where many mistakes are made and secrets are kept from new breeders. If a valuable stud or bitch begins to throw serious hereditary problems within a line, the dog should be eliminated from your breeding program. You are doing the breed a great injustice if your attitude is *"All I need is one good male in a litter and it doesn't matter if the rest are lousy."*

It does matter, and your actions may cause many people many problems.

The three accepted forms of inbreeding practiced by most breeders are:

- Mating sire to his daughter and producing stock with three-quarters of the genetic makeup of the sire. This is to intensify his qualities.

- Mating the dam to her own son or sons successively. This increases the genetic makeup of the dam. With a good brood, this promises a lot.

- Brother and sister mating, but this is the least promising, since you are working with unknown quantities instead of the sire-and-dam matings, where you already know what their offspring are like.

Selecting and Maintaining the Stud Dog

The dog you select as a stud should have certain things going for him. First, he should be masculine in appearance and, to at least your appraisal, conform closely to the breed standard. A major mistake made by breeders is to keep a dog that is overdone in some feature in the hope he can overcome a bitch with deficiencies in these areas. It doesn't work that way! Breeding an oversize dog to a small bitch in the hope of getting average size puppies is a futile effort. The hallmark of a good breeder, one who understands basic genetics, is breeding to dogs who conform to the standard. Extremes should be avoided like the plague. They only add complications to a breeding program down the road.

Second, it is extremely important that the stud dog come from an unbroken line of producers on both his sire's and dam's side. By unbroken it is meant that at least his sire, grandfather and great grandfather should have produced ten or more champions each. If his sire is still young he may not have hit that mark, but from reading the magazines and seeing his offspring an intelligent breeder can tell if he is going to make it. This unbroken line helps to ensure that he is likely to be homozygous for his good traits. An unbroken producing bitch line is frosting on the cake. It's usually more difficult to find because bitches have fewer offspring. So, when a dog is found that has unbroken producing lines for three generations on his sire's and dam's side, there is an excellent chance of having a prepotent stud.

Third, is appearance. Let's face it, if the male is not constructed right or if his color is not quite right, he is not going to be a great show dog. While the dog doesn't have to be a great show winner to attract the bitches, it helps. Believe me, it helps. Of course there are outstanding examples of non-titled dogs being excellent studs. However, they are few and far between.

There is more to breeding than just dropping a bitch in season into the stud dog's pen and hoping for the best.

First off, let's talk about a subject that never seems to be addressed in the literature about stud dogs, the psyche of the dog. Young stud dogs need to be brought along slowly. If he is a show dog to begin with, he is most likely outgoing an the "gung ho" type. If he is not, please do not think about using him at stud. Behavior traits such as shyness and lack of aggressiveness are transmitted to the next generation just as beautiful necks or slipped stifles are.

He should be taught to get along with other male dogs. Do not put him in with an older male too early on. If you do, there is a good likelihood that he will be intimidated and it may harm his prospects of being a good stud. Good stud dogs have to be aggressive in the breeding box. Dogs who have been intimidated early seldom shape up. However, running, playing and even puppy fighting with littermates or slightly older puppies doesn't seem to have a detrimental effect.

The young male, until he is old enough to stand up for himself, should be quartered first with puppies his own age and then introduced to older bitches as kennel mates. It's not a good idea to keep him in a pen by himself. Socialization is extremely important. Time for play as a puppy and a companion to keep him from boredom helps his growth and development.

His quarters and food should present no special problems. Serious breeders all feed their dogs a nourishing and balanced diet. Study after study in colleges of veterinary medicine and by nutritionists at major dog food companies, have shown that the major brands of dry dog food come as close to meeting the total needs of the dog as any elaborately concocted breeder's formula. Each of you has probably learned to add three drops of this and two teaspoons of that, but honestly, a good dry food does the trick. Many breeders spice up the basic diet with their own version of goodies, including table scraps, to break up the monotony or to stimulate a finicky eater. However, for the most part, this is more cosmetic than nutritional. If it makes you feel better, feed him those extra goodies. Do not get him fat and out of condition. That could do terrible things to his libido.

A very important aspect of being the owner of a stud dog is to make sure he can produce puppies. Therefore, at around eleven-twelve months of age it's a good idea to trundle him off to the vet's for a check on his sperm count. This will tell you if he is producing enough viable sperm cells to make sure he can fertilize eggs in the ovum of a bitch. Sometimes it is found that while a stud produces spermatazoa, they are not active. The chances of this dog being able to fertilize an egg is markedly reduced. While this problem is usually found in older dogs, it happens often enough in young animals to be of concern. Thus the sperm count exam is important, and should be done yearly.

Since we are dealing with the breeding of a warm-blooded mammal, there is need to be concerned with his general health. Sexual contact with a variety of bitches exposes the dog to a wide variety of minor infections and some major ones. Some, if not promptly identified and treated, can lead to sterility—and there goes the farm! Other non-sexual infections and illnesses, such as urinary infections, stones, etc., can also reduce a dog's ability to sire puppies. Since it is not desirable for any of these things to happen, stud dog owners need to watch their young Romeos like a hawk.

*Top: Seven week old Blood-
hounds, bred by Judi Soulé,
photo by Teresa Coffey*

*Middle left: One year old
Keeshond, bred and owned by
Joanee Fraser*

Middle right: Min Pin

*Bottom: 12 week old Keeshond,
Joanee Fraser*

It's a good idea to have your vet check all incoming bitches. While checking them for obvious signs of infection, especially brucellosis, he can also run a smear to see when they are ready to breed. The dog should also be checked frequently to see if there is any type of discharge from his penis. A dog at regular stud should not have a discharge. Usually he will lick himself frequently to keep the area clean. After breeding it is also a good idea to rinse off the area with a clean saline solution. Your vet may also advise flushing out the penile area after breeding using a special solution.

The testicles and penis are the male organs of reproduction. Testicles are housed in a sac called the scrotum. The AKC will not allow dogs who are cryptorchids (neither testicle descended) nor monorchids (a dog that has only one testicle descended) to be shown.

The male's testicles are outside the body because the internal heat of the body would curtail the production of sperm. There is a special muscle that keeps them close to the body for warmth in cold weather and relaxes and lets them down to get cooled in hot weather.

In the male fetus the gonads, or sex organs, develop in the abdominal cavity—migrating during gestation toward their eventual position. Shortly before birth they hover over an opening in the muscular structure of the pubic area through which they will descend to reach the scrotal sac. This external position is vital to the fertility of the animal, for production of live sperm can only proceed at a temperamental several degrees cooler than normal body temperature. The glandular tissue of the testes are nourished and supported by arteries, veins, nerves, connective tissue and duct work, collectively known as the spermatic cord. The scrotum acts as a thermostat. As noted above, there are many involuntary muscle fibers within it that are stimulated to contract with the environmental temperature pulling the testes closer to the body for warmth. Contraction also occurs as a result of any stimulus which might be interpreted by the dog as a threat of physical harm—sight of a strange dog, being picked up, etc. This contraction does not force the testicles back up into the abdominal cavity of the adult dog because the inguinal rings have tightened and will not allow them to be drawn back up. The tightening of the rings usually occurs at about ten months of age.

There are a number of reasons why a dog may be a monorchid or cryptorchid. For example the size of the opening through the muscles may be too small to allow for easy passage of the testes, or the spermatic cord may not be long enough for the testes to remain in the scrotum most of the time, and as the proportions of the inguinal ring and testes change in the growing puppy, the time comes when the testes may be trapped above the ring as they grow at different rates. Also there exists a fibrous muscular band which attracts both to the testes and scrotal wall, gradually shortening and actually guiding the testes in their descent. Possibly this structure could be at fault.

The important thing about all of this is to help the prospective stud dog owner learn about the anatomy of the reproduction organs of the dog. From the foregoing, is it any wonder that many puppies are described as being down one day and up the next?

Next time you place that favorite male puppy on the grooming table, be wary when probing for all of his standard equipment. The scrotal muscles may contract and the still generous inguinal rings may allow the disappearance of the parts sought.

Great luck, a youngster has been found that has "IT" and it is decided to let the world share in the good fortune of owning him. It's a good idea to get him started on the right foot with a cooperative, experienced bitch, on of your own preferably. By introducing the young and inexperienced stud to a "woman of the world," his first experience will result in an easy and successful breeding. Like all males, his ego will soar as a result. This is important. He needs to have the feeling of accomplishment and success. A feisty, difficult bitch the first time around could very well frustrate the youngster and, as a result, he may not be too enthusiastic about future breedings. Remember, we want a confident and aggressive stud dog in the breeding box. There will be difficult bitches to come so it's best to bring him along slow and easy until he will be a match for these fearsome females.

When the bitch is ready to breed (as your stud gains experience he will not pay too much attention to her until she is really ready) both animals should be allowed to exercise and relieve themselves just before being brought together. It's also a good idea not to feed them before mating. Bring the bitch in first. The place should be quiet and away from noise and other dogs. Spend a few minutes petting her and telling her how wonderful she is. Then bring the dog in on a lead. Do not allow him to come lunging in and make a frustrated leap at her. This can cause her to panic and bite him out of fear.

Another Keeshond from
Joanee Fraser

After a few minutes of pirouetting around together—she throwing her vulva in his face and he, with his ears curled on top of his head, trying to lick fore and aft—take off the lead. Allow them to court for a few minutes. She should tell you she is ready by being coquettish and continually backing into the dog.

Now comes the important time for the future success of the young stud. The dog needs to learn the owner is there to help and should not back away from breeding the bitch just because someone is holding her.

Having planned ahead, there will be a large non-skid rug on the floor. Place the bitch on the rug, add a little Vaseline around the vulva and face her rump toward the dog. Pat her on the fanny to encourage the dog to come ahead. Generally speaking, he will. As a rule he will lick her again around the vulva. Some dogs are truly considerate lovers, they will go around to the front and gently lick at the bitches' eyes and ears. These are true gentlemen. However, this will get him nowhere, so again encourage him to come around to where the action is. If he is unsure of himself, lift the bitch's rear and dangle it in front of the dog's nose.

By now, encouraged and emboldened, the male will mount the bitch from the rear and begin to slowly probe for the opening to the vagina. Once he discovers it, he will begin to move more rapidly. This is a critical time. Some young dogs are so far off the target they never get near the right opening. It's time to gently reposition the bitch so he can have a better angle. This may occur any number of times. He may get frustrated and back off. Don't get excited, this is normal in a young dog. He may even get so excited and confused that he swings around and tries to breed her from the front. This approach never ends successfully.

If your stud is getting all hot and bothered and not having much success, take a break. Put the dog back by himself for a couple of hours. Don't let him wear himself out. This lack of success can make him lose interest. Pet him and tell him how great he is. At the end of that time, try again. The approach should be the same. If it happens a second time, the bitch may not be ready. And if after twenty minutes of fruitless endeavor you do not have a tie, there is always tomorrow. Do not work the young dog to the point of exhaustion. When the next day rolls around you can begin again, giving him maximum encouragement. Don't let him fool around again or he will learn bad habits and think that he had to perform these antics before breeding the bitch.

Get him back on track. Show him the business end again, and encourage him to proceed. By now you have noticed a red, bone-like protuberance sticking out from the penis sheath. This, of course, is the penis itself. As a dog continues to probe and finds the opening, he will begin to move frantically. As he moves in this fashion, a section just behind the pointed penis bone begins to swell. It is capable of great enlargement. This enlargement of the bulbous takes place due to its filling with blood, and it becomes some three times larger than the rest of the penis. In this way, the dog, once having made penetration, is "tied" to the bitch; it is entirely due to the male, the bitch having no part in the initial tying.

When a tie has occurred, the semen is pumped in spurts into the vagina. The bitch then helps to keep the penis enlarged as she begins to have a series of pulsating waves which cause a slight tightening and relaxing of the vagina. Some males will stay tied for up to sixty minutes and others as little as five. A five-minute successful tie is just as satisfactory as a longer one, because the semen has moved up through the uterus and fallopian tubes to the ovarian capsules by the end of five minutes.

Once the dog and bitch are successfully tied, the male characteristically tries to lift his rear leg over the bitch to keep the tie in a back to back position. Some dogs merely slide off the back of the bitch and maintain a tie facing in the same direction. One thing you can count on, they will not stay in one position for any length of time. If someone were to chart the moves of a dog and a bitch during a thirty minute tie, it would look like break dancing at its best. Because of this it may be a good idea to have two people involved at this point: one at the bitch's head and one at the male's.

Every now and then a fractious bitch will be sent for breeding. She can be frightened about being shipped, or just plain spooked by a variety of things. Certainly one doesn't want a stud to be bitten by a frightened bitch, nor to have one's own fingers lacerated (yes, even a frightened Pug may bite!). The easiest solution is to muzzle the bitch's jaws. Usually an extra pair of firm hands will gently restrain the bitch from doing any harm to you or the stud. If absolutely necessary, a wire muzzle can protect you from snapping teeth.

After the tie has been broken, there sometimes will be a rush of fluid from the bitch. Don't worry about it, the sperm is well on its way up the fallopian tubes. Gently move the bitch to a quite pen, apart from other dogs, and give her fresh water and an opportunity to relieve herself. The dog should be petted and told how well he has done. This is a good time to flush out his sheath, and if your vet has recommended any medication, apply it now. Then, the dog, too, should be put in a separate quiet pen with fresh water. It is not a good idea to put him back with a group of male dogs. The opportunity for a serious fight is greatest at this time. The other dogs smell him and get quite upset that it wasn't their turn.

How often can a dog be used at stud? If the dog is in good condition, he should be able to be used every day for a week. Some serious breeders who, when faced with many bitches to be bred to a popular stud, have used the dog in the morning and the evening for at least three days. If a dog is used regularly, he can be used from day-to-day for a long time. However, if a dog is seldom used, he should not be expected to be able to service day after day for any great length of time.

Nature is most generous with sperm. In one good mating a dog may discharge millions, and by and large, a copious amount of sperm is produced in dogs who are used regularly.

All this Olympian activity may be possible for a short time, but for good health and good management, three times a week in normal use seems about right for the average stud. Of course, most breeders would give their eyeteeth for such a popular dog. An individual bitch should be serviced twice—once every other day—for the best chance at conception.

For some breeders to breed to a stud of their choice is often difficult, especially in countries that have quarantine restrictions. In the U.S., the basic cost of shipping, the possibility of the dog being booked, the chance of making connections with a popular stud who is out on circuit being campaigned, etc., are some of the problems that can produce a great deal of frustration. The use of frozen sperm opens up many new possibilities. Owners of popular stud dogs should definitely look into it. At the time of this writing, there are a number of AKC-sanctioned collection stations. There should be many more in the future.

Collecting sperm from dogs is not like collecting from cattle. One collection from the latter produces enough to inseminate over 100 cows. The largest amount collected, at one time, over the many years of research in dogs was twenty-two vials. Usually two to three vials are used to breed a bitch on two to three occasions while she is in season.

The estimated time to store enough semen to inseminate thirty bitches differs by age, health, and sperm quantity and quality. Estimate approximately a month for a young dog, approximately three months for a dog of eight or nine years of age or older. Collection is still time-consuming.

It doesn't take one long to recognize that, in the early stages, those males of outstanding quality will make up the main reservoir of the sperm bank. It is suggested by the collection centers that collection be done at a young age—three to five years.

Limitations in quality and quantity due to old age lengthen the period necessary to store enough sperm for even a few bitches. In addition, the daily routine of a dog's life may limit freezability. The settling down in an new environment, changes in diet/water, minor health problems, etc. It is also not uncommon to get poor freeze results from a stud dog that has not been used for a month or longer. For the dog, once he settles down, the process of collection is a pleasant experience.

Now, for a most important item: How much should be charged for the dog's services? A good rule of thumb says that for a young unproven stud, charge 65%-75% of the average being charged. Don't include the Mr. Big's who have already sired twenty or more champions in your calculations. Their fees are elevated based upon accomplishment. You are charging a fee based upon hope and good bloodlines. After the dog has sired at least five champions, boost his fee to the average being charged. If he should prove to be a *prepotent* stud and sires some 115 champion offspring, a price more commensurate with his siring abilities should be set. Don't be afraid to ask a price above the average. Th average breeder, like the average buyer of goods, equates a good price with a good product.

What am I going to be when I grow up?

Chapter 4

Having Puppies

Whether this is your first litter or your next litter, this information should be helpful to you in delivering a healthy litter of puppies and being a good caretaker to your little mother.

Let's back up a few weeks from the actual delivery and mention that your breeding female should have been in good health with no unusual vaginal discharge before breeding. Her vaccinations should be up to date before she is bred. She should be a good quality bitch, not necessarily a Champion, but sound of body and leg. You should certainly study the AKC Standard for your breed before you buy your foundation bitch.

Some breeders will want you to have a Brucellosis test on your bitch before breeding, and you are perfectly within your rights to ask if the stud has been tested as well.

To determine the approximate best time for breeding, the bitch should be presented to a veterinarian for a vaginal smear at about five days after the first sign of color and swelling. There are some bitches who come into heat and are ready for breeding before they are willing to accept the male, and in these cases, you or your veterinarian will have to do an artificial insemination. Usually, the best times for breeding are about the tenth, twelfth, and fourteenth day of color. Your veterinarian can teach you how to read the changes of the cornified cells under a microscope. Some breeders use diabetic testape, which starts to turn green when the breeding time is right, after being inserted carefully at the opening of the vulva. I personally have used both approaches and have had no missed pregnancies as long as the stud was viable. There is no clinical, medical proof that

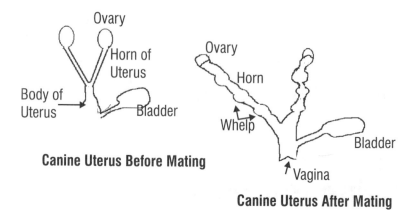

Canine Uterus Before Mating

Canine Uterus After Mating

the testape is a good guide, but it does turn green at the most promising time for breeding.

Ovulation testape, available from the Revival catalog is manufactured by Wysong. The toll-free phone number to request the catalog is (800) 786-4751, Fax (712) 737-5566.

Handling a mating is not always a simple task. Many people try to breed two animals with no success, causing much frustration and possible harm to the stud. Don't just put dog and bitch down together and expect nature to take its course. To do so is letting yourself in for big problems—either to the stud if the bitch attacks him, or to the bitch if the dog is overly aggressive.

Do seek professional help in getting the dogs bred. A professional breeder will be able to guide you regarding the best approach to mating, with safety considerations for your bitch and the stud dog. In some instances, the bitch ovulates before she is willing to accept the male, and in those cases, artificial insemination may be the only answer. In this situation, ovulation testing by your veterinarian is the key to determining the correct breeding time. Fortunately, these instances are rare and probably not worth all the extra effort and expense involved. The period of normal heat is usually one week coming in, one week in heat, and one week going out. The ova (eggs) are ready to be fertilized as they reach the uterus and break down if not fertilized within forty-eight hours. The male sperm live up to seven days.

There is a device developed in Poland, called an Ovulation Detector. The URL on the Internet is: www.draminski.com.pl/. Marjorie Winebrenner is the United States distributor at mwine@serv2fwi.com. Her phone number is (219) 925-0185, and she reports that the device is extremely accurate. It uses a probe that tests the vaginal secretions and tells you when ovulation is near, when the exact day to breed is, whether or not it's a false heat, and so forth. The cost is approximately $350.

This might be an answer for someone having a problem finding the right timing to get their female bred. There are no other accessories to buy. It must be cleaned well and sterilized each time.

There are, however, reasons for doing an artificial insemination, such as the size of the dog as compared to the female. Some females just plain want to remain a virgin forever, and that doesn't mean that they aren't going to be good mothers. Of course, sperm banks store frozen sperm. The best place to get information on that source is The Saeger SI Clinic, 329 Sioux, Park Forest, IL 60466. Phone (708) 748-0954. This clinic will also sell you an AI kit with instructions on performing an artificial insemination. *DO NOT USE A FEEDING TUBE TO INSEMINATE. TO DO SO COULD CAUSE GREAT PAIN IF THE TUBE ACCIDENTALLY GOES INTO THE CERVIX.* The pipette that comes with the AI kit from Dr. Saeger's Clinic is a bit more rigid. When you feel it slip over the pelvic area, it is where it belongs. I don't do an AI unless I have to, but I do not hesitate to do it if there is no choice. The result has been many live puppies.

Another service for AI and reproductive related products is International Canine Genetics, 271 Great Valley Parkway, Malvern, PA 19355. Phone (800) 248-8099 or (215) 640-1244

To do an AI with larger breeds, you will need someone to hold the bitch, and it would be a good idea to put a muzzle on her. Collecting from the dog can be done in the same manner. Elevation of the rear of the bitch for at least ten minutes after inserting the sperm in the vagina is recommended, and then two hours of crating is advised.

The average time of gestation (pregnant with pups) is sixty-three days, however anytime from fifty-six days to seventy-two days should be okay provided none of the *danger signals* listed later are apparent. See the following *Perpetual Whelping Calendar* on page 36 for more information.

Equipment Needed

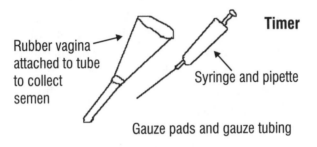

Rubber vagina attached to tube to collect semen

Timer

Syringe and pipette

Gauze pads and gauze tubing

Make sure all equipment is thoroughly dry and clean.

Allow dog and bitch to sniff each other and grasp penis between thumb and forefinger and massage making sure the sheath is behind the bulbous glands. Slip the collection sheath in place over the penis.

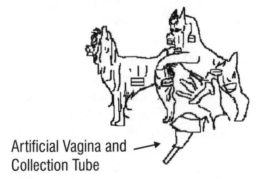

Artificial Vagina and Collection Tube

After collection for five minutes and holding your left hand around the tube to keep the collection warm, have your helper put the male in a safe place and elevate the rear of the female. Draw the semen from the collection tube with the syringe and pipette and insert it vaginally over the pelvic ridge. Slowly deposit the seminal fluid. Holding the bitch upright, remove the syringe and put your finger over the pipette to keep fluid from coming out.

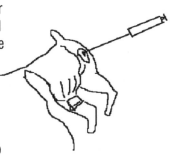

Reinsert syringe and inject air to help the flow of seminal fluid in the right direction. Remove the pipette.

Simulate "tie" by putting your gloved finger into the vaginal canal with the bitch's rear still elevated. After five minutes, put cold wet compress over the vulva and keep rear elevated for another ten minutes.

Crate the bitch for two hours after AI breeding.

Perpetual Whelping Calendar

Date Bred	Date due to whelp	Date Bred	Date Bred	Date Bred	Date due to whelp	Date Bred	Date due to whelp	Date Bred	Date due to whelp	Date Bred	Date due to whelp
January	March	February	April	March	May	April	June	May	July	June	August
1	5	1	5	1	3	1	3	1	3	1	3
2	6	2	6	2	4	2	4	2	4	2	4
3	7	3	7	3	5	3	5	3	5	3	5
4	8	4	8	4	6	4	6	4	6	4	6
5	9	5	9	5	7	5	7	5	7	5	7
6	10	6	10	6	8	6	8	6	8	6	8
7	11	7	11	7	9	7	9	7	9	7	9
8	12	8	12	8	10	8	10	8	10	8	10
9	1	9	13	9	11	9	11	9	11	9	11
10	14	10	14	10	12	10	12	10	12	10	12
11	15	11	15	11	13	11	13	11	13	11	13
12	16	12	16	12	14	12	14	12	14	12	14
13	17	13	17	13	15	13	15	13	15	13	15
14	18	14	18	14	16	14	16	14	16	14	16
15	19	15	19	15	17	15	17	15	17	15	17
16	20	16	20	16	18	16	18	16	18	16	18
17	21	17	21	17	19	17	19	17	19	17	19
18	22	18	22	18	20	18	20	18	20	18	20
19	23	19	23	19	21	19	21	19	21	19	21
20	24	20	24	20	22	20	22	20	22	20	22
21	25	21	25	21	23	21	23	21	23	21	23
22	26	22	26	22	24	22	24	22	24	22	24
23	27	23	27	23	25	23	25	23	25	23	25
24	28	24	28	24	26	24	26	24	26	24	26
25	29	25	29	25	27	25	27	25	27	25	27
26	30	26	30	26	28	26	28	26	28	26	28
27	31	27	1	27	29	27	29	27	29	27	29
28	1	28	2	28	30	28	30	28	30	28	30
29	2			29	31	29	1	29	31	29	31
30	3			30	1	30	2	30	1	30	1
31	4			31	2			31	2		

Perpetual Whelping Calendar

Date Bred	Date due to whelp	Date Bred	Date Bred	Date Bred	Date due to whelp	Date Bred	Date due to whelp	Date Bred	Date due to whelp	Date Bred	Date due to whelp
July	September	August	October	September	November	October	December	November	January	December	February
1	2	1	3	1	3	1	3	1	3	1	2
2	3	2	4	2	4	2	4	2	4	2	3
3	4	3	5	3	5	3	5	3	5	3	4
4	5	4	6	4	6	4	6	4	6	4	5
5	6	5	7	5	7	5	7	5	7	5	6
6	7	6	8	6	8	6	8	6	8	6	7
7	8	7	9	7	9	7	9	7	9	7	8
8	9	8	10	8	10	8	10	8	10	8	9
9	10	9	11	9	11	9	11	9	11	9	10
10	11	10	12	10	12	10	12	10	12	10	11
11	12	11	13	11	13	11	13	11	13	11	12
12	13	12	14	12	14	12	14	12	14	12	13
13	14	13	15	13	15	13	15	13	15	13	14
14	15	14	16	14	16	14	16	14	16	14	15
15	16	15	17	15	17	15	17	15	17	15	16
16	17	16	18	16	18	16	18	16	18	16	17
17	18	17	19	17	18	17	19	17	19	17	18
18	19	18	20	18	20	18	20	18	20	18	19
19	20	19	21	19	21	19	21	19	21	19	20
20	21	20	22	20	22	20	22	20	22	20	21
21	22	21	23	21	23	21	23	21	23	21	22
22	23	22	24	22	24	22	24	22	24	22	23
23	24	23	25	23	25	23	25	23	25	23	24
24	25	24	26	24	26	24	26	24	26	24	25
25	26	25	27	25	27	25	27	25	27	25	26
26	27	26	28	26	28	26	28	26	28	26	27
27	28	27	29	27	29	27	29	27	29	27	28
28	29	28	30	28	30	28	30	28	30	28	1
29	30	29	31	29	31	29	31	29	31	29	2
30	1	30	1	30	1	30	1	30	1	30	3
31	2	31	2			31	2	31		31	4

Your veterinarian can examine your bitch and palpate her at thirty to thirty-five days in an effort to determine her pregnancy, or if you are too anxious to wait, many veterinarians offer an ultrasound service to determine if she is pregnant. They usually can, at that time, determine if there is more than one pup. The cost of this service varies; you might want to find out first what the cost is, because your curiosity may not be worth the price you will be charged.

Some signs of pregnancy are: loss of appetite during the third or fourth week for a day or so, up to a week. Don't let this go on too long. If she seems thin or if her *gums lose their color*, start feeding her with a syringe to keep up her strength. A good formula for this is either Esbilac with an added egg yolk or the following homemade formula.

> l can evaporated milk
> l can (equal amount) Pedialyte plain (or Gatorade plain)
> (or 1 1/2 cups boiled water, 4 teaspoons Karo syrup, dash salt)
> 1 egg yolk
>
> Put these items (or the substitutes) in a blender; warm to body temperature; add Gerber's Baby Rice to thicken, or use the syringe to feed her with the Nursing Mom Pudding Recipe.

You may notice that your pregnant bitch will throw up a bit now and then, and there may be some swelling at her breasts. Usually, by the sixth and seventh weeks, it is pretty obvious to even the most inexperienced first-time breeder that she is in whelp. If there is no sign of pregnancy and you are in serious doubt that she is pregnant, take her one week before her first due date—NOT EARLIER—and allow the veterinarian to X-ray her to see if there is more than one pup in the uterus. If there is one pup, there is a possibility that she may need a Cesarean Section at whelping time. An X ray is a very good diagnostic tool for the veterinarian and for you so you know approximately with how many pups you are dealing.

Keep the hair around the vulva short, and keep the vulva clean using a furacin solution and cotton ball or cotton tipped swabs. A mucous vaginal discharge is normal during pregnancy and is no problem as long as it isn't green, yellow, or foul smelling.

She should be fed fifty percent more food after five or six weeks, when you are confident she is in whelp, in divided meals (two times a day) or twenty-five percent more food three times a day and Pet Tabs as well as Solid Gold Concep, which contains raspberry leaf tea. According to James Duke Ph.D., one of the foremost experts on herbs and their uses, wrote: "I'm sold on raspberry for complaints of pregnancy. One study identified a chemical in raspberry that relaxes the uterus. For centuries, women prone to miscarriage have been urged to drink raspberry leaf tea throughout their pregnancy to help them carry the baby to term." From *The Green Pharmacy.*

James Balch M.D., another authority on natural health and nutrition, supported red raspberry leaf tea and claims that it decreases menstrual bleeding, relaxes uterine and intestinal spasms, and strengthens uterine walls. It also promotes healthy bones, teeth, and skin, helps with diarrhea and relieves female disorders such as morning sickness, hot flashes, and cramps. It can be combined with peppermint for nausea and heals canker sores.

You should get your pregnant female used to staying in a confined area as her whelping time approaches and when you cannot watch her activities regularly. Otherwise, she may make her nest where you cannot find it or have puppies all over the place so that they can become chilled and die. Do get her used to the area that you set up for her to have her puppies and nurse them, a whelping box that is low enough for her to get in and out of easily but not so low that the pups can roll out and chill. Choose an area that is draft free and away from heavy people traffic. *Please tape the carpet or heavy toweling or sheepskin to the bottom of the box with duct tape rolled so it is sticky on both sides.* If you don't, the mother may paw up the pads and accidentally smother or jump on a pup and injure it.

It's okay to use a heating pad (with chewproof cord if possible), **but do not cover the entire area with heat!** It's better to tape the heating pad to the edge of the outside of the whelping box covering only, at the *most* one-third of the area. Too much heat will make the mother uncomfortable and keep the pups from cuddling to her.

With a large litter, three or more pups, it usually isn't necessary to have a heating pad. Another alternative is a chill chaser at least eight feet above the whelping area. Be careful to monitor temperature where pups and mother are lying, especially if using a heat lamp chill chaser.

One week before her first due date, check your maternity supplies listed next, and be sure you have everything you may need for the BIG DAY!

Whelping Supplies

A whelping nest can be the bottom half of a fiberglass crate or a more elaborate one with a "pig rail" to keep the pups from being smothered. Many dog catalogs offer these fiberglass "nests" with a "pig rail." Size, of course, depends on the size of the expectant mom. It should be big enough for her to lie down in, with sides high enough that the pups won't tumble out. Another alternative is the Dura-Whelp corrugated plastic whelping box along with the Therma-Whelp heat emitter (no light—just heat) and cradle.

The directions suggest keeping the cradle temperature between 85 and 95 degrees. The pups get on and off the cradle as they want and seem very contented on it. Some users feel that the mom seems much more comfortable in the box with this heating system than she did with the old heat lamp and/or heating pads.

Other Supplies:

- A scale (the Homs, model number 28 is an excellent scale with ounce measurements that are very easy to read)

- Or the new digital scales which show ounces very clearly.

- Nutri-Cal high calorie dietary supplement

- Clean, dry towels (preferably hand towels and wash cloths)

- Sterile three-inch gauze pads to dry inside pups' mouths

- Alcohol to sterilize instruments and hands

- Betadine Skin Cleanser

- Several hemostats (Kelly forceps—7") at least three straight and one curved, to clamp umbilical cord if necessary

- Iodine to apply to umbilical cord to aid in drying and kill germs

- Sterile cotton balls, baby bottles and preemie nipples, small Bordon nursing bottles.

- Tube feeding kit—No. 5 toy feeding tube for toys. No 8 for larger breeds.

- Glucose solution
  1 teaspoon (5cc) white corn syrup
  A few grains of salt
  4 tablespoons (60cc) boiled water

- Esbilac or other formula, Just Born
  Esbilac and goats milk with equal parts water
  Or 1 can evaporated milk
  Mix with equal parts Pedialyte and one egg yolk mixed well in blender

- Rectal thermometer and KY Jelly or intimate moisturizer

- Room thermometer to monitor temperature of whelping area which should be approximately 80 degrees Fahrenheit and reduce daily

- Syringes—10cc and 20cc—for giving medicine and measuring formula

- Pure glycerin, which is good to use for a quick enema

- Eyedroppers

- Bay Rum or Camphorated Oil to dry up mother's milk

- Blood stop powder

- Cotton thread or dental floss

- Silver nitrate sticks to stop bleeding at umbilical and when removing dew claws and tails

- Nasal syringe (infants) to suction nose and mouth

- Sterile surgical gloves

- Several pieces of cardboard at least 8 x 11 and Vet wrap (2")

Medications

Amoxicillin
Consult your veterinarian for dosage, depending on weight of dog. (Normal dose is 5 mg/pound, two times day.) A toy dog usually needs 50 mg, and a large breed like a Dane uses 250 mg, two times per day.

Dopram V
Respiratory stimulant; can be used sub- lingually (under tongue) on depressed pup.

Temaril P Prednisolone
Antihistamine/This is a combination drug that many vets still use for respiratory problems.

Lactinex granules or yogurt

Lixotinic
Appetite stimulant, iron source

Pet Nutri Drops
High Energy Nutritional Aid. Can be obtained from BoviDr Laboratories, Inc. Phone (800) 658-4016

Terramycin Opthalmic

Make sure there is good footing in the whelping box. If footing is inadequate, the pups could develop "swimmers" problems (a muscular deficiency usually caused by inadequate footing). Swimmer pups are usually about three to four weeks old, very fat, and full of milk. They extend their legs out spread eagled, and have a hard time getting up on their feet. Taping one-half inch aerated tape in a figure eight pattern near the top of the legs, holding the legs together, usually helps them to "get up" on all four. I have seen one case, and my vet showed me how to tape the legs together. Within a few days, the pup was up on all four legs.

A heating pad can be taped to the outside (one-quarter or one-third) of the box so the dam and pups can get away from the heat if they want to. Firm footing should be taped to the box so the nesting dam cannot disturb it and injure a pup. She will want a couple of hand towels to push around and arrange while she is nesting. Do **not** use indoor outdoor carpeting as it can become toxic when urinated on!

One Week Before Whelping

You should start taking the dam's temperature rectally five to seven days before she is due to whelp. The normal temperature should be approximately 101.4 degrees. When the temperature begins to drop under 100 degrees or lower, you usually will note that it stays low before whelping. When it goes under 99 degrees and remains in the 98 to 99 degree range for twenty-four hours, it is a good indication that whelping time is very close. This is not *always* the case. There are exceptions to every rule where the temperature will rise for some reason before whelping, but these are the *exceptions*. A mucous discharge is normal, but a green or odorous discharge is a sign of trouble, and a veterinarian should be consulted. In any event, as soon as the temperature starts to drop, you should call your veterinarian and be sure that someone will be available for you in case you need veterinary assistance or a cesarean section. A green discharge could indicate premature placental separation, or it could indicate an infection.

After the first pup is passed, it is normal to see some green discharge from the afterbirth.

A cesarean section is an **Emergency**. Don't leave your bitch with a veterinarian who wants to wait until after office hours to take care of your laboring bitch. Ask your veterinarian ahead of time if he considers a cesarean section an emergency. If he does not, keep looking for a vet that does.

When the Temperature Has Dropped

Bathe pregnant bitch with Plexadine shampoo or Betadine shampoo or surgical scrub, and rinse thoroughly. Clip the hair on her abdomen around all the nipples, with a surgical blade—#40 or #30. Be sure her nails are clipped short so she doesn't tear them when nesting (scratching and tearing at paper and towels). When the temperature drops below 99 degrees and stays there for twelve hours, you can be pretty sure that whelping time is upon you. This doesn't mean that your bitch won't start labor at 100 or 99 degrees, but it means that it is a *good indication* that

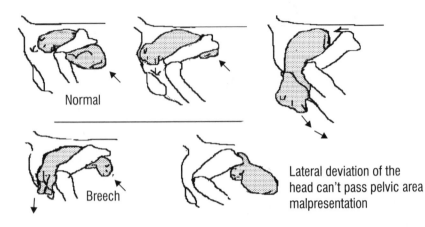

Normal

Breech

Lateral deviation of the head can't pass pelvic area malpresentation

whelping time is near. Make notes of happenings and the time. You may need this information later. Even if you don't need it, it keeps you busy while you nervously wait, and you do lose track of time when you are a nervous wreck!

Stages of Labor

First Stage   Uterine contractions, dilation of cervix, abdominal discomfort, panting; may last three to six hours. The dam may refuse to eat and may have loose stools or a water bag may appear.

Dam in labor. First pup's water bag visible at vulva.

Second Stage   Expulsion of the fetal sac (water bag). This is no reason to panic. The dam may take long naps with one or more water bags just lying at the vulva with occasional contractions for two or three hours and still be okay. If she is pushing steadily for an hour with no results and nothing is in the vaginal canal, you should get in touch with your vet.

The pup's head or tail may be presented first. It is perfectly normal to have posterior presentation. Do not interfere too quickly. Encourage her to continue pushing. If she stops pushing and the water bag is broken and the

Posterior presentation. Dam stopped pushing. Downward pressure applied with warm, wet washcloth.

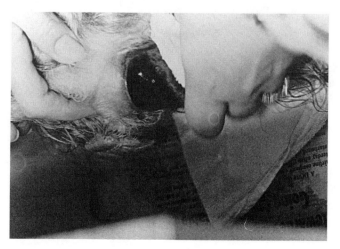

pup is more than halfway out, you may want to grasp the pup with a warm wet wash cloth and apply pressure (don't pull) to encourage her to push out the rest of the pup. If that doesn't work, then it is okay to use some KY on your gloved finger and work it around the vaginal opening while applying pressure in the direction of natural birthing.

Sometimes you are able to hook a finger on the shoulders and carefully work the pup out. If the pup is presented head first and the bitch *stops pushing after the head is out*, you should break the sac, dry out the mouth, syringe the nose, use KY around the vaginal area and apply pressure to the head *without pulling* and try to work your fingers around the shoulders to help her pass that part of the pup. *Don't pull on the head.* Just *apply pressure* until you can hook the shoulder, and then you can pull when the dam is pushing.

Progressive slow withdrawal of cord and placenta with hemostat.

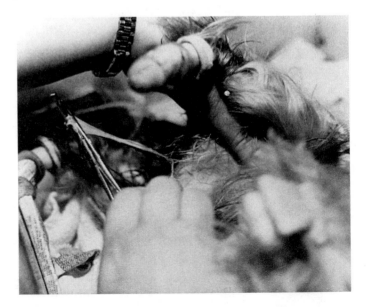

If the pup has been passed, it is good to dry it, even if it is still attached, syringe the nose and mouth, blot the pup's mouth with the sterile gauze, and stimulate with rough wash cloths or hand towels to get the pup crying. The pup may begin nursing at this point even with the placenta (afterbirth) still in the vagina of the dam. Leave the placenta and cord alone for awhile. She will probably pass the placenta within the next half hour. Watch her and keep the pup warm and free from being knocked about by her if she is jumping around. If the dam breaks the sac and licks and stimulates the pup, that's fine! If she doesn't, then you must interfere. You can use your hemostat to clamp about an inch from the puppy's belly and a second hemostat one more inch down on the cord towards the vulva to keep the cord from going back in. Use *dull* scissors or your fingernails to cut the cord between the two hemostats.

Be careful to keep the hemostat pressed against the pup's belly so you do not pull it away from the belly and cause a hernia or pull out the intestines. (*In the event the intestines are accidentally pulled out by you or the dam, do put a sterile, cold, wet compress over the intestines and get the pup to a veterinarian RIGHT AWAY!*)

Keep the pup's head down while you are working on the pup. If you see any bleeding at the pup's naval cord, you may apply a silver nitrate stick to stop the bleeding. Have someone hold the other hemostat, which is still attached to the cord and placenta if it is still inside the bitch. This can be taken care of later after the pup is out of danger. If the pup is not breathing, a slow handshake action while holding the pup in a head down, standing position should facilitate removal of fluids. Make sure you support the neck. It is the most fragile part of the pup. Rub the puppy briskly with a rough hand towel using your thumbs back and forth in the area of the lungs, or use mouth to mouth resuscitation to get the pup breathing in short quick breaths. After the pup is crying and breathing, towel dry, and quickly tie the cord between the belly and the hemostat (approx 3/4" from belly), and place the pup with its dam (or in a warm box or incubator if she is laboring and rough with a subsequent pup). Using a respiratory stimulant is more effective after the pup has taken its first breath, but if you cannot get the pup breathing and crying, a couple drops of Dopram V sublingually (under the tongue) may help. Continue massaging the chest area between your thumbs and shaking down the pup. If you have oxygen, it may help at this point, especially if the pup is gasping or if the breathing sounds raspy or congested.

After the pup is dried, crying, and sounds clear of congestion, it's time to get back to the mother. By applying pressure, turning the hemostat, and wrapping the cord around the hemostat, you can withdraw the placenta if it is still within the mother. If you lose it, don't panic; she will probably pass it with the next pup. Also, don't be surprised if she eats it. Some people feel it provides lots of nourishment for her, and perhaps it does, but I try to dispose of it, because a well fed and properly nourished

Pup all the way out, breathing okay, and dried off. Cord clamped for easy withdrawal.

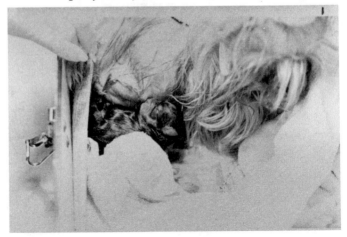

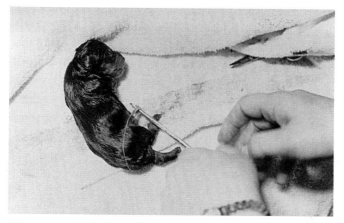

New pup, cord clampled and cut, ready to be tied off and have iodine applied.

mother doesn't need it, and it could give her a bout of diarrhea.

If you have a pup coming out back legs first—about forty percent of puppies do—he may get hung up in the birth canal. If he does, he's going to try to breathe with his head still in the uterus. Any mucous in his lungs will reduce his capacity for oxygen exchange even further.

To clear his lungs, after you've syringed his nose and mouth, and if shaking down hasn't done it, lay him, secured with gauze from a two inch roll or Vet-wrap, on heavy cardboard, head down at a forty-five degree angle, and leave him in that position for about twenty minutes. Put him under a heat lamp or gooseneck with 100 watt bulb so he won't chill. This position will help drain out the fluid. He doesn't like the position so he cries; when he cries, his chest expands, and that's exactly what you want. This method works great after a cesarean section so that you can go from pup to pup particularly if you have no helper. I always have my "board" ready in the incubator. Don't swing the puppy too violently in "shaking down," because if you do, his brain can bang against the skull and cause hemorrhage.

Third Stage   Expulsion of the fetal membranes. The placenta (after-birth) should pass after each pup. Please observe if a placenta has not passed for each pup and notify your vet. The bitch *should* have an injection of Posterior Oxytocin Pituitary (POP) if she has retained a placenta. As a matter of fact, we always give it to be sure the uterus contracts and to increase milk letdown within twelve to twenty-four hours of the whelping.

It is not necessary to do a cesarean section to remove the placentas. Believe it or not, I've heard of this being done. An injection of POP (oxytocin) usually helps the bitch to pass the placenta.

Complications

If the dam has been pushing hard and steady for half an hour and there is no pup in sight, put on a surgical sterile glove and insert your finger in the vaginal canal to feel if there is a pup in the canal. This is called "feathering" and sometimes will make the bitch get down to business and push some more. If the pup is right there, another few pushes should get it out. If not, alert your vet immediately.

Other danger signs before, during, and after whelping—Call Your Vet

- Constant *hard* labor for more than an hour with no results
- Green or odorous discharge from the vulva
- An interval of two hours between pups with occasional hard labor
- Any part of a pup stuck or protruding from the vaginal canal
- One hour of hard labor and no puppies
- Three hours of no labor between pups and you think there is another pup

It is a good idea to try to get the first pup or two nursing, because this will cause a release of natural oxytocin and may help her to begin contractions again to deliver the remaining pups.

Cesarean Section

A decision on a cesarean section is not simple. One vet will try to "pull" a pup that is stuck in a posterior position, and another may decide that a cesarean section will give the pup that is stuck and the pups behind it a better chance of survival. The stress and extra pushing for a "stuck" pup could very well cause fatal respiratory distress in the pups behind the one that is stuck.

The good thing about "pulling" a pup is that if you get it out, your bitch will not have had to go through serious surgery and the resulting adhesions. Even if the pup dies, you can always breed the dam again. The other side of the coin is that, even with a vet's skilled hands, you may not be able to get the pup out, and you may still need to have a cesarean section done. Thought should be given to the condition and the age of the pregnant bitch when this decision is made.

Each situation is different, and you and your vet will have to make a decision with which you can live. The most important decision you can make about a cesarean section is what anesthesia your vet uses. The drug of choice is Isoflurane, which is a gas anesthesia and does not further depress the bitch or the pups. *Fatalities using injectable barbiturates have been numerous.*

Cesarean section single-ton Keeshond pup at four weeks.

Causes of Difficult Birth—Dystocia

Fetal oversize, malpresentation, and abnormality of maternal pelvis are some of the reasons for difficult deliveries of pups. Sometimes a lack of exercise can contribute to poor abdominal muscles, which can affect proper contractions. A low hormonal imbalance otherwise known as *Uterine Inertia,* or exhaustion and nervous inhibition can cause difficult births.

Posterior Oxytocin Pituitary (POP)

Advantages	POP can stimulate uterine contractions if the uterus is sensitive. The cervix must be completely dilated prior to giving POP. It is usually suggested *only* after the first pup has been born. It does increase milk letdown.
Disadvantages	POP can cause placental separation and make delivery of pups much more urgent causing a lack of oxygen to the pup(s); therefore, time becomes critical for delivery of live pups. If used improperly, it can cause a ruptured uterus. Always speak to your vet before the use of POP.

Ectopic Pregnancy

Ectopic pregnancy occurs when a fetus develops outside of the uterus because of a uterine rupture either from a previous pregnancy or some kind of trauma to the abdomen. Because of the lack of blood supply, the result is usually mummification of the fetus involved.

Postnatal Care of the Dam

Her vaginal discharge, which should be red and/or dark in the beginning and may be mixed with some green stuff, should gradually fade. We prefer to give POP within twelve to twenty-four hours of the end of whelping. This will cause the uterus to contract, thus emptying it of any membranes that could cause infection; it also increases the milk letdown.

Any vaginal discharge that is odorous, green, or filled with pus should be reported to your veterinarian immediately. Keep the vaginal area clean with Furacin or another antibiotic solution, and keep hair in that area clipped very short.

If the dam has had a cesarean section, allow your vet to remove the stitches. He will examine the abdomen of the bitch at that time and physically examine her. If she is in "show wraps" because of long hair, be careful that they are packaged very tightly so that a puppy doesn't get hung up in the wraps or in the hair!

Make sure that her nipples are flowing and breasts are not becoming hard. The pups won't nurse on the nipple with a hard breast. You may have to use very warm compresses and gently knead off the excess milk in order to get them to use that nipple. Pay attention to this, because the dam could get mastitis, an acute mammary infection. The milk could become toxic, which leads to hand raising pups, which is no picnic!

To dry up her milk at weaning time, a twenty-four hour fast and cold compresses twice a day for a few days are in order (see weaning). If she doesn't have enough milk, the following mix is good to improve milk supply, if it is a large litter.

Mix large 4 cup size vanilla pudding, 1/2 cup of sugar, 4 cups of milk, and 4 egg yolks. Cook on low heat to a pudding consistency, and offer to your new mom (at body temperature please)! I have never had this recipe cause diarrhea, and it definitely brings in an abundance of milk. Let her eat as much of it as she wants to, probably 20 cc or more twice a day for a small (ten pound or under) dog, in addition to regular food.

If you don't have a large 4 cup package of vanilla pudding on hand you can mix the following in a saucepan and cook on medium heat to pudding consistency.

2/3 cup sugar
6 tablespoons cornstarch
1/2 teaspoon salt
4 cups milk (or one can evaporated milk plus equal parts water to make quart)
4 egg yolks
2 teaspoons vanilla
Feed with a syringe, on a spoon, or let her eat it from a bowl.

Eclampsia (Milk Fever)

Symptoms   The nursing bitch may have rapid breathing, restlessness, nervousness, and whining. She may stagger and develop stiff limbs and exhibit elevated body temperature. The bitch may be unable to rise, lie with extended legs, salivate, and sound congested. Untreated, it can lead to convulsions and death. Most common during the first three weeks of lactation, eclampsia can occur up to six weeks after delivery.

Cause   Too low a calcium level due to malfunction of the pituitary gland, mostly common in the small- or medium-sized breeds.

Treatment   A cold compress to the tummy will help on the way to the vet if there is a high fever. The emergency treatment by the vet is to give a calcium solution by intravenous injection. Reoccurrence is common. Remove pups, and bottle feed so that the bitch is not again depleted of calcium from nursing.

Prevention   Give a calcium tablet with vitamin D supplement after whelping until weaning time, or calcium injectable as recommended by your vet. Even then, the possibility of eclampsia exists, so it is a good idea to supplement a litter of three or more after three weeks of age in small breeds and six or more in larger breeds to cut down the drain on the mother.

Your vet may want you to supplement with oral calcium prior to an eclampsia episode, *but not before whelping.*

Dr. Dale Heisler states, "If you give calcium supplement during gestation the body says 'Hey, why should I release any calcium into the bloodstream as I'm getting it from an outside source. I think I'll just shut down and not do any work.' Then the puppies are born, more calcium is needed for milk. The body says 'OK, I"ll do the best I can, but you've got to realize that I have been shut down for several weeks. It will take me a few days to catch up.' All of a sudden Eclampsia results. The moral of the story: Don't give any calcium supplement during gestation. A Pet Tab is OK. Increase the food during the last three weeks of gestation. After the puppies are born, feed her all the food she wants to keep the milk supply up. Definitely give a Pet Tab during nursing."

Amoxicillin is sometimes suggested by your vet to use on a nursing mom, and I have administered this with no problem. It is excreted in small amounts but has not been known to harm the pups. Of course if you don't have to use any types of medication on pregnant and nursing dogs, that is ideal, but sometimes we are not left with any other option. However, under no circumstances should penicillin be administered to a nursing or pregnant mom. It could cause Fading Puppy Disease.

Uterine Prolapse

Signs	Bitch pushes uterus out.
Cause	Overstraining with labor. Giving POP too close to whelping time, for instance right after whelping. It is best to wait a few hours before giving POP. It will work for milk letdown and contracting the uterus if given to the bitch within twenty-four hours of delivery of the last pup.
Treatment	Cover uterus with wet sterile dressing and get *immediate* veterinary attention.

Socialization While Nursing

Never allow nursing mothers to visit one another while they are nursing. Also, "Daddy" does not have to come to visit his puppies either. It is *not unusual* for a nursing mother to ravage another mother's babies. It happens. Why take a chance?

Litter of ten 3-day-old German Short-haired Pointers
Owners: Greg and Leslie Sorenson, Ardrossan, Alberta, Canada

Chapter 5 🐾

Birth to Six Weeks

Birth Weight and Survival

A newborn puppy is immature when born. The eyes and ears open at ten to fourteen days. The average puppy can stand by the tenth day and walk by the twenty-first day. Voluntary control of urination and defecation usually occurs between sixteen and twenty-one days.

The best guide to survival capability is birth weight. Average birth weight of toy dogs: three to six ounces (average litter—two to four pups). Average birth weight of large dogs is four to eight ounces (average litter —six to nine pups) Puppies that are twenty-five percent below the average birth weight have a higher mortality rate. Birth weight equals immaturity, and immediate steps should be taken with those puppies if survival is to be accomplished.

Cornell Normal Physiologic Values

For Young Puppies

Weight gain	Twofold increase per 8-10 days
Body temperature	Weeks 1-2: 94-99 degrees Fahrenheit Weeks 3-4: 100 degrees Fahrenheit
Water requirement	2-3 ounces per pound per day, turnover about two times that of adult
Caloric requirement	60-100 kcal per pd per day Newborn pups become hypoglycemic if not fed for 24 hours, especially toy breeds.
Respiratory rates	15-35 per minute
Heart Rate	Approx 220 per minute
Sucking Reflex	Usually strong at birth. Weak in physically immature, abnormal or chilled puppies.
Shivering Reflex	Develops 6-8 days after birth
Muscle Tone	Firm; puppies stand upright at three weeks with normal tone and postural reflexes; walking and running by four weeks.
Eyes open	10-16 days
Visual perception	Absent less than three weeks; present at four weeks.
Hyperkinesia (activated sleep)	Normal one-three weeks; disappears after four weeks; body twitching

Care of the Normal Newborn Puppy

Ideally, pups should nurse within twenty-three to twenty-four hours to insure maximal transfer of immunity (ingestion of colostrum). To monitor food intake and proper growth response, mark each pup with a spot of nail polish—on head, neck, back or tail (four pups). Weigh pups daily within the first week. Puppies should gain five to ten percent of birth weight each day.

At birth, the puppies' temperature is below the normal adult temperature. For the first two weeks 94-99 degrees Fahrenheit and 97-100 degrees Fahrenheit at two to four weeks. Temperature in the whelping area should be approximately 80-85 degrees Fahrenheit for the first week and can be maintained by infrared heating lamps about eight feet above the whelping area.

Some breeders use plain one hundred watt light bulbs in a safe gooseneck lamp a couple of feet above the nest. A heating pad can be taped to the bottom one-third of the nest as described previously in Whelping Supplies, on page 40.

You should encourage the pups to nurse by putting them on the nipples, opening the mouth if necessary to assist them in locating the nipples. The tongue should be curled around the nipple and the mouth "latched" on with suction. Being observant is probably the most important thing you can do. Check the pups' skin by pinching it together at the back of the

Dehydration check: If skin stays together, pup needs rehydration

neck; it should go right back in place when you let go. If it doesn't, the pup may be dehydrating. Check the pups to see if the meconium (dark waxy substance that plugs the rectum of newborns) has been removed by the dam. You can do this by using a cotton ball dipped in warm water to massage next to the rectum. The procedure should cause the puppy to pass this stuff. If not removed, the meconium can harden and cause the pup to stop nursing and die. If a pup is not being "diapered" by his mother, it needs to be diapered by the caretaker. The same method of using a cotton ball or Kleenex dipped in warm water and massaging the genital area and rectum will make the pup eliminate. The pup will die if his or her urine and stool are not passed.

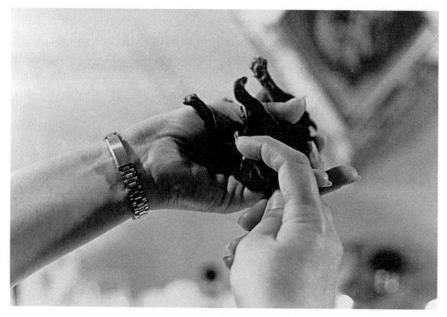

Diapering a female pup

Check the dam's milk flow, making sure the nipples are not clogged, the milk is rich and creamy, and that all nipples are flowing—even the ones that are up high and may not be used regularly. Do this every other day or so. If the milk has an off color and is extremely sticky to the touch or yellow or greenish, immediately have the veterinarian look at it under the microscope. Don't take no for an answer. *Have it checked under the microscope*. Toxic milk can cause your pups a lot of trouble in a day or so. It's better to be sure.

If your puppies lose weight on any day or show no increase in weight for a two-day period, supplemental feeding should begin, either by stomach tube or nursing bottle. As you observe your pups, be sure to watch for the one that gets pushed easily off the nipple. Check this pup for a cleft palate as pups with this problem never seem to nurse properly. A cleft palate (see illustration) is an opening in the roof of the mouth. Usually the pup will have milk coming out the nose when this condition exists. Most veterinarians agree that this problem is best handled by putting the pup down.

Cleft Palate: Opening in the roof of the mouth

Hare lip is an opening from the nose extending to the opening in the roof of the mouth which is the cleft palate.

If the pup is just being pushed off because of its size, then you must regularly be sure you are putting the tiny one on a nipple that has milk. Don't let that pup suck on a nipple with no milk, which they often do. The alternative is to immediately supplement that pup with a Bordon's nursing bottle or regular preemie nipple depending on the size of the pup. A recipe for formula is provided under Whelping Supplies, on page 40.

Adequately fed healthy pups will lie with heads extended and show an occasional muscle twitch (activated sleep) as they sleep. The jerking or twitching is necessary for muscle development. Lack of activated sleep may cause "flat" puppies. In addition, excessive vitamin D can cause poor muscle tone and possibly flat puppies and "swimmers." Be sure the pups have good footing so they can crawl successfully to the dam to nurse.

If the pups are awakened, they yawn, are not vocal, and have good muscle tone. Hungry pups, if not warm, are usually vocal. Crying reflects stress or pain, discomfort, and chilling. Failure to nurse results in depleted glycogen (sugar) stores in the liver causing hypoglycemia.

Tails and dew claws are best removed either when they are five days old or four ounces, whichever is first. For the Yorkies, I use the 5 1/2" Kelly straight hemostat pinch-and-twist method on the tail removing two-thirds of the tail (as illustrated). Pinch off the dew claws with a 5 1/2" Kelly curved hemostat and cauterize with a silver nitrate stick. This method was demonstrated to me by a poodle breeder many years ago. I prefer to twist the hemostat and just as you feel it break away, lift the hemostat up and a little string (or muscle) comes away with the tail. Or, you may twist the tail, and just before it comes loose, release the hemostat and pull up, thereby removing that little muscle, which poodle breeders swear helps keep the tails up!

There is very little fussing when it is done this way, and I don't have to worry about taking my little ones to the vet's office and undergoing a surgical procedure of cutting and stitching. I feel there is less trauma to the pups this way. (Probably I'm more traumatized than they). It is desirable to remove the dewclaws, front and back, on a long-haired dog so that after

1.

2.

Tie tubegauze tightly to base of tail.

Turn pup and pinch off dew claws and rear with curved hemostat and cauterize with silver nitrate stick.

3.

4.

Clamp with straight hemostat 1/8 to 1/4 inch above the tan.

Twist off 2/3 of tail either by twisting hemostat or tail. Seal with vet glue.

they grow up and the long hair grows in, the claws are not accidentally ripped off when their hair is being combed—a very good reason!

To have a nice clean removal of dew claws on a smooth-coated dog, like the Italian Greyhound for instance, tie a twelve to fourteen inch piece of unwaxed dental floss with a loop, slip it around the dew claw, tighten it, and hold for ten to fifteen seconds. It swells some. Pop the piece up with a pull. If there is any bleeding, use a silver nitrate stick to cauterize the area. I have not done it this way, but I have seen it done, and it is quick and sterile and effective. However, if you are squeamish about this procedure, have the vet do it for you rather than doing it wrong and causing trauma to the pups and mother. Most vets like to suture all dew claw removals to avoid having a hairless scar. This "breeders" method "may" or may not leave a scar so that would be my vet's only concern.

If all is well and the puppies are gaining weight and nursing and, the dam is doing a good job, you really don't have to do much but observe and check on the diapering job (same routine as removing the meconium) until three and one-half to four weeks.

As you weigh the pups, observe the eyes, ears, and docked tail so that if there is a problem, you can catch it early. The closed eyes should not be swollen or bulging. If they are, it may indicate an infection, and applying Terramycin Opthalmic at the eye openings may help clear it up. (I always have Terramycin Opthalmic on hand for mild conjunctivitis of adults). A docked tail may become swollen and infected. If this happens, you should soak that pup's back end with the tail in warm salt water three times a day for a few days, ten minutes or so at a time, keeping the tail gently squeezed open so that any pus can drain.

This is usually a local infection and may not require antibiotics.

Care of the Orphan Puppy

Hand Feeding

Tube Feeding   Using a No. 5 catheter French feeding tube for a toy dog and No. 8 for larger breeds, measure the pup from the end of the rib cage to the nose, mark the spot on the tube, and then fill with formula or glucose. Insert the tube over the tongue and down into the tummy *slowly*. If the pup can still cry, you can be sure you have inserted it correctly. I want to assure you that it is very difficult to insert the tube into the trachea. Press the syringe and slowly deposit the body temperature contents into the tummy. Withdraw the tube slowly, and wash generously with clean, clear water. Spinning the tube above your head will help clear the contents. Be sure to diaper as the pup cannot eliminate on its own.

(5 cc = 1 teaspoon or 15 cc = 1 tablespoon). This ratio is to be figured on a weight per day basis and the quantities of feedings that make the pup feel comfortably full.

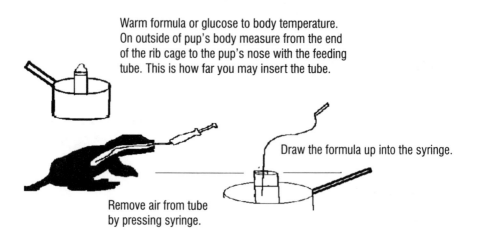

Warm formula or glucose to body temperature. On outside of pup's body measure from the end of the rib cage to the pup's nose with the feeding tube. This is how far you may insert the tube.

Draw the formula up into the syringe.

Remove air from tube by pressing syringe.

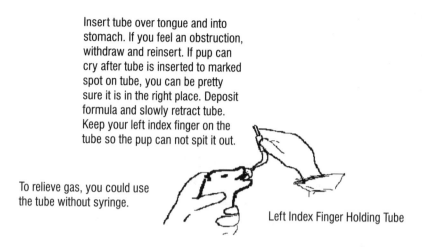

Insert tube over tongue and into stomach. If you feel an obstruction, withdraw and reinsert. If pup can cry after tube is inserted to marked spot on tube, you can be pretty sure it is in the right place. Deposit formula and slowly retract tube. Keep your left index finger on the tube so the pup can not spit it out.

To relieve gas, you could use the tube without syringe.

Left Index Finger Holding Tube

A six-ounce pup, for instance, would be fed 45 cc daily (12 feedings of 3.75 cc per feeding). The formula is 7.5 cc per ounce daily x weight of pup. Don't start off with more than 2 cc for the first feeding; in fact, I usually start with one cc each hour for a toy dog and gradually go to 5 or 6 feedings per day.

Bottle Feeding the Orphan Puppy

If bottle feeding, the pup will usually drop off the nipple when full. Gently pat the pup to help relieve gas that may have formed while bottle feeding. Don't squeeze formula into the mouth; let the pup "go onto the nipple" to nurse.

Critical Periods For Puppy

For the first twenty days

The puppy needs Warmth, Food, Sleep, and Mother, with as little handling by humans as possible. Just weigh them and be sure they are diapered.

Fourth week (21-28 days)

The puppy needs little else but Warmth, Food, Sleep, and Mother. All senses are functioning, and the pup is aware of littermates. It is extremely critical that puppy has contact with littermates and that introduction to human society is instituted slowly, quietly, and with control.

Fifth through seventh weeks (29-49 days)

Now is a good time to socialize within the litter and with humans in their own territory. Puppy begins to respond to voices and is able to recognize people as different than canines. About this time the Mother has had enough of them and weaning can be done.

Eighth through twelfth weeks (50-84 days)

This is a good time to separate them from each other with a divider, but they should be close enough that they can see each other. Human socialization brings the "new mother image," and they can have supervised play with children. They start to establish a permanent bond with people, and they can have gentle discipline. Housebreaking can begin. Introduction to other humans is very important but must be closely supervised to minimize adverse conditioning. Expose to different noises a little at a time, and give lots of encouragement.

Thirteenth through sixteenth weeks (85-112 days)

The puppy needs Love, Attention, Discipline, Socialization, and Security. Puppy's mind is being influenced, and he can establish himself as a dominant being. Bad experiences with leash training can leave long lasting impressions. Leash train with great care. Praise for correct behavior is a valuable tool and shapes positive attitudes. Sixteen weeks is the perfect time to begin leash training. Be sure it is fun for the puppy. Follow him around for awhile and laugh and talk with lots of happy encouragement and good treats!

Care of the Sick Puppy

Do not give formula to a weak or sick pup as he cannot digest it.

Sugar water (glucose solution) is absorbed quickly and gives immediate energy to a sick or weak puppy. Pedialyte can be substituted for glucose solution. Crying for more than fifteen minutes reflects trouble. Possible causes are chilling, dehydration, and inability to nurse. Water constitutes 82% of the weight of a newborn pup, and the skin and body structures constitute 25% of the weight at birth. Pet Nutra drops should be started immediately.

Failure to regularly intake water or exposure to low humidity or high heat causes dehydration. The skin loses elasticity and when pulled together fails to go back into place. See illustration, page 59. The sick puppy should be hand fed with nursing bottles or a stomach tube. The pup must be stimulated for urination and bowel movement (diapering) before and after each feeding. A gentle massage of the genital area and anus is essential at least until 16 days of age.

Institute supplemental feeding with 2 cc glucose at two hour intervals. Place puppy in incubator with oxygen flow and maintain at ninety degrees Fahrenheit and fifty percent humidity for twenty-four hours. Instigate antibiotic therapy if needed. Amoxicillin is 5 mg per pound, two times a day. Have the vet check the mother's milk under the microscope to be sure it is not toxic.

Chilling

Chilled pup syndrome is the number one cause of puppy mortality. Rectal temperature of newborn puppies can drop as much as eight degrees Fahrenheit. The newborn loses body weight through conduction, convection, and evaporation. The small amount of subcutaneous fat makes it difficult for newborns to conserve body heat and the shivering reflex is not operating in the newborn.

Some signs of chilling are: bitch culling, pushing pup away, and ignoring its cries. The bitch senses cold skin temperature.

Increased activity in pup and vocalization (crying pup) indicates stress from loss of litter comfort and chilling or hunger. As the chilling becomes severe—temperatures below ninety-four degrees Fahrenheit— activity diminishes, cries become weaker, and body feels cold. When the rectal temperature reaches seventy degrees Fahrenheit, the puppy is motionless with slow respiration or an occasional gasp for oxygen.

Puppies can survive up to twelve hours of chilling and will recover if warmed slowly. Using body heat is the best method for slow warming. For instance, put the puppy in the pocket of a close-fitting garment or in a bra between the cleavage. If you don't have a bra or cleavage, find someone who does to help! Gentle massage will also help stimulate circulation. Less effective, but adequate means for mild chilling are incubators, lamps, and hot water bottles. Rapid warming can cause subcutaneous hemorrhage and death, so *go slow!*

Diarrhea and Treatment

Prior to the third week of life, most instances of diarrhea are related to food intake. Excessive food intake overwhelms the digestive enzymes and diarrhea develops.

Treatment   Restrict food intake to glucose solution every two to three hours and use 1 cc of Milk of Magnesia two times every three hours to neutralize intestine for twenty-four hours on a four-to- five ounce pup. Dilute formula to half water and gradually work back to full strength.

Constipation

A crying pup could indicate one that is constipated. Using an eyedropper filled with pure glycerine, insert in pup's rectum, and release a couple of drops (one-quarter cc). Massage anal area. Warm water can also be used and administered rectally with an eyedropper.

Pups With Respiratory Problems

The first thirty-six hours are the most critical. Posterior presentations at birth and premature placenta separations will initiate respiratory effort in the puppy while it is still in the uterus. This respiratory effort brings placental fluids into the pharynx and trachea.

Aspiration of fluids from each pup should be routine at delivery. Oxygen enriched air is necessary for pups having difficulty breathing. If a pup is very congested, you should instigate Amoxicillin therapy and a couple drops of Benadryl (for infants) or Temaril P (If you have it, a few granules in the glucose solution is sufficient once a day for two days.) Check with your veterinarian because this Temaril P is a prescription drug used for respiratory problems.

A perfectly healthy pup can inhale milk from the mother's breast or from a baby bottle nipple on which the flow is too fast or from dropper feedings. Any time you see fluid in the nose, at least during the first twenty-eight days, or hear any congestion or gasping, the pup should be treated as a "sick pup," fed glucose, and treated with antibiotics and antihistamines to keep it from going into a secondary infection, which would end in inhalation pneumonia from which puppies almost never recover. Tube feeding is a must with such a pup if you are going to save it.

Neonatal Dermatitis

The signs are crusty lesions on the head and neck caused by staph infection due to failure of the bitch to clean up dried remnants of placental fluid on the skin. The area becomes infected and causes environmental contamination, which can spread to the bitch and other pups.

Treatment   Use Panalog sparingly on the affected area and consider the administration of antibiotics. Cleansing with Betadine shampoo or Plexadine shampoo may be necessary.

Prevention   Sanitation

Colic

The signs of colic are easy to recognize: a hard stomach, piteous wailing unlike a normal hunger whimper, and the pup stops nursing. The hard stomach comes from accumulated gas. These pups should never be placed on a heating pad as heat makes gas expand. Heating pads must be used with great care and never cover the entire nest. If too much area is covered with the heating pad, the resultant steady heat can dehydrate the pups.

Colic can also come from the bitch's milk going bad, stress, and unknown causes. First, act quickly to relieve the gas and get the bowels open and working. Two or three drops of Milk of Magnesia on the tongue three times a day will help soothe the stomach and bowels. Inserting an eyedropper with pure glycerine rectally and squeezing a few drops can help the pup to expel the gas and hard stool. Or use a warm water enema (one cc = one dropperful for a four to five ounce pup). Sometimes inserting a stomach tube orally in the same manner as you would "tube feed" (but without the syringe) will expel trapped gas and relieve the pain. Also, a couple of drops of Mylicon, which you can get from your drug store, (it is used for preemie babies) is great for relieving gas and bloated tummies.

A colicky pup can result from a stressed out dam who is ignoring her pup if she is able to wander about the house and not get down to business nursing and caring for her babies. Keep the dam confined and pay attention to her attitude. She may need special attention or even a dose of

Valium for a couple of days to relax her. (Check with your vet for dosage.) I don't recommend nursing mamas visiting each other's litters. I strongly feel they should be kept separate, the exception being properly marking a pup and having another mother "adopt" it if she has ample milk. Even then, once the pups are settled in their nest, I don't feel they should be disturbed by the other animals in the household.

Herpes Virus

Herpes affects puppies between five and twenty-one days of age. The signs are soft, odorless, greenish-yellow stools, loss of appetite, constant crying, lack of coordination, and death. The signs may appear over a two week period. The virus is transmitted from the affected bitch's vagina during birth.

Treatment   Expose affected litter to 100 degrees Fahrenheit for four hours followed by 90 to 95 degrees Fahrenheit for twenty hours. Adequate fluids at frequent intervals are necessary to avoid dehydration. (See sick puppy.)

Replication is quite depressed at these high temperatures. Puppies that survive may have kidney diseases apparent by eight to ten months of age. Suspect dead pups should be autopsied. Bitches can be bred again without harm to subsequent litters.

Foster Mothers

There are times that the natural mother cannot or will not nurse her pups. At that time, if you are lucky and have another female "in milk"—whether she is just finishing nursing her own or has room in her nest for another pup or had a "false pregnancy" that resulted in "full breasts with milk"—it is possible to have the female nurse "foster pups." I find that by squirting the foster mother's milk all over the pups and\or spreading the pup with Nutri-cal, the foster mother will usually accept these pups without a problem. Watch these "adopted pups" carefully to be sure they are being diapered. Some adoptive mothers will draw the line at diapering their "adopted pups."

Weaning the Pups

Removing the dam from the pups at three to three and one half weeks for an hour or so and then offering them a weaning formula two times a day helps the dam out and gets them started lapping. For some very fat pups where there is an abundance of milk from the dam, you may be wasting your time, but it's good to try anyway. Let the dam in to clean up the leftovers and clean up the pups. In some cases, the mother will refuse to let them nurse at about four weeks and start to dry up her own milk. If that is the case, let nature take its course!

Weaning Formulas

(all served at body temperature)

- Pedigree Puppy Canned Food or Science Diet Canned Growth (mashed) and Warm Water or

- Soak kibble in warm water or "zap" in the microwave for thirty seconds and mash into a gruel any one of the following or other quality dry foods:

- Pedigree Puppy, Science Diet Growth (Small Bites) dry, or Custom Care (new natural dog food by Science Diet), or Purina O N E Lamb and Rice. There are many very good foods on the market today. I prefer to use a kibble with a natural preservative. Though I have never had any problems with my dogs that I consider to be dietary in origin, I prefer to err on the side of safety.

For very tiny pups:

- The formula shown in Whelping Supplies, on page 40
- Plus Gerber's Rice Cereal and strained baby lamb

The formula is good to keep a very tiny puppy well fed so that the worry of hypoglycemia is lessened. "Nursing Mom's Pudding" is very good for tiny pups that are not eating enough to maintain their proper sugar level and weight.

The human contact with the pups at this early age—coaxing them to eat—is strongly recommended and facilitates development of adult canine behavior that results in better social integration of the pup to human.

By the fifth and sixth weeks, offer three times a day. By the end of the sixth week, the mother can be kept away completely, and pups should be fed four times a day. As you are increasing the feedings for the pups, start to decrease the quantity of food given the dam to minimize mammary complications at complete weaning.

On weaning day, withhold food from the bitch twenty-four hours and limit the supply of water. Massage her breasts with Bay Rum, from the pharmacy, or camphorated oil to aid in drying up her milk. If you cannot find camphorated oil, mix four ounces of spirits of camphor in sixteen ounces of mineral oil to massage on the breasts and dry up milk.

On the second day, feed her only twenty-five percent of her normal maintenance diet (nmd). Third day, feed fifty percent nmd; fourth day, feed seventy-five percent nmd, and fifth day, feed maintenance level as prior to breeding. This restricted feeding at weaning will prevent mastitis due to abrupt weaning and preserve the breasts for future nursing chores.

Toxic Milk Syndrome

Effects of toxic milk are commonly seen between three and fourteen days of age.

Symptoms: Pups are uncomfortable, vocal, bloating, and straining, and anus is red and swollen. Generally occurs following metritis in bitch.

Treatment: Puppies should be removed from bitch, given glucose and fluids until bloating is relieved, then raised as "orphan pups." The bitch needs veterinary care and antibiotic therapy.

Prevention: Check the color and flow of the milk at whelping time. If there are any doubts, have the vet check for bacteria under the microscope. The milk should look creamy and rich and never grayish, greenish, or sticky and yellowish. Check the flow of milk regularly, and be sure none of the nipples are clogged.

Chapter 6 🐾

Six Weeks to Twelve Weeks

Erect Ears

The ears of some breeds, like Yorkies, certain Terrier whose ears fold over, Pugs, and Collies sometimes need to be taped. The ears should be trimmed on the edge about halfway down each side, then use a clipper (a hair clipper, such as is used to trim the hair on the back of the neck, is available in your local drug store.) with a surgical blade, about halfway down the front and back of each ear. This is usually started at about four weeks, but if your puppy's ears are still not up, you must take off the hair, massage them regularly, say once a day, to keep the circulation going, and tape them as shown.

Sometimes you can take a brown paper bag, cut it to the shape of the ear, and glue it on the shaved front of the ear with eyelash adhesive. It may be enough of a prop to keep the ears up. If this doesn't work for you then, the method of taping as illustrated on the following pages may work.

Other ears that need taping after cropping are Boxers, Affenpinschers, Great Danes, Min-Pins, Dobermans, and some others. The taping procedure involved in these cases varies, and your vet or breeder should demonstrate how it is done. For example, we used the cardboard from tampons to prop our Great Dane ears and used aerated tape and a metal bridge between the ears.

For "small dogs," like the Yorkie, that need upright ears, Flexible Collodian (obtained from your pharmacy) is a good glue (invisible bandage) to use to paint the ears. You can dip "netting," like bridal veil netting, in the Collodian and paint it on the ears. It lasts for a while and is a

Tape: Sticky side out

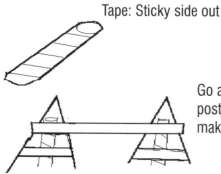

Go around each ear to secure post and then tape across to make bridge front and back.

good support, but it is a bit messy to remove. You must be careful to take away all the flaking, or it can pull the ear down again as the hair begins to grow.

A dental absorber is a good post for propping the ear of a toy dog. Wrap some aerated Johnson & Johnson tape backwards so the sticky side is out, and insert on the base of the ear as support and wrap more aerated tape as shown. Then tape a bridge between the ears to hold them up, being careful they are in a natural position.

You can keep the ears taped for a week, but then even if they haven't come loose, you must remove them and make sure the pup's ears are dry and clean. Whether they are up or not, leave them alone for a day or two. Retape them if they fall again.

Bonnie Braun, fellow breeder, uses the tape for package wrapping, Scotch # 893. Clip the ear hair to the skin. Cut two pieces of tape about three inches (one for each ear) and two pieces about four and one-half inches. These two will hold the ears together. Hold the pup between you knees with him facing away from you. If he wiggles place him lower till you have the shoulders between the knees. See illustrations.

After taking the tape down in a few days, smell the ear. If there is an odor, you may want to ask your veterinarian for some Tresaderm, or Otomax for an ear yeast infection, which is common. If the ear is odorous or looks swollen, don't retape until you've corrected the situation or seen a vet.

If you are taping the ears on a litter of pups, please separate the pups first. This is very important anyway as pups can "bully" each other, and those little needle teeth can be very painful.

Separating your pups at seven weeks with a divider gives them a chance to develop their own personality, plus it encourages them to start "bonding" with humans rather than becoming a "pack animal."

Food and Nutrition

Keep the Science Diet Growth (Small Bites), or whatever other dry food you are using, available all the time as well as water, as you are feeding the gruel (weaning formula). Most puppies start eating the small bites on their own as soon as they can handle it. It's small enough that they shouldn't choke on it. Once you are sure they are eating the dry food, start feeding them only two times a day with canned Science Diet Growth at body temperature, mashed slightly with a fork and a little warm water, mixed with water softened kibble.

Immunization Shots

Giving the DHP CPV + Corona at 8 weeks, 12 weeks, 16 weeks and 20 weeks is recommended by most veterinarians I know and is a good regimen, which I have used with no problems. The passive immunity the pup has received from its mother usually is over by 16 weeks. Many vets agree that it is unnecessary to give the Lepto part of the vaccine to toy dogs, but they like to include it when the dog reaches one year of age. Some vets don't give the Lepto part of the vaccine to toy dogs at all, because it is very painful and exposure for toy dogs is minimal.

Hypoglycemia

Many puppies are lost unnecessarily each year, simply because breeders know too little about hypoglycemia, and many veterinarians find it difficult to diagnose. My vet's opinion is that too few background facts are given to a vet when the sick puppy is brought in for help. Usually the puppy is comatose the first time a vet sees him, and since the animal usually responds immediately to intravenous or subcutaneous dextrose injections, the vet often diagnoses the problem as acute viral hepatitis or encephalitis. The reaction is the same in all of these cases.

However, in a young puppy, or a very tiny toy dog, this condition is usually hypoglycemia, brought on by stress or shock in some form. Also, it usually occurs in puppies from four to five months of age but can occur in mature toy breeds when they are subjected to stress.

The stress usually causing this condition is:

1. Overhandling young puppies and not letting them get enough rest and sleep.

2. A puppy refuses to eat for a period of more than eight hours due to change of home and/or food.

3. Exposure to low room temperatures for a period of time or sleeping in drafts.

The puppy will appear limp and lifeless with the gums and tongue usually grayish blue in color. Often the eyes are unfocused and barely open. They may appear to be slightly sunken in. Temperature will be subnormal and the puppy will shiver and tremble in the early stages. As the condition worsens, the puppy either goes into a coma or convulsions. Hypoglycemia is a metabolic disorder, and death can result, unless properly diagnosed and *cared for immediately*, if the case is severe. The level of the blood sugar must be raised at once and the stress condition treated.

My vet recommends an injection of 5-10 cc of a five percent solution of dextrose with added B-12. He gives this subcutaneously, as it provides a longer lasting action, and it is almost impossible to locate a vein in a tiny puppy. A new product that works marvelously for a sick pup or dog is Pet Nutradrops. It gets into the bloodstream faster than any other vitamin with "miraculous" results. If you haven't become acquainted with it yet, please go to www.tcsn.net/terriyork/nutra.htm or call (800) 658-4016. Be sure to have it in your first aid kit and whelping kit.

With the dextrose or glucose, my vet also gives an injection for shock and stress. He said that many vets use a form of cortosteroid for this stress factor. It is produced under many trade names, but your vet will be sure to have it on hand. When these injections are given in time, the puppy may regain consciousness promptly. If the seizure is bad or not *cared for in time*, the puppy may *remain in a coma for days*. When this happens, you must feed him, keep him warm and quiet, and see that he has proper eliminations. Don't let him lay for long periods on one side, but keep moving from one side to the other at least every hour.

Usually the bowels will move without help, but an older puppy may struggle to be supported erect on his feet for elimination. Check carefully for urination as the pup is in trouble if the kidneys cease to function. Wash genital area with cotton soaked with warm water if the puppy is comatose. If partially mobile, put his feet on a towel at the edge of a wash basin or in the tub with adequate footing. Support him with one hand, and turn the water on. Hearing the running water usually makes him urinate.

Also, mix the glucose solution shown in "Whelping Supplies" on page 40 or mix honey, sugar or corn syrup with equal amounts of water and feed 10 cc with a syringe four times a day. I prefer Karo syrup to honey, which has a tendency to cause diarrhea.

When hypoglycemia is caught in time, there is no reason why a puppy won't come out of it and never have it again if the stress factor is eliminated. Even if this never occurs to your puppy or adult, it is important that you know about it to aid your vet in diagnosing the problem. This usually affects tiny toy breeds and most of them outgrow this danger by six months of age. However, it can happen to a small dog even as an adult, and careful attention must be paid to the diet of any small or tiny toy dog.

Litter of Golden Retrievers from Fireside's Welsh Springers

This is their cutest stage

Chapter 7 🐾

Twelve Weeks to Six Months

Veterinary Approval of Your Puppy

The breeder from whom you purchase your puppy should give you the opportunity to have your veterinarian examine the puppy to be sure it is in good health before the sale becomes final. Usually forty-eight hours during the week or seventy-two hours over a weekend is enough time for you to make an appointment and have this done.

Some veterinarians do suggest surgery for "luxating patellas." Don't do it. Surgery is not to be undertaken unless the dog is lame. In that case you should probably take the pup back to the breeder immediately or at least inform the breeder that the dog is lame. Complete rest of the leg will probably ease the situation, if the dog was not lame at the time you bought him. Don't let the new puppy jump off of furniture or run like crazy on slippery floors. These things *can* injure a leg on a toy dog. With long-haired dogs, keep the hair around the pads of their feet trimmed so they have adequate traction on slippery floors. Read the information about "patellas," and then make an educated decision.

Food and Nutrition

It is important to follow the diet the breeder has given you, assuming it is a good one. There are many fine dog foods on the market today. You can't go wrong feeding the diet many veterinarians recommend, Science Diet Growth, Small Bites and Science Diet Growth canned.

It is okay to feed only one canned-food meal a day after four months if the puppy is "chowing" down on the dry food. Keep the dry food and water available at all times. The tiny breeds should continue to be fed at least two warm meals a day until they are more than six months of age.

It's a good idea to also give your very tiny puppies one inch of Nutri-Cal twice a day. Ask your veterinarian for it. Most handle it, or you can get it at most farm supply or pet supply houses with no prescription. If you have a tiny, carefully read the section on hypoglycemia!

Sorting and Culling Pets from Show and Breeding Quality

I, personally, wouldn't buy a show dog of any breed until it was at least ten months old. I would guess that the offspring in most breeds won't "fall apart" after that age. However, if you were looking at a Dalmatian puppy, for instance, you would want to keep in mind that this breed has a very extended growth/maturity pattern. A Dal could "fall apart" any time between three months and nine months and not "come together" again until after he/she was a year old. Many times, I'm told, a Dal doesn't and moreover, *shouldn't look* adult until it reaches full maturity, which would be close to three years old. Dals that look "mature" at close to a year often don't look very appealing by the time they are three or so.

Not too much can be determined before three months of age as far as picking the puppies that you would like to keep for your breeding plans. However, by twelve weeks, the personalities begin to be apparent and sometimes at this age one can start "culling" or eliminating the dogs that will not be desirable for breeding or showing. For instance, if the bite is going off at twelve weeks, it could indicate that this will be a permanent problem. Some breeders feel very strongly that an undershot jaw at twelve weeks in a breed that should have scissors bites is nothing to worry about, but my experience has been that this will probably at the "best" be a "level" bite. I prefer to keep and show only those dogs with full dentition and scissors bites, or the bite suggested by the AKC Standard for each breed.

I would also like to point out that "culling," according to the dictionary definition, means "to select only the best to keep for breeding plans." There has been a "connotation" to some that "culling" means to kill or to put down.

Wire Hair Pointing Griffon owned by Meg Romanowski

This has never been my intended use of this word. A dictionary referral will explain it further to you. I would never put to sleep any puppy that has a good quality of life expectancy. There is almost always a good home to find and all breeders should make sure that every living thing for which they are responsible should have a "quality" life. This is a breeder's responsibility for bringing these little ones into the world.

Lead Training

Whether you are training your puppy for show or pet walking, the best age to start "following the puppy around" is approximately four months. They have a natural curiosity at this age but still want to follow you for the most part, and they love to follow your feet. This should be encouraged. My friend, exhibitor Joan Gordon of the famous Wildweir Kennels, tells me that all their puppies are encouraged to follow their heels as they give treats. While doing this she puts a leash on and persuades them to walk, with no jerking or pulling, and off they go. Use a very lightweight lead without a big heavy clunky clasp for small dogs especially.

I make my own puppy leads out of a curtain rod plastic ring and six feet of silk ribbon. It slips over their head in a loop and is very lightweight. It is my opinion that they don't seem to blame you when the collar tightens up if they run the wrong way. With a loose lead and plenty of happy encouragement, they will soon start following you with the aid of "goodies." These may take the form of Rollover or RedBarn (Call (800) 775-3849 or (310) 493-3412 and ask them to send you a sample.) or other quick small treats and furry squeaky toys or a favorite play toy. It is a mistake to use a harness on show dogs because they have a tendency to "sniff" the ground when a harness is used. Many pet people prefer a harness for toy dogs, in particular, because there have been surprising large dog attacks, and if the small dog is on a harness, it is easier to quickly pull it up out of harm's way. It is unfortunate that any dogs are allowed to run loose and off leash, but it does happen in many communities, and much too often the small dog is seriously injured or killed. Don't walk your dogs where large dogs run loose. If you see one approaching, do shout in a firm, loud voice, "Noooooooo Staaaaaaaaaaaay." It may halt the large dog if you are loud and firm enough, however, it is better to be safe than sorry. Walk your dog only in safe places. Carrying something to "distract" the intruder, like a can of coins, might work to halt the attack temporarily.

For show pups and pet pups (in case they become show pups) from eight weeks on we practice standing the small dog on the table and standing still on leash for bigger dogs. Get every visitor to touch them and go over them. It doesn't matter if they are not standing exactly right, just so they understand "Stand...Stay." Matches and/or handling classes are very helpful for the puppy's socialization, but local parks can be beneficial if you have no other choice! Many All Breed Clubs have handling classes.

Stool Eating (Coprophagy)

This is a very unpleasant behavior out of which puppies usually grow. However, for those that have developed this habit, adding one ounce of tomato juice or three banana slices to their food each day may help. They say a lack of potassium can be the reason. Another suggested additive for their food is "Oral Ectoral" or another organic phosphate product, but few health food stores carry it anymore. I've heard that "Forbid" has met with some success. Also, adding some meat tenderizer to the food is a good way to discourage this practice; just sprinkle a little on their food.

Chapter 8

Six Months To One Year

Veterinary Approval Of Your Show Puppy

If the breeder did not give you an X ray of your puppy's hip area, now is the time for your veterinarian to contact the breeder's veterinarian to see if one was taken and have it forwarded to your veterinarian. You want to certify that your show puppy is free from Legg Perthes, (usually apparent at eight to eleven months) and hip dysplasia (in larger breeds) and has a general health examination.

If the dog has luxating patellas at this early age, whether he is good enough for breeding is debatable, depending upon the degree of luxation. Do not let the veterinarian help you decide to operate if the dog is not lame. Bear in mind that a surgically corrected dog cannot be shown. Furthermore, operating on the patellas very seldom corrects the problem. Some show dogs have finished their championships with luxating patellas. There are varying degrees of luxation, and as long as the dog is not lame, leave it alone. (See page 141 for more on luxating patellas.)

Choosing a Handler

The best way to find a handler is to go to the shows and observe your breed being shown. Check the catalog and find the names and addresses of the handler that you feel has made a good presentation of the dog. Try to find where that handler is "set up" for grooming, and ask him/her when would be a good time to talk about handling fees. Ask for a rate card and for the address of the kennel. It is usually best to have a handler nearby so that you can visit the place your dog will be kept and see the conditions. This will be your dog's home away from home, and if you can manage a few surprise visits to the shows and to the kennel, you will know how well your dog is being cared for and presented.

Food and Nutrition

A good basic diet for your puppy, as mentioned previously, is Science Diet Canned Growth, Science Diet Growth Dry Kibble, or Eukanuba, all of which are now made in very small bites for toy dogs. After three months, I feed Science Diet Growth Kibble which I leave available all day dry and feed the following once a day:

- Dry kibble covered with water, add canned Science Diet Growth and make a liverwurst gravy, just enough to flavor the broth. Microwave two to three minutes, let sit until body temperature and serve.

Siberian Huskies

Photos courtesy of Susan Malmstrom

They come in all shapes and sizes!

Teeth Cleaning

As soon as you get your puppy, you should get him used to your fingers in his mouth. Put a piece of gauze dipped in a tooth cleaning preparation (not for people but for dogs), such as Hexarinse or Nolvadent, and rub his teeth and gums every chance you get. That way by the time he is a young adult, you will be able to start scaling and brushing his teeth regularly and thereby save the teeth and gums from periodontal disease. I have found that my dogs are "intimidated" when I stick them in the laundry tub for their bath, and it's a good time to scale their teeth. Scaling and brushing is especially important for small dogs as it seems they are more prone to early tooth loss if proper care isn't taken, but there is no reason to lose the teeth on your toy dogs if you keep their teeth free from plaque. Nolvadent is a good teeth cleaning product or just plain salt water. Once a week, put one drop of Glyoxide (people mouth product) on each side of your dogs mouth next to the molars. It will kill the bacteria and help keep down the plaque. Your dog will have better breath and a healthier mouth. The expense and risk of anesthetizing your dog is reduced if you keep the teeth clean. Don't forget that infection from bad gums and dirty teeth can go through his whole system—resulting in a sick dog!

Watch for the arrival of the second or adult teeth, particularly in toy dogs. Very often, the long-rooted baby teeth are retained. In this case, you should have your veterinarian remove them if they are messing up a good bite, or if they haven't been shed by eight to nine months of age. To retain them beyond that point is only inviting tooth decay. Have your veterinarian remove baby teeth if they remain, and **be sure to ask what kind of anesthesia** your veterinarian chooses. Isoflurane is the safest anesthesia to use for toy dogs. There are some vets who continue to use Pentabarb to anesthetize dogs. This method is decades behind and kills toy dogs. *Do not under any circumstances allow your vet to use pentabarb or injectables to anesthesize your toy dog. If your vet won't use Isoflurane, find another veterinarian.* Usually the incisors (front teeth) shed with no problem, but the canines quite often have long roots and have to be removed by the vet. Have him or her check back molars also and flip out the ones that head to the inside of the mouth. Sometimes they can become infected and cause serious problems for the little guys!

Japanese Chin puppies everywhere...

Photos provided courtesy of
Barbara Latimer

My vet has used both ultrasound and hand scaling to clean teeth; his preference is hand scaling. The ultrasound works well in the little cracks and crevices of the tooth, but for the flat surfaces—both outer and inner—they are about the same.

According to my vet, the main problem with the ultrasound is that you constantly need to keep the spray of water moving. If you stay in one area of the tooth for too long, you cause heat to build up, which can damage the pulp cavity. With hand scaling you need to be sure you have sharp instruments. Take care not to scrape too hard and damage the enamel.

With both types the most important part is the polishing. With each method you will leave microscopic crevices in which bacteria and plaque can build up. Polishing smooths these crevices flat. Once cleaned a good homecare plan is important, as mentioned previously.

A new oral rinse, Hexarinse, is available now for the prevention of plaque, calculus, and gum disease. It's a soothing, refreshing, and highly palatable rinse containing chlorhexidine gluconate, cetylpyridinium chloride, and zinc. The antimicrobial activity of the chlorhexidine and cetylpyridinium chloride, combined with the antiplaque and anticalculus properties of zinc, can aid in the prevention of tooth and gum disease and leave your dog with clean breath and relief of minor gum irritation.

Chapter 9

Grooming

Grooming your pet depends on the breed. Be sure to get information from your breeder on the grooming for your breed. Double coated dogs like Pomeranians and Pekinese are usually just brushed and powdered. Very little trimming is done. They do shed.

Silky, long-haired dogs, like Maltese and Yorkies, are treated pretty much like human hair. They do not shed and, therefore, are recommended for people with allergies, as is the poodle and a few other breeds. The hair on the Yorkie ears should be trimmed with a clipper or scissors about halfway down the ear. I recommend the Wahl Rechargeable Beard and Mustache Trimmer for this, available at most drug stores.

If you don't keep upright ears on Yorkies trimmed, they will flop, and even with taping, may not come up again if the weight of the hair has broken the tissues of the ear. In the case of the drop-ear, long-haired dogs like the Shih Tzu or Maltese, ear infections can be a problem if the hair in the ear is not removed. These long-haired dogs should be bathed every seven to ten days, using a good tear-free shampoo and a conditioner. Rinse thoroughly and blow the hair dry after spraying with a detangler like Focus 21 Hair and Skin Plasma or Sensational Hair Detangler.

For quick cleanups on long-haired dogs, especially at the backsides when stool is loose, there are products like Mr. Groom Cleaning Powder with silicone, or plain talcum powder, or cornstarch, which you put on and brush through the hair, after removing as much of the material as possible. This will work to keep them clean until you have time to give them a bath.

The very best supplies you can get for any long-haired dog are available from SENPROCO. Call them for a list of their products at (800) 748-1777 and #1 All Systems, available through www.cherrybrook.com or phone (800) 524-0820. Another new product that I just tried is the Absolutely Natural Four Pack: shampoo, conditioner, hair glossifier, and grooming aid. (800) 772-2559 (www.absolutelynatural.com). I cannot recommend these too highly—great stuff! One of the most complete lines of animal products is Omaha Animal Supply, and the phone is (800) 367-4444. On long-haired breeds, if the ears get filled with hair, which can become matted, you should sprinkle on an antibiotic ear powder and then remove the hair by plucking it out with a hemostat and fingers. Many different brands of ear powder are available. The powder will make it less painful to pluck these hairs for the dog and easier for you to grip them. It can leave a harsh residue around the ears, which can make the hair brittle, so I suggest doing it before bathing. After bathing, use R7 Ear Cleaner or Nolvasan Otic Ear Cleaner, or a similar ear product to prevent swimmers ear infection. It is also a good idea to put cotton in the ear before bathing to prevent water getting into the ear.

I feel it is a good idea to empty the anal glands every time you bathe your dog while it is soaped up. Get your breeder or veterinarian to show you how. It is important that you do this properly so that you do not cause an infection in that area by squeezing inwards, but it is easy to do and should be part of regular grooming. You may see your dog scooting around on his backside. I've heard people say that this means the dog has worms, but that isn't true. It *usually* means that the dog needs his or her anal glands emptied. He or she is uncomfortable, and the glands are clogged and could become infected.

Keeping the nails trimmed short is another necessity if you want to keep the coat from being matted and destroyed. Long nails and/or fleas can damage a coat beyond belief overnight and cause a great deal of discomfort to your pet. Use a good quality citrus flea shampoo and spray. The best way to get rid of fleas is to fumigate the premises and shampoo all dogs and spray all cats with a good flea spray at the same time. The saliva from one flea bite can cause an allergic reaction that will torture the dog for months, and you may have to obtain prednisone from the vet to stop the reaction. Fleas can also make a dog (especially toy dogs) anemic as they are "blood suckers." A good citruscide shampoo, like Mr.

All dolled up and ready for a show!

Photos courtesy of Alice Ruiz

Christian's Australian Citrus Shampoo (obtained from Cherrybrook at www.cherrybrook.com), works well.

The supermarket kind of treatments are generally too harsh for any dog and particularly toy dogs. Flea collars are not wise because they have been suspected of doing liver damage. I would also suggest spraying the dog with Adams Flea & Tick Spray with fourteen day residual action, after the bath but while still wet, being careful not to get it in the eyes; then blow dry.

For heavily infested flea areas, some breeders have been successful using the Frontline and Advantage. The Frontline pill is good at sterilizing adults, thereby preventing egg laying, but it does not kill adult fleas, so they will bite. Advantage kills adults and young as well as larvae. Some people prefer Frontline because it kills ticks also, and it does not wash off with shampooing, while Advantage will.

If using Advantage, always bathe animals before applying. You can reapply after three weeks or the second shampoo. For dogs that are washed more frequently, due to being shown and groomed, Frontline may be better as it lasts through several shampoos. However, there have been some reports of allergic reactions from Frontline.

The grooming of show dogs of any breed is a lot more complicated. The long-haired dog is usually lightly oiled with a product like #1 All System Conditioner and Hemectant Oil or Bio Groom Super Cream and then wrapped with tissue wraps, rice paper wraps, or silk organza wraps. In between bath grooming should always be done with a moisturizer spray. Do not brush a dry coat.

A beautiful Yorkshire Terrier and a doll made from her hair. Owned by Elizabeth Shaw, Australia

Chapter 10 🐾

Housebreaking

Get yourself a Puppy Playspace Exercise Pen so that you have a place to put the puppy indoors to urinate. A plastic storage box for blankets is an excellent litter box in which you can put paper and a "piddle pad." It might be a good idea to start out with the lid from the box for a young puppy because jumping in and out of the box can be a little difficult for a tiny new puppy. I don't encourage the use of newspapers because the urine doesn't absorb fast enough, and those little feet get wet and "inky" from the newsprint and make the floor dirty. Many people are successful with small or medium sized dogs in using an old throw rug over the paper at the door; others use plastic lining on the floor and put an exercise pen over it and put puppies in when it is likely they will need to relieve themselves such as after napping, after eating and first thing in the morning. End rolls of newspaper (uninked) are great for use in pens and can usually be purchased inexpensively at your local newspaper plant. It can be cut to fit the pen and doesn't make everything, including the dog, dirty from the newsprint. With bigger breeds, crate training is your best solution in housebreaking. I followed the crate training rules with my Great Dane. Thankfully, she only made one mistake; it was a "lake."

When correcting the puppy for "going in the wrong place," don't forget to watch that puppy and "praise with a happy, happy voice" when he or she happens to go in the right place. That praise will leave a better impression than the scolding, because unless you catch puppy in the act, he or she probably won't know why you're bent out of shape and hollering. Your voice is all you need to "discipline" any dog. A "bad dog" harsh voice is sufficient.

A Puppy Playspace, or exercise pen, comes in handy when you are traveling and need to set up a potty spot at a motel. When visiting friends, it protects the pup from over fondling by young children. Also in the case of long-haired toy dogs, who wants to get out the blow dryer every time they go out to urinate in bad weather? So you will be happy you invested in a collapsible Playspace.

In *Pet USA* catalog, there is a new litter box system that uses litter that is scented to attract puppies to the box. Three sides of the plastic box are six inches high, and the fourth side has a lowered opening (smack dab in the middle) for ease of entry. This means all four corners are six inches high. The box also comes in two sizes.

- Small (30" L x 21" W x 6" H)—$34.97
  Holds ten pounds of litter.

- Large (41" L x 30" W x 6" H)—$44.97
  Holds twenty pounds of litter. Litter costs $9.97 per ten pounds.

I think this would eliminate those "near misses" and "leg lift" problems. You could use scented wee wee pads, instead of the litter. Litter is the flushable type. The toll free number for Pet USA is (800) 4-PET-USA.

When the puppy makes a mistake on your carpet, do not spray with ammonia because it smells like urine. You can use Massengill Douche Powder for cleanups (two heaping teaspoons to one quart of warm water) in the rug shampooer or in a spray bottle for an area freshener. Another good remedy for cleanup of puddles is to sponge up the puddle and spray with white vinegar.

Five week old Shih Tzu pups with dad.

Breeder: T. Ford

Ten Commandments of Housebreaking

1. **Thou shalt not bring home a puppy or adult dog and expect it to know immediately where the potty is.** Every time they move from one home to another, they need to be taught where to go.

2. **Thou shalt not expect a young puppy of eight-sixteen weeks to be housebroken.** That's like expecting a one-year-old child to be completely potty-trained. It just isn't going to happen.

3. **Thou shalt not allow the new puppy to urinate all over the house, run loose, and then wonder why the dog goes back to the same spot to urinate.** You will have to disinfect the house thoroughly where he has done his business. White vinegar in the water will help neutralize the smell because he/she will go back to the spot that smells.

4. **Thou shalt not yell at the pup (dog) when he/she goes in the wrong spot.** Better than yelling, you need to clean it up thoroughly and put the dog where he or she is supposed to go. Dogs and most animals learn much better by the praise and reward system.

5. **Thou shalt not keep the six months or younger confined for long periods of time.** They are too young, until at least six months to hold it for that long. Take them out to urinate frequently, and generously praise and reward them for going where you want them to.

6. **Thou shalt not put a long-haired, single-coated toy dog out in the rain to urinate unless you want to use a hair dryer when it comes back in.** To do so could cause a chill and tonsilitis and/or tracheobronchitis.

7. **Thou shalt not expect an unneutered or unspayed dog to have proper potty manners.** In many cases, it is only natural that they (boys and girls) leave calling cards and scents for the other sex to notice. Chin up; if they were goats, they would constantly PEE on their heads to make themselves attractive to the opposite sex.

8. **Thou shalt have a potty place gated off for your young puppy at least until six months of age.** It's unrealistic to expect a young puppy to be completely trained until then.

9.   **Thou shalt spend a lot of time watching the dog when the dog is new to the house to correct bad habits before they start.**

10. **Thou shalt read these commandments instead of being angry at the dog and mend your ways.** The dog wants nothing more than to please you.

Crate Training

Cages are cruel. Not true. A crate is an indoor doghouse, just big enough for the dog to stand up, lie down, and turn around in. It is your dog's den, home, and place to feel safe.

When you go shopping, or when your pup is very young, it's a good place to keep him out of trouble. However, don't expect a very young puppy to stay in there for long periods of time. Keep the time crated to short intervals and extend them a little at a time as the pup gets older. They cannot be expected to hold their water for eight to sixteen hours at a time when just a young baby. Take this into consideration when your pup is very young. If you must be gone for an extended period of time, leave the door open and keep a place outside the crate where the puppy is allowed to urinate on papers or on a piddle pad in an exercise pen or puppy play pen. The crate is the dog's "space" in the house. This should be a place where your puppy feels safe. It's his or her house. He or she should be made to feel secure in his house so he or she can sleep while owners do what they must do. When you return in a few hours, your dog will not have destroyed the house and it will be a happy reunion. Honest, dogs love their crates. When you leave, they will probably just go to sleep, and you will not come home to "destruction," such as chewed cords and windowsills.

How long can puppy stay in there?

For a few hours while you go shopping or overnight in the crate next to your bed so you can sleep without worrying about what the pup is up to. If you are going to be gone for a longer period of time, you should get a pet gate and confine the dog to a gated area, where he or she cannot pull lamps off tables or get at any electrical cords, like in a utility room or a kitchen. Sometimes there is a covered secure spot in your yard that can be used if the weather is good, like a deck or fenced in area where the dog can play without escaping and where no one can get in and steal him or her! Having a place to keep your dog away from small children is a blessing your dog will appreciate.

Dogs need to interact with their people. Never tie them up or leave them out on the deck or yard for too long without being there to talk to them and interact with them. Dogs are social animals and need this contact. They need to feel that they are a part of the family; that means being in the house, even when the family may not be in the house. If you deprive your dog of that feeling of belonging and being part of the family, it can do great psychological damage to the animal, and he or she can become neurotic or psychotic. Problems with digging, fence jumping, and barking are just a few of the ways neurosis can manifest itself.

It is deplorable to buy a dog and chain it outside all the time because you are too tired, busy, or lazy to train it. You must invest some time and lots of praise to have a canine companion that will be devoted to you for a lifetime. It is worth the time you will invest.

When dogs are young, they all go through destructive behavior. Most of them outgrow it, and eventually you will feel safe leaving them alone in the house.

Remember that if you allow the dog to "go" all over the house when it first comes to your home, he or she will go back to the source of the smell. Normally, a dog does not urinate or defecate where he or she sleeps, because then he or she would have to lie next to it.

Crates aren't cheap, but sometimes you can pick up one secondhand without having to put out a lot of money. Check the classifieds or at yard sales.

Buying a crate

Most pet shops, dog shows, or kennel supply houses carry crates. The price depends on where you purchase the crate and the size of the dog. You will probably spend anywhere from $40 to $80 for a crate (depending on breed size), but it will last for a lifetime. The fibreglass or plastic ones are easier to keep clean as they won't rust, like wire crates, and they aren't as noisy as the wire collapsible crates are. Considering that this is the safest way for your dog to travel, you have bought him his "dog house" and "car seat" in one package.

Your dog's crate should be just big enough for him to stand up, lie down, and turn around in—no bigger. The reason for this is so that he can't piddle in one corner and sleep in the opposite corner. This teaches the dog control.

How do I know what size crate to get?

Just stand the dog next to the crate, if he is full grown, and make sure the crate extends about four inches above the shoulders and four inches from each side and from front and back of the dog—big enough for him to turn around in and lie down in. If he is a puppy, you'll have to estimate his full-grown size. Place a cardboard box inside to make it just comfortable for him. Keep changing the size of the box as he grows. Some brand names of plastic dog crates are: VariKennel, Kennel Cab, and Sky Kennel.

Where is the best place to put the crate?

The busiest room in the house, wherever the family congregates.

The dog keeps crying when in the crate. Now what?

Most dogs "hate" being confined in the beginning, but with a little time to realize they will not be in there forever, your dog will love the peace and safety of its crate. If the dog cries, just tap the crate and say "No. Quiet now!" in a firm voice. Keep repeating this, and don't give in! Puppies cannot be expected to go for long periods of time without relieving themselves, so the time confined must be for short periods. Praise the puppy for going in the crate, and give him a treat when he or she goes in willingly. If he doesn't, then give him a push into the crate a treat, and a "good boy (or girl)" verbal command and shut the door. After puppy is quiet in the crate for a few minutes, return and open the door and allow him or her to go use the bathroom spot outside of the crate that you've designated. Make sure the exercise area is sturdy enough that he or she cannot knock it down. As the puppy gets older, he or she will be able to "hold it" longer and by six months should be able to spend an entire night without having to relieve himself. Be sure to let the puppy go potty before you shut it in the crate for the night. DO NOT let the puppy out when he or she is crying!! If you do, you have just taught the puppy that it can get its way by being vocal. Always wait until the puppy is quiet before you let it out of the crate. The exception to that rule is when you get home after the puppy has been in the crate for a while. The excitement of your return will make your puppy need to "go," so you should take it immediately to the designated "spot" and praise exuberantly when he or she does the right thing. Do this same thing in the morning, after the puppy has been crated at night.

Crate training the adult dog is a little harder, but patience, persistence, and a set of earplugs should get you through it. Put the dog's bed and toys into the crate and throw in a treat that he/she loves, and say "bedtime" or "crate time." Tell your animal how wonderful it is for going "in the crate." Play for a minute, and then close the door when the dog is comfortable in the crate. Do this a few times, and use the same command each time. Put the dog in there if it refuses, and praise it for going to the crate. Good boy (or girl)!

Keep repeating this command and getting him or her in the crate until the dog realizes it will get a reward for going in the crate and that eventually you will let it out. You must be consistent. Once the dog will go in on command, and you can leave it there for a few minutes without crying, you can increase the amount of time that the dog is in the crate, a little bit more each time. Always be sure your dog has been to the "potty" before crating. With small dogs, it's sometimes easier in the beginning to put them in the crate at eye level at night, like on your night table.

Taking Trips

Now that your dog is crate trained, it will be easier to take him or her along on trips, and he or she will handle the stress of being shipped, if necessary, and will be safe in a vehicle. You can leave your dog in the hotel room without worry that the maid might come in and accidentally allow your dog to "take off." Used to being in the crate, the dog will sleep while you are gone.

Helping Your New Dog Adjust To Your Home

Set up a schedule and follow it consistently

Always feed, walk, socialize, and put out your dog at the same time. Like the rest of us, dogs feel much more comfort able if they know what to expect. Follow this schedule for at least four to six months, as it will take the dog some time to feel "at home."

Be consistent

Not just with the schedule, but with everything you do with your dog. Decide on the rules by which the dog will live, and then stick to those rules. Dogs learn much more quickly and behave much better if you are consistent in your actions and expectations.

Consistency must start the minute you get the dog home. Everyone in the household needs to agree on the rules for the dog, how those rules will be taught, and how they will be enforced. This means that you will need to be prepared for the dog before it comes home. Be fair to the dog; don't obtain him or her on the spur of the moment. Be ready for him. Dogs don't just walk in the front door and say to themselves, "Oh, there's the potty." They need to be trained in where to relieve themselves, even if they are already housebroken. A new house means new rules, and you must teach the rules.

Don't get angry

Anger doesn't teach. It may be understood as a threat or a challenge by the dog. It doesn't lead to the desired response. Deal with disobedience by using quick, matter fact corrections. Don't involve your emotions. Many problem behaviors are not the result of the dog's attempt "to get even" but rather the result of being bored, lonesome, frightened, or having learned to get attention by an undesirable means.

Puppies at rest and play!

Photos courtesy of Eric Newman, Yorba Linda, CA

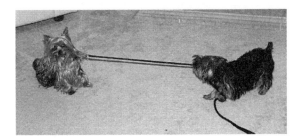

Be the Pack leader

A leader is clear, concise, and consistent. Dogs understand and need to have a pack leader. If you don't assert your right to that position, the dog will naturally move into the leadership role. That means that the sofa, the garbage, the Thanksgiving turkey, and the new pair of shoes you just bought are the dog's. In short, he or she is in control. Leaders don't come when called. Leaders may bark when and for as long as they want. Leaders may bite. Think about it.

Enroll in training classes

Training classes help you communicate with your dog. Learning to obey when there are lots of other dogs and people around helps build confidence in both the dog and owner. Owners who work with their dogs find that the mental exercise is just as important as physical exercise for keeping the dog from becoming bored. It is a proven fact that people who put in the effort to obedience train their dogs and maintain the training have fewer problems with their dogs. An added bonus is the working bond that develops between the dog and the owner when they spend time training together. Just because you own a small dog doesn't mean that obedience training is unnecessary. Do be sure that your instructor is mindful of the fact that you have a small dog and separates the classes by sizes or at least moves them separately in the classes until all the dogs are "under control."

Use Praise

Praise is the reward the dog receives for obeying your command. There are simple rules for giving praise/rewards:

- Make the reward immediate. Praise delayed equals praise denied.
- Reward the dog only for obedience. He doesn't get any praise without earning it.
- Praise should be short-term. Only a few seconds of patting is enough.
- Don't use food as the only type of reward.

Little Orphan Andy (deer) and Little Tuffy, CDX
Photo courtesy of Bonnie Braun

Be positive

Tell the dog what you want him to do instead of what you don't want. It is easier for the dog to understand one positive command (like "down") instead of a series of negative commands (don't chase the cat, don't jump on the sofa, don't bark). Being positive enforces the idea that you are the leader because you give and enforce commands.

- Giving commands gives definite direction.

- Obedience earns a reward (praise) for the dog.

- It puts you in control.

Let your dog be a dog

Enjoy, train, and have fun with your dog. Do not expect him or her to make decisions. That's your job—you're the leader. Expect him or her to act like a dog—nothing more, but certainly nothing less.

Dogs are intelligent, energetic, and very adaptable. Given the right training and respect for the qualities that have made them "man's best friend" for thousands of years, dogs can become very good companions and valued members of the household. Without training, proper care, or an understanding of how dogs think, feel, and react, these four-footed creatures can become problems for both owner and neighborhood and not give the pleasure that good training can create.

Three pound Yorkie "herding" sheep
Photo courtesy of Bonnie Sustich

Chapter 11

General Health Care

It is important that you work with your veterinarian in the health care maintenance of your dog. Choose a vet who is willing to work with you and who genuinely cares about your dog.

Addison's Disease

(From www.vetinfo.com)

The Facts You Need To Know

Symptoms: Most less than seven years of age. Seventy percent are female. Weakness, depression, collapse, slow heart rate, shock (in acute or end state disease), off and on loss of appetite, vomiting, diarrhea, muscle weakness, depression (chronic)

Diagnosis: ACTH Stimulation test.

Treatment: Intravenous fluids and glucocorticoid (Cortisone), mineralcorticoid (Florinef)

Prognosis: Good. Animals need life-long glucocorticoid and mineralcorticoid supplementation. Periodic blood work needed to monitor treatment.

What Is Addison's Disease?

Addison's disease is a severe or total deficiency of the hormones made in the adrenal cortex, caused by a destruction of the adrenal cortex. There are normally two adrenal glands, located above each kidney. The adrenal glands are really two endocrine (ductless or hormone-producing) glands in one. The inner part of the adrenal (called the medulla) produces epinephrine (also called adrenaline), which is produced at times of stress and helps the body respond to "fight or flight" situations by raising the pulse rate, adjusting blood flow, and raising blood sugar. However, the absence of the adrenal medulla and epinephrine does not cause disease.

In contrast, the outer portion of the adrenal, the cortex, is more critical. The adrenal cortex makes two important steroid hormones, cortisol and aldosterone. Cortisol mobilizes nutrients, modifies the body's response to inflammation, stimulates the liver to raise the blood sugar, and also helps to control the amount of water in the body. Aldosterone regulates salt and water levels, which affect blood volume and blood pressure. Cortisol production is regulated by another hormone, adrenocorticotrophic hormone (ACTH), made in the pituitary gland, which is located just below the brain. Classical Addison's disease results from a loss of both cortisol and aldosterone secretion due to the near total or total destruction of both adrenal glands. This condition is also called primary adrenal insufficiency. If ACTH is deficient, there will not be enough cortisol produced, although aldosterone may remain adequate. This is secondary adrenal insufficiency, which is distinctly different from, but similar to, Addison's disease, since both include a loss of cortisol secretion.

What Causes Addison's Disease?

When Dr. Thomas Addison first described this disease in London in 1855, the most common cause was tuberculosis. This remained the leading cause until the middle of the twentieth century when antibiotics progressively reduced TB's incidence.

Since then, Addison's disease primarily results from an autoimmune reaction in which the body's immune system erroneously makes antibodies against the cells of the adrenal cortex and slowly destroys them. That process takes months to years. There are also several less common causes of Addison's disease: other chronic infections besides tuberculosis, especially certain fungal infections; invasion of the adrenal by cancer cells that have spread from another part of the body, especially the breast; CMV virus in association with acquired immunodeficiency syndrome (AIDS); rarely, hemorrhage into the adrenals during shock; and the surgical removal of both adrenals.

It is more easily treated than Cushings, the overproduction of hormones, which is the exact opposite disease. In Addison's the patient does not supply enough natural cortisone, which will also affect the testosterone levels. Both are expensive diseases to treat, but the chances of finding a balance of the medications is better with Addison's. If caught early enough, before too much damage has occurred to the kidneys and heart, it can be treated by medications, but the medication and testing will required for the rest of the patient's life.

Aerosol Dangers

Most aerosol sprays give directions not to inhale the fumes. They can, indeed, be dangerous to pets. Any disinfectant sprays used to treat crates, pens, and beds of dogs and cats should be perfectly dry before the pet is allowed to enter or use them. I find it's better to use the pump spray cleaners, but still be sure they are dry before the pet enters and inhales any mist from them.

Allergies

Inhaled allergies

A classic sign of atopy (inhaled allergies) is chewing of the feet. Why do dogs chew their feet if they have a food allergy? Probably because the dog is also allergic to things that he inhales through the air. That's why allergies can be tough to pin down. The only way to know exactly to what the dog is allergic is to do skin testing. The thing to remember is that if the owner is unwilling to give allergy injections for the rest of the dog's life, there is no point in spending the time, money, and effort to determine the allergens. People have tried serum testing to tell about allergens but the results have not been consistent. To deal with food allergy, the market is flooded with different types of food. The current idea is to use a home-cooked diet with no extras, only several basic ingredients. Use this diet only for eight weeks. If the allergy goes away, go back on the regular diet, and the symptoms should reappear. Also no chew sticks, Pet Tabs, or other treats.

Hypoallergenic diets

Some new choices are duck and potato, lamb and potato, venison and potato, and rabbit and potato. IVD Diet Innovation Veterinary Diet, Corona, California, phone 1-800-359-4IVD.

Symptoms: Classic symptom is chewing feet and legs.

Treatment: Non-allergic food. NO TREATS!!

Allergy—Flea

Symptoms: Biting and scratching at various parts of the body and sores

Treatment: Treat the premises using flea products from your vet like Program or Advantage, or keep the pet sprayed with repellant like Adams Flea and Tick Repellant spray. Get rid of fleas on the premises—house and lawn—with fumigation and/or Malathion on the lawn.

Anal Glands

Many groomers will automatically express the anal glands while the dog is in the bath. Some dogs seem to need to have the glands expressed on a regular basis, some never need to have them expressed their entire lives. Anal sac abscesses occur more regularly on small dogs but very rarely on large dogs. Expressing the glands should not increase secretions. My vet has suggested that if the dog is scooting, express; if not, leave things be.

If the anal glands become infected, they must be treated locally with warm compresses and antiseptics or antibiotic creams and oral antibiotics. If you cannot clear up the infection and it becomes chronic, it sometimes becomes necessary to remove the glands surgically. It's a good idea to do a culture and sensitivity test to be sure the right antibiotic is being used.

As the dog gets older, anal glands can become impacted. The anal sacs are on each side and slightly below and to the side of the rectum. It is usually possible to feel them if they are full. If you grasp either side of the rectum and squeeze firmly outward, there should be a liquid that may be gray, tan, brown or black, all of which are normal. If blood is present after squeezing the anal sacs, you should consult your veterinarian as this may indicate an infection.

Anasarca

Edema may be localized or generalized. Severe generalized edema is called anasarca. Bulldogs have a higher-than-normal record of producing anasarca puppies. The fetus often weighs two to three times what the normal pup weighs, and because they are bigger, they cannot pass through the pelvic opening of the birth canal. If the anasarca puppy is first in line to be born, then a cesarean section is absolutely necessary.

This can be determined by an ultrasound. Usually, these puppies do not live more than a few minutes. This is one reason why most bulldog puppies are born by cesarean section. It is suspected that the condition is inherited, but repeat breedings may not produce more anasarca puppies.

The anasarca puppy is usually robust, and it is possible for them to survive, though it requires a lot of hard work.

Anesthesia

I am told that vets cannot use injectable barbiturates in sight hounds as they don't metabolize it and will die, and that boxers cannot tolerate Ace Promezine.

Dr. Dale Heisler's personal preference is Telazol. Isoflurane is expensive, so some practices use it for the small and high risk dogs and use Metafane for the routine procedures. Injectable anesthesia are dosed according to body weight. Animals with widely differing percentages of body fat may respond somewhat differently to them. Rarely is there any significant problem. Dr. Heisler's tiny Yorkie, who weighed 1.9 pounds, received Isoflurane. She was masked down, and then intubated, rather than getting a risky injection.

Dr. Steve Robinson uses Isoflurane for all inhalation anesthesia. For very short procedures and for induction of anesthesia, he uses either a combination of diazepam and ketamine or a medication called propofol. For most toy dogs he simply masks them down.

The most important decision you can make regarding anesthesia for surgery or dental work is what kind of anesthesia your vet will use. For very small dogs, it is better to mask them down with Isoflurane, according to both of these vets.

Antibiotic Therapy

It is very important that any antibiotic therapy is carried out for the full term. It can be very dangerous to discontinue it too quickly just because the patient is feeling better. Do not quit the antibiotic until the full length of treatment is completed.

The best method of antibiotic therapy is, of course, having a culture done so you know that the antibiotic you are using is the "right one" for the germ with which you are dealing. However, there are times when a broad spectrum antibiotic is necessary for the benefit of a very sick dog when time is crucial.

Recently, there has been some discussion of Baytril causing problems in some canine patients, so if you and your vet are planning to use this drug, discuss the side effects thoroughly with the vet.

Auto Immune Diseases

Most veterinarians are familiar with Dr. Jean Dodds, a specialist in auto immune diseases. Her research indicates that in hemolytic anemia, a destruction of red blood cells occurs due to, in basic terms, the presence of antibodies that stick to the cells and cause reactions within the body that ultimately destroy the cells. In other words, the body mistakes the RBCs (red blood cells) for a substance that is toxic or foreign depending upon the etiology of the disorder. This may be an immune reaction with unknown etiology or may be precipitated by a primary stimulus such as the presence of a virus, parasite in the blood, a medication (often penicillin or sulfa preparations) or some other toxin.

Symptoms: Lethargy, progressing to coma within hours. The presence of jaundice is usually an indication that the illness has progressed to a more acute level and the prognosis is diminished.

Treatment: Prednisone. Watch the color of mucous membranes and have your vet routinely monitor platelet levels; administer small doses of prednisone when needed.

Reference—Dr. Jean Dodds, *The Immune System and Disease Resistance*

Prognosis: Dependent upon the cause of the anemia, the severity of the progression, and the dog's general health. For example, if an adverse reaction to the medication precipitated the anemia, one might expect rapid improvement, whereas if the cause if not external in origin, suppression is more difficult.

Bladder Control

Some dogs sleep so soundly that the muscle that controls urination relaxes so they urinate while sleeping. A medication that can control this, phenylpropanolamine is given daily or another medication, DES, is given once a week. Consult with your vet if the problem continues.

Bladder Incontinence

A dog with an incontinence problem can be treated with one-half to one mg Stilbesterol every seven to fourteen days, and that should solve the problem. Many dogs are on it for years with no difficulties. It's very inexpensive. Some dogs can be taken off after four to six months of treatment with no recurrence of the problem.

Bladder Stones

If your dog is diagnosed with bladder stones, the stones were analyzed, and surgery was done, you have two options to prevent future problems.

1. If the next stone is struvite, you can feed SD diet and the stone should dissolve in six to ten weeks.

2. You can do the surgery to remove the stone, have it analyzed, and then go on the proper diet to prevent future problems. A special diet will not *always* prevent problems down the road. You also need blood work to document any other problems. Kidney Diet (KD) at this point in time will not help much. Remember if your dog goes on a special diet there are to be NO TREATS, which would undermine the diet. You might also consider using distilled water rather than regular tap water as drinking water. The bottom line is you have two choices: diet to dissolve or surgery.

Bloat

(From www.vetinfo.com and Dr. Dale Heisler)

Symptoms:	Nonproductive vomiting attempts, excessive salivation, abdominal distention, restlessness, difficulty breathing, weakness, and collapse.
Diagnosis:	Usually on physical confirmation with radiograph No one knows the cause, but it usually affects deep-chested dogs, and it seems that intake of large volumes of food and water make the situation worse, as well as overexertion after eating or delayed emptying of the stomach.
Treatment:	There still is not a firm consensus on the best way to treat this problem when it occurs and not much concrete information on the causes, although it is widely accepted that large deep-chested dogs are at the greatest risk. The vet will try to pass a stomach tube to decompress the stomach. If it can't be done, then decompressing the stomach with 16-18 gauge needle inserted through the skin into the stomach is next. Most require surgery to decompress, rotate, and reposition the stomach. The stomach is attached to the abdominal wall to prevent recurrence. There are many short-term complications and possible death. If surgery is done, bloat "probably" won't reoccur. If the stomach is tubed only and no surgery is done, it usually reoccurs.

The problem is twofold.

1. Gastric dilation: overdistention of the stomach with fluid, gas, or food.

2. Gastric volvulus: twisting of the stomach in a counter-clockwise direction.

The above can lead to a number of secondary problems, including shock, blood-clotting abnormalities, cardiac heartbeat abnormalities, and death in approximately one-third of the cases.

This enlargement of the abdomen or bloat should be treated as an absolute emergency. Most owners are familiar with the available emergency clinics for "after hours." When I bought my Great Dane, the breeder cautioned me to always feed her in her crate and keep her crated for at least one-half hour after she ate, to help prevent this condition.

Bordetella

Bordetella is the most common cause of tracheobronchitis (kennel cough) in dogs. If your dogs are exposed to a kennel situation or indoor shows where many dogs congregate, it would be wise to vaccinate for Bordetella twice a year, either with the intranasal or subcutaneous vaccination for this disease.

Brachycephalic Breeds

Brachycephalic breeds such as the Pekinese, Shih Tzu, Japanese Chin, Bulldogs and pugs have some medical problems that are relative to their very short muzzles and comparatively large heads. Cleft palates on pups at birth are common, as are cesarean sections because of the large heads desired in the breed. Because of their airway, they do not do well in climates where heat and humidity prevail, and those with heavy coats fare even worse.

These dogs have an elongated soft palate (the top of the inner mouth); therefore, these breeds have a problem when they must undergo surgery and be intubated. When they are waking up, they must regain total control of their airway following surgery, and be licking and swallowing. The tube should remain in the airway until they regain this control. If the tube is taken out too early, that elongated soft palate can close their airway and render them unable to breathe. My vet feels that the endotracheal tube is ready to be pulled when the brachycephalic breed is ready to chew it out.

These are not breeds to own if you have weather extremes or no air conditioning. The short muzzle causes a strain on the upper respiratory tract during the heat of the day, and when combined with a tremendous coat, it is a deadly combination. If weather is extremely hot, ice packs would be a necessity where there is no air conditioning.

Shih Tzu and Pekinese are very close to the ground and are prone to injury to their large eyes. It is imperative to keep the hair trained to grow away from the eye. Eye problems need immediate attention to prevent the loss of the eye.

Brucellosis

A specific contagious disease primarily affecting cattle, swine, sheep, goats, and dogs, brucellosis is caused by bacteria of the *Brucella* genus characterized by abortion in the female and, to a lesser extent, infection of the sex glands of the male and infertility in both sexes.

While dogs occasionally become infected, these are sporadic happenings, and the dogs usually are closely associated with infected herds of domestic livestock.

Brucella canis organism can be disseminated among dogs closely kenneled, especially at the time of breeding or when abortions occur.

Transmission is congenital or venereal or by ingestion of infective materials. All ages and both sexes appear to be equally susceptible.

The clinical feature is abortion during the last trimester of pregnancy. Stillbirths and conception failure are predominant features of the disease.

Button Tumors

A button tumor is known as a histiocytoma. The majority occur on the face, ears, and front legs. They are red, raised, hairless, and rarely exceed one inch in diameter. One appeared on a show dog of mine, and my vet told me to wait and see, because this kind of tumor usually goes away; it did. However, the wait and see approach is not always the right one. In one instance, the tumor turned out to be a mass cell tumor. Now my answer would be to remove it and do a histopath to be sure it is not malignant.

Cardiomyopathy

There are two different types of cardiomyopathy, *dilated and hypertrophic.*

Symptoms: Fluid around the heart, difficulty breathing, coughing, respiratory distress, exercise intolerance, weight loss

Treatment: You may need to use Enacard longterm to help the heart muscle. The problem will get worse over time; the question is how quickly. Treatment is usually done with Lasix, Digoxil, Enacard, anti-arrhythmic drops if heartbeat is irregular, and antibiotics. With hypertrophic cardiomyopathy, there is increased muscle wall thickness, which decreases the size of the ventricle, and there is a heart murmur and weak femoral pulse. The treatment would be Lasix, Beta blockers (Indural), and Enacard.

Prognosis: The heart will not return to normal.

Treatment and prognosis is about the same in both types of cardiomyopathy.

Cataracts

A cataract is defined as any spot on the lens, regardless of size, that does not allow light to pass through. Cataracts can be confined to a single area within the lens or affect the entire structure. They were identified in dogs as early as 1925. Some cataracts are clearly visible to the naked eye, appearing as white flecks within the eye, or giving a milky gray or bluish-white cast to the lens behind the pupil. They result in varying degrees of blindness. Aging animals often have a graying of the lens, which should not be mistaken for a cataract.

Cataracts are classified as primary or secondary. Primary cataracts usually result from a (presumed) recessive gene and typically appear at an early age. Usually both eyes are affected, though not necessarily with symmetrical development. Primary cataracts do not always advance to cause total blindness and are sometimes associated with other ocular diseases.

Secondary cataracts are generally associated with other hereditary eye diseases where the nutrition of the lens is disturbed, as with diabetes. They can also develop secondary to Progressive Retinal Atrophy (PRA) or lens luxation. Cataracts can also be acquired as a result of trauma.

Before you decide on surgery for cataracts, your vet may wish to perform an ERG (electro- retinogram) to determine if there is any retinal damage in the back of the eye. It makes no sense to do cataract surgery and then find out that the dog is still blind due to retinal disease. Prior to surgery, make sure the dog is in good health. Seeing an eye specialist for an evaluation would be a good idea. Recently, a client told me of laser eye surgery on a twelve-year-old dog, which worked, and now the little dog that was bumping into things and appeared frightened is playful as a puppy again. Prior to surgery the dog should be built up and be in otherwise good health.

Cleft Palates

Symptoms: Puppies that have this crack or opening in the roof of the mouth usually cannot nurse without inhaling the milk, which "usually" leads to aspiration pneumonia. Sometimes a hare lip is also present.

Causes: Cleft palates can be inherited and/or acquired by toxins. Infectious disease exposure during the twenty-fifth to twenty-eighth days of pregnancy may induce cleft palates.

Some cleft palates can be surgically fixed, but the surgery is very complicated and respiratory problems may persist. Genetics probably plays a role in cleft palates. If there are only one or two in a litter, then it is probably genetic, but if a large percentage of the litter is affected, then it would be more likely that a toxic condition may have caused the problems.

Coccidiosis

Coccidiosis is a disease of young dogs and cats. Symptoms are diarrhea, mucous mixed with blood in the stool, especially brought on by stress of some kind like moving to a new environment. It is a microscopic intestinal parasite. The symptoms of the disease may vary from mild diarrhea to severe infections causing bloody diarrhea, loss of appetite, weakness, or weight loss. Severe outbreaks are the exception. The course of the disease may vary from a few days to ten days. Coccidiosis is seldom fatal, except where it is complicated with some other infectious or parasitic disease.

Generally the disease can be controlled with good sanitation and the proper medication. Fecal examinations should be made and the animal should be medicated.

Colitis

Definition: A large number of inflammatory cells in the intestines. Another name for it is "inflammatory bowel disease." It is similar to Crohn's disease and ulcerative colitis in humans. The cause is unknown.

Symptoms: Increased frequency of defecation, and stool is bloody and filled with mucous.

Diagnosis: Endoscopy with biopsy

Treatment: Diet of high quality protein and high fiber. Drugs of choice are prednisone, flagyl, and amoxicillin. Dramatic results can be obtained by switching the pet with colitis to Prescription Diet (D/D) (rice and Salmon).

Culture Program

There are many reasons why both the male and female should be cultured, including abortion, absorption, or failure to conceive and Fading Puppy Syndrome. I highly recommend the B.D.M.L. (Breeder's Diagnostic Microbiology Laboratory) for culture, identification, and sensitivity testing so that the proper antibiotics can be used, if necessary. The bacterial identification is absolutely necessary in some cases to prevent further puppy loss and reproductive diseases. The culture program is explained in full in *Form, Function & Fancy*, by Sandy Lemire, as well as in her new book, *Yorkies-Head to Tail*.

The culture sticks can be purchased from BDML lab. Contact through readtaintor@networld.com.

Cushing's Disease

Symptoms: Cushing's (hyperadrenocoticism) is a very complicated disease. In addition to increased water consumption, possible signs are increased appetite, decreased appetite, panting, abdominal distention, and lethargy. Primary clinical signs are increased water intake and increased urination. Secondary problems are infection and congestive heart failure.

Diagnosis: Blood tests

Presumptive diagnosis is usually based on clinical signs and abnormal results on a routine blood chem panel.

Definitive diagnosis is based on low dose dexamenthone suppression test and ACTH stimulation test.

Treatment: Consists of using either Lysodren or Anapryl. Each medication has its own pluses and minuses. The choice depends on the patient and the owner.

Prognosis: Good to excellent for normal life for about two years. Most common cause of death is pulmonary embolism. A new medication, Anipiyl, hopefully will extend life past two years.

Cushing's Syndrome is an excess of glucocortisone in the system and is eighty-five percent pituitary gland dependent due to overproduction of ACTH (hormone that stimulates cortisone production).

Adrenal gland tumors account for fifteen percent (Fifty percent of these tumors are benign.) It can also result from excess cortisone usage orally, topically, or by injection. If pituitary dependent, it should be treated medically. If it is an adrenal tumor, treat surgically. A secondary disease is always possible in other organ systems. A chance of hypertension is associated with Cushing's disease leading to retinal damage and blindness. Cataracts are more common in dogs with Cushing's disease but these things have obvious clinical symptoms on an exam.

Diabetes Mellitus

There are two types: Type 1 requires insulin and diet control; Type 2 can be diet controlled.

Signs:
Early symptoms include voluminous discharge of urine in a given period, chronic excessive intake of water, gluttony, and weight loss.

Later symptoms include loss of appetite, laziness, depression, and vomiting. Obesity with recent weight loss is typical for most cases.

It is believed to be an autoimmune disorder just as in people. Animals may develop this disease as a result of some other disease, such as chronic pancreatitis. (more common in small, overweight, middle-aged dogs and Siamese cats). It can be triggered by viral infection.

Diarrhea Control

Pepto Bismol, flavored with Nutrical, one ml per pound, given three times a day, would be a good first resort. Another choice is Imodium one to two cc per 4 pounds three times a day, or one tablet per twenty-five to forty pounds, or Kaopectate one ml per pound two to four times a day.

Aspirin is okay to give to dogs for pain as directed by your veterinarian, but Tylenol can be *fatal*!

Other medications that may work for the first signs of diarrhea are Fastrack and Children's Cherry Flavored Kaopectate. Many products work fine, but I prefer to treat with Kaolin, which you can get from your veterinarian or from Omaha Vet Supply, (800) 367-4444. Dosage for a five-pound dog would be three cc every three hours. It is a good mixture, and I give it three times and then as needed (3 cc per dose for a four to six pound dog). Check with your vet for dosages. Do not use over-the-counter remedies unless you have checked with your vet. Pepto Bismol contains an aspirin-like ingredient that some vets feel is not safe for dogs or for some people with aspirin allergies. However, my vet still prefers using Pepto Bismol over Kaopectate, and I have used it on adult dogs with no side effects.

Adding cooked rice to the dog's present food may help. Sometimes changing diet will cause diarrhea, and you must back up to what the dog was eating and make changes slowly. A change of water also can cause a bout of diarrhea. If you see mucous in the stool, it is a good idea to take a stool sample to your veterinarian. For some dogs with a touchy stomach or colitis, just add a heaping tablespoon of canned pumpkin (body temperature) to their food each day. It adds fiber and helps in some cases. I have seen dramatic results in a dog with colitis that was switched totally to Prescription Diet Rice and Salmon. Nothing else seemed to help her, but this diet fed exclusively did. (See Enteritis for severe diarrhea problems).

Dog Bites

(from www.bestdogs.com, January 1999)

"A unique bacteria is found in animal bites."

Researchers have found that life-threatening bacteria unique to dog and cat bites are more prevalent in the animal bites than researchers had expected. The scientists found the bacteria, *Pasteurella multocida*, which has the potential to cause blood stream and joint infections and meningitis, in seventy-five percent of cat bites and fifty percent of dog bites.

"As opposed to the usual stuff that causes infections, these infections are a different animal," said Dr. David Talan, of the UCLA Medical School in Olive View, California. Talan and colleagues studied 110 emergency room patients treated for dog and cat bites at eighteen hospitals around the country. Their study was published in *The New England Journal of Medicine*. "The bacteria are quite unique," said Talan, of a type not usually seen by physicians in other types of skin infections. "We were struck with how rapidly these things (infections) happen, sometimes within eight hours," he said. Animal bites account for 300,000 emergency room visits each year in the United States, leading to 10,000 hospital admissions and twenty deaths, mostly among small children. Ninety percent of animal bites come from dogs and cats, and up to eighteen percent of dog bites and twenty-eight percent to eighty percent of cat bites become infected.

Talan said the study is the first comprehensive look at the bacteria in dog and cat bites. While the existence of pasteurella has been noted in the medical literature before, it was not acknowledged to be so prevalent.

Dr. Gary Fleisher, of Children's Hospital in Boston, said the study used "a more careful culturing method" to give the best picture of what's contained in an animal bite.

For parents, the good news is that bite infections can be very effectively treated with of antibiotics, and there has been no sign that such infections are resistant to antimicrobial treatments. In an accompanying editorial, Fleisher said even apparently minor bite wounds require "careful exploration" by physicians, because injuries that may appear to be superficial could actually be covering up more serious problems, such as lacerated tendons, vessels, or nerves. Talan, an emergency room physician, advised parents to carefully watch any animal bite for redness, swelling and pain, even if the possibility of rabies has been ruled out.

Dry Skin

Dry skin can be caused by many different things. It can be dietary, in which case a little vegetable oil or olive oil added to the food will help. Don't give a lot of oil all at once. If you start with about a quarter teaspoon and gradually increase it to a half teaspoon for a small dog, you shouldn't have a problem. Any sudden changes to the diet will probably cause a bout of diarrhea.

If your dog's skin looks dry, it could be the result of leaving some of the shampoo in the coat after bathing. Be sure you rinse the hair thoroughly and that the conditioner you use is not burning the skin. Years ago, many breeders used Alpha Keri bath oil on long coats, and dry skin was a resultant problem. A great product that I have used for dry skin and brittle coat is Tomlyn's Nova Pearl Skin Moisturizer, available at www.cherry-brook.com and Omaha Supply (800) 367-4444. Of course, if you cannot eliminate the problem, and it is recurring, then you may want to have your vet do a skin scraping and culture, particularly if the dog is scratching.

Ear Infection

Symptoms: Scratching at ears, odor, scabs in ears

Treatment: Check for ear mites. Get a culture and sensitivity swab of the ear and in the mean time use Otomax ointment (not Animax ointment). It could be a bad yeast infection in which case the Otomax will work better. The swab results will tell you if bacteria are present and what antibiotic would solve the problem. Consider a 1:1 or 1:3 dilution of vinegar to water as an ear wash, which can kill bacteria, especially Pseudomonas, a tough bacteria to eliminate. Always put a piece of cotton in the ears at bath time to prevent "Swimmer's" ear and infection. Use a good ear cleansing product like Nolvasan Otic Solution or R7 Ear Cleaner in the ears after bathing.

Eye Tearing

Symptoms: Excessive tearing and staining around the eyes.

Diagnosis: Vet exam may indicate blocked tear ducts or mild infection.

Treatment: Your vet may prescribe Tripoptic-S by Pfizer or other relevant medication. This can sometimes produce dramatic results. It contains bacitracin, neomycin, and polymyxin with hydrocortisone acetate 1%. The hydrocortisone shrinks the swelling of the tear ducts and may allow the tears to start flowing again naturally.

First Aid

In all cases, be sure to consult *Hands-on Dog Care: The Complete Book of Canine First Aid,* by Sue Copeland and John Hamil, DVM, (Doral Publishing, 2000) for immediate, detailed help.
Reference: Judy Carey, Consumer Affairs, with advice from pet expert, Jack Bloch, D.V.M.

Burns

Fortunately, because of their hair coats, dogs do not have many problems with burns. Usually, when dogs are burned, it is because of human stupidity, not that of the animal.

Immediately after a burn happens, get the dog into cold water. If the entire dog is involved, get him into a bathtub of water with ice cubes in it. Immerse the dog. Butter, lard, and other substances should not be put on burns, because they trap the heat and make the burn more severe. Sometimes a little of the hair will come out later. Things like A & D ointment work well to prevent this. If it is a superficial burn, you can care for it in this manner.

However, if the area is large or it is a group two or three burn, give the dog the cold water treatment, then get him to the veterinarian, because he may go into shock, which is something you as a dog owner cannot treat.

Head Blows

It's a good idea to have "coffee extract" on hand for a "cold conk," which renders a dog unconscious. A bit of coffee extract under the tongue might bring the dog around.

Heat Exhaustion or Heat Stroke

Symptoms: The first sign is excessive panting. An overheated dog is one thing, but heatstroke is another. With true heatstroke, the mucous membranes will be deep red to blue and very dry.

Diagnosis: The history is very important. Was the dog in a hot car, in the direct sun, or under a dryer too long? A "hot" dog is treated differently than a dog with heatstroke. Many times a fine line separates the two.

Treatment: When a dog becomes overheated, apply an ice pack to the stomach and apply wet towels on the body to bring down the temperature. Get the dog out of the sun and into the shade, air conditioning, or a cool bath. If this doesn't help bring down the temperature, you had better get veterinary attention immediately. You can offer the dog a couple of wet ice cubes lick on. If you have a thermometer, take the dog's temperature. Anything higher than 106-107 degrees Fahrenheit is a serious emergency.

Get immediate veterinary attention. The vet will usually use intravenous fluids and cool water and high-dose cortisone. If the temperature hasn't remained too high for a long period of time, the prognosis is good for recovery.

Ingested Glass

A well circulated first aid remedy for ingesting holiday decorations (glass ornaments) is to dip cotton balls into half-and-half cream and feed them to your dog. This may help work the glass and/or staples through the intestines without injury. Make sure you get real cotton balls for your first aid kit. It is a good idea to keep a quart of "half and half" in the freezer for such an emergency. Two soaked balls should be sufficient for dogs under ten pounds, and dogs ten to fifty pounds should probably have three to five soaked balls. On larger breeds, five to seven soaked cotton balls might do the trick.

Some veterinarians use this approach before they consider surgery, in the hope that the cotton will work its way through the digestive track and wrap itself around the glass or staples. Please see your veterinarian immediately and tell him what you suspect and how you have treated the situation. You will have to carefully check the dog's stool for a few days. If you see any fresh blood or a tarry appearance, return immediately to the vet for further evaluation.

Insect Bites

Symptoms: Bite marks, swelling, hives, weakness, pain, panting, breathing problems, vomiting

Treatment: If pet is weak, vomiting, or having breathing difficulties, take it to your vet immediately. Remove the stinger, if visible, by scraping it out with a dull knife. Do not use tweezers. Apply ice.

Poisoning

Symptoms: Excess salivation, vomiting, weakness, twitching, collapse, pale gums and tongue.

Treatment: Contact your vet or poison control center immediately. Take pet and sample of poison, if possible, to vet.

Shock

The first thing you will notice in diagnosing shock is a decrease in blood pressure. There are two ways you can recognize this. Lift up the gum and look at the mucous membrane of the mouth. If you have not done this before, look at your normal dog. Pinch the membrane. The tissues should blanch out, and immediately return to a normal, pink color.

An animal in shock has pale mucous membranes. Sometimes they are sheet-white. If so, the dog needs immediate attention. Sometimes they are marginal and, if pinched, the color comes back right away. This is a good indication that the animal has substantial blood pressure. If you pinch it and it is more than a minute before the color returns, the dog is probably in shock.

Learn how to palpate, or feel, the pulse of the dog. This can best be done in the femoral artery, which runs down the inside of the dog's thigh. It is a firm, evenly rising, evenly falling beat. A dog in shock has a rapid pulse that is very weak. If the pulse is rapid and weak and the mucous membranes are pale, then call the vet's office immediately and tell them that you think the dog is in shock and why you think he is in shock. The vet will then know that the animal needs treatment right away. You must get emergency treatment immediately.

Skunk Spray

Symptoms: Unmistakable skunk odor

Treatment: Flush pet's eyes with lukewarm water. Using an eyedropper or saturated cloth, apply warm olive oil (or any other food-grade oil) or over-the-counter artificial tears into eyes for protection. Neutralize the smell by soaking the entire body with tomato juice. Other solutions may do the trick; check with your vet. Allow to dry, and then bathe thoroughly. The process may have to be repeated several times to eliminate all odor. A trip to your groomer might be a good next step.

Wound (Minor)

Symptoms: Small cut or puncture, may or may not be bleeding.

Treatment: Clip hair away from area and wash gently with soap and water. Flush with hydrogen peroxide, and use an antibiotic cream. If bleeding, apply direct pressure. Consult your vet if bleeding continues.

Wound (Major)

Symptoms: Bleeding injury deeper or wider than a small puncture.

Treatment: Apply pressure over wound with clean, dry cloth, and take pet to your vet. Freshly sutured areas heal faster and better than open wounds.

Make Your Own Pet First Aid Kit

Any type of small box works well to hold supplies. Include the following:

- bandage scissors
- 2 gauze rolls
- 6 gauze pads
- l adhesive tape roll
- chemical ice pack
- rectal thermometer
- antiseptic lotion
- antibiotic ointment
- tweezers
- hydrogen peroxide to clean wounds and also to induce vomiting if poison is ingested. (5-10 ml twice, thirty minutes apart)

Flea and Tick Control

Fleas

Flea infestation has become reasonably easy to control in the last few years, since the advent of drugs that interfere with the life cycle of the fleas. Formerly, flea dips, collars, and sprays were only temporary measures directed at killing the flea on and around the animal. Naturally, as soon as Kitty or Fido went outside again, new fleas soon found a new home. Control of flea infestations is important, not only for the comfort of your pet, but for yours as well. Having a house, especially with carpets, professionally fumigated because of an infestation of fleas is an experience you don't want to repeat. Another important reason for control of fleas is that cats, dogs, and people frequently develop an allergy to flea saliva. Flea bite allergy may cause severe itching and dermatitis with extensive damage to the skin, often followed by a secondary bacterial infection. Additionally, there are some very dangerous infectious agents transmitted by fleas and other internal parasites that use the flea as a means of transmission to a new host.

The cat flea is responsible for the most severe allergies in cats, dogs, and humans.

My vet tells me that his family has small dogs, which are never outside, and nine cats, which are all outdoors. Since he began using the flea control programs that interfere with the flea's life cycle, their animals have been completely flea free. Two of their cats come in the house regularly, and they have not had a single flea in the house since initiating this treatment more than two years ago. His bigger dogs are on Top Spot. Talk to your veterinarian about starting this treatment if you haven't already. The difference in Advantage, Program, and the other flea programs is as follows:

Program: Oral tablet given once a month that prevents flea eggs from hatching.

Advantage: Applied to skin once a month to kill fleas. Not absorbed into the system, stays in the skin, and will wash off after repeated bathing. It is water-based in skin.

Top Spot: Applied to skin once a month to kill fleas AND ticks. Stays in skin and is not absorbed into the system. It is less likely to wash off due to being oil-gland based in the skin.

In summary, if you don't have any fleas, use Program to prevent infestation. Use Advantage or spray as needed. If you already have a flea problem, use Advantage and Program together because they do two different things.

- Top Spot may last three months, depending on in which part of the country you live.

- Bio Spot is an over-the-counter medication that people are unhappy with. It contains permethrin, a synthetic insecticide.

Just remember this: Program—Flea Eggs, Advantage or Top Spot—Adult Fleas.

There are numerous new products on the market. Consult your vet for the one best suited for your dog.

Ticks

The other major ectoparasite found in dogs and cats is the tick. Ticks are responsible for the transmission of a number of serious diseases in both pets and people. Dips, dusts, and sprays are the most commonly used eradication methods. Most control programs are designed to reduce the free living stage of the tick in the environment. For most people and pets, ticks are less of a problem than fleas. For additional information, see Ticks on page 161.

Flea Allergy Dermatitis

The most common allergic skin disease in the dog develops when certain dogs become hypersensitive to flea bites. The allergic agent is contained in the saliva or mouth parts of the flea and is injected into the dog when the flea feeds. Commonly called "summer eczema," the disease usually occurs during the warm months.

The disease begins near the tail on the rump of the dog. The patient will scratch or rub this area intensely causing the hair to fall out and often ulcerating the skin. In severe cases, the hair loss can become more generalized and involve large areas of the body. Although the disease occurs more commonly in the summer months, many dogs show signs of the disease all year. The flea can complete its life cycle in the home environment and thus can cause constant irritation to hypersensitive dogs.

Therapy is aimed at flea control on the dog, on other pets, and in the dog's environment. In addition, specific therapy can be instituted to control the signs in affected dogs. Cortisone-type drugs (prednisolone) will relieve the symptoms of the allergic reaction.

New products now on the market for flea control, like Advantage, Frontline, and others, are very valuable in the control of fleas. Some allergies have been reported, but they seem to work on most dogs. Depending on the type of exposure your dog has, you may want to try these products.

Giardia

Giardia is a protozoan parasite that lives in the intestine of affected animals. There may be several species of this parasite, and they are difficult to find in a fecal examination.

Symptoms: Signs of giardia include weight loss, inability to gain weight appropriately during growth, diarrhea, vomiting, lack of appetite, and greasy appearing stools.

Treatment: Sanitation of the premises with disinfectants, Lysol, and bleach. Keep premises clean and dry. The drug of choice for the affected animal is Flagyl. Washing hands often after handling an infected animal is important. Humans can be infected with this bacterial parasite also, and a doctor should be consulted if asymptomatic.

Glaucoma

Glaucoma is one of the leading causes of blindness in dogs.

Symptoms: Excessive tear production, dilated pupil, cloudy cornea, enlarged globe, increased interocular pressure. Discharge from the eye, pain and squinting of the eye, corneal fluid build-up, dilated pupil that does not constrict when light is shined in it. Blindness and visible enlargement of the eye. By definition glaucoma is an increased pressure in the eye, and the only way to confirm is to measure the pressure in the eyes.

Treatment: Medical emergency if there is hope to retain vision. (Fifty percent chance of that at best) Hyperosmotic agents given Intravenously or by mouth to draw the fluid out of the eye. Carbonic anhydrase inhibitors to decrease fluid production in the eye. If pressure is really high, your vet can insert a 30 gauge needle in the eye and draw fluid off. Long-term medical therapy usually doesn't last. Surgery is needed.

Surgery: 1) destroys some of the tissue that produces fluid in the eye, 2) increases the out-flow tract so the fluid can drain from the eye better.

Prognosis: Chances of having a functional eye, even with surgery are small. You are trying to maintain the eye in a pain-free state so the animal can function. Many times removal of the eye is the only option. If it happens in one eye, most likely it will happen in the other eye at a later date. The other eye can be treated before it shows signs, but glaucoma will probably result anyway.

Heart Murmur

Symptoms: Signs of heart problems are coughing, fatigue, and fainting spells.

Treatment: If a heart murmur is suspected, an ultrasound of the heart and an X ray would be suggested. If you can only afford one, then choose the ultrasound. Continue to monitor the murmur.

Prognosis: It may disappear or stay the same for years, and the patient may live to a ripe old age, but it needs to be monitored.

Heart Problem

An electrical condition in the heart can best be described in this manner. A puppy can have a massive heart attack, like a "short circuit," though not the same as in people.

The heart beats as it does because there are several areas of the heart that send and receive electrical impulses so that all four chambers in the heart beat in the proper sequence rather than randomly. These electrical impulses are on the microscopic, cellular level, so you do not see any external signs of a problem. In some cases, the electrical system of the heart short-circuits causing the heart to stop beating properly, with the result being death.

Nothing can be done to prevent this, but thankfully, the condition is extremely rare.

Heartworm

Heartworm treatment has changed dramatically over the last two years. Many vets now use Immiticide to treat a dog who has adult heartworm, which is an arsenic that is much safer and more effective than caparsolate, which has been used for years and years.

In a large dog, all that is required are two injections in the lumbar muscles along the spine, given twenty-four hours apart. Not only safer, this treatment is more effective in killing adult heartworms. One month after taking your dog home, give him medication to kill immature heartworms. After that, practice heartworm prevention year round forever and ever.

Today heartworm prevention medication is commonly used throughout the country.

Hemorrhagic Gastric Enteritis

Hemorrhagic Gastric Enteritis is a serious threat to all dogs, but particularly dangerous to the smaller breeds.

Is it Parvo, Corona, Giardia, or Cambylobacter Enteritis? Any kind of bacterial diarrhea can quickly dehydrate an animal, and the smaller dogs are in great peril as they have little weight to lose before they are dehydrated and need intravenous rehydration.

Your dog can be infected by a walk in the park or at a dog show or other congregation of dogs. Between two and ten days from exposure, your dog can come down with this problem, starting with vomiting, lethargy, refusing to eat, and progressing to mucous-covered stool, loose stools, profuse diarrhea, and bloody diarrhea.

Though it is important that your dog is placed on wide spectrum antibiotics, it is also important to first do a culture so that you know exactly what bacteria you are treating.

Many cases of Hemorrhagic Gastric Enteritis are treated with a combination of Amoxicillin and Flagyl. Both these drugs will probably be recommended by your veterinarian at the first sign of bloody diarrhea and vomiting. DO NOT waste time, particularly with the smaller breeds, as they have few reserves from which to deplete fluid through diarrhea, especially bloody diarrhea. I have seen severe bloody diarrhea, *bright red* blood, stopped after administering Amoxicillin, as my vet instructed, along with kaopectolin or another antidiarrheal agent from your vet. In a more severe case, he had me give Flagyl at the same time. Consult your veterinarian for proper dosage by weight.

Hernias

Umbilical hernias are common and are genetic. Inguinal are genetic but rare. To quote *Ettinger Book Of Internal Medicine*, "Improper transection of the umbilical cord at birth may result in failure of the umbilical ring to close naturally. However, it is unlikely that this mechanism is involved in the majority of cases."

Hip Dysplasia

Hip Dysplasia is an abnormality in the development of the hip joint. When dogs exhibit clinical signs of this problem they usually are lame on one or both rear limbs. Severe arthritis can develop as a result of the malformation of the hip joint and this results in pain as the disease progresses. Many young dogs exhibit pain during or shortly after the growth period, often before arthritic changes appear to be present. It is not unusual for this pain to appear to disappear for several years and then to return when arthritic changes become obvious.

Dogs with hip dysplasia appear to be born with normal hips and then to develop the disease later. This is an inherited condition, but not all dogs with the genetic tendency will develop clinical signs and the degree of hip dysplasia which develops does not always seem to correlate well with expectations based on the parent's condition. Multiple genetic factors are involved and environmental factors also play a role in determining the degree of hip dysplasia. Dogs with no genetic predisposition do not develop hip dysplasia.

At present, the strongest link to contributing factors other than genetic predisposition appears to be to rapid growth and weight gain. In a recent study done in Labrador retrievers a significant reduction in the development of clinical hip dysplasia occurred in a group of puppies fed twenty-five percent less than a control group which was allowed to eat free choice. It is likely that the laxity in the hip joints is aggravated by the rapid weight gain.

If feeding practices are altered to reduce hip dysplasia in a litter of puppies, it is probably best to use a puppy food and feed smaller quantities than to switch to an adult dog food. The calcium/phosphorous to calorie ratios in adult dog food are such that the puppy will usually end up with higher than desired total calcium or phosphorous intake by eating an adult food. This occurs because more of these foods are necessary to meet the caloric needs of puppies, even when feeding to keep the puppy thin.

If clinical signs of hip dysplasia occur in young dogs, such as lameness, difficulty standing or walking after getting up, decreased activity or a bunny-hop gait, it is often possible to help them medically or surgically. X-ray confirmation of the presence of hip dysplasia prior to treatment is necessary.

Once a determination is made that hip dysplasia is present, a treatment plan is necessary. For dogs that exhibit clinical signs at less than a year of age, aggressive treatment may help alleviate later suffering. Surgical reconstruction of the hip joint is helpful if done during the growth stages. For puppies with clinical signs at a young age, this surgery should be strongly considered. It has a high success rate when done at the proper time.

Dogs that exhibit clinical signs after the growth phase require a different approach to treatment. It is necessary to determine if the disorder can be managed by medical treatment enough to keep the dog comfortable. If so, aspirin is probably the best choice for initial medical treatment. If medical treatment is insufficient then surgical repair is possible.

Regular exercise can be very helpful and weight loss can have dramatic effects on the amount of discomfort a dog experiences.

Working with your vet to come to the best solution for your dog and your situation will enable you and your dog to enjoy life to its fullest, despite the presence of hip dysplasia.

Hypoglycemia

Hypoglycemia is a low blood sugar condition that affects some toy dogs, particularly the tiny ones, very seriously. This is discussed in detail in Chapter 6, Six Weeks to Twelve Weeks. The Nursing Mothers Formula is a pudding recipe that helps to keep up the strength and blood sugar of "tinies" who are "off" their food and need nourishment along with the glucose formula.

Kidney Incontinence

All breeds can have kidney incontinence. In an older spayed female dog, the problem is a lack of estrogen as estrogen controls the bladder sphincter muscle.

My vet indicated that this can be treated with diethylstilbesterol one mg. The standard treatment is to give a capsule once per day for three to five days then one capsule every seven to fourteen days as needed for control. Some dogs can go off it after awhile; others must remain on it forever. It can cause bone marrow problems if used too frequently. This drug is hard to find, but Dr. Dale Heisler recommends contacting Red Oak Drug at (800) 551-1991 in Red Oak, Texas.

Kidney Infections

When a kidney infection is diagnosed, your vet may suggest Clavamox. If that does not work he may recommend using a low dose of Tribrissen at night long term. According to my vet, that is what women who have interstitial cystitis do. Your vet can collect urine samples directly from the bladder with a syringe. This can be very difficult, though, if the bladder is nearly empty. Otherwise, believe it or not, most animals tolerate it very well.

The vet can also pass a urinary catheter, but there may be some contamination if not very careful. A "catch" sample or even one syringed off the floor is okay for dipstick analysis and urine specific gravity. You can even examine the sediment for crystals, casts, and all types of cells. Therefore, a sample so obtained is still useful. Almost one hundred percent of the time, a vet will do a urine culture by cystocentesis. This fancy word means that the vet will use a small gauge needle (25 gauge) withdraw a urine sample. This is the only way to be sure that you do not get a contaminated sample. During a kidney infection, the only treat I would give is a Nylabone. Any treat of any sort could affect the special diet you are using. You must stick exclusively to the diet your vet recommends. With an acidic urine, crystals will be less likely to form or will dissolve if they do. CD is used for both dogs and cats to prevent crystal formation, since it produces an acidic urine. It contains chicken, rice, corn, and liver.

Kidney Stones

Obstruction can occur in the ureter leading directly from the kidney due to a stone forming in the kidney and then blocking the urethra when passed. A large number of stones can block outflow of urine from the bladder. Stones can travel through the urethra after leaving the bladder. Problems are more prevalent in males than in females due to smaller diameter and longer urethra.

A common spot for blockage is at the end of the penis. Microscopic crystals form small stones, which can be passed, but if the small stones get together and form a larger stone, it cannot be passed.

Symptoms:
: Straining to urinate with little urine flow, blood in the urine, urinary leakage, inappropriate urination, not eating, vomiting, and depression

Stone types:
: Struvite, calcium oxalate, urate, cystine, calcium phosphate, silica. Struvite is most common, generally, except in Dalmations where most are urate. With struvite, Hill's SD diet may be helpful in dissolving them.

  Calcium Oxalate: Remove surgically

  Urate: Feed Hill's UD and allopurinol to dissolve or surgically remove.

  Cystine: Feed UD and 2-MPG or surgical removal

  Calcium phosphate: Surgical removal

  Silica: Surgical removal

Prevention:
: All stones need dietary management, medication, and increased water intake. Many dogs are prone to new stone formation, despite medical and dietary management. You will want to have the stone analyzed. Sometimes there is one type of stone in the center and a different type on the outside. It is best to use a lab that does a lot of stone classification. Stones that are present with a liver shunt are usually urate stones. Diets can control further stone formation, but you must have the stone analyzed to determine the type, since different stones are treated with different diets.

Dalmatian breeders have had experience with kidney function problems; however, the stone problems experienced by Dalmatians are a different stone than those with which most other dog owners are dealing. Most are concerned with acidifying the urine, to prevent *struvite* stones. Dalmation owners are concerned with *urate* stones, which arise from the fact that Dalmatians have *high acid* urine. Dalmatians' stone problems would be more analogous to those experienced by *humans* than those experienced by other dogs. So the solution you might recommend for any other breed of dog with stones would probably be *disastrous* for a Dalmatian.

Leather Ear—Black Ear

Leather ear, slick ear, English ear, or black ear affects some toy dogs, namely Yorkies, rather seriously. It can be responsible for hair loss on the ears, hocks, and the end of the tail and leaves a slimy black substance in those places. Some people think it is a fungus; some think it is a "rabbit mite." Frankly, having spent hundreds of dollars to cure it, I can't tell you what it is, but I can tell you how to keep dogs from getting it or how to get rid of it once they've "got it."

At the first sign of black around the edges of the ear, wipe the ear with "dog-o-dontic pads" dipped in alcohol. Bathe in Betadine or Plexadine shampoo, paying particular attention to the ears, end of tail, and hocks. Use Nolvasan Otic Solution regularly in the ears. Cover the ears, hocks, and end of tail with a thin coating of Lotrimin 1%—no other kind of Lotrimin—every day until the problem is solved! You will notice the ear begin to get very dry. Stop using the Lotrimin if the ears get too dry.

Joan Gordon of Wildweir Kennels tells me she has had success in curing leather ear by using Noxema on the ears. Best Ear Relief Wash has been suggested by some vets. Other breeders suggest using RID, a human product. The "drying" properties of most of these products are what helps.

Another product I recently have used for this problem is #1 All Systems Tea Tree Oil, and I'm happy to say that it works! It is also really good to spray on "wrappers" for those long-haired dogs that like to remove the wrappers, as it is not too tasty.

Softer-coated dogs never seem to have a problem with leather ear but the silky coated dog with a lower skin temperature seems to have a problem when colder weather and high humidity prevail. Keep the dogs warm and wash them at least once a week using Betadine or Iodine shampoo in those areas that are susceptible.

You will be in control if you follow these instructions. It is also a good idea to have your veterinarian do a thyroid function test on dogs with these symptoms, because some dogs with this problem also have a low thyroid function and medication may help the situation.

Legg Perthes

Legg Perthes is a disease of the bone, namely the head of the femur, which starts to disintegrate and can cause the dog to become lame. The first sign that you may notice is that the dog will not put full weight on the affected rear leg. As he refuses to use this leg, the muscles can start to atrophy, and you can begin to feel a big difference in the size of the thigh muscles on the rear legs. When your veterinarian X-rays the hip area, he or she can usually point out the loss of bone on the head of the femur. You will plainly see the deterioration. Your veterinarian can surgically correct the problem by removing the head of the femur. The dogs recuperate very well from this surgery, and after a very brief convalescent period, the hair grows back and the dogs compensate for the difference in the length of the leg. You would never know that most of them had an operation.

Obviously, such an animal *should not be shown or bred*, however, it is easy for judges to discover this surgery. All they have to do is put their thumbs on the hocks of these corrected dogs and gently extend their legs, it is obvious that one leg is shorter than the other by about one-half inch.

My veterinarian believes this to be an inherited disease, as it is inherited in people. There are cases where traumatic injury is suspected, but the weakness or disease in a nonprogressive state was probably always there. You don't have to be a board certified radiologist to see it on the X ray. Usually both hips are not affected at the same time, so you can compare the normal and the abnormal.

Liver Shunt

During gestation, the placenta delivers blood with food and oxygen from the dam through the umbilical vein. This means that in the fetus, circulation is the reverse of circulation after birth, because the fetus veins have the oxygenated blood and arteries return unoxygenated blood to the heart. In order to make this work there is a shunt from the liver's venous circulation to the arterial circulation. At birth the pressure of the circulatory system changes as respiration occurs. This shuts the shunt which eventually disappears.

If this reverse in circulation doesn't happen for some reason, the liver is deprived of a blood supply and doesn't develop properly after birth. Many puppies can live with the small functioning part of the liver for some time, but eventually have problems and usually die if the problem is not corrected. It is possible to surgically close the shunt and sometimes this works well.

If you suspect a shunt problem check with your vet. The diagnosis of a suspected problem with the vein carrying blood from the digestive organs to the liver is often done in three stages. The first is checking blood and urine samples. If these are suggestive of a shunt problem the second stage tests, consisting of pre and post bile acid tests and an ammonia challenge test are performed. My veterinarian explained to me that these two tests help determine the functional capacity of the liver. The third stage consists of an ultrasound or nuclear scan to try to locate and determine the extent of the shunt.

Treatment and prognosis of shunts depends upon their location and severity. A single congenital single shunt outside of the liver that is caught early is a good candidate for surgery according to Dr. Brinson. Shunt problems inside the liver must be treated medically

The medical treatment is aimed at reducing the amount of ammonia circulating in the body and decreasing symptoms. A low protein diet and lactulose to reduce absorption of ammonia are usually prescribed. If left untreated the symptoms will get progressively worse and eventually the pet will die.

The symptoms can start to appear at almost any age. Such afflicted dogs are usually very thin and who pick at their food. They not only have a poor appetite but they can become lethargic, dizzy and stagger. They may try to climb out of their pen. They may also throw their heads back after eating and may walk along walls and seizure.

This is not a new disease but one which came attention of Yorkshire Terrier, Maltese, and Cairn Terrier breeders and others in the 80's and 90's. Many breeders feel it is an inherited problem and that the only way to eliminate it is to remove the affected dogs and carriers from the breeding pool

The University of California at Davis Veterinary School is currently collecting swabs of normal dogs and their pedigrees to establish the normal DNA of healthy dogs. The AKC Canine Research Foundation is making great strides in genetic studies in many breeds for inherited disease. The work is being greatly facilitated by the national Canine Genome project. You can get up-to-date information at the following site :

www.vhl.ucdavis.edu/research/canine/

There is a list of veterinarians that have successfully performed surgery on liver shunt cases and you can find information about it at the following sites:

www.shooterdog.com/alexfaq3.htm#LS
www.design.klever.net/~mrbroome/shunt.html

In the meantime eliminating these dogs and their siblings from your breeding program puts you ahead of the game.

Loss of Appetite

Dogs have difficulty if they go without eating for more than twenty-four hours. Dogs can starve themselves, become hypoglycemic, and lose so much weight they could die. You must find out why they are not eating and feed with a syringe if necessary, but do not ignore this sign that something is wrong! My dogs will eat almost anything unless they are sick, as long as I mix a liverwurst gravy with their food.

Luxating Patellas

Many dogs live their whole lives with luxating patellas and are never lame. A "luxating patella" would be best described as a "trick knee," which can move out of place if injured by jumping, walking in a hole, or running on slippery floors. Toy dogs are prone to this kind of injury because of their diminutive size. No matter how firm the knees seem as puppies, toy dogs are liable to injure their knees, depending on the degree of luxation. The groove in the knee where the knee fits is sometimes shallow, and the knees can be very wobbly. Most breeders try to breed away from this. The taller, more fine-boned dogs seem to be more prone to this injury.

Sometimes, if the knee pops out and stretches the ligaments that hold it in place, it becomes a chronic problem, and the dog becomes lame. In this case, the first treatment would be to keep the dog crated for a week or two and supervise the activity—no jumping from furniture or up and down behind a gate on a slippery floor. In conjunction with restricted movement, the dog should be given prednisolone to reduce the inflammation. My vet suggests one-half of a 5 mg tablet two times a day for three days, one-half of a 5 mg tablet one time per day for three days and then one-half of a 5 mg tablet every other day four times during the crated convalescent time. Check with your vet for the dosage and this prescription medication. Usually this period of rest will be all that is necessary to correct the situation.

Depending on the degree of luxation, and how shallow the groove, it can be a problem for the dog. In these cases, the vet may suggest surgery.

Surgery is very seldom the answer and should only be done by an orthopedic surgeon if the dog is lame. My vet believes that if surgery is done for a luxating patella on a dog that is not lame, that dog will have problems with arthritis from the surgery five years later.

Some show dogs have finished their title with a luxating patella, but using these dogs in your breeding program should depend on the degree of luxation. I would certainly think twice about breeding a dog with a luxating patella, and consult with your veterinarian about its severity.

Lymphangiectasia

Lymphangiectasia and Inflammatory Bowel Disease are two different conditions. The only real treatment for lymphangiectasia is to control the diet by using low levels of medium chained fats and higher levels of high quality protein. Lymphangiectasia is a disease of the intestinal lymph vessels that is associated with malabsorption.

Symptoms: Edema, putting on weight

Treatment: Prednisone, dietary

Prognosis: Long-term prognosis is poor.

Lymphosarcoma

Lymphosarcoma is very rare. As far as my vets know, there is no genetic link. Two genetic diseases are: Lymphedema, a developmental problem in the lymph system allowing tissue edema, and lymph node hypoplasia, a condition in which there is decreased lymphoid tissue in the lymph nodes. Both are very rare.

Mammary Cancer

You can greatly decrease the odds that your beloved pet will develop mammary tumors by spaying before the first heat. I would say that about ninety-five percent of veterinarians would prefer to spay prior to the first heat, as a precaution to prevent mammary cancer.

In the dog, mammary tumors are most common in intact females but, on rare occasions, may be seen in the male. Ovariectomy (spaying) before the first estrus (heat) period reduces the risk of mammary neoplasia (tumors) to less than one percent of the risk in intact females. If the dog is spayed after the first estrus, the risk is approximately eight percent of the intact female. Dogs spayed after the second heat have about the same risk of developing mammary tumors as intact females. In dogs, the mammary glands closest to the tail (posterior) are the most common sites of mammary tumors. The good news for dogs is that only about fifty percent of mammary tumors are malignant. Therefore, by having your young female cat or dog spayed, you can dramatically reduce the chances of her developing mammary tumors, in addition to reducing the population of unwanted kittens and puppies, many of which may end up in animal shelters, where they may be euthanized.

Treatment of already developed mammary tumors is generally surgical removal of the affected area. As in humans, the amount of tissue removed, either a simple removal of the isolated tumor or removal of the mammary gland and its associated lymphatic drainage, depends upon how much the tumors have spread. For older pets, the risk of anesthesia and surgery may outweigh the risk of the tumors themselves. This decision should be discussed with your pet's veterinarian after a through examination, which may include radiographs to determine if the tumors have spread to the lungs.

Here is some data to explain why it is better to spay your pet female or male.

■ If spayed prior to the first heat, there is a 1 in 100 chance that the dog will develop mammary tumors in its life.

■ If done after the first heat there is a 1 out 12 chance that the dog will develop mammary tumors.

■ If done after the second heat there is a 1 in 4 chance that the dog will develop tumors.

■ If spayed after 2-1/2 years of age, there is no protective effect of the surgery on developing tumors. Basically, you hope tumors do not occur, but according to my vet there is a fairly good chance of that happening.

Mange and Mites

Sarcoptic mange is contagious to other dogs and people. Scabies is caused by the sarcoptic mange mite, and demodex is caused by the demodectic mange mite.

Treatment consists of weekly dipping with Paramite dip for four to six weeks, or use a new product called Revolution that you apply to the skin once per month for two months.

Cheyletiella rasguri is the common species of mite affecting dogs, while *Cheyletiella prasitovorax* is the species found on rabbits. Both species of mites can interchangeably transfer to man, dogs, cats, and rabbits. It is not yet clear how long the mites survive on another host.

Simple scurfy dandruff with pruritus in young puppies is highly suggestive of *Cheyletiella* dermatitis. Skin scrapings and routine examinations are prudent if mites are suspected.

Sarcaptic mange is easier to treat than demodex mange. You must treat the environment, too. Use a Paramite dip once a week for four weeks, or you can use Ivermectin.

Demodex mange is not contagious to people or other dogs. That's the good news. The bad news is that the disease can be controlled but never cured. These dogs will have mites for the rest of their lives. You could have a single episode with the mites or there may be persistent flare ups. Though there are several ways to treat this problem, it can be frustrating and expensive. Antibiotics, shampoos, and dips are helpful. If the disease is not too far gone, try treating for awhile. Just remember it may be a life-long problem. The infested dogs should be neutered or spayed and never bred.

Sometimes a liver disease can be an underlying cause in many cases of demodex that occur in adult dogs that do not have a history of chronic infection. You also have to rule out other systemic illnesses. Complete blood cell counts and general serum chemistry testing is a good idea. Sometimes ear infections accompany demodecosis.

Treatment: Maricarmen-Mitoban is the only currently approved medication for demodectic mange. It is not unusual for dogs to look worse after dipping with Mitoban. It kills the mites, they die in the hair follicles, and there is often additional hair loss. Antibiotic therapy for secondary infections is very important in the success of therapy for demodecosis.

The heritability of demodecosis is established in some breeds. Many puppies develop localized demodecosis lesions (confined to the head or a couple of areas on the body) and eventually outgrow it as their immune system strengthens. When a puppy does not outgrow the mange or when it spreads to several sites on the body, it is most likely to be generalized demodex and more likely to be an inherited condition.

The breeds with a known tendency to develop demodecosis include the Shar-pei, West Highland White Terrier, Scottish terrier, English bulldog, Boston terrier, Great Dane, Weimaraner, Airedale, Malamute, and Afghan.

Cushing's disease seems to predispose dogs to demodecosis, as does liver disease.

If the dog is treated and the condition is resolved, it is probably not inherited.

Metritis

Pyometritis in the bitch can occur spontaneously; secondary to an infectious disease process; as a post-partum (after whelping) metritis, or a mismating injection of estrogen, especially estradiol; as a post breeding or artificial insemination infection. This disease most commonly occurs in bitches, starting at three to four years of age. The incidence increases with age and is increased in bitches with several nonpregnant cycles (false pregnancies resulting). Virtually every intact bitch can develop cystic endometrial pyometritis complex. Therefore, if they are not intended for breeding, they should be spayed prior to three years of age. Some veterinarians feel that it is best to spay them before the onset of the first heat (anytime from six months to one year) and that this will also decrease the chance of mammary cancer later in life.

The ideal breeding age of the bitch is prior to three years of age. Acute endometritis and metritis in the bitch are usually diseases of the postpartum period following retained placentas or fetuses, obstetric manipulations, dystocia (difficult delivery), or abortions. They may occasionally follow mating or artificial insemination if sanitary procedures are not followed. The postpartum uterus is frequently enlarged and flaccid. The bitch is usually depressed and has an odorous vaginal discharge, which may be brown and thick. Frequently, a bitch with a vaginal infection will ignore her newborns.

Estrogen therapy, especially estradiol cypionate, is used in the bitch for mismating within five days of breeding. Following this treatment, some animals have developed pyometritis. A mismating injection is not recommended by this breeder, as the consequences are more serious than putting down or finding homes for unwanted puppies.

The "classic" signs of pyometra are increased water intake and urination, depression, and lethargy. Fever may be present, especially in advanced cases. Sometimes a vaginal discharge is present, sometimes not. Anytime a bitch is "off" after being in season, watch for these signs. The time varies, but observe roughly at two to three weeks. Usually it affects older bitches but can occur in younger ones. It can be very sneaky; the animal may become critical before the owner recognizes it is ill. Once diagnosed, it must be treated at *once*. Spaying is the best option. Waiting to treat with antibiotics can result in a ruptured uterus and a fatality. An old adage in veterinary medicine is "don't let the sun set on a case of pyometria." Once you decide you will no longer be breeding your bitch, have her spayed as soon as possible. If you have concerns about spaying, discuss them with your vet, and make a decision. I think it's better to spay a young healthy dog than do surgery on a critically ill older dog.

Cheque drops, which are used to stop estrus, are suspected of causing pyometria. They are not recommended by any of the five vets with whom I have consulted.

Ovulation

Cheque drops have been around for a very long time. If heat cycles are already irregular, Cheque drops may not be called for. The is Cheque (Rx); the generic name is mibolerone. It is not recommended for use in a bitch intended for future breeding, as it may cause problems with future fertility.

Vaginal infections, increased body odor, abnormal behavior, urinary incontinence, riding behavior, oily skin and liver damage may also occur. The medication must be started at least thirty days prior to the time the next estrus would occur in order to be effective. If there is any chance the bitch is pregnant, this medication must not be used as it can cause birth defects.

An alternative medication with fewer side effects, although not entirely free of problems, is megestrol acetate (Ovaban Rx). This pill can be given at the start of the estrus to delay it awhile or given in anticipation of estrus over a longer period of time.

Pancreatitis

To determine whether the patient has pancreatitis, or a liver shunt, it is necessary to have your vet do a chemscreen to check amylase and lipase enzymes. Do pre- and post-bile acids for shunt. Pancreatitis, which is an inflammation of the pancreas, is often fatal in dogs, and it must be aggressively treated. Once the disease has advanced too far, nothing can be done. However, many dogs have been successfully treated for it. Too much fat in the diet is one of the main causes of this disease. Recognizing the dog's illness and presenting it for prompt treatment is important. Symptoms include severe abdominal pain, loss of appetite, bloating, lethargy, vomiting and diarrhea. Intravenous fluids to avoid dehydration are a must as a dog can have *nothing* by mouth until the crisis is past.

Often fresh frozen plasma and artificial blood volume expanders like Hetastarch are used. Research has shown that even the scent of food can trigger pancreatic enzymes. My vet keeps pancreatitis dogs out of the area where other pets are being fed. Strict compliance with your vet's diet orders is important to prevent reoccurrence.

Pano

Symptoms: Pano can strike any breed although it is mostly found in the larger breeds of dogs. It is commonly found in Rottweilers. Pano is a pain that can move from joint to joint. Your pet may be lame in the front one day and then experience pain in a rear leg. Pano usually appears in younger dogs. In Rotties, it tends to appear anywhere between four and eight months. It can last up to a year. Although the dog appears to be lame, your vet won't be able to see anything on X rays or by physical exam. Pano can move from leg to leg and makes your dogs limp or lame.

Treatment: Lots of forced crate rest and waiting it out. The vet may put the dog on Rimadyl and vitamin C therapy. Too much vitamin C will give dogs loose stool. Usually by six months of age, they take about 4,000 units a day, and it seems to decrease Pano substantially. Some breeders feel that this daily dosage of Vitamin C helps the problem. Restricted activity is the best solution. There is no real cure; the dogs just outgrow it. It is like growing pains in young children. As their joints are growing sometimes pain is involved.

Prognosis: In time it will pass, but it can take two to eight months depending on the individual dog.

Parasites

Taking a stool specimen to your veterinarian once a year, or whenever you see something unusual, is a good idea. If you see what looks like dried rice at the rectum of your dog, and/or what looks like "rice moving about in the stool," your dog probably has tapeworm, which comes from swallowing fleas. Your veterinarian can give one injection, or the right tablet dosage, of Droncit.

If you see what looks like spaghetti noodles in the stool, that is probably round worms, which can be treated with Nemex. Other common parasites are not seen in the stool but are manifested by blood and mucous in the stool. Don't just buy an all-around wormer from the supermarket or pet shop. These can be *deadly* or *harmful* to your dog.

Preventive worming for dogs who are exposed regularly to congregations of dogs is in order.

- Puppies three to six weeks— Your vet may prescribe Nemex II with Repeat in three weeks and Alternate with Albon three to five days.

- Adults— Same as above, once a year. Panacur is also a good all-around wormer, which is used for three days and covers just about any parasite. Liquid Panacur is available from your veterinarian and the dosage I use is one cc per five pounds. Panacur is also available in granules from your vet.

For parasite control in your yard, lime sweetens the soil, helps eliminate urine odor, and helps kill parasites that may be lurking in the soil—worm eggs and coccidia. I have never heard that it bothers the dogs' feet.

Caution is indicated in the use of lime, because if it gets in the eyes it can cause serious problems. Make sure that you keep the dogs off a lime-treated yard for a few days. Lime is good to control worm eggs, just be sure that it is watered down well after putting it down, and don't let dogs on it until it is dry. My vet described very nasty corneal ulcers, which took weeks to heal, from when dogs were let back on a "limed" yard.

Parvo

If your dog has been confirmed with Parvo virus, follow these rules. As the virus is not airborne, and is acquired from direct dog-to-dog contact or from people handling a parvo dog and then infecting another dog by handling it, always feed and handle the healthy puppies before the sick ones. Clean. Clean. Clean. The virus will still be shed in the stool for awhile, so you have to keep the dogs as far apart as possible. Wash everything with bleach, and plan on this kind of quarantine for at least a month.

Pneumonia

Pneumonia is a secondary infection of the lungs that sometimes occurs afer a viral upper-respiratory infection, or due to bacteria. It takes advantage of a dog's weakened resistance. The lungs start filling with fluid and may cause the heart to beat overtime since oxygen is not correctly getting in the blood. Other contributing factors can include stress, aspiration, shipping/showing, causing exposure to powerful bacteria that can cause pneumonia in otherwise healthy, unstressed dogs.

Symptoms: Fever, lack of appetite, cough, discharge of pus from nostrils, depression, and rapid or labored breathing. The cough may be harsh and shallow, or deep and moist. It may be self-perpetuating, in that one cough seems to bring on another one.

Treatment: Support and administration of appropriate antibiotics.

Poisons

National Animal Poison Control Center at (800) 548-2423 or (900) 680-0000.

Symptoms: All non-specific including vomiting, diarrhea, weight loss, seizures, not eating, bleeding for no reason, heart rate abnormalities, kidney failure, liver failure, and death.

Treatment: To induce vomiting, food grade hydrogen peroxide can be used—one teaspoon (five ml) for a toy dog, if you suspect poison was swallowed. Consult your veterinarian immediately.

Poisonous plants:

More than seven hundred species of plants are known to possess poisonous principles that can threaten man and animal alike. It is impossible to list them all, so we will touch upon commonly found plants that can produce serious or fatal results when taken in small doses.

- In hyacinths and daffodils, the danger lies in the bulbs, which can cause intense digestive upset. Even a small amount of narcissus can produce poisoning in man. The climbing or glory lily has caused digestive upset accompanied by symptoms of nervous excitement.

- Oleander and poinsettia are extremely dangerous. A single leaf of either can be lethal to children. Oleander contains a poisonous principle similar to digitalis in its effect on the heart, and it also produces severe digestive upset. Poinsettia contains an acrid, burning juice that could severely injure sensitive digestive system tissue.

- Dumbcane and philodendron, as well as other members of the arum family, contain small, needle-like crystals that become embedded, through biting into the plant, in the tissues of the tongue and mouth. This causes intense burning and irritation. Although most cases prove uncomfortable, but not dangerous, death can occur if there is severe enough swelling at the base of the tongue to block air passages of the throat.

- Rosary pea or precatory bean seeds and castor bean seeds, sometimes found in the home, are extremely dangerous. One precatory bean seed has caused death, and one or two castor bean seeds can be a lethal dose for an adult. These seeds are very attractive and are used frequently in tropical countries in jewelry and other ornaments. They are a favorite souvenir item, brought home from trips by tourists, and care should be taken that they are not left around where children or animals could chew them.

- Mistletoe, commonly found in homes during the Christmas holidays, is believed to be quite poisonous, as the berries contain an active toxic principle.

The above are commonly found in homes. The world of outside poisons is another whole episode.

Other poisons:

Snail bait caused a close call for one of my toy dog friends, and *chocolate* can and has caused death when eaten by dogs. An ingredient in chocolate called theobromine affects dogs' hearts and can cause cardiac arrhythmias, hyperactivity, tremors, seizures, comas, and even death if eaten in quantity. Veterinarians may induce vomiting or give a substance called "activated charcoal," which helps absorb the toxic chemical. A fatal dose for a small dog, such as a Chihuahua, would be just a half-ounce to an ounce of baking chocolate or four to ten ounces of milk chocolate. For a larger dog, such as a Labrador retriever, a fatal dose would be four to eight ounces of baking chocolate or two to four pounds of milk chocolate.

Don't leave Cordohyde leads lying around for pups to chew on as this can cause inflammation of the mouth and severe salivation!

Progressive Retinal Atrophy

The Canine Eye Registry Foundation (CERF) is an organization devoted to tracking and hopefully eliminating inherited eye disorders in purebred dogs. Any ocular disease that is heritable is of interest to them, not just progressive retinal atrophy (PRA). The importance of CERF testing probably varies a little from breed to breed, but almost all breeds have an eye problem to which they are prone. Miniature schnauzers are susceptible to congenital cataracts that are believed to be passed genetically through an autosomal recessive mode of inheritance.

If you would like more information about CERF and its registry, you can contact them by writing: Canine Eye Registration Foundation (CERF), 1235 SCC-A, Purdue University, West Lafayette, IN 47907-1235.

It is true that the ophthalmologist may examine a dog that does not have a visible condition at the time of exam. Remember that cataracts tend to show up during middle age after many dogs have been bred several times. Despite this, an attempt to help limit the occurrence of heritable diseases seems worthwhile.

One of the first symptoms of PRA is the loss of night vision. This can appear as early as eight months of age but often does not show up until the dog is three to five years old. Owners often notice their dog is reluctant to go outside at night. In a dim room, they may not want to jump on or off furniture and may not go up or down stairs. As the disease progresses, the pupils become increasingly dilated, causing a noticeable "shine" to their eyes, and the lens may become cloudy.

Dogs do not feel any pain or discomfort with the disease, however there is no cure or treatment, so owners must learn to live with their dog's condition. As vision deteriorates, affected dogs adjust as long as their environment remains constant.

Since PRA is a progressively degenerative disease, it is highly recommended that dogs have their eyes examined on an annual basis, starting at approximately six months of age and continuing until eight years of age. This is especially true of dogs that are being used for breeding purposes, however, to benefit the genetic health of the breed, test all litter mates and offspring as well.

Puppy Strangles

The medical term for this disease is Bacterial Lymphadenitis It is a cellulitis of the head and neck and swelling of the cervical lymph nodes that occurs in four-to-twelve-week-old puppies. It may be heritable in the sense that several dogs in the litter can be affected. It is an autoimmune not a bacterial problem. The vet will probably use antibiotics in addition to cortisone to cover all bases. It won't reoccur, and a full recovery is likely. There will probably be no major skin or coat defects.

Reverse Sneezing

Symptoms: Snorting noise when excited or exercising. The problem occurs more in dogs with long, soft palettes. It could be compared to a person clearing their throat. Sometimes the dogs will cough up a small amount of white mucous.

Treatment: Calm the dog down and within a few minutes everything is back to normal. Not life-threatening or serious, it does sound bad if you don't know what it is.

Ringworm

Ringworm is a fungal infection of the skin that shows up as circular or irregular areas of hair loss on the face, body, and/or legs. The skin in affected areas is usually dry and scaly. This disease can be transmitted from animal to animal, from soil to animal, and from animal to man. Definitive diagnosis is best achieved through culture and identification of the fungal agent. Your veterinarian should pass a "Woods light" over your dog, and it should confirm the diagnosis immediately. Many chronic diseases that do not readily respond to treatment are mistakenly diagnosed as fungal infections. These mistakes can be avoided by the use of fungal cultures. Fungal skin disease is not common in the older animal.

Therapy is specific and will result in complete remission of the disease. Topical and systemic drugs are used. Griseofulvicin is a specific oral drug that will resolve this disease problem, but use of this drug is contraindicated in breeding animals. Allow your veterinarian to make this decision.

Betadine Surgical Scrub baths can't hurt and have been known to be very helpful in control of skin fungus conditions.

Seizures

Many dogs of all ages start having seizures for no reason. They can have seizures if there are heart problems that lead to poor oxygenation of the blood; the seizure occurs due to lack of oxygen to the brain.

A seizure is a short-circuit in the electrical activity in the brain, most times due to overstimulation. Convulsive seizures appear to be inherited as a recessive gene in certain breeds of dogs. Even though the EKG at the hospital looks all right, there could have been abnormal rates or rhythms during the seizure.

Most of the time you can't get a seizure during the EKG. Starting some heart medication may help with the seizure problem. While rare, you can't rule out a brain tumor. There are many causes of seizures, not only low blood sugar. Depending on the age and size of the dog, a blood sample could be taken to check for the various causes. You may want to try and run a few basic tests with a few drops of blood. As with diabetic humans, a blood sugar can be run on one drop of blood that will rule in or out low blood sugar as a cause for seizures. Diagnosis could be a liver shunt, epilepsy, kidney disease, other liver disease, or heart abnormality. You have to do the best you can considering age and size. You need to get a physical exam and some blood work done to find out the cause for the seizures. One cause for seizures in an older dog is early heart failure. After exercise, the heart can't meet the oxygen demands of the body, and the dog passes out for a short period of time. When oxygen levels increase, then the animal returns to normal. You can also get seizures due to abnormal liver function, diabetes, or low blood sugar just to name a few. That is why the blood work and physical are necessary. Inherited epilepsy usually shows up between one and three years of age, but it can occur earlier or later. Since there are many causes of seizure activity, it is hard to be sure of the problem. We generally assume it is present when lab work checks out "normal" and we can't find an apparent cause in the history or clinical exam. That is the closest we can come to a diagnosis of congenital epilepsy.

Skin Problems

Symptoms:	Bumps in the groin area that look like pimples, red and raised with a white head that pops if you scratch it; scratching and itching
Treatment:	Bald spots, crusty lesions, and blisters could be caused by bacterial infections. Protecting the eyes and nose, try bathing the dog with Betadine Scrub or Plexadine Shampoo every third day twice and then again in a week, leaving the shampoo sitting on the skin for at least one full minute each time. If this doesn't clear up the problem,

then veterinary aid should be sought. Bald round spots could also indicate ringworm, and Plexadine Shampoo is also the best thing to do for common ringworm. If the situation continues, see a veterinarian, as this kind of thing can be very contagious.

Your veterinarian will probably advise the following: Cefadroxil, 100 mg tablets, for a five- to six-pound dog give half in the morning and half at night. After one month's treatment, it may be gone and then come back. Sometimes repeating the treatment a second time is necessary.

Diagnosis: Staph bacteria infection on the skin. It could progress to a Staph hypersensitivity.

Secondary treatment:

1. Another thirty days of antibiotics (Keflex, Clavamox, Tribrissen, almost any one will do)

2. Weekly medicated shampoos (NuSal T, Pyoben, Chlorhexadine)

3. If there is dry skin, use a fatty acid supplement by mouth (DermCaps, EFA)

4. If scratching a lot, Prednisone is indicated in low doses every second or third day.

5. If skin is dry, use a spray-on conditioner (Focus 21 Skin & Hair Sea Plazma) or Nova Pearls by Tomlyn. Dry skin can be caused by over bathing and by winter months' heat with lack of humidity, which can cause scratching.

6. If problem continues, consider Staph Phage Lysate, which is used with bacterial hypersensitivity. It is staph bacteria that is rendered non-pathogenic and then it is injected on a regular basis (just like allergy shots). Your dog will develop antibodies against this staph bacteria and hopefully cure the staph skin infection.

There are a number of breeds that are prone to skin problems. Thin, flat scabs are certainly associated with an infection. Allergies, parasites (fleas, mites, etc.), fungal diseases, and underlying hormonal disease (hypothyroidism) are varying problems that can manifest themselves clinically with skin disorders. Take your dog to your regular veterinarian and have your vet perform a skin scraping, fungal culture, and possible blood test for thyroid level and treat accordingly. He/she most likely will prescribe antibiotics, medicated shampoos, and possible hormonal replacement therapy if warranted.

There are times that a bacterial infection has an underlying cause, such as allergies, immune mediated disease, systemic illness or skin parasites. Checking for these conditions may be necessary if the problem continues. There are veterinary dermatologists, and it can be worth the drive to one for difficult skin problems. They see the resistant and atypical cases of skin disease and often pick up patterns of disease not apparent to a general practitioner, or they do specialized testing not available at all veterinary offices.

Sporadic Wheezing

Symptoms:	Congestion, constant clearing of throat, wheezing sound
Diagnosis:	It could be an upper respiratory infection or bacterial and/or viral infection and is usually accompanied by coughing and/or sneezing. Generally lasts only about a week to ten days. The body is exposed to a staggering amount of potential disease-causing organisms (pathogens) almost every moment, however, most otherwise healthy animals, including humans, do not become infected by these pathogens. Many of these pathogens are airborne and may be present in the next breath you or your pet inhale. The complex system of airways, which warm and moisten every breath, trap many of these potential disease organisms. Small hairs, called cilia, present in the nasal mucosa, which lines the respiratory passages, also help to trap these small airborne particles and keep them from reaching the lungs.

If, despite all these protective measures, pathogens reach the lungs and cause pneumonia, there is a decrease in available oxygen transport via the lungs and a decrease in the amount of air able to reach the lungs. Sometimes it leads to fluid in the lungs. In the lungs and smaller respiratory passages, this "fluid" may be due to the body's response to infectious organisms or, more rarely, inhaled chemicals. Naturally, the presence of edema makes obtaining sufficient oxygen more difficult, and a wheezing sound may be heard as air attempts to pass by such swelling.

Treatment: A sound of trying to clear the throat "could be" swollen tonsils, ingested fibers and hair, and even a genetic narrowing of the respiratory passages, but only a through physical exam can pinpoint the exact cause(s) for sporadic wheezing. Have the vet check this out at the next routine visit, unless the wheezing is constant and accompanied by a copious nasal discharge, and then you should see your vet as soon as possible for treatment.

Sparse Coat

A sparse coat may be the result of a thyroid problem. Have your veterinarian do a thyroid function test on your dog. If you find him to be abnormal (*anything under 2.0 should be treated as "low thyroid" condition*), a simple thyroid function tablet each day will do wonders for his coat and health. Sperm production and ovulation can be affected adversely if your dog has a thyroid function problem.

Stool Eating

There appears to be some connection between stressful and unsanitary rearing practices and the incidence of coprophagia.

There are several theories as to why dogs eat feces ranging from:

- It is instinctive, mother eats her puppies' feces.

- Protection in the wild—removing their scent so predators cannot locate them

- Nutritional deficiency

- Boredom

- It just tastes good to them!

As disgusting as it is to us humans, it really is more common than we imagine. Remedies range from adding B vitamins to the diet, using Accent sprinkled on the dog's food, and using products such as "Forbid," which are available in pet supply catalogs and stores. What works for one dog may or may not work for another.

In short, the only sure-fire way to prevent this is by picking up after your dog as quickly as possible and disposing of the "tasty tidbit."

Simple aversion therapy can be done by letting the dog approach the stool on a long lead. If he starts sniffing it, give a strong leash check. If he passes by, praise him.

Adding an alfalfa tablet, or Deter, is a safe, good-tasting and effective method designed and tested to eliminate coprophagia (eating of feces) in dogs. Call (888) USA-PETS (872-7387) or visit www.petmedexpress.com.

Strokes or Seizures

Symptoms: Difficulty standing, stumbling, falling, bumping into things, uncontrolled urination, generally agitated, but calmed down. Gums were pink, and vision seemed okay, but not interested in food and seem disoriented, rests comfortably after episodes, but sometimes there is a slight tilt to the head.

Diagnosis: Dogs do not have strokes per se. They can have some vascular problems, but these are rare. One of several things may be going on:

1. Old age vestibular disease: For some reason dogs develop a problem in their middle and inner ear that causes them to become disoriented, stagger, and almost always tilt the head. Watch the eyes closely, and see if you see any constant motion back and forth of the eyes. If you see it, this is what it is.

2. Early seizure activity: Seizures are basically abnormal electrical brain activity that can lead to abnormal behavior and gait problems.

3. Bacterial or viral infection in the brain: Rare but does occur. Physical exam and blood work necessary. Not a good prognosis.

4. Internal medicine problem: Kidney failure, liver failure, diabetes, Addison's disease. Need blood work.

Treatment: Try and get some fluids into the dog to help avoid dehydration. You can give an aspirin one tablet per 60 pounds, twice daily. You should get an appointment as soon as possible for a physical and hopefully some blood work.

Swallowing Foreign Objects

Be sure to check merchandise that you've bought, hand made or otherwise, for pins and needles, because they can do a lot of expensive and painful damage to the intestines of your dog. Also be very careful about staples that you remove from things that you bring into the house. Don't let them fall on the floor. They, too, can cause serious problems in the intestines. Be sure to dispose of them safely and properly.

Most squeaky toys are non-toxic, but young puppies with their little needle teeth could get the squeakie out and swallow it. They may throw it up, but it could become an obstruction in the intestines. Supervise their playtime with toys, and remove anything that looks loose.

Stress Management

Stress can affect the tinies more than the larger breeds. It would behoove you to protect them from stressful situations. For example, crate them or put them in a safe place when small children visit, if they are not used to youngsters. Pay particular attention to their eating habits if things have changed in their lives such as new animals entering their world or when other members of the family, which they are not used to, arrive for a visit. At this point, you might want to "crate." (See "Crate Training," page 96)

Swimming Pools

Some people enjoy taking their dogs swimming. However, be aware that some breeds must be taught what a swimming pool is about; otherwise, they may walk off the edge into a pool thinking they can walk on water, silently struggle and drown. Teach them how to reach   the steps to get out.

Testicles Not Descending

When puppies are first born, the testicles are in the abdomen. As they get older, they move down to the scrotum where they stay. However, in some cases, the testicles remain in the abdomen. These testicles have a higher rate of tumor formation but it is usually confined to the testicle itself. In small dogs, the testicles are probably the size of a small pea, and it sometimes is hard to find them until the dog has matured. Testicles that remain in the abdomen will not produce sperm but will produce testosterone, so you will still see male behavior patterns such as marking territory. Wait until your puppy is about a year old before discarding him as a intact dog. There is an outside chance that the testicles will descend. At one year, if they haven't descended, you should consider surgical removal. Dogs without both testicles cannot be shown at AKC shows. It is a disqualification.

Thyroid Conditions

Symptoms:	The dog may have scaly and flaky skin, sparse coat, and, in general, an "unthrifty look." In some breeds this will also go hand in hand with the "slimy leather ear." (see Leather Ear, page 137).
Diagnosis:	Poor blood flow can occur with hypothyroidism. Areas furthest away from the heart are the worst. (ears, hocks, elbows, tail, and nose). This leads to cooler temperatures in those areas leading to hair loss and skin changes.
Treatment:	Generally a blood test should be taken to determine the thyroid function.

Prognosis: Proper medication can keep the condition under control, and in many cases improve hormonal function and hair and nail growth.

Ticks

Rocky Mountain Spotted Fever

Symptoms: Highest occurrence is in the eastern United States. Fever, not eating, lameness from joint/muscle pain, vomiting, diarrhea, small hemorrhages of skin and mucus membranes, edema of limbs, increased lymph node size. Usually occurs in March or October.

Diagnosis: With a blood test

Treatment: Doxycycline for seven to ten days

Prognosis: There is a rapid response in the first twenty-four to forty-eight hours. It is fatal if untreated. Recovered dogs are immune for six to twelve months.

Ehrlichiosis

World Wide Tick Disease

Symptoms: Depression, weight loss, fever, not eating, bleeding tendencies; causes decreased platelets, red blood cells, and white blood cells.

Treatment: Doxycycline for fourteen to twenty-one days

Diagnosis: Blood test must be taken.

Lyme Disease

Mainly north east United States

Symptoms: Fever, not eating, joint and muscle pain, minimal joint swelling. Bites from infected ticks may not appear for two to five months. Clinical signs five to nine days after attachment.

Diagnosis: Blood test to diagnose; usually run a complete tick-borne disease profile if any of them are possible. Tick paralysis. You may see acute, rapidly progressive paralysis.

Treatment: Doxycycline fourteen to twenty-eight days. Improvement within twenty-four hours of tick removal.

Lyme vaccine seems to cause more reactions than the average vaccine. Unless you are finding ticks on your dog on a regular basis or the dog spends a lot of time outside, I would skip the vaccine and just check for ticks on a daily basis. If you are finding them, either use Top Spot to kill ticks or get the vaccine. Lyme disease may be contracted by humans as well.

Tonsillitis

Symptoms: 1) Chronic recurrent tonsillitis that is unresponsive to antibiotics 2) Acute tonsillar enlargement causing mechanical interference with swallowing or air flow and 3) Tumors. Acute tonsillitis is usually not an indication for surgery, because surgical intervention may lead to spread of the infection.

Treatment: Antibiotic therapy is usually sufficient. Dr. Heisler states that "In eighteen years I have done two tonsillectomies. If you fit into one of the above categories, then do surgery. If not, leave well enough alone."

Many breeds are prone to tonsillitis when the weather changes and there are severe temperature fluctuations. A tiny toy dog can die from secondary infections of tonsillitis if left untreated.

It is important that you know the symptoms and treatment for this because the symptoms can be confused with other gastritis problems, which could waste valuable time in treatment. Small dogs cannot afford to lose too much weight, particularly the tiny ones.

The first sign of tonsillitis is refusal to eat that progresses to lethargy and swelling of the salivary glands (just below the jawbone connection). If you can open the mouth and depress the tongue, you will see that the tonsils are inflamed and enlarged, the back of the tongue is affected and red, and swallowing is difficult. If left untreated, the dog will swallow mucous and the next sign you'll see is mucous in the stool. Depending on the size of the dog, this can progress to severe gastritis and thereby produce mucous stool and later bloody stool. The dog does not necessarily run a fever through this episode.

If the dog is very small, that is, a three or four pound dog, and you delay going to the veterinarian, you could have a very sick dog who may be too weak to stand or might start convulsing.

The dog as presented to the vet could be suffering from any one of many different diseases, so the first thing he or she may do is suggest a blood test and fecal test to rule out any infectious diseases or parasites. Rather than weakening an already weak dog, mix the formula for a pregnant sick bitch (See Whelping and Sick Puppy) or the Nursing Mother Pudding and syringe the dog to keep up its strength. Also give Pepto Bismol mixed with Nutri-Cal to coat the stomach. Ask your vet to check the throat and salivary glands on your dog to rule out tonsillitis before taking blood. If the tonsils are inflamed, my vet advises treating the dog as follows:

- 50 mg Amoxicillin two times a day for ten days (ten pound dog and under)

- 250 mg Amoxicillin two times a day for ten days (160 pound Great Dane)

- 1/4 Temaril P (toy dog) two times a day for three days, one time a day for two days, every other day three times.

- Do not give Temaril P or any steroid if pregnant.

Temaril P is a combination drug, and your vet can prescribe it to help your dog to recovery. The Amoxicillin will attack the infected throat and the Temaril P is an antihistamine with prednisolone which will reduce the inflammation so the dog will start to eat again. Within a day or so if the dog isn't any better, start blood tests and whatever else is necessary. If Amoxicillin is going to work, you should see results in twenty-four hours. Any antibiotic therapy must be continued for the full duration of seven to ten days. Don't stop giving it mid-way. To do so means that the next time you need that antibiotic, it may not work!

Do not allow your dog to go without eating for more than one day without seeking a solution. Mix the gruel, and see if the dog keeps it down. Remember your last sore throat and how hard it was to swallow. Dogs won't eat if their throats hurt!

Tracheobronchitis (Infectious)

Kennel Cough

Symptoms: A mild, self-limiting disease involving the trachea and bronchi of dogs of any age. It spreads rapidly among animals that are closely confined in hospitals, kennels, or any indoor congregation of dogs, particularly benched shows. Exchanging air in a cloistered area tends to exchange airborne diseases. Environmental factors such as cold, drafts, and high humidity apparently increase susceptibility to the disease.

The incubation period is five to ten days. The outstanding sign is a harsh, dry cough that is aggravated by activity or excitement. The coughing is followed by retching or gagging in attempts to clear small amounts of mucous from the throat. Reverse sneezing is noted in some cases. Gentle pressure over the larynx or trachea will induce a cough. Body temperature is normal in the early stages but may be elevated as secondary bacterial invasion takes place. The most severe signs are noted during the first five days but continue in some degree for ten to twenty days.

Treatment: Keep warm (not hot) and quiet. Use an expectorant like Benadryl Children's Antihistamine/Nasal Decongestant (dosage 1 to 1-1/2 ml two times a day (for small dogs under ten pounds). Though antibiotics have no effect on the primary disease, which it will have to run its course, they may be used to good effect in controlling secondary bacterial infection, which could lead to pneumonia if unchecked. Amoxicillin is my veterinarian's choice as a primary antibiotic. Check with your vet for dosage based on weight.

- 50 mg two times per day for ten days.(toy dogs ten pounds and under)

- 250 mg two times per day for ten days (large dogs like Danes 160 pounds)

Whether or not to vaccinate your dogs against Bordetella (another respiratory disease) probably depends on your exposure. If they are to be kenneled or shown at indoor shows during the cold winter months, then it is probably a very good idea to have your veterinarian give this vaccination, which is very effective. It may give your dog a mild case of the disease but can be beneficial if the exposure is a threat.

Travel Sickness (Motion Sickness)

Dog people have been told for years to use ACE Promezine tablets for travel sickness. I personally have used this with no problems, especially for long trips in a motor home. The dog sleeps but is "aware." There are, however, some problems with the use of Ace, but they are not really associated with certain breeds. It does lower blood pressure so any dogs on vasodialators (Vasotec) for heart disease can have their pressure bottom out. Also the dosage listed on the bottle is too high. Dr. Dale doesn't use the tablets at any more than 0.5 mg per pound. The largest injectable dose that he has given is 0.3 cc, whereas, the dosage listed on the bottle says 1 cc per ten pounds. It also lowers the seizure threshold so any dogs on medication for seizures or those that have an occasional seizure can't use this drug. Some people don't like to use it due to the sedation; other people want the sedation. I would suggest never using it without your veterinarian detailing careful dosages. Other drugs for travel sickness are Centrine and Dramamine. I have been told that Boxers have a problem with even mild tranquilizers. They are not safe. Their blood pressure and body temperature goes way down and will not come back up, resulting in death.

Ulcers

Ulcers are not bacterial but are a virus. You just live with them and maintain them with certain medications. It's possible there is a genetic predisposition to them like cancer. When the right stimuli comes into contact with the virus, it springs into action. If it does not go away, the vet can keep it under control with Doxycycline, Zantac, and Flagyl, giving medication for the remainder of the dog's life. It would be foolish to breed a dog that is on these medications constantly, therefore spaying is sometimes required for a bitch. In humans, they treat with routing antibiotics intravenously, but it would be almost impossible to do this with dogs, so they treat with oral medication.

Humans and animals are affected differently by bacteria. If a bitch gets sick while pregnant and loses the pups, it's possible that the E coli made her sick and the antibiotics to kill the E coli let the heliobactor take over. This is even more difficult to get rid of. Sometimes extended use of antibiotics will cure the ulcerated stomach. Whether this bacteria can spread to other dogs on the premises is unknown, but it is believed to be contagious.

Carafate is used as a natural bandage to the ulcer, and Cimetidine (Tagamet) is used to decrease acid production. Reglan is sometimes used to control vomiting. Sometimes Amoxicillin, an antibiotic, is also prescribed in treatment of ulcers.

A healthy intestinal cleansing and bacterial balance for the intestines in ulcer therapy is Echinacea, from a health food store, mixed in water.

Vaccinations

Dr. Dale Heisler recommends: DHLPP, Corona, Bordetella, and Rabies. He likes to give the DHLPP and in a week the Corona and Bordetella and the final series at sixteen to eighteen weeks. He also advises dosing with one baby aspirin per fifteen pounds twice daily. It can be dissolved in water.

My program of vaccination has been six weeks, nine weeks, twelve weeks and sixteen weeks with DA2 PP + CPV + CORONA (NO LEPTO) Puppyshot, and then annually with this combination. But recently my vet told me to change it to eight, twelve, and sixteen weeks, the more recent theory being that we are "over vaccinating." Your pup should be vaccinated by four to six months against rabies. Rabies vaccinations are repeated in three-year intervals after the pup reaches one year of age. Leptospirosis vaccine is a part of some of the combination shots that dogs receive. Many veterinarians do not feel it is necessary to give the "lepto" part of the shot to toy dogs. It is very painful and in some instances has caused the toy dogs to go into anaphylactic shock. It is my understanding that the only way your dog can get Leptospirosis is if it drinks from a pool of water where an animal infected with the disease has urinated. Very few toy dogs under a year of age have any chance of being exposed to this problem, but if you think the exposure is a clear danger, then you should take the chance of including it in your vaccinations.

If a dog has a reaction to a vaccine 99% of the time it is the lepto, therefore, in future vaccinations the lepto can be left out of the vaccine. When the dog has had a reaction, you may only want to give one vaccine a day, wait a few days and give another until all are given. This will help rule out that other one percent of vaccine reactions.

Rabies

The veterinarians used to give the rabies injection as an intramuscular shot in the leg, which caused some pain and great discomfort for many of the smaller breeds. Now they give it at the back of the neck, but because of the antigens in this shot, it is wise to give it subcutaneously, especially on long-coated dogs, as far down on the side as you can, because an allergic reaction can cause a permanent bald spot!

Vomiting

Causes of Chronic Vomiting

1. Systemic—diabetes mellitus, uremia, pancreatitis, liver disease, drug therapy, lead poisoning, heartworm disease, central nervous system lesions

2. Gastrointestinal—Stomach

3. Chronic Gastritis—simple strophic, helicobacter

4. Foreign body, Ulcer, Mass—abscess, granuloma, neoplasia, extragastric obstruction, gastric motility disorder, chronic GDV

5. Gastrointestinal— Small Intestine

6. Inflammatory bowel disease, Partial obstruction—stagnant loop syndrome, neoplasia, foreign body, infiltrative, lymphosarcoma, histoplasmosis, phycomycosis, ulcer, giardia.

Helicobacter—Chronic Vomiting

If vomiting continues for more than five to seven days, or episodes occur periodically, it should be classified as chronic. Occasional vomiting (two to three times per week), in an otherwise healthy pet, may only require dietary adjustment and simple management changes. However, vomiting associated with weight loss, lack of appetite, and lethargy should be considered serious and be thoroughly evaluated in a diagnostic work-up by your veterinarian.

History, physical examination, and routine laboratory evaluation will guide the diagnostic plan.

Symptoms: Salivation, depression, anxiety, and vomiting.

Profuse and protracted vomiting can lead to dehydration, loss of electrolytes (chloride, sodium, and potassium). Mild vomiting will usually maintain normal acid-base status, while severe vomiting can lead not only to dehydration, but it can cause weight loss and aspiration pneumonia.

The time interval between eating and vomiting may be helpful in establishing the diagnosis. Vomiting "undigested" food eight or more hours after eating suggests delayed gastric emptying. Vomiting occurring immediately after eating may indicate gastritis.

The history is important because nonsteroidal anti-inflammatory drugs can cause vomiting as can hair ingestion with dogs that excessively groom themselves. The occasional feeding of table scraps or other dietary indiscretion could be an underlying cause of recurrent vomiting. Paying attention to the nature of the vomiting "act" may be helpful to your vet in the diagnosis.

Chronic vomiting may be associated with weight loss, unthrifty appearance, and a dull, dry hair coat. Clinical signs such as loss of skin turgor, dry mucous membranes, cold extremities (feet, ears) may indicate dehydration. Dehydration occurs most often with frequent severe episodes of vomiting. Diarrhea may be present and contributes to the dehydration. Some animals with chronic intermittent vomiting can retain water and/or food between episodes. Evidence of weight loss and dehydration may not be present in these dogs.

The normal stomach cannot be palpated abdominally. However, gastric enlargement, secondary to chronic outflow obstruction, can be severe enough to allow abdominal palpation. Thickened bowel wall (inflammatory bowel disease or diffuse lymphosarcoma), a dilated loop of bowel (partial intestinal obstruction), a foreign body, bunched intestines, abdominal pain, or enlarged lymph nodes may be detected.

However, many animals with chronic vomiting have a normal physical examination.

The *Diagnostic plan* is to do multiple fecal examinations for parasites, especially if diarrhea is present. If the history and physical examination are normal, fecal examinations negative, and dietary discretion is eliminated, in some cases a bland and easily digested diet may eliminate the vomiting. If all these things fail, tests are indicated to evaluate the gastrointestinal causes of vomiting, to identify a systemic cause. Doing an endoscopic examination is minimally invasive, rapid to perform, and only rarely fails to identify a gastrointestinal cause for vomiting. It allows identification and removal of foreign bodies and detection and directed biopsy of masses and irregular, eroded, or ulcerated mucous membranes. Sometimes your vet will want to do a routine radiograph or abdominal ultrasound prior to the endoscopic exam. Ultrasound may identify an abdominal mass or gastric or intestinal tumor.

Helicobacter is the single largest cause of chronic gastritis and peptic ulceration in humans, and it is associated with an increased risk of gastric lymphoma and adenocarcinoma. Spiral bacteria were described in 1896 in humans and several animal species. They were rediscovered in 1983 as a cause of peptic ulceration. This organism lives in gastric mucus. The immune system does not remove the organisms, and infection can be lifelong without treatment. Some infections do not cause clinical signs.

Treatment: Standard treatment is Omeprazole with Amoxicillin, Metronidazole (Flagyl), and Pepto Bismol for two weeks. Sometimes Zantac or Tagamet is also used.

Vomiting—Upset Tummy

Symptoms: Vomiting

Diagnosis: Has there been any change in the regular diet or new treats or table food that may have upset the stomach? These are some of the most common causes of throwing up food.

Treatment: No food for the first twenty-four hours. Give Pepto Bismol one to two teaspoons two to three times a day. No water for the first twelve hours. After provide ice cubes, and let the dog lap up water as they melt. If this does not solve the problem, seek veterinary attention, as the dog may need antibiotic therapy.

There have been some occasions when people complain about dogs throwing up yellow foam. This can be caused by an empty stomach, and more meals per day may help.

If dogs throw up food after eating, it could be because they ate too fast or too much. In this case, put the dog on a fast for twelve hours giving Pepto Bismol and just Nutrical on the roof of the mouth, and feed again. If the dog continues to throw up, your veterinarian should be consulted immediately, especially if diarrhea is also involved. They lose fluids too quickly with vomiting and diarrhea. (See Enteritis, page 132).

von Willebrand's Disease

Symptoms: An inherited bleeding disorder. Bleeding increases after surgery and trauma. Bleeding of mucosa is intermittent.

Diagnosis: A blood test will tell you if it's von Willebrand's Disease. Apparently it also strikes poodles, Welsh Terriers, and Dobermans.

Treatment: To treat a bleeding episode: transfusion of plasma or whole blood. Periodic blood counts done to monitor red blood cell numbers and iron levels. Do not give aspirin or anything that could inhibit clotting. Avoid elective surgery. Don't breed dogs affected. Hypothyroidism can make this disease worse.

Trying to weed out the dogs who are carriers is a problem in any breed. Carriers are dogs who have the defective gene on one chromosome but a normal gene on the other and don't bleed, but can pass the defective gene on to their puppies.

DNA tests have now been developed for the type III von Willebrand's Disease of Scotties, the type I von Willebrand's Disease of Dobermans, and the type III von Willebrand's Disease for Shelties. These DNA tests can be done at any age. Taken from mouth swabs collected by the breeder/owner (the swabs pick up cells from inside the mouth that provide the DNA), the tests unambiguously classify dogs for the rest of their lives into affected, carrier, and clear animals. With results from this test, the breeder can rapidly eliminate the von Willebrand's Disease gene from the breed. If a particularly valuable dog turns out to be a carrier, it can be bred to a clear animal and non-carrier puppies saved for the next round of breeding.

The test is remarkably easy to get done and is reasonably priced, considering that it is a definitive lifetime determiner of the von Willebrand genetic type of the dog tested.

Vet Gen, 3728 Plaza Drive, Suite 1, Ann Arbor, Michigan 48108
(800) 4-VETGEN (800) 483-8436 / fax (734) 669-8441

Appendix A

Genetics

Inherited Diseases

Breeding carrier to affected, and affected to affected should be avoided if at all possible. The first breeding produces fifty percent affected on average, and the second produces one hundred percent affected animals. There should be two initial objectives of the breeding program. One objective should be to produce as few affected animals as possible, because each is a health risk. That doesn't mean we believe affected puppies should be put down. Those that don't die of the disease and can live normal lives should be neutered and carefully placed in pet homes. The second objective of the breeding program should be to gradually reduce the gene and disease frequency. The kinds of breedings involving the mating of an affected animal, as listed at the first of this paragraph, tend to increase the disease gene frequency, whereas clear to clear and clear to carrier breedings tend to decrease frequency.

To further raise the awareness and standards of breeders, VetGen is helping the Orthopedic Foundation for Animals (OFA) establish a von Willebrand's Disease registry for Dobermans, and the University of California at Davis is preparing to do a DNA identification on liver shunt affected Yorkshire Terriers. AKC Canine Health Foundation is making tremendous strides in other genetic diseases' DNA identification. By registering the results of the von Willebrand's Disease and liver shunt DNA testing on their dogs, breeders stand to benefit at the point of sale when selling either carrier or clear puppies when the DNA marker is identified.

In summary, breeders are approaching the advantageous position of being able to begin eliminating one of the significant diseases in their breed.

- *Dogs that are "clear."* This finding indicates that the gene is not present in your dog. Therefore, when used for breeding, a clear dog will not pass on the disease gene.

- *Dogs that are "carriers."* This finding indicates that one copy of the disease gene is present in your dog, but that it will not exhibit disease symptoms. Carriers will not have medical problems as a result. Dogs with carrier status can be enjoyed without the fear of developing medical problems but will pass on the disease gene fifty percent of the time.

- *Dogs that are "affected."* This finding indicates that two copies of the disease gene are present in the dog. Unfortunately, the dog will be medically affected by the disease. Appropriate treatment should be pursued by consulting a veterinarian.

Suggestions to Improved Planned Breedings
by Dr. Carmen L. Battaglia

Check the following when screening study dogs:

1. Frequency of the desired traits occurring among his ancestors (three generation pedigree)

2. Frequency of the desired traits found among his littermates

3. Number of carriers, affected littermates, and ancestors in his three generation pedigree

4. Number of pups produced with desired traits

Steps to eliminate carriers:

1. Not repeat the breeding

2. Not use the sire/dam again

3. Test the offspring and not breed from carriers

4. Exclude littermates of those affected

5. Not breed to close relatives of those affected

Characteristics of Good Brood Bitches:

1. Whelps naturally without problems

2. Milk supply sufficient to support litter size

3. Encourages puppies to nurse

4. Careful and calm with pups

5. Is attentive with pups

Hopefully, the ongoing Canine Genome Project will allow us to identify marker genes for all the major inherited genetic diseases. This project, closely allied with the Human Genome Project, is already producing startling results.

For further information, see *Standard Book of Dog Breeding* by Dr. Alvin Grossman.

Appendix B 🐾

Food and Nutrition

Homemade Diets by Hills Pet Products, Inc.

Canine Restricted Protein Diet

> 1/4 lb. ground beef (do not use lean round chuck)
> 2 cups cooked rice
> 1 hard-cooked egg, finely chopped
> 3 slices white bread, crumbled
> 1 teaspoon calcium carbonate
> Balanced vitamin-mineral

Cook beef in skillet, stirring, until lightly browned. Stir in remaining ingredients and mix well. This mixture is somewhat dry and its palatability can be improved by adding a little water (not milk) Keep covered in refrigerator. Yield 1-1/4 lb.

Analysis

- Protein   6.4%
- Carbohydrate   21.0%
- Fat   5.0%
- *Calories 740 Kcal/pound

This diet supplies 17% protein calories, 30% fat calories, and 53% carbohydrate calories.

Feeding Guide

Feed sufficient amount to maintain normal body weight.

Body weight	Approximately Daily Feeding
5 lb	1/4 lb
10 lb	1/2 lb

Canine Soft Bland Diet

1/2 cup Cream of Wheat, cooked to make about 2 cups
1 1/2 cups creamed cottage cheese
1 large hard-cooked egg
2 tablespoons dried brewers yeast
3 tablespoons granulated sugar
2 tablespoon corn oil
1 tablespoon potassium chloride
2 teaspoons dicalcium phosphate

Cook Cream of Wheat according to package directions. Cool. Add remaining ingredients and balanced vitamin-mineral supplement and mix well. Keep covered in refrigerator. Yield: 2 lbs.

Analysis

- Protein   7.0%
- Carbohydrate   9.6%
- Calories   422Kcal/lb
- Fat   2.7%
- Moisture   78.0%

Feeding Guide

Feed sufficient amount to maintain normal body weight.

Body Weight	Approximate Daily Feeding
5 lb	2/3 lb
10 lb	1 lb

Canine Low Salt Diet

1/4 lb ground round or other lean beef
2 cups cooked rice
1 tablespoon corn oil
2 teaspoons dicalcium phosphate

Balanced vitamin mineral supplement in a quantity sufficient to provide the daily requirement for each vitamin and trace mineral. Cook beef in a skillet, stirring until lightly browned. Add remaining ingredients and mix well. Keep covered in the refrigerator. Yield: 1 pound

Analysis

- Protein   8.0%
- Carbohydrate   16.0%
- Calories   700 Kcal./lb.
- Fat   5.6%
- *Sodium   .01%

This diet contains approximately 50 mg. sodium/100 gm. dry diet. Veterinary cardiologists recommend a ration containing not more than 50 mg. sodium/100gr dry diet for dogs with congestive heart failure.

Feeding Guide

Feed sufficient amount to maintain normal body weight

Body Weight	Approximate Daily Feeding
5 lb	1/3 lb
10 lb	1/2 lb

Canine Reducing Diet

> 1/4 lb ground round or other lean beef
> 1/2 cup cottage cheese (uncreamed)
> 2 cups drained canned carrots
> 2 cups drained canned green beans
> 1 1/2 teaspoons dicalcium phosphate

Cook beef in skillet, stirring until lightly browned; pour off fat and cool. Add remaining ingredients and balanced vitamin-mineral supplement and mix well. Keep covered in refrigerator. Yield: 1 3/4 lbs.

Analysis

- Protein   7.0%
- Carbohydrate 5.0%
- Calories   300 Kcal/lb.
- Fat   2.0%
- Moisture   85.0%

Feeding Guide

Optimal

Body Weight	Approximate Daily Feeding
5 lb	1/2 lb
10 lb	2/3 lb

Snacking and scavenging should be absolutely forbidden during the reducing period. However, since many obese dogs are accustomed to begging (and receiving) an occasional tidbit of raw vegetable will add only roughage, vitamins and minerals, not appreciable calories.

Canine Hypoallergenic Diet

1/4 lb diced lamb
1 cup cooked rice
1 teaspoon corn oil
1 1/2 teaspoons dicalcium phosphate

Balanced vitamin-mineral supplement in a quantity sufficient to provide the daily requirement for each vitamin and trace mineral. Trim fat from lamb. Cook thoroughly (braise or roast) without seasoning. Add remaining ingredients and mix well. Keep covered in refrigerator. Yield: 3/4 lb.

Analysis

- Protein   10.0%
- Carbohydrate 15.3%
- Calories   800Kcal/lb
- Fat   8.0%
- Moisture 65.0%

Feeding Guide

Feed sufficient amount to maintain normal body weight.

Body Weight	Approximate Daily Feeding
5 lb	1/3 lb
10 lb	1/2 lb

If the allergy is suspected to be food induced, maintain the patient on this diet and distilled water. Then expose the patient to foods, one at a time, beginning with tap water, to discover offending materials. The aim of this provocative exposure is to determine foods the patient CAN eat rather than those the patient cannot eat.

Canine Ultra Low Protein Diet

5 oz or 2 1/2 cups dry instant rice
1 oz corn oil
2 large hard cooked eggs
1/4 teaspoon calcium carbonate

Balanced vitamin mineral supplement in a quantity sufficient to provide the daily requirements. Cook rice as per package instructions. Add other ingredients and mix well. Refrigerate between feedings. Yield: 1 1/4 lb.

Analysis

- Moisture   68.6%
- Fat   6.7%
- Ash   1.9%
- Phosphorus   0.05%
- Protein   3.5%
- Carbohydrate   19.3%
- Calcium   0.10%
- *Calories   720 Kcal/lb

This diet supplies 12% protein calories, 38% fat calories and 50% carbohydrate calories.

Raw Meat Diet

Some breeders are feeding a Raw Meat diet, and though I have never tried it, I was going to offer some information on it, but it met with some severe opposition with five vets across the country that I have discussed it with.

I do not have any objections personally to the raw meat diets, but also have no "proven" benefits of it, so for the time being, I choose to leave it to the Raw Meat Experts.

1. There are no proven benefits of raw meat over cooked meat in home-made diets.

2. To be safe, these vets advise cooking the meat to eliminate toxoplasmosis, salmonellosis and E coli infections. These are probably the most common food borne diseases that affect dogs when they are fed raw meat, although other problems are reported.

Toxoplasmosis is a parasite whose cysts live in the muscle of cattle, pigs and other creatures. If meat is not cooked enough the cysts live and can infect dogs or humans exposed to them. In an immune compromised patient this is a much worse problem than in patients with normal immune systems. E coli and Salmonella are bacterial infections. In most cases they are the result of food contamination by infected workers who handle the meat during processing. I am not aware of any studies that really specify the risk to dogs of these illnesses to dogs but they are frequently implicated in food poisoning deaths in humans. We know that dogs do get infections from these bacteria, and it is therefore reasonable to assume that there is a risk that probably approximates that of humans but may be smaller or larger than the risk to people. The bacteria would be more likely to cause serious illness in an immune compromised patient.

Appendix C

Microchips

Microchips used to track lost dogs, are available through a variety of companies. Check with your vet. The initial setup costs about $400 and includes the chipper, twenty-five chips and the reader and complete instructions with a phone number for help. All the chips are registered to the your kennel. Although I've heard of chips migrating, this is not the norm. The chips in general do not migrate. I have heard of chips that have been injected a little to the left of the area recommended to inject, which is between the shoulder blades, but the reader will and does pick up the chip from almost any location. The reader is run from the head to the base of the tail looking for chips and should find any chip that may have migrated from in proper implantation.

Avid company provides "friendship chips" which allows a breeder to chip an animal and provide a transfer for any new owner. They also will sell friendship chips, which require $15.00 registration through Avid, to anyone that wants to chip their own dog or a breeder that has not got enough dogs to warrant the complete setup. But if a breeder chips all their dogs and plans on chipping puppies they may have to sell or have to ship, it will save them money in the long run to have their own setup. Then you can just buy chips from them when you run out of chips. They are approximately $12.00 per chip when you purchase at least three chips at a time. Avid also provides free universal chip readers to any humane society or rescue organization that calls them and sets up and agrees to scan any animals that comes through their facility.

Rescue groups I know fill out an application and do this with their rescue dogs picked up. A Universal reader will read all chips, and Avid provides Universal readers for vets, humane societies, etc. You really need to have a reader because for inspection, by licensing departments, animal regulation and/or American Kennel Club, you can show them the papers and the ship number and then scan the dog and your identification is complete.

Bibliography

Books

The Dog Judge's Handbook, by Sari B. Tietjen, (Howell Book House, Inc., 1980), out of print.

Form, Function, & Fancy, by Sandra Lemire (self-published).

Hands-On Dog Care: The Complete Book of Canine First Aid, by Sue Copeland and John Hamil, DVM, (Doral Publishing, 2000), ISBN: ISBN: 0-944875-68-8.

How to Buy Your Toy Dog and Raise it Inexpensively, by Terri Shumsky, (self-published, 1993)

The Nicholas Guide to Dog Judging, by A. K. Nicholas, (Howell Book House, Inc., 1979), out of print.

Standard Book of Dog Breeding, by Dr. Alvin Grossman (Doral Publishing, 1992), ISBN: 0-944875-18-1.

Winning with Pure Bred Dogs: Success by Design, by Dr. Alvin Grossman and Beverly Grossman (Doral Publishing, 1997), ISBN: 0-944875-17-3.

Yorkies Head to Tail, The Essential Care Guide, by Sandra Lemire (Paper Chase Press, 1999), ISBN: 1-879706-8-30.

Websites

www.vetinfo.com

Addison's Disease
www.vetinfo.com/dencyclopedia/deaddisons.html

Dog Bites
www.bestdogs.com, January 1999

Liver Shunt
www.vhl.ucdavis.edu/research/canine/
www.shooterdog.com/alexfaq3.htm#LS
www.design.klever.net/~mrbroome/shunt.html

Puppy Mills
www.puppymillrescue.com
http://members.tripod.com/~rescues/

Raw meat diet
http://secondchanceranch.org/rawmeat.html#safe

Miscellaneous References

Judy Carey, Consumer Affairs, with advice from pet expert, Jack Bloch, D.V.M.

Dr. Jean Dodds, *The Immune System and Disease Resistance*

Dr. David Talan & Associates

Aileen Martello, article on Inbreeding and Linebreeding, *Dog World*, 197?

Suggestions or Improved Planned Breedings, by Dr. Carmen L. Battaglia

Index

A

Addisons's Disease 105
Adjusting to your home 100
Aerosol dangers 107
Allergies 107
  flea saliva 127
Amoxicillin 42
  colitis 117
  eclampsia 55
  kennel cough 164
  respiratory problems in pups 68
  tonsillitis 163
  treating enteritis 132
  ulcers 166
Anal glands 90, 108
Anasarca 109
Anesthesia 86, 109
  cesarean section 51
  mammary cancer 143
  with teeth cleaning 86
Antibiotic therapy 110
Antibiotics
  treatment of kennel cough 164
  treatment of mange 144
  treatment of pneumonia 149
  treatment of skin problems 155
  treatment of strangles 152
  treatment of ulcers 166
  with tonsillitis 162

Appetite loss 38, 70, 105, 117, 119, 139-140
Artificial insemination 33
Aspirin
  diarrhea control 119
  hip dysplasia 134
  seizures 159
Auto Immune diseases 110

B

Backyard breeders 9
Bacterial infection 156
Birth weight 57
Black ear 137
Bladder
  control 111
  incontinence 111
  stones 111
Bloat 112
Bordetella 113
Bottle feeding orphan puppy 65
Brachycephalic breeds 113
Breed Standard 15
Breeders 14
  finding 1, 4
  kennel clubs 9
  show champions 4